DIGITAL STRATEGIES AND ORGANIZATIONAL TRANSFORMATION

Digital Transformation: Accelerating Organizational Intelligence

Print ISSN: 2811-0552
Online ISSN: 2811-0560

Series Editor: Jay Liebowitz *(Seton Hall University, USA)*

According to a report released by Veritis in 2021 "the global digital transformation market size is anticipated to reach USD 1009.8 billion by 2025 from USD 469.8 billion in 2020. The demand for digital transformation services is expected to rise at a Compound Annual Growth Rate (CAGR) of around 16.5% over the forecast period from 2021 to 2025. The growing adoption of digital technologies, including Artificial Intelligence (AI), cloud computing, big data, the Internet of Things (IoT), and Machine Learning (ML), is driving the growth of the digital transformation market." To be competitive in today's fast-changing marketplace, organizations need to apply the "alphabet" of digital transformation.

The focus of the book series is unique and will cover the various perspectives on organizational digital transformation, namely business & management, technology, legal and ethics, and social aspects.

Published:

Vol. 4 *Digital Strategies and Organizational Transformation*
edited by G Reza Djavanshir

Vol. 3 *Doing Well and Doing Good: Human-Centered Digital Transformation Leadership*
by Cheryl Flink, Liora Gross and William Pasmore

Vol. 2 *Digital Transformation Demystified*
by Frank Granito

Vol. 1 *Digital Transformation for the University of the Future*
edited by Jay Liebowitz

Digital Transformation
Accelerating Organizational Intelligence
– Volume 4

DIGITAL STRATEGIES AND ORGANIZATIONAL TRANSFORMATION

G. Reza Djavanshir, Sc.D.
Johns Hopkins University, USA

World Scientific

NEW JERSEY • LONDON • SINGAPORE • BEIJING • SHANGHAI • HONG KONG • TAIPEI • CHENNAI • TOKYO

Published by

World Scientific Publishing Co. Pte. Ltd.
5 Toh Tuck Link, Singapore 596224
USA office: 27 Warren Street, Suite 401-402, Hackensack, NJ 07601
UK office: 57 Shelton Street, Covent Garden, London WC2H 9HE

Library of Congress Cataloging-in-Publication Data
Names: Djavanshir, G. Reza, editor.
Title: Digital strategies and organizational transformation /
G. Reza Djavanshir, Sc.D., Johns Hopkins University, USA.
Description: New Jersey : World Scientific, 2023. | Series: Digital transformation: accelerating organizational intelligence, 2811-0552 ; Vol. 4 | Includes bibliographical references and index.
Identifiers: LCCN 2022061306 | ISBN 9789811271977 (hardcover) |
ISBN 9789811271984 (ebook) | ISBN 9789811271991 (ebook other)
Subjects: LCSH: Technological innovations--Management. | Information technology--Management. |
Organizational change. | Strategic planning.
Classification: LCC HD45 .D4898 2023 | DDC 658.5/14--dc23/eng/20230104
LC record available at https://lccn.loc.gov/2022061306

British Library Cataloguing-in-Publication Data
A catalogue record for this book is available from the British Library.

For any available supplementary material, please visit
https://www.worldscientific.com/worldscibooks/10.1142/13298#t=suppl

Desk Editors: Nimal Koliyat/Thaheera Althaf

Typeset by Stallion Press
Email: enquiries@stallionpress.com

This book is dedicated to my wife
Gissou Tabatabi
and to my entire family — my
sisters and brother

https://doi.org/10.1142/9789811271984_fmatter

About the Editor

G. Reza Djavanshir is a full Professor and Academic Program Director at the Johns Hopkins Carey Business School. He joined the Johns Hopkins University in 2002. He has received numerous awards including Dean's Awards for Faculty Excellence for several years and an Excellence in Teaching Award from Johns Hopkins University's Students Association. Professor Djavanshir is also Associate Editor-in-Chief of *IEEE Computer Society ITPro* and Editor of 3 other journals. Prior to joining Johns Hopkins University in 2002, he held the positions of Sr. Scientist, Chief Engineering, and executive positions of Vice President at Citicorp and Sr. Technologist (now Citigroup). He received his Doctor of Science degree in Systems Engineering from the George Washington University.

https://doi.org/10.1142/9789811271984_fmatter

About the Contributors

Javad Abed joined the Johns Hopkins Carey Business School in 2020. He is Assistant Professor of Information Systems in the practice track. Dr. Abed has taught a variety of courses including the technical and managerial aspects of information systems. His research interests are in diverse settings involving behavioral and design science issues in the information systems field.

Stephen J. Andriole is an American information technology professional and Professor at Villanova University who has designed and developed a variety of interactive computer-based systems for industry and government, from positions in academia (Professor, Chairman, R&D Center Director), government (Director of Cybernetics Technology at DARPA), and industry (CIO, CTO, SVP, Director, and CEO). Dr. Andriole is well known for the design and development of a global crisis warning system — the Early Warning & Monitoring System — whose output appeared in President Ronald Reagan's Daily Briefing Book. His research portfolio while at DARPA included early funding of the MIT Architecture Machine Group now known as the MIT Media Lab, research in artificial intelligence at Yale University and Carnegie-Mellon University, computer simulation, computer-aided decision analysis, and computer-based crisis management. At DARPA, he funded one of the first research programs in counter-terrorism crisis management. Andriole is also well known for the design and development of the United States' first totally online Master's program in information systems (MSIS), with the support of Alfred P. Sloan Foundation while at Drexel University. He was also the principal architect of the investment strategy of Safeguard

Scientifics, Inc. (NYSE: SFE) that led to multiple Initial Public Offerings (IPOs) of Internet companies with a total market capitalization of over $100B. He has also published over 35 books and 500 articles on artificial intelligence and machine learning, information systems engineering, defense command and control, interactive systems design and development, human–computer interaction, venture investing, technology due to diligence, social media, emerging technology, and information technology. He is a Fellow of the Cutter Consortium, was a charter member of the U.S. government's Senior Executive Service (SES), has received the Defense Meritorious Civilian Service Award for his work at DARPA, and was awarded an Honorary Doctorate from La Salle University in 2000. He currently holds the Thomas G. Labrecque Chair of Business Technology at Villanova University's School of Business where he teaches AI and machine learning, strategic technology, innovation, business consulting, entrepreneurialism, and technology management (from: https://en.wikipedia.org/wiki/Steve_Andriole).

Robert Cohen is Adjunct Professor at Seton Hall University. He teaches in the areas of both computer science and business management. His previous experience includes executive technology management at Prudential Financial for over 23 years. As a former Chief Information Officer (CIO), he directed various technology functions for Prudential's Investment and Asset Management businesses. He managed and provided leadership on significant large-scale software development projects across various global businesses. Prior to Prudential, his experience included working at several financial services companies including Bankers Trust (NY), Crum & Forster (NJ), and Mutual of NY. He earned a Master's degree in computer science from Montclair State University and an MBA from Rutgers University.

Dian Huang is a graduate student at the Carey Business School of Johns Hopkins University. She has a BEng degree in cybersecurity (2021) and an MS degree in Information Systems (2022). She has work experience in data security in China Telecom, providing customers with a variety of solutions for securing data.

Shreyas Iyer received his Bachelor of Science (BSc) degree in the field of Electronics and Communication Engineering from PES University of Bangalore, India, in 2020. He received his Master of Science degree in

Information Systems from the Johns Hopkins University in 2022, and then joined IBM to work as a Cloud Engineer. His research interests lie in the area of data science, artificial intelligence, and machine learning in business applications. He has collaborated actively with his teammates in several other data science and machine learning-related projects.

Ruchin Kansal has dedicated his energy and resources to advise companies on leadership and change, growth strategy, and innovation. He is a Member of Faculty of the Department of Management and Director of the No. 1 ranked Business Leadership Center, Stillman School of Business, at Seton Hall University. Previously, he served as the SVP and Global Head of Strategy for Digital Services at Siemens Healthineers, as Head of Business Innovation at Boehringer Ingelheim Pharmaceuticals Inc., and as a management consultant with Deloitte and Capgemini. He is the co-author of *Redefining Innovation: Embracing the 80-80 Rule to Ignite Growth in the Biopharmaceutical Industry*; Co-Editor of *In The Lead*; Lead Researcher of Future of Leadership Survey; and a host of 30 minutes on Comcast Channel 23 Danbury. He is also the Project Director of The 5th Industrial Revolution — a graduate-level course on radical innovation, and a narrative project exploring the intersection of human existence, health technology, and space. He was invited to the Obama White House to share best practices for engaging patients in research in support of the Presidential Precision Medicine initiative. He was recognized with the Top 40 Healthcare Transformers Award by Medical, Marketing, and Media in 2016 and Boehringer Ingelheim President's Award for developing the company's first Patient Engagement Strategy. He is a member of the Board of Trustees for Cyrenius H. Booth Library, Newtown, CT. He has served as a board member for Stanford Medicine X (2014–2017) and Weston Education Foundation. With a passion to develop future leaders, Professor Kansal founded Kansal & Company which coaches leaders and companies to lead with purpose and with courage. Further, he advises companies on design thinking, growth strategy, innovation and change. He is married to Gunjan, a physician, and has a son, Neil, who is in college. The father and son team loves to restore cars for adventure travel.

Dongwon Lee is Assistant Professor and Researcher at the Hong Kong University of Science and Technology. Previously, Dr. Lee was Lecturer and Graduate Assistant at Robert H. Smith School of Business, University of Maryland, 2012–2017, Researcher at Korea Advanced Institute of Science and Technology (KAIST), 2008–2012; and Researcher at Electronics and Telecommunications Research Institute (ETRI), 2006.

Xiangyu Lei received his Master's degree in Information Systems from Carey Business School of the Johns Hopkins University (2022), and a Bachelor's degree in Mathematics at Xi'an Jiaotong University (2021). He has research experience in Multi-objective optimization.

Frederic Lemieux currently serves as Faculty Director and Professor at Georgetown University. He oversees a vast portfolio of graduate degrees including a Master's in Applied Intelligence, a Master's in Cybersecurity Risk Management, and a Master's in Technology Management. Dr. Lemieux has also published extensively on topics related to intelligence, cybersecurity, and disruptive technologies, including artificial intelligence and digital transformation. Dr. Lemieux has presented his research at numerous international conferences and has been invited as a keynote speaker on a frequent basis.

Xiaoyue Li received her Bachelor of Business Administration degree in the field of finance from the Chinese University of Hong Kong, Shenzhen, in 2021. She received her Master of Science degree in the field of Information Systems from Johns Hopkins University in 2022. In 2022, she joined Alibaba as a risk strategist. She focused on data analytics in the fintech area and risk management in transaction processes.

Hsueh-Yao Lu graduated with a Master of Science degree in Information Systems from Johns Hopkins University. Lu is a Data Analyst focusing on the application of data in business intelligence. Lu's strengths include defining customer needs, performing data analyses, and constructing visualizations. As a former research and industry analyst at Issuer Pixel, Lu constructed 6 industry taxonomies which contributed to doubling their user base and raising 300K for the company.

Angelica Marotta of MIT received her Bachelor's degree in Computer Science from the University of Pisa, a Graduate Certificate in Cyber Security, and a Master's degree in Justice Studies with a specialization in Cyber Security from Southern New Hampshire University. Dr. Marotta received her PhD in Cybersecurity from the University of South Wales,

United Kingdom. Dr. Marotta is also a Certified Information Security Management System Auditor (ISO/IEC 270001). She is currently an affiliated researcher in Cybersecurity at the MIT Sloan (CAMS) Center at the Massachusetts Institute of Technology (MIT). Her research explores several topics, including cybersecurity culture, risk management, and regulatory compliance. In addition to her research activity, she teaches Ethical Management in Public Safety in the Homeland Security and Emergency Management program at Thomas Edison State University in Trenton, New Jersey. She is also a dissertation supervisor and teacher in the MSc Digital Transformation program at the University of Hull, UK. Dr. Marotta is a frequent presenter at international conferences and has authored/co-authored several papers on cyber insurance, risk management, cybersecurity culture, AI bias, robotics, and compliance. She earned several professional distinctions, including winning the 2021 Best Paper Award at the IACIS (International Association for Computer Information Systems) Europe Conference.

Sunil Mithas is a World Class Scholar and Professor at the Muma College of Business at the University of South Florida. He is also a Visiting Professorial Fellow at the School of Information Systems, Technology and Management, at the UNSW, Sydney. Previously, Mithas was the Ralph J. Tyser Professor of Information Systems at the Robert H. Smith School of Business at the University of Maryland, where he was Co-Director of the Center for Digital Innovation, Technology and Strategy and the Center for Excellence in Service. He has held visiting positions at the University of New South Wales (UNSW) Business School, Sydney; the University of Mannheim, Germany; Hong Kong University of Science and Technology (HKUST), Hong Kong; and the Graduate School of Management at the University of California, Davis. Identified as an MSI Young Scholar by the Marketing Science Institute, Professor Mithas is among the top information systems scholars in the world. His research published in top journals and conferences has won multiple best paper awards and has featured in practice-oriented publications such as *MIT Sloan Management Review*, *Bloomberg*, and *CIO.com*. Dr. Mithas is a Senior Editor of *MIS Quarterly* and Department Editor of *Production and Operations Management* and *Management Business Review*. He serves on, or has served on, the editorial boards of *Information Systems Research* and *Journal of Management Information Systems*. He is the author of two books *Digital Intelligence: What Every Smart*

Manager Must Have for Success in an Information Age and *Making the Elephant Dance: The Tata Way to Innovate, Transform and Globalize.* He has consulted and conducted research with a range of organizations including A. T. Kearney, Ernst & Young, Johnson & Johnson, the Social Security Administration, and the Tata Group. He is a frequent keynote speaker at industry events for senior leaders and at academic conferences and professional associations. More details are available at https://www.usf.edu/business/about/bios/mithas-sunil.aspx.

Josh Morton is Lecturer in Strategy and Innovation at Leeds University Business School, University of Leeds, UK. He teaches strategy and innovation at different levels of study, including to business leaders. Dr. Morton's research focuses on the work of strategists and top managers in organizations, with a particular interest in strategic agility, open forms organizing, and digital strategy and innovation.

Albert T. Mubako is Senior Systems Application Products Consultant and a qualified business model innovation and research professional with over 21 years of work experience. He holds a Doctor of Management degree in Management and eBusiness (DMgt) and a Master's degree in Business Administration (MBA) with an Information Systems major. His consultancy and research interests are in digital business innovation, digital transformation strategy, disruptive technologies, Internet of Things, mobility, big data, and e-Learning. He obtained his Doctorate of Management degree in e-Business, Advanced Management, and Strategy from the Swiss Management Centre University, where he investigated and developed a framework for supporting digital business strategy in consumer-focused industries. He is the co-author of *The Definitive Guide to a Digital Business Strategy*, which facilitates a strategically channeled digital approach to business challenges. Dr. Mubako holds certifications in Systems Applications Products (SAP), TOGAF, Cloud Credential Council (CCC) Internet of Things, and Certified Digital Transformation Executive (CDTE). Mubako co-founded and leads the Institute for Digital Business Strategy with a focus on emerging transformative technology and business improvement. He has facilitated Digital Transformation courses at the University of Maryland Baltimore County (UMBC) and Smart City Management programs at the Zigurat Institute of Global Technology (Spain). He is an academic thinker with business acumen, connecting the dots, and bringing it all together for clarity and action.

John Palfreyman has worked at a European and global level in IBM as leader of emerging technology businesses. Palfreyman currently focuses on the business application of Blockchain, working directly with customers and through enablement of IBM practitioners and partners. Palfreyman founded Palfreyman Ventures in July 2017 offering informed, objective advice for the application of new technologies for sustained business advantage. Dr. Palfreyman has also worked as Non-Executive Director of Novus Property Solutions and is currently Associate Faculty Lecturer at Leeds University Business School and Lecturer and Associate at Salford University Professional Development.

Jeffrey S. Ray is Director II, Engineering Systems, for BAE Systems serving as Chief Engineer on a large networking and cloud engineering program. He holds BS and MS degrees in Engineering from the University of Maryland College Park, a Juris Doctor degree from the University of Maryland School of Law, an MS degree from the George Washington University (GWU) in Engineering Management, and a Doctor of Management degree from Swiss Management Center (SMC) University. At Leidos, Dr. Ray served as Program Manager conducting the project start-up of the Advanced Battle Management System (ABMS) Digital Infrastructure (DI) program, served as Principal Systems Engineer for the Leidos Innovation Center (LInC), and was a member of the Leidos Systems Engineering Center of Excellence. Dr. Ray holds certifications from Certified Systems Engineering Professional (CSEP), Project Management Professional (PMP), Six Sigma Black Belt, and Certified Digital Transformation Executive (CDTE), is a licensed Attorney at Law, a registered Professional Engineer (PE), and an instrument-rated private pilot with detailed knowledge of the National Airspace System (NAS). He is a member of INCOSE, PMI, is a Co-Director of the Institute of Digital Business Strategy (IDBS), and mentors international doctoral candidates through the dissertation process. Dr. Ray is Professor, Member of the Graduate Faculty, and supports the Systems Engineering and Engineering Management Advisory Boards at UMBC. He teaches graduate-level courses in Project Management (PM), Systems Engineering (SE), and Organizational Learning, and has developed and presented numerous SE training courses to the NAS. Dr. Ray has 38 years of PM and SE experience that includes broad-based problem-solving related to the structured acquisition of military and IT systems. He stood up and managed a Systems Integration and Test Lab (SITL) for 12 years at Northrup Grumman and has an expert level of understanding related to the testing and qualification of large, complex, software-intensive systems, and brings structured process controls to software development, integration, and test activities. Dr. Ray's technical skills include all aspects of SE, defining systems and functional architectures, C4ISR architecting, project planning and control, scheduling, budget forecasting, earned value management (EVM) status reporting, developing force protection, first responder, airborne ISR, CBRNE sensing and alert reporting systems, and qualification of integrated C4ISR and CBRNE software applications. Dr. Ray co-authored the book *The Definitive Guide to a Digital Business Strategy*, and authored over 30 research papers related to management, engineering, organizational learning, and marketplace analysis topics.

Shahdrick Samson is a value creation and results-driven Senior Business and Technology Executive with international leadership experience and proven expertise in transforming large global organizations. He has corporate, government, and professional services experience, specializing in business and technology to vastly improve global operations, spanning multiple industries including financial services, healthcare, and public sector. Samson has closely collaborated with many key players including CxOs and Board Members, bringing technical clarity and strategic direction to large global organizations, complex programs and projects, and cross-functional teams that impacted multi-billion-dollar operations. Samson enabled employers and clients to successfully embrace digital transformation and emerging technologies to solve convoluted business problems and experience exponential growth, profitability, and regulatory compliance through high-performing technology strategies, solutions, products, and services in both the corporate and government world including AIG, Bank of America, BNP Paribas, Dell | EMC, Fannie Mae, FedEx, Fidelity Investments, Freddie Mac, Morgan Stanley, and government agencies.

Hector Santiago was awarded a Doctor of Science (DSc) degree in Information Assurance/Cybersecurity in 2014 from Capitol Technology University (CTU) (Maryland, USA) and holds three Master's degrees in Strategic Intelligence (National Intelligence University, Washington, D.C.), Business Administration (Liberty University, Virginia), and Telecommunications & Information Systems Management (CTU). Dr. Santiago has been an Adjunct Professor teaching cybersecurity to grad students at Johns Hopkins Carey Business School since 2018. He currently works as a Cyber Threat

Intelligence Analyst for the US Federal Deposit Insurance Corporation (FDIC) — a role he enjoys as he enters his 23rd year of service to the US government and military. Distinctions include being the creator of the US Department of Homeland Security's (DHS) PEREGRINE Data Analytics Program and the DHS non-Forensic Attribution Methodology (nFAM), as well as the co-developer of the DHS DANTE Cybersecurity Database and US Department of Commerce Supply Chain Risk Management Program.

Tanush Sharanarthi received his Bachelor of Science (BSc) degree in the field of Electronics and Communication Engineering from People's Education Society (PES) University of Bangalore, India, in 2020. He received his Master of Science degree in Information Systems from the Johns Hopkins University in 2022, and then joined IBM to work as an AI Engineer. Previously, he worked for about 2 years as a Software Engineer at the Global Digital Technology Center in Bangalore, building products to enable the digital transformation and enhancement of the company's global supply chain. His research interests lie in the areas of Machine Learning and Artificial Intelligence and he has worked on multiple projects in the field.

Barney Tan is Head of School and Professor at the School of Information Systems and Technology Management (SISTM), UNSW Business School. He graduated with a PhD in Information Systems from the National University of Singapore, and was formerly Professor of Strategic Information Systems and Deputy Head of the Discipline of Business Information Systems at the University of Sydney.

Yumeng Zhuang has a Master's degree in Information Systems from Carey Business School of the Johns Hopkins University (2022). She graduated with a BS degree in both Accountancy and Information Systems from University of Illinois at Urbana-Champaign (2021). She has work experience as a junior consultant for the big four accounting firms.

Chuyun Zou got his Master's degree in Information Systems from Carey Business School of the Johns Hopkins University (2022). He also has a BS degree in Business Information Management from the University of California, Irvine (2020), and an MS degree in Business and Data Analytics from the City University of Hong Kong (2021). He has work experience as a program implementation consultant and data analyst.

https://doi.org/10.1142/9789811271984_fmatter

Acknowledgments

The idea of this book was suggested by my best friend and colleague Professor Jay Liebowitz last year. So, I am particularly grateful to his suggestions and support. I would also like to express my gratitude to each individual contributor and reviewer, specifically Meghan 'Dell. Finally, I am thankful to my family members — especially my beloved and patient wife Gissou Tabatabi for her unwavering love — and Dr. Aida Ahari for their support and inspiration in finishing this book.

https://doi.org/10.1142/9789811271984_fmatter

Contents

https://doi.org/10.1142/9789811271984_0001

Chapter 1

Introduction

G. Reza Djavanshir

Johns Hopkins University, Baltimore, MD, USA
rj@jhu.edu

Over the past several years, digital strategy has become a common term within all industries and academia. Moreover, its impact on organizational transformation has become a high priority for executives and academic researchers. In other words, the implementation of digital strategy is transforming our organizations and industries. It will also make significant contributions to improve organizations' value creation processes and national economies.

In general, a strategy is a plan of actions and policies that can help in successfully achieving objectives within given environments. In the context of digital strategy, this translates into a plan of actions and policies designed to achieve organizational objectives by analyzing the environment, planning, and implementing digital initiatives. However, the successful implementation of a digital strategy requires the necessary organizational transformation that enables its seamless integration, as well as effective and efficient operations during its value creation process.

The implementation of digital strategies is transforming all types of organizations and services, including government, healthcare, financial services, supply chain management, and manufacturing.

In the healthcare sector, for instance, AI-enabled frontier technologies are helping to save lives, diagnose diseases, and extend life expectancy. In education, virtual learning environments and distance learning have opened up new pedagogic delivery mediums to students who would otherwise be excluded. Government services are also becoming more accessible and efficient by using digital products and services, and data analytics algorithms enable accurate policies and strategic planning.

Today, many organizations are using machine learning and convoluted neural network (CNN) algorithms for pattern recognition and to gain insights in big data, make decisions, and suggest actions. AI-based systems can continuously learn how to imitate natural human cognitive functions. Moreover, AI solutions can learn users' behaviors and understand their unique needs to make decisions for them. This has the potential to create unique, highly differentiated customer value propositions and radically improve organizational processes. Therefore, the right digital technology will greatly outperform competitors (Gray, 2017).

To better understand the transformative impacts of digital strategies on organizational operations, Microsoft sponsored research asking Harvard Business Review Analytical Services to study the digital transformation of organizations (Gray, 2017). This study is based on a survey of 537 *Harvard Business Review* readers from different sizes and types of organizations (Gray, 2017). The survey found that businesses are not simply deploying digital technologies to improve their efficiencies; rather, firms are developing new business models and strategies to develop new revenue sources and improve market share.

The survey shows that the areas where digital technologies are having major impacts are ranked as follows: improving customer service (53%); increasing productivity (52%); developing new services (50%); business models (42%) and products (41%); and increasing revenue (40%) (Gray, 2017). The survey also demonstrates the growing consensus among experts that business organizations should identify which core capabilities they need to differentiate and focus their strategies to transform these core business capabilities.

In the aftermath of pandemic-related supply chain problems, the need for implementing a digital strategy in managing the supply chain is inevitably rising, as is the demand for better business strategies. Digital technologies can provide effective interfaces and efficient services for various segments of given supply chains.

In manufacturing systems, increasing the efficiencies and the effectiveness of manufacturing processes and improving customers' experiences are some of the positive outcomes of implementing a digital strategy. In financial organizations, AI-based FinTech and particularly blockchain can minimize errors and maximize customers' experiences.

Moreover, the need for organizational transformation to align to the implementation of the digital strategy and the challenges of making the transformation to create a technology-intensive production process are illustrated by a case study of "MacroMed" (a pseudonym), a large medical products manufacturer (Brynjolfsson *et al.*, 1997). In a plan to provide better product customization, MacroMed made a large investment in technology-intensive manufacturing. This investment includes giving workers the authority to make decisions about process and workflow innovation, improved interactions with customers and suppliers, and changes in skills, processes, culture, and structure (Brynjolfsson and Hitt, 2000).

Therefore, given the tremendous opportunities involved in today's global economy and interconnected world, this book looks at the concepts of digital strategy and organizational transformation. It includes chapters written by respected subject experts within academia and industry to provide an in-depth understanding of digital strategy and organizational transformation and to discuss the digital opportunities and challenges before us.

In Chapter 2, Reza Djavanshir discusses the roles of institutionalized normative and cultural factors in successful implementations of digital strategies and organizational changes in developing economies. Specifically, the author discusses the systemic barriers in developing economies, as well as the roles of informal institutions such as normative and cultural factors and how they can impede their efforts to gain benefits from digital technologies. The chapter discusses the weaknesses in developing economies' regulative, normative, and cultural institutions that create resistance to changes needed for the successful implementation of digital strategies and organizational transformations. Finally, it provides policy recommendations on how to improve the institutional weaknesses within developing economies and what policies they may need to formulate and implement in order to benefit from their efforts in digital strategies.

In Chapter 3, Dongwon Lee, Barney Tan, and Sunil Mithas provide interesting insights into some nomenclatures used within the context of digital technologies and digital strategy, the role of technology in digital transformation, how it unfolds, and how incumbents and entrants should manage digital transformation. Their goal in this chapter is to review some of the recent work in this domain and provide their viewpoint on this topic, building on their prior and related work.

In Chapter 4, Angelica Marotta examines the role of risk perception in determining people's cyber risk-taking behaviors and the related implications for cyber insurance policies and dynamics. Her study provides a high-level analysis of the existing risk perception literature through a detailed examination of social, demographic, economic, cultural, psychological, and performance factors. The findings of the author's research suggest that the nature of the relationship between risk perceptions and cyber insurance benefits may be influenced primarily by an organization's ability to keep its risk profile stable over time. More specifically, the cultural dimension of risk perception has been identified as one of the areas where risk reduction strategies have the most significant potential for lowering cyber insurance costs. The findings of this study can assist businesses and insurance companies in directing training efforts and forecasting organizational reactions to cyber threats as they navigate digital transformation.

In Chapter 5, Steve Andriole says that most digital transformations do not disrupt business processes or whole business models. Instead, they're "incremental," or just as often part of planned technology "modernization" initiatives. These kinds of projects are safer, less risky, less expensive, and "politically" protective of executive reputations, which is perhaps why a vast majority of digital transformation projects focus on incremental changes or modernization. The author says that digital transformation projects that are truly transformative are targeted at replacing or automating business processes, or replacing or automating whole business models — which are the riskier, more expensive, and more politically dangerous projects than incremental and modernization ones. Impact follows risk: Incremental and modernization projects are easily less impactful than disruptive ones. According to Andriole, companies should decide how and where they want to "transform," acknowledging the likely return on their digital transformation investments. But eventually, because of the trajectories of technology and business, all companies will have to pursue more disruptive transformation.

In Chapter 6, Frederic Lemieux discusses the opportunities and challenges associated with digital transformation and artificial intelligence (AI).

According to the author, the adoption of AI is booming and was accelerated during the pandemic of 2020, directly impacting the pace of digital transformation across industry verticals. So, he writes, it is now critical to explore current and emerging challenges as well as opportunities offered by AI solutions to better understand how organizations and society could be affected. First, this chapter examines the evolution of computerization and its influence on AI. Second, the author scrutinizes how AI performance has been harnessed through digital solutions that are transforming numerous industries. Third, the author addresses fundamental ethical and moral challenges that derive from the application of AI in real life and its implications for human beings. Finally, he discusses the challenges of securing and protecting AI solutions against cyberattacks. The chapter concludes with the future of AI as it relates to technology convergence with cloud computing, IoT, and eventually quantum computing.

In Chapter 7, John Palfreyman and Josh Morton attempt to clarify some confusion regarding what steps organizations should follow to achieve improved business values. The authors outline seven steps in a conceptual process model, the digital transformation loop, which organizations can adopt for what they call "agile digital transformation." Their aim is to offer a compelling and comprehensive conceptualization which illustrates the challenges faced by organizations and poses questions they need to reflect upon to realize value from the agile use of digital technology. Finally, the authors argue that agile digital transformation must be part of achieving a clear strategic vision and should drive sustained and demonstrable business value.

In Chapter 8, Robert Cohen argues that as part of a digital strategy, machine learning (ML) has become a common toolset and capability across many businesses. However, the operational aspects of machine learning (MLOps) are often overlooked for ML projects until they are already installed and being executed in the business environment. This chapter provides a review of MLOps products and vendors to give data scientists the ability to set up the appropriate ML infrastructure in a proactive manner.

In Chapter 9, Javad Abed studies the role of digital technology in changing social relationships and looks at the role of IoT in developing new means for leveraging relationships between IoT systems. Abed argues that advancements in technology allow humans to add many interesting features to everyday devices. As humans, we can tackle many problems in complex societies and manage the complexity of networked social systems. Sociability is a vital human capability that improves our social lives and manages social interactions. Adding this feature to smart devices can facilitate the management of complex and networked IoT settings. People can improve the relationship between social and smart devices in different ways. He argues that, nowadays, researchers are investigating the future generations of IoT, namely, social IoT. This study aims to develop a new method for updating and leveraging the friendships between IoT devices by using social IoT and social networking principles. The author utilizes a design science approach to propose a novel friendship management method for social IoT that is able to effectively evaluate and manage the relationships between devices. The new friendship development and updating models use the basic concepts of Knapp's relational stage theory. In this chapter, a new simulation tool for evaluating the new friendship mechanism is proposed. The evaluation results show that the proposed method performs effectively and can enhance network navigability, service composition, and service discovery.

In Chapter 10, Hector Santiago discusses how the most pressing need in cybersecurity could propel the development of quantum computing. His chapter proffers that the biggest ongoing challenge currently facing cybersecurity professionals (namely, ransomware) can potentially be mitigated by the expected benefits of quantum computing, a technology still in the nascent stages of demonstrating reliable and repeatable network defense support to broader commercial industries, particularly industries based in the United States. The author demonstrates that the commercial losses from ransomware (both incurred and expected) by US entities may be enough to justify the need for a concerted near-term "sprint" by US stakeholders to develop a quantum-based defensive capability with deliberate speed. Santiago's work highlights the competition among leaders in the quantum computing development space, the consequences to national defense and business health of not having defensive quantum computing capabilities, and the global shifts in political and commercial influence that would likely result depending on which nation-state eventually establishes dominance in the quantum computing space. Scientific and economic challenges to the development of quantum computing capabilities in the current environment are also explored alongside the benefits of investing at certain points along the innovation cycle of quantum computing technology.

In Chapter 11, Shahdrick Samson discusses the role of digital disruption in growing businesses. He argues that traditional methods no longer seem effective and are detrimental to survival. So, how well a business becomes digital and adapts to the rapidly changing market forces will to a great extent determine how much market share it will gain in comparison to its competitors. He argues that while becoming digital is not an easy or an inexpensive journey, it is an essential one. It requires a firm commitment and dedication of resources to be truly successful. However, the rewards for undertaking such a journey are well worth the efforts and will determine the new set of market leaders.

In Chapter 12, Tanush Sharanarthi *et al.* study the application of deep learning in car damage detection.

This chapter proposes a car damage detection model using convolutional neural networks. The authors argue that the automobile industry can utilize cameras to catch the defects in vehicles and provide better-quality inspection than manual methods. AI-based machines using computer vision will help make the entire supply chain process more efficient and reliable. The proposed model uses the VGG-16 convolutional neural network that is optimized to provide the best accuracy and minimal loss. The model is trained and validated with a dataset containing images of vehicles that have no defects and ones that are damaged. Results of their study show the potential of such a model being widely used in the industry since it can accurately detect damages for a diverse set of vehicles.

In Chapter 13, Lei *et al.* study AI-IoT systems' roles in the transformation of the manufacturing industry. They say that starting with cloud computing (the foundation of IoT), and combining it with AI, adds an essential capability to connected systems: action. In industrial scenes, AI-IoT is mainly used to achieve specific functions related to machine prediction and data processing, in addition to intelligent industrial robots, industrial vision detection, perception identification, and positioning. The authors use Bosch's AI-IoT transformation example to illustrate how AI-IoT technologies can help a company in manufacturing and supply chain management in the real world and analyze four forces that drive the AI-IoT transformation. Finally, they conduct a SWOT analysis to provide a comprehensive view of how AI-IoT can renovate smart manufacturing and what we should pay attention to as we integrate it into manufacturing.

In Chapter 14, Albert Mubako and Jeffrey S. Ray present a model for digitally transforming a business by first performing a digital maturity assessment of current capabilities, describing the maturity levels of the digital environment to define a starting point to base future modifications on, and then applying a Digital Business Strategy Model (DBSM) to ensure that required inputs and outputs for developing a Digital Business strategy (DBS) will create and capture value for the firm from emerging digital technologies. A solution and cultural intelligence-driven approach is enabled through strategic alignment of a firm's organizational structure, infrastructure architecture, and the innovation strategy being pursued. Their recommended digital transformation process will overcome sponsor hesitancy to make the investment required to modernize corporate infrastructures. Organizational learning must be part of a comprehensive digital transformation effort. Finally, they present an enhanced organizational learning model with recommended practical implementation steps to ensure smart organizational transformation.

Finally, in Chapter 15, Ruchin Kansal provides an experiential case study about digital transformation and organizational change. When it comes to digital transformation, the healthcare industry lags behind. The lack of adoption of digital products, services, and business models highlights the author's case. Despite the evidence that the rate of change is accelerating, such as in the hospital sector, true transformation will happen once digital skill sets are fully incorporated in the training and development of the healthcare workforce and its leadership. In the meantime, healthcare leaders should take pragmatic steps to enable the digital transformation of their respective organizations.

References

Brynjolfsson, E., Renshaw, A.A. and Van Alstyne, M. (1997). The matrix of change. *MIT Sloan Management Review*, Winter, pp. 37–54.

Brynjolfsson, E. and Hitt, L.M. (2000). Beyond computation: Information technology, organizational transformation and business performance. *Journal of Economic Perspectives*, 14(4), 23–48.

Gray, P. (2017). The digital transformation of business. A Harvard Business Review Analytic Services Report.

https://doi.org/10.1142/9789811271984_0002

Chapter 2

Digital Technology Strategy and Cultural Factors in Developing Economies

G. Reza Djavanshir

Johns Hopkins University, Baltimore, MD, USA
rj@jhu.edu

This chapter discusses the roles of normative factors that minimize the resistance to the successful implementation of digital strategies and organizational changes. A particular emphasis is made to discuss the roles of institutionalized normative and cultural factors in successful implementations of digital strategies and organizational changes in developing economies. Specifically, the chapter will discuss the systemic barriers in developing economies, as well as the roles of informal institutions such as normative and cultural factors and how they can impede their efforts to the benefits gained from digital technologies. The chapter will focus on discussing the weaknesses in developing economies' regulative, normative, and cultural factors that create resistance to changes needed for the successful implementation of digital strategies and organizational transformations.

Finally, this chapter will provide policy recommendations on how to improve the institutional weaknesses within developing economies and what policies they may need to formulate and implement in order to benefit from their efforts in digital strategies.

1. Introduction

Businesses and organizations in developing economies spend billions of dollars to develop, acquire, and implement digital technologies in order to improve their productivity and create the required organizational transformation to offer new products and improved services. In many cases, businesses and organizations are typically successful in formulating their digital technology strategies, but they often fail to take full advantage of their technology implementation in ways that create productive activities and allow them to compete in today's global business ecosystem. In other words, they fail to create the kind of competitive advantages that they planned for in their digital strategies.

Digital technology strategy and organizational transformation form a systemic approach rather than simple technology acquisition, integration, and implementation; it embraces a broad range of institutionalized cultural and normative factors within any organization. Moreover, digital technology strategy in any organization is a complex, nonlinear process. Its success depends not only on seamless integration with the organization's structure and its ecosystem but its technology strategy also needs to be synchronized with the structure, processes, and functional operations of the given organization (Prahalad and Krishan, 2002).

Furthermore, digital strategies and their required organizational transformations need well-planned congruence among the functional groups within the organization that supports it. This means that in order for an organization to realize the benefits of digital technology, it must ensure that its employees will adapt it without any resistance. Therefore, the successful planning and implementation of digital strategies require one to consider the important role of cultural and normative elements that are institutionalized over a long period within an organization and how they cause resistance to the adoptions of new technologies. In this chapter, we will call these two critical elements cultural and normative factors.

Both normative and cultural institutional elements play critical roles in minimizing the resistance to the implementation of digital strategies. Critical factors in normative and cultural institutions include employees' propensity toward using the new technology, and their ability to learn and adapt to the norms and dynamics of a changing organization. These two institutional factors are critical because they directly impact employees' motivation to learn quickly and synthesize their own knowledge, talents, and skill sets with new technology in order to create a unique amalgam of core capabilities.

In any organization, cultural and normative factors can be thought of as the invisible "hands" (rules) of the game. These are reflected in an organization's routines, values, norms, legitimate (acceptable) behaviors, and codes of conduct. In other words, they define "the general habits of action and thoughts" (Veblen, 1915) that are accepted and practiced in an organization. These norms and other cultural factors also determine the level of trust among the individuals, which impacts the sense of cooperation among the people (Fukuyama, 2004). Moreover, normative and cultural factors in an organization impact the creation of the kind of meaningful interactions between individuals that can result in entrepreneurial activities (Audretsch and Aldridge, 2012). So, in light of the impact of cultural and normative factors in organizational transformations, it is clear that in order to succeed in their digital strategy and business development efforts, organizations need supporting cultural and normative institutional factors that are synchronized with their technology-driven organizational transformations. It is also important that an organization's cultural and normative elements complement its digital strategies and its transformation efforts. In other words, if cultural and normative factors within an organization are not synchronized with the organization's transformation efforts, non-compliant behaviors proliferate, which can cause inertias in the organization's transformation efforts. The result is a failed digital technology strategy.

This chapter attempts to elaborate on the importance of cultural and normative inertias that work to prevent businesses and organizations from benefiting from their digital strategies and organizational transformation efforts. It discusses how cultural and normative institutional forces maintain their influence on the complex processes of digital technology strategy implementations and organizational transformation processes. The following section lays out the theoretical framework and discusses cultural and normative institutional inertias in organizations and businesses. This section also describes how businesses and organizations can build effective capabilities and benefit from their digital strategy.

2. Theoretical Foundations: Institutional Theories

A successful implementation of the digital strategy and organizational transformation is a complex, nonlinear process which requires institutional changes within a given organization (Cohen, 2004; Freeman, 1994, 2002, 2010). As such, institutional theory can provide an appropriate framework for addressing the organizational contexts that shape the implementation, use, and effective operation of the digital technology. Institutional theory can be applied to focus on the role of the cultural and normative elements that surround organizations and individuals (North, 1990; Scott, 2008).

The cultural and normative institutional factors that impact an organization's technology-driven transformation include attitudes toward adapting a new technology and new ways of conducting business. In general, this includes a comprehensive unlearning and learning process: unlearning dominant logics, behaviors, norms, cultural values, attitudes, routines, and actions that are problematic in successful implementations of digital strategies and creating resistance to organizational change.

In general, individuals' preferences are manifested in their cultural values, and attitudes are shaped during their education processes. Attitudes toward risk-taking are determined by an individual's cultural background (Audretsch *et al.*, 2007, 2014). Scott (2008) enumerates the importance of normative and cultural elements of institutions. The normative pillar includes the uncodified attitudes in organizations (Welter *et al.*, 2004). When such normative expectations and attitudes are broadly diffused, they tend to "take on a rule-like status in norms, actions, and behaviors (Covaleski and Dirsmith, 1988; see also Baughn *et al.*, 2006)." As Scott (2008) notes, institutional elements shape stability, order, and predictability to individuals' behaviors. The different institutional elements provide different forms of stability. While the underlying "logic" of the cultural element of conformity is instrumental to the shared image of working together in an organization, the logic of the normative pillar is the "appropriateness" of any decision, action, or behavior (Baughn *et al.*, 2006; Scott, 1995).

Thus, this chapter follows the approaches employed by North (1990), Malerba and Nelson (2012), Nelson and Nelson (2002), Aidis and Estrin (2014), Freeman (1986, 1994, 2010), Baumol (1990), and Bell and Pavitt (1993), and builds on a theoretical framework primarily based on the theories of institutions articulated by Scott (2008), DiMaggio and Powell (1991), Zucker (1991), and Abramovitz (1986). Institutional theory provides a powerful approach in explaining the impact of cultural and normative institutions on the behavior of individuals and on organizational decision-making. The rationale for applying institutional theory in this chapter is that it explains the forces and inertias that impact the behaviors of individuals in organizations.

Furthermore, for businesses in developing economies, institutionalized cultural and normative factors coupled with education and training are at the heart of building capabilities not only for scientific discovery, innovation, and technological development but also for adapting, operating, and using a new technology within any business. To succeed, these organizations need well-trained, competent employees who are surrounded by the required cultural and normative institutional elements. In fact, the quality of an organization's employees' technical competency is often highly impacted by its normative and cultural institutions.

Porter (1998) makes the point that businesses cannot compete on sophisticated products and services without well-educated employees and well-informed customers. Formal education and training, along with membership in professional networks, professional publications, and trade associations, are effective mechanisms to develop such well-trained, tech-savvy employees who are adaptive to organizational change: those who have the "know-how," the "know-why," and other necessary cultural and normative elements. Professional networks, trade associations, education, and training institutions not only train competent technologists and managers but also help employees learn accepted norms and behaviors that become institutionalized among members of the group and manifest themselves in their preferences, attitudes, discourse, and codes of conduct (Williamson, 1979).

Involving employees, training them, and creating incentives for change, combined with changes in their normative and cultural elements, enable employees to be part of the organizational change process that is required for the successful execution of a technology strategy and organizational transformation. This also minimizes their resistance to change in adapting, using, and operating the new technology. Furthermore, employees' participation in the organizational change process makes them part of the new solution rather than being an element of a problem. Finally, this helps align and synchronize the organization's digital strategy with its transformation process.

However, the required changes in cultural and normative factors within an organization can take a long time to be fully adapted or institutionalized, as to a large extent these are determined by individuals' educational backgrounds and the surrounding normative and cultural factors. As such, it takes a long time to change or modify people's dominant preferences, attitudes, and values. However, leadership can also influence and shape employees' preferences by creating and fostering incentives and minimizing the fear of change among employees.

Employees feel uncertainty when facing new technology and organizational changes. When confronting a situation of risk and uncertainty, people tend to mimic the behavior of other people facing a similar situation (Liang *et al.*, 2007). Particularly, when an organization has unclear operating procedures, policies, and processes of implementing a new digital strategy and its required organizational changes, or when a new technology's implementation process, operating procedures, and policies are misunderstood among the employees, they may mimic the behaviors of their peers in other organizations whom they perceive as successful. Mimicking, therefore, is often associated with joining the successful "crowd" (Staw and Epstein, 2000). If the "crowd" prefers the new technology to other legacy and other professional alternatives, others may be encouraged to follow this path.

The process of institutionalizing new norms and cultural elements in organizations is complex. It begins with understanding the problem along with benefits of the new norms and organizational culture. The next step is unlearning the old norms, dominant logics, behaviors, attitudes, routines, and actions and learning the new ones that support digital strategies and organizational changes. Finally, through a long process of learning, repeated actions, and internalization, the new norms and cultural elements become institutionalized (DiMaggio and Powell, 1991; Scott, 2008).

An organization's training systems, its internal communications, and participation in professional associations are critical to institutionalizing new organizational norms and culture and improving the capabilities needed to utilize the new technology. A lack of effective technical and organizational capabilities results in loss of financial capital and waste of valuable human capabilities.

Capability building is the main objective of training. It focuses on developing technical, managerial, and organizational competences that organizations need in order to achieve their desired goals of using and operating any new technology and achieving their organizational transformations. Thus, building technical capability that meets the international standards and operating procedures should be the main objective of any technology strategy (Cohen, 2004; Millman, 1990). In addition to effective training systems, efforts such as workshops, seminars, and memberships in professional networks can build organizational capabilities that training efforts depend on. In the following sub-sections of this chapter, we attempt to outline the specific capabilities that organizations need to focus on in order to succeed in their digital technology strategy.

2.1 *Capability to make cultural changes*

This is a critical factor, because in order for organizations to make technological changes, they must also have the necessary capabilities to make the required normative and cultural institutional changes (Abramovitz, 1986). In a seminal article about "Catching up, forging ahead, and falling behind," Abramotivz (1986) argues that, historically, a socio-economic system that succeeds in achieving its technological and business development goals is one that creates the capability to make cultural institutional and technical changes.

The process of building capabilities in organizations is complex and nonlinear. Organizational capabilities include the capability to make not only cultural changes but also technical capabilities. A study by Dahlman *et al.* (1987) shows that the success of organizations in their change efforts has also been partly due to their governments' consistent policies on technology and education policies. This means that in order to be successful, governments need to formulate policies to build the required technical and social capabilities. These capabilities together will enable them to make the necessary technological and organizational changes they need in order to create core competencies and establish a competitive advantage in the global economy.

2.2 *Diminishing incentives and misuse of talent*

One of the major objectives of digital technologies is to develop opportunities for new business ventures (Audretsch *et al.*, 2007, 2014). Indeed, the importance of incentives in new business development is a well-understood concept. Baumol (1990) notes that norms and cultural factors play major roles in creating the incentive structure in a given economy. Formal norms and cultural factors impact incentive structures that, in turn, influence the dynamics of new technological activities. However, in some developing economies, the incentive structure makes it more lucrative for an individual to engage in opportunistic behaviors than in productive applications of technological activities. That is, individuals in a nation's talent pool may be driven to get involved in unproductive behaviors that serve their immediate interests (North, 1990), instead of putting their talents, skills, and capabilities into productive, technology-driven business activities. This is a major problem in some developing economies with inefficient formal and informal institutions, to the extent that it diminishes the incentives for engaging in productive business activities. Thus, it results in the misallocation of talent and creates adverse effects for a nation's technological business activities.

2.3 *Lack of accurate information*

The ability to access undistorted and accurate information is the lifeblood of not only scientific, technological, and business activities but also of making decisions about allocating resources, structuring contracts, and reducing risk and uncertainty, among other areas (Djavanshir, 2015). In some developing economies, access to undistorted information is difficult due to politics, while this is crucial for discovering and capitalizing on new business development opportunities (Audretsch *et al.*, 2014). In fact, in some developing economies, the ability to access accurate information is a systemic problem that stems from weak institutions. Inaccurate information can create weak banking and financial credit systems in developing countries, resulting in improper lending by public and private banking and credit institutions. For Audretsch *et al.* (2007), accurate information is critical to credit markets; when information is highly asymmetrical, credit rationing can emerge. In their seminal work, Audretsch *et al.* (2007) argue that because the cost of obtaining accurate information depends on the size of the organization, new and small firms become more exposed to asymmetric information and therefore to credit rationing. Thus, the lack of accurate information can become an entry barrier to young and small ventures in a nation. Moreover, Auerswald (2007) makes the case that information problems can not only cause costly and incomplete contract but can also be a source for market failures in technological business activities. Thus, in developing economies, firms with access to accurate information are better positioned to adopt appropriate technology, make the appropriate organizational changes, and reduce the risks of inaccurate decisions, incomplete contracts, and market failures.

Therefore, policy makers in developing economies should formulate consistent policies with effective enforcement mechanisms that place high penalties on sources of inaccurate and distorted information. They should also work to create a public information repository or bank. These measures can serve to minimize the level of inaccuracy and asymmetry in their country's information, and enable people to access undistorted information (Djavanshir, 2015).

2.4 *Business registration problem*

Start-ups and small companies make up a majority of the firms in developing economies. However, obtaining business licenses with minimum cost and within minimal time is critical to the success of digital strategies in developing economies. This is true because businesses in developing economies need to compete in the global economy. Some of the major challenges that new start-up companies face in these nations relate to obtaining business licenses, registering patents, and obtaining intellectual property rights with minimum cost and within minimal time. This is a major problem in many developing economies because it effectively creates a barrier to entry for start-up technology businesses. Therefore, public policy makers should formulate policies with effective enforcement mechanisms that minimize the required time and monetary cost of registering patents, registering intellectual property, and starting new businesses.

2.5 *Normative and cultural factors*

In general, normative and cultural institutional contexts define the norms, beliefs, culture, and default values that are deeply encoded in any social setting, including organizations (Djavanshir, 2015). These normative and cultural factors play a critical role in determining how people behave, interact, trust, and relate with each other, and how they learn and use their knowledge and capabilities (Lundvall *et al.*, 2002). Norms define the legitimate or accepted behaviors and routines (repeated patterns of behaviors that are taken for granted). Cultural factors define the behavioral maps or scripts for an individual. Employing Hofstede's (1991) metaphor, they are the "operating system of the mind" (see also Scott, 2008). Cultural elements also define the shared image of life, unquestioned assumptions, or default values of an individual's activities (Gharajedaghi, 2007). Scott (2008) notes that individuals organize their material world based on their mental categories. This means that cultural elements create an internalized microcosm of the world in an individual's mind, which serves as the information processing agent and determines an individual's preferences and attitudes, and how they organize, interpret, encode, prioritize, evaluate, and respond to events (Markus and Zajonc, 1985). Additionally, norms and cultural factors are mutually reinforcing, and they create social obligations for an individual (March and Olsen, 1984). These elements not only impact an individual's goals, routines, and organizational activities but also influence the processes of strategy formulation, planning, and implementation (DiMaggio and Powell, 1991; Scott, 2008). The following paragraphs outline some impacts of normative and cultural institutions in digital technology strategies in developing economies.

Cultural and normative institutions play an important role in enabling technologists, businesses, and individuals to effective and efficient use of talent pools and to enhance business opportunity (Aidis and Estrin, 2014; Hills *et al.*, 1997). Thus, the roles of normative and cultural institutions are critical to the effective implementation of their digital technology strategies. However, due to a lack of effective rules of law policies in some developing economies, social networks and personal connections can sometimes create mechanisms to circumvent the rule of law. That is, some individuals may attempt to ignore the law by taking advantage of their close connections and ties with influential people. Thus, in the absence of effective and consistent enforcement of rules and laws, personal connections can penetrate all branches of government, creating favoritism and corruption. In many developing economies, normative and cultural elements are heavily influenced by "tribal" or group identities. Close cultural bonds between the group members define their legitimacy, and members seek to achieve recognition from groupmates or tribe leaders who monopolize political and economic power (Fukuyama, 2004). Clan and tribe leaders define the map of "reality" in loyal members' minds and provide scripts for their "legitimate" (accepted) behaviors. This script or map for group members' behaviors becomes the set of institutionalized norms and cultural elements of the group. These behaviors act as their own reinforcing mechanisms.

Tribal networks also create a culture of inspection and punishments, in which obedience and following the rules of a tribe's clan become a routine habit (Aidis and Estrin, 2014). Thus, the tribe suppresses risk-taking and independent actions among the loyal members, bypassing the law. In any economy, respect for the law, contracts, and property rights is considered critical to conducting business. Specifically, for technology-driven business strategies, protection of intellectual property rights and honoring contracts are the key elements that secure investments. Moreover, technology companies may depend on obtaining financial credit, raising capital, and bearing high risks.

All of these activities require transactional trusts: protecting contracts and intellectual property rights with effective and consistent enforcement (Aidis and Erstin, 2014). However, in some developing economies, there is a weak propensity toward respecting the rule of law, honoring contracts, and protecting intellectual property. Thus, some individuals may try to bypass the law and contracts by taking advantage of their ties to government officials or through bribery, extortion, and other illegal activities. These norms and attitudes can create major problems for the success of digital strategies. For example, violation of intellectual property and copyrights, software piracy, and breach of contract diminish the incentives for individuals to engage in technological business activities. Policy makers should formulate laws and policies that establish the rule of law and respect for contracts and property rights, and ensure that they are strictly and consistently enforced. Further, their media, education, and training systems should actively promote norms and attitudes related to respecting the law, contracts, and property rights.

2.6 *Direct and indirect discrimination against women*

In many developing economies, women represent an untapped professional talent pool, where women's level of involvement in technology-driven business activities is significantly low. This may stem from the nation's normative and cultural values that directly or indirectly discriminate against women. Thus, one of the major challenges in such countries is the incorporation of women into business activities.

Developing economies should address the issue of equal treatment and equal rights for women, not only from a human rights point of view but also because countries that discriminate against women deprive themselves of the talents, knowledge, skills, and efforts of a large part of their population. Moreover, discrimination against women creates major inertia in the ability of business and government organizations to involve women in their business development processes (Aidis *et al.*, 2007). Aidis *et al.* (2007) suggest that if a nation's population is to contribute to its business development efforts, it is important that women, along with men, fully participate in business development efforts. Moreover, Welter *et al.* (2004) argue that women-owned businesses are important for several reasons. First, they tend to employ and engage other women more frequently, which reduces the impact of discrimination against women in the labor force. Second, women business owners can become role models for later generations. Third, by encouraging women to engage in business and technological activities, developing economies could see more successes through increased innovation capabilities and entrepreneurship development.

However, according to Welter *et al.* (2004), in many developing economies, this kind of discrimination against women is manifested in different forms. For example, even when gender equality is legally or constitutionally endorsed in a given developing economy, there may exist differences in role allocations or implicit discrimination against women. This may stem from traditional attitudes of society that forbid women from carrying out certain activities (Welter *et al.*, 2004). Differing "appropriate" jobs or normative expectations for men and women may be manifested in work preference, as children are taught which career choices are deemed appropriate for their gender (Baughn *et al.*, 2006; Harriman, 1985; Hisrich, 1986). Thus, as Baughn *et al.* (2006) note, these traditional norms and cultural values have led to gender-segregated labor forces, involving both horizontal (in which women are clustered in different occupations from their male counterparts) and vertical (in which women are more frequently found at lower levels of occupations) labor market segregation. Gender inequality creates forces that may decrease the level of female participation in entrepreneurship (and technology transfer and development) efforts, thus diminishing the effectiveness of the country's efforts to catch up with developed economies (Baughn *et al.*, 2006).

Baughn *et al.* (2006) examine national characteristics related to attitudes toward women and the relative rates of women to men engaged in entrepreneurship in different countries. They suggest that anti-discrimination laws and government policies play critical roles in eliminating gender discrimination. Although changes in regulative institutions and policies can be implemented in a short period of time, norms and cultural values take much longer to be changed. Therefore, in these economies, policy makers should take greater steps toward accelerating the pace of eliminating gender discrimination and increasing the rate at which women engage in all activities of the country's development processes. Moreover, in some developing economies, the education and training systems should strongly and actively oppose all kinds of discrimination. The media in these countries can also play a critical role in eliminating the discriminatory norms, attitudes, and cultural values (Djavanshir, 2015). All these cultural values impact the successful implementation of digital strategies in developing economies.

2.7 *Trust and social capital*

In any economy, successful businesses are those that have established trust and a sense of cooperation with their stakeholders, customers, suppliers, distributors, creditors, and even competitors. Trust and social capital increase the efficiency, effectiveness, and productivity of any business activities. Audretsch and Aldridge (2012) define social capital as "cooperative interactions and social networking among people." Therefore, trust and social capital make a developing economy more conducive to business investment and create an efficient process of benefiting from technology-driven business strategies. Podolny (2009) suggests that individuals usually trust each other if they share the same values and if they make sure that their expectations are met. However, there are many elements that erode trust and cooperation. These include corruption, lack of fairness, lack of transparency, inconsistent behaviors, and disparity between the credibility of a message and the credibility of its messenger. In many developing economies, lack of trust and social capital can be a major problem in their business activities, mostly due to ineffective and inconsistent enforcement of laws, contracts, intellectual property rights, corruption, tribal norms, and lack of transparency and fairness.

Fukuyama (1995) argues that to build an efficient economy, developing economies not only need to integrate digital technological advancements into their businesses but they also need to build nationwide trust networks. However, the strength of any nationwide trust network depends on the strength of their norms and cultural values. Thus, these two institutional elements are critical to digital technology-enabled business processes. Nevertheless, some developing economies have low levels of trust and sense of cooperation outside their tribal networks. This lower level of nationwide trust and cooperation can be detrimental to the successful implementation of their digital technology strategy. In this regard, trust becomes a critical factor to reduce the transaction costs by providing a necessary means to enforce policies, laws, and business contracts.

3. Policy Recommendations

Digital strategies and organizational transformation face unique challenges in developing economies. These challenges include a lack of capability to effective implementation; resistance to organizational change due to institutionalized norms and cultural factors; lack of business opportunities and incentives to start new digital ventures; scarcity of resources; lack of access to credit, loans, and financing; and the need for capability building.

These challenges partly stem from formal and informal institutions (normative and cultural factors) in developing economies. Thus, policy makers should not only create ways to ensure the effective enforcement of laws, contracts, and intellectual property rights but they should also engage in removing the cultural and normative factors that prevent them from successful implementation of their digital strategies and organizational changes.

Therefore, from a policy perspective, businesses and organizations in developing economies should work together to come up with policies and recommendations on employees' training, capability building, and creating incentives to minimize the resistance to organizational change. Policy makers should also build the necessary infrastructure to support these digital strategies.

Thus, to support the successful implementation of digital strategies and to minimize the resistance to organizational transformations, the following points are a summary of policy recommendations:

(1) Before formulating policies to embark on any digital strategy, allocate some time to test and reexamine the underlying assumptions to be used in formulating the technology strategies and required organizational changes. My experience shows that policies and strategies that are formulated hesitantly and in reaction to an ongoing situation result in failure.
(2) To gain the organizational stakeholders' support, focus on communicating and showing the benefits of the new technology and its accompanying organizational changes. Emphasize the difference between a "zero-sum game" (win–loss) and a "positive-sum game" (win–win) where all parties benefit (Bailey and Rehman, 2022).
(3) Create incentives to gain employee support.

(4) Embark on continuous cultural training to minimize the normative and cultural factors that create resistance to changes.
(5) Conduct trainings for capability building in digital technology strategy formulation and implementation. This includes trainings in organizational change and transformations.
(6) Create an organizational culture that promotes a sense of belonging among the employees and involves employees to gain their support. One of the critical factors for any technology strategy's success is the support of the stakeholders.
(7) Hire outside consultants to identify the sources of weakness and resistance to changes within the organization. The best sources for soliciting these are the mid-level managers within the organization.

4. Conclusion

This chapter has attempted to outline the impacts of normative and cultural factors that minimize the resistance to the successful implementation of digital strategies and related organizational changes; in particular, this chapter discussed the roles of institutionalized normative and cultural factors in successful implementations of digital strategies and organizational changes in developing economies.

This chapter discussed the systemic barriers in developing economies, as well as the roles of informal institutions such as normative and cultural factors and how they can impede their efforts to the benefits gained from digital technologies. The chapter specifically focused on discussing the weaknesses in developing economies' regulative, normative, and cultural factors that create resistance to changes needed for the successful implementation of digital strategies and organizational transformations.

Finally, this chapter provided some policy recommendations on how to improve the institutional weaknesses within developing economies and what policies they may need to formulate and implement in order to benefit from their efforts in digital strategies.

For further study, we recommend investigating which mechanisms are effective in extracting undistorted and reliable data from developing economies, and whether data analytics might be a way of accomplishing this. Moreover, future research may study and analyze what other mechanisms may exist that developing economies can employ to minimize the impacts of resistance to change in these countries.

References

Aidis, R. and Estrin, S. (2014). Institutions, incentive, and entrepreneurship. In Acs, Z.J., Szerb, L., and Autio, E. (eds.), *Global Entrepreneurship and Development Index* (pp. 27–37). Washington, DC: CreateSpace Independent Publishing Platform, The Global Entrepreneurship and Development Institute.

Aidis, R., Welter, F., Smallbone, D., and Isakova, N. (2007). Female entrepreneurship in transition economies: The case of Lithuania and Ukraine. *Feminist Economics*, 13(2), 157–183.

Audretsch, D.B. and Aldridge, D. (2012). Transnational social capital and scientists entrepreneurship. In Audretsch, D.B. (ed.), *Public Policy in the Entrepreneurial Society* (pp. 193–200). Cheltenham, UK and Northampton, MA: Edward Elgar.

Audretsch, D.B., Grilo, I., and Thurik, A.R. (2007). Explaining entrepreneurship and the role of policy: A framework. In Audretsch, D.B., Grilo, I., and Thurik, A.R. (eds.), *Handbook of Research on Entrepreneurship Policy* (pp. 1–18). Cheltenham, UK and Northampton, MA: Edward Elgar.

Audretsch, D.B., Lehmann, E.E., and Wright, M. (2014). Technology transfer in a global economy. *Journal of Technology Transfer*, 39, 301–312.

Auerswald, P.E. (2007). The simple economics of entrepreneurship: Market failure reconsidered. In Audretsch, D.B., Grilo, I., and Thurik, A.R. (eds.), *Handbook of Research on Entrepreneurship Policy* (pp. 18–35). Cheltenham, UK and Northampton, MA: Edward Elgar.

Bailey, J.R. and Rehman, S. (2022). How to overcome return-to-office resistance. *Harvard Business Review*. https://hbr.org/2022/02/how-to-overcome-return-to-office-resistance.

Baughn, C., Chua, B.-L., and Kent, L.E. (2006). The normative context for women's participation in entrepreneurship: A multicountry study. *Entrepreneurship Theory and Practice*, 30(5), 687–708.

Baumol, W. (1990). Entrepreneurship: Productive, unproductive and destructive. *Journal of Political Economy*, 98, 893–921.

Bell, M. and Pavitt, K.L.R. (1993). Industrial and corporate change. *Oxford Journal*, 2(2), 157–210.

Cohen, G. (2004). *Technology Transfer: Strategic Management in Developing Countries*. New Delhi and London: Sage.

Covaleski, M.A. and Dirsmith, M.W. (1988). An institutional perspective on the rise, social transformation, and fall of a university budget category. *Administrative Science Quarterly*, 33, 562–587.

Dahlman, C.J., Ross-Larson, B., and Westphal, L.E. (1987). Managing technological development: Lessons from the newly industrializing countries. *World Development*, 15(6), 1373–1388.

DiMaggio, P.J. and Powell, W.W. (1991). The iron cage revisited: Institutional isomorphism and collective rationality in organizational fields. In Powell, W.W. and DiMaggio, P.J. (eds.), *The New Institutionalism in Organizational Analysis* (pp. 63–82). Chicago, IL: University of Chicago Press.

Djavanshir, G.R. (2015). The institutional inertias that constrain technology-driven economic development. In Phan, P.H. (ed.), *Academic Entrepreneurship* (pp. 185–205). Johns Hopkins Series on Entrepreneurship.

Freeman, C. (1986). The diffusion of innovations — Microelectronic technology. In Roy, R. and Wield, D. (eds.), *Product Design and Technological Innovation* (pp. 193–200). London: Open University Press.

Freeman, C. (1994). The economics of technical change: A critical survey article. *Cambridge Journal of Economics*, 18(5), 463–514.

Freeman, C. (2002). Continental, national and sub-national innovation systems — Complementarity and economic growth. *Research Policy*, 31, 191–211.

Freeman, C. (2010). Formal scientific and technological institutions in the National System of Innovation. In *National Systems of Innovation: Toward a Theory of Innovation and Interactive Learning* (pp. 173–188). UK: Anthem Press.

Fukuyama, F. (1995). *Trust: The Social Virtue and Creation of Prosperity*. New York: Free Press Paperbacks.

Fukuyama, F. (2004). *State Building Governance and World Order in the 21st Century*. Ithaca, NY: Cornell University Press.

Gharajedaghi, J. (2007). *Systems Thinking, Managing Chaos and Complexity: A Platform for Designing Business Architecture*, 2nd edn. Amsterdam: B.H. Elsevier.

Harriman, A. (1985). *Women/Men/Management*. New York: Praeger.

Hills, G., Lumpkin, G., and Singh, R. (1997). Opportunity recognition: Perceptions and behaviors of entrepreneurs. In Reynolds, P., Autio, E., Brush, C.G., *et al.* (eds.), *Frontiers of Entrepreneurships Research* (pp. 203–218). Wellesley, MA: Babson College.

Hisrich, R. (1986). The woman entrepreneur: Characteristics, skills, problems, and prescriptions for success. In Sexton, D. and Smilor, R. (eds.), *The Art and Science of Entrepreneurship* (pp. 61–84). Cambridge, MA: Ballinger Publishing.

Hofstede, G. (1991). *Culture and Organizations: Software of the Mind*. New York: McGraw Hill.

Liang, H., Saraf, N., Hu, Q., and Xue, Y. (2007). Assimilation of enterprise systems: The effect of institutional pressures and mediating role of top management. *MIS Quarterly*, 31(1), 59–87.

Lundvall, B.-K., Johnson, B.E., Andersen, S., and Dalum, B. (2002). National systems of production, innovation and competence building. *Research Policy*, 31, 213–231.

Malerba, F. and Nelson, R.R. (eds.) (2012). *Economic Development as a Learning Process: Variation across Sectoral Systems*. Cheltenham, UK and Northampton, MA: Edward Elgar.

March, J.G. and Olson, J.P. (1984). The new institutionalism: Organizational factors in political life. *American Political Science Review*, 78, 734–749.

Markus, H. and Zajonc, R.B. (1985). The cognitive perspective in social psychology. In Lindzey, G. and Aronson, E. (eds.), *Handbook of Social Psychology* (pp. 137–230), Vol. 1, 3rd edn. New York: Random House.

Nelson, R.R. and Nelson, K. (2002). Technology, institutions, and innovation systems. *Research Policy*, 31, 265–272.

North, D.C. (1990). *Institutions, Institutional Changes and Economic Performance*. Cambridge: Cambridge University Press.

Podolny, J.M. (2009). The buck stops (and starts) at business school. *Harvard Business Review*, 87(6), 62–67.

Porter, M.E. (1998). Clusters and the new economics of competition. *Harvard Business Review*, 76(6), 77–90.

Prahalad, C.K. and Krishnan, M.S. (2002). The dynamic synchronization of strategy and information technology. MIT Sloan Management Review, July 15.

Scott, W.R. (1995). *Institutions and Organizations*. Thousand Oaks, CA: Sage.

Scott, W.R. (2008). *Institutions and Organizations*, 3rd edn. Thousand Oaks, CA: Sage.

Staw, B.M. and Epstein, L.D. (2000). What bandwagons bring — Effects of popular management techniques on corporate performance, reputation and CEO pay. *Administrative Science Quarterly*, 45(3), 523–556.

Welter, F., Smallbone, D., Isakova, N., Aculai, E., and Schakirova, N. (2004). Women entrepreneurs in Ukraine, Republic of Moldova and Uzbekistan: Results of a comparative study. In UNECE (ed.), *Access to Financing and ICT: Women Entrepreneurs in the ECE Region* (pp. 39–52). Geneva: United Nations.

Williamson, O.E. (1979). *Markets and Hierarchies: Analysis and Antitrust Implications*. New York: Free Press.

Zucker, L.G. (1991). Postscript: Microfoundations of institutional thought. In Powell, W.W. and DiMaggio, P.J. (eds.), *The New Institutionalism in Organizational Analysis* (pp. 83–107). Chicago, IL: University of Chicago Press.

https://doi.org/10.1142/9789811271984_0003

Chapter 3

Driving Digital Transformation*

Dongwon Lee[†,¶], Barney Tan[‡,||], and Sunil Mithas[§,]**

[†]*The Hong Kong University of Science and Technology, Kowloon, Hong Kong*
[‡]*The University of New South Wales, Sydney, NSW, Australia*
[§]*University of South Florida, Tampa, FL, USA*
[¶]*dongwon@ust.hk*
[||]*barney.tan@unsw.edu.au*
[**]*smithas@usf.edu*

Due to the proliferation of digital technologies in recent decades, digital transformation has emerged as an important phenomenon in both academia and industry (Tabrizi *et al.*, 2019). However, despite much hype about digital transformation in the media and managerial articles, there is a great deal of fuzziness on what the term means, the role of technology in digital transformation, how it unfolds, and how incumbents and entrants should manage digital transformations. Our goal in this chapter

*This chapter is a derivative work, and is adapted from and draws on the authors' research and prior work, extensively updating and contemporizing some of the examples. In particular, the chapter draws on some fragments of the book, *Digital Intelligence: What Every Smart Manager Must Have for Success in an Information Age*. [Mithas, S. 2016. *Digital Intelligence: What Every Smart Manager Must Have for Success in an Information Age*. Gurgaon, Haryana, India: Portfolio Penguin].

is to review some of the recent work in this domain and provide our viewpoint on this topic, building on our prior and related work (Mithas, 2016).

1. Digital Transformation: Scope and Definition

Some view digital transformation as the strategic deployment of information technology (IT) to modify or substantively enhance business processes and practices to help the organization compete effectively in an increasingly digital world (Wessel *et al.*, 2021). Others view it as a process that aims to improve an entity by triggering significant changes to its properties through combinations of atoms, bits, information, computing, communication, and connectivity technologies (Vial, 2019).

We view digital transformation as different from other forms of organizational change in at least three important ways. First, the technologies involved, such as big data analytics, blockchain, the Internet of Things, or artificial intelligence (AI), seem very different from earlier forms of IT in terms of their capabilities (e.g., enablement of sensing, analytics, collaboration, and execution), scale, and extent of connectivity (see Hanelt *et al.*, 2021; Mithas *et al.*, 2022). Second, digital technologies in digital transformation cannot be restricted to the boundaries of a specific firm or industry, but involve a wider ecosystem or business network (Bharadwaj *et al.*, 2013) as compared to being more focused on change within an organization in relation to the adoption and use of enterprise IT systems. The overarching digital infrastructures and platforms are open, flexible, and ready for use by anyone, not just by companies (Parker *et al.*, 2016; Tilson *et al.*, 2010). Third, the consequences of digital transformation appear to extend beyond those of previous IT-enabled organizational change, which were usually associated with a particular business practice or incremental change within an organization, while consequences of digital transformation include the emergence of new digital business models even in non-digital industries (Hanelt *et al.*, 2021; Vial, 2019).

And yet, in spite of the general acknowledgment that digital transformation is a distinct phenomenon driven by novel forms of IT, whose implications are more expansive and far reaching than other technology-enabled phenomena seen previously (Wessel *et al.*, 2021), there is currently a lack of consensus on the scope and definition of digital transformation (Hanelt *et al.*, 2021). For instance, what is the difference between digital transformation and other "digital x" phenomena such as digital disruption, digitalization, or digital innovation (see Avital *et al.*, 2019)? The lack of a precise definition and conceptualization of digital transformation gives rise to the risk that the term could be used as a label for most technology-enabled phenomena, rendering it a meaningless catch-all buzzword (Bockshecker *et al.*, 2018).

As such, to clarify our discussion for the remainder of this chapter, we go back to the dictionary definition of the term "transformation," which the Merriam-Webster dictionary defines as "a complete or major change in someone's or something's appearance or form."[1] More specifically, we see digital transformation as distinct from digital innovation, which is defined as "the creation or adoption, and exploitation of an inherently unbounded, value-adding novelty (e.g., product, service, process, or business model) through the incorporation of digital technology" (Hund *et al.*, 2021), because transformation implies the modification of an existing, as opposed to the creation of a new, object.

In addition, digital transformation is also distinct from digital disruption because the latter implies the wholesale replacement or substitution of the existing object (see Riemer and Johnston, 2019). What is common, however, among digital transformation, digital innovation, and digital disruption is the fact they are all underpinned by digital technologies, and may be conceived as discrete processes under the umbrella of digitalization or digitization (i.e., two terms that are often used interchangeably; see Lyytinen and Yoo, 2002; Yoo *et al.*, 2012).

2. The Role of Technology in Digital Transformation

Technology and organizational change tend to go hand in hand, and radical changes in technologies often cause significant transformations in business activities. For instance, it took the emergence of newer transportation and communication technologies (e.g., railways, the telegraph, the telephone) and newer sources of energy (e.g., coal) to catalyze the growth of the modern multi-unit enterprise (Chandler, 1977; Landes, 2005). Successful digital transformation typically comes not from implementing new technologies but through transforming (1) customer experience,

[1] See https://www.merriam-webster.com/dictionary/transformation.

(2) operational processes, and (3) business models to take advantage of the possibilities that technologies provide (Westerman *et al.*, 2011).

Transforming customer experience through digital technologies enables customer analytics, digitally enhanced selling, predictive marketing, streamlined customer processes, omni-channel, and self-service. For example, Home Depot decided to pursue a more comprehensive digital transformation approach in late 2017 (Elsworth *et al.*, 2020). Its goal was to enhance the online shopping experience and provide customers with the highest-quality products and services through a seamless process across all of its sales channels. Home Depot subsequently invested $11 billion over three years to improve both its in-store and online shopping experience and hired about 1,000 IT professionals to improve customer experience. They developed its backend and distribution channels as well as a robust IT department to utilize customer data more effectively. As a result, Home Depot was able to reduce costs by tracking local trends and maintaining adequate inventory levels, and it has a positive stock market perception, with its stock value over the last five years rising from $135 to $415[2] (Elsworth *et al.*, 2020).

Transforming operational processes through digital technologies allows process digitization, remote working, operational transparency, and ultimately data-driven decision-making. To illustrate, Honeywell, a large American multinational conglomerate, has helped many companies improve their digital presence and capabilities. But Honeywell itself realized that it needed to begin to transform digitally when Darius Adamczyk became CEO in 2017 with a digital-first vision[3] (Ajao, 2021). Managing a wide-ranging multinational company could be inefficient, especially given a digital infrastructure that Adamczyk described as "a bit of an IT mess."[4] Thus, he invested heavily to improve the digital infrastructure for strengthening, streamlining, and standardizing the company's systems and processes, which enabled Honeywell's leaders to harness large amounts of data to make better informed decisions and execute those decisions more quickly and decisively (Ajao, 2021). By digitizing and streamlining its internal processes, Honeywell could build quality products and relationships. Using new digitized internal solutions and customer data, the company now offers technology solutions to its customers and has reinvented

[2] https://www.marketwatch.com/investing/stock/hd/charts?mod=mw_quote_advanced.

[3] https://www.ey.com/en_gl/ceo/thriving-in-the-digital-era-at-honeywell.

[4] https://www.ey.com/en_gl/ceo/thriving-in-the-digital-era-at-honeywell.

its industrial process. For example, Honeywell Forge helps its customers manage the connection of IT systems with operation systems running manufacturing sites, buildings, and other installations by providing real-time data and visual intelligence.[5] Consequently, in the past five years, Honeywell's stock prices have grown from $115 to over $210.[6]

Transforming business models through digital technologies enables digitally enhanced business processes, new digital products and services, the reshaping of organizational boundaries, and the global delivery of products and services. Microsoft, for example, has been known for its Windows and Office Suites and achieved success in its first three decades by licensing its software (Wu and Na, 2020). Since Satya Nadella became CEO in 2014, the company decided to rethink its strategy from licensing proprietary software platforms and applications to focus on Azure-based cloud services (Wu and Na, 2020). Azure provides three layers of cloud computing services: infrastructure as a service (IaaS), platform as a service (PaaS), and software as a service (SaaS) for building, managing, deploying, and testing applications and services (Wu and Na, 2020). In addition, Azure supports open-source programming languages and operating systems instead of resisting the open-source movement. In 2018, Microsoft acquired GitHub for $7.5 billion in support of open-source software and communities. Microsoft's transformation has fueled its growth with a market cap of $2.4 trillion and stock prices that skyrocketed from $38 in 2014 to $315 in Jan 2022.[7] Without these changes, these accomplishments may not have been possible.

3. Digital Transformation: Phases and Stages of Maturity

Digital transformation is widely conceived as an iterative process (Chanias *et al.*, 2019) that is made up of a number of phases. While different specifications of its constituent phases exist in the literature (e.g., Boston Consulting Group, 2016; Verhoef *et al.*, 2021), it may be helpful to make a distinction between phases for digital transformation at the industry level and at the firm level.

---

[5] https://www.honeywellforge.ai.

[6] https://www.marketwatch.com/investing/stock/hon/charts?mod=mw_quote_advanced.

[7] https://www.marketwatch.com/investing/stock/msft/charts?mod=mw_quote_advanced.

At the industry level, prior work identifies three phases for industry transformation in general: *trigger*, *experimentation*, and *shakeout* (Porter and Rivkin, 2000). In the *trigger* phase, most digital transformations are typically driven by, or originate from, technological developments, evolving consumer preferences, regulatory changes, and entrepreneurial activities prompted by business leaders, new entrants, or competition (Vial, 2019). Regarding technology as a trigger, the changes brought about by IT tend to be evident across almost all sectors of the economy. Day and Schoemaker (2000b) distinguish between emerging and established technologies, arguing that emerging technologies are associated with much greater ambiguity regarding infrastructure, markets/customers, and industry than established technologies. But it must also be recognized that technology alone is insufficient to bring about a transformation (Tabrizi *et al.*, 2019). Successful transformations require managerial choices and actions. For example, when Alibaba, China's e-commerce giant, was competing with eBay, which entered the C2C sector in China first and had a 70% market share prior to the entry of Alibaba's Taobao.com, it was not cutting-edge technologies that enabled Alibaba to digitally transform the C2C business model. Instead, it was a considered an adaptation of how transactions were enabled by digital technologies in line with the preferences of the Chinese market (e.g., allowing buyers and sellers to haggle over prices) that allowed Alibaba to beat eBay and assume the role of the market leader (Tan *et al.*, 2015).

The workings of other forms of triggers are apparent and commonplace as well. For example, changes in consumer tastes may explain the transition from CDs to MP3s (Riemer and Johnston, 2019), while the deregulation of the airline industry in the United States has brought significant changes in its wake. Evidence from emerging economies such as China and India also attests to the transformational role of government regulations and interventions (or lack thereof) in business activities (see Muthukannan *et al.*, 2020). Likewise, the role of entrepreneurs is evident in the changes brought by new businesses or start-ups, which often use newer technologies or combinations of existing technologies to their advantage to bring about digital transformation (Nambisan *et al.*, 2019).

The most important digital transformation triggers tend to be those that affect the relative position of players (Porter and Rivkin, 2000). Dramatic changes in relative position do not come from operational excellence alone; operational excellence only shifts the productivity frontier. Truly transformative changes confront existing companies with difficult trade-offs; if there are no trade-offs, such technological changes merely shift the productivity frontier.

The next phase after the trigger phase is the *experimentation* phase, which involves a trial-and-error search for a new overarching formula for competitive success. In this phase, many players would compete for key markets with alternative technologies and standards. Digital ecosystems may be established to serve as information conduits and the basis of virtual alliances, and "keystone" (Iansiti and Levien, 2004) or core entities (Pierce, 2009) within the ecosystem such as venture capitalists and government agencies may play an important role in this phase, which tends to be characterized by operational risks and a lack of information. A common dilemma is whether to improve relative position but undermine future industry structure (Porter and Rivkin, 2000). The markets for fintech, cryptocurrencies, and AI products are just some examples of sectors undergoing digital transformation that are currently in this phase.

The process of digital transformation typically culminates in a *shakeout* phase, in which a dominant pattern emerges, only to be thwarted again by another trigger for a subsequent iteration of digital transformation. Arguably, the music industry experienced a shakeout after Apple entered with iPod and iTunes, making the company a dominant player in the online retail music space (see Riemer and Johnston, 2019). iTunes itself has now been superseded by streaming services such as Spotify, Tidal, and Apple's own Apple Music (see Eriksson *et al.*, 2019). Other examples include the industries that have had to contend with the emergence of digital platforms that are based on the sharing economy paradigm. Traditional businesses in the taxi and hotel industries, for instance, have had to respond to threats imposed by platforms such as Uber (Cramer and Krueger, 2016) and Airbnb (Chang and Sokol, 2020). This has resulted in a market *shakeout* characterized by the demise of organizations that are unable to adapt to the new competitive equilibrium, which stems from the measures and subsequent countermeasures of the traditional and new players.

A second way to understand phases of digital transformation can be from the perspective of the organization. Kane *et al.* (2015) emphasize digital maturity as a gradual process that unfolds across the organization over time and propose three phases of digital maturity: early, developing, and maturing phases, with respect to barriers, strategy, culture, talent development, and leadership. In practice, the global leader in management consulting, McKinsey, has provided a different conceptualization of the process with three stages of digital transformation and ten guiding principles (Catlin *et al.*, 2017). McKinsey's three stages of digital transformation are the (1) defining value, (2) launch and acceleration, and (3) scaling up stages. Boston Consulting Group has also conceived digital transformation as a journey with four critical steps: (1) educate on the landscape, (2) crystallize a plan for how to move forward, (3) accelerate successful initiatives, and (4) scale up and transform the entire organization (Boston Consulting Group, 2016). A key commonality of these distinct conceptualizations is that digital transformation is seen as an iterative process, and organizations have to understand their starting position in order to plan for the right path forward by aligning digital technology and business (Saldanha *et al.*, 2020).

4. Managing Emerging Technologies and Digital Transformation

Incumbents have always had a particularly difficult time navigating and responding to transformations that involve IT. The networked nature of emerging technologies has made that even more difficult because now it is not only the incumbent that has to respond but the partners in its business network as well (Ansari and Krop, 2012).

The history of the computer industry is also replete with cases of incumbent inertia and resistance. For example, IBM decided not to enter the mainframe business initially because of a 1948 forecast about a very low demand for computers (less than a dozen or so) based on the amount of computing done in the world at that time. Decades later, it had a difficult time entering the PC business, and when it did, it made poor choices that would later incapacitate the company. It also did not recognize Xerox's potential and refused to buy it, and it passed an opportunity to buy 10% of Intel's equity (Day and Schoemaker, 2000b; Day *et al.*, 2000).

Other internationally renowned organizations across an array of industries have also fallen prey to such tendencies. Kodak, for example, was founded in 1880 and rated among the five most valuable brands in the world until the 1990s. It built one of the first digital cameras in 1975 but failed to adapt its business model because it wanted to cling on to its lucrative film business. Worldwide camera sales showed negligible quantities of digital cameras in 1995 but more than 20 million were sold in 2005, overtaking sales of conventional film cameras (*The Economist*, 2012).

In a similar vein, Microsoft reportedly killed its search engine project called Keywords in 2000 after two months of experimentation, fearing that this new business "would cannibalize other revenue streams," before Google figured out a way to combine search with advertising. Microsoft also declined to acquire Overture in 2003, which was eventually bought by Yahoo (Guth, 2009). Some suggest that Yahoo also made a mistake early on when it preferred its lower-quality search engine to the better-performing Google search engine because it wanted surfers to stick around on its own website, even if it did not provide the most relevant search results to users.

More recent examples include the failure of incumbents, such as taxi companies (e.g., Cramer and Krueger, 2016) and hotel chains (see Chang and Sokol, 2020), to adapt to the platformization of businesses and the emergence of the sharing economy. Even in the financial sector (which is notoriously resistant to change), the hegemony of banks and financial institutions is now being threatened by the proliferation of financial innovations (Anand and Mantrala, 2019), and these incumbents have to carefully consider if they are to imitate (Chen *et al.*, 2019), take over (Dranev *et al.*, 2019), or form strategic partnerships (Muthukannan and Gozman, 2019) with the new fintech start-ups.

However, not all the missteps related to emerging technologies and industry transformations can be blamed on managerial negligence, complacency, or ignorance. Industry changes happen slowly at times and may be abruptly brought about by forces that are below the incumbents' radars. Do incumbents always lag behind when it comes to emerging technologies? The answer is "no," and to understand this, some make a distinction between sustaining and "disruptive" innovations. We must forewarn the readers that despite the hype that "disruptive innovations" have received, there are significant questions about their underlying ideas and the key premises, and stories in the trade press have also provided anecdotal evidence against the hype associated with the label "disruption" (King and Baatartogtokh, 2015; Lepore, 2014).

Incumbents are usually good at managing transformations that pertain to sustaining technologies. Tushman and Anderson (1986) characterize such technologies as "competence-enhancing." These are the technologies that correspond to the current dominant customers' value. Even if there is a radical discontinuous change in these technologies and it does not threaten the business models of incumbents, chances are that incumbents will find a way to succeed with such transformations. According to Porter (1985), a desirable technological change has several features. First, it lowers costs or enhances differentiation and makes a technological lead sustainable. Second, it shifts costs or uniqueness in favor of a firm. Third, pioneering the technology translates into early-mover advantages, in addition to those advantages inherent in the technology itself. Finally, it improves overall industry structure.

More difficult, however, are the digital transformations that pertain to what are known as "disruptive" or "competence-destroying" innovations. Note that the word "disruptive technology" is not used here. Technologies are typically neutral — they can be sustaining and disruptive at the same time when viewed from the perspective of incumbents or entrants. Sometimes, a technology can appear to be both sustaining and disruptive. Consider video on demand from the perspective of cable providers: This technology is needed for the cable providers' internet or data business, but it potentially cannibalizes their own on-demand services.

"Disruptive" here refers to a technology's potential to cause turmoil to the established ways in which current industry players create value and limit their ability to thwart entrants that are not vested in current industry practices or business models. This is one of the critical downsides of disruptive innovations — namely, it brings new types of competitors that have no regard for the current set of rules (Argyres *et al.*, 2019). Incumbent music players had a difficult time dealing with iTunes because Apple was not invested in \$15 music CDs (Riemer and Johnston, 2019). Likewise, Blockbuster had a difficult time competing with Netflix because Netflix was not wedded to the idea of charging late fees, and its business model did not depend on late fees.

According to proponents of the theory of disruptive innovation, disruptive innovations are those whose performance trajectory is typically below the current market needs and far below the performance trajectory of the sustaining innovations. Typically, these innovations are not valued by mainstream customers and they initially have lower profit margins. Disruptive innovations arise because of a simple dynamic: Technologies almost always improve more quickly than the ability of humans and markets to absorb those technologies. And when they do, revolutionary change unfolds in the form of punctuated equilibrium (Gersick, 1991).

Disruptive innovations are different from radical, discontinuous, and sustaining innovations. The latter make quantum improvements in the technology trajectory but do not create heart-wrenching trade-offs for incumbents in the same way that disruptive innovations do. For example, Internet Explorer (a browser) was a radical but sustaining innovation for

Microsoft, but Java is disruptive because it makes Microsoft's operating system less valuable. This is the primary reason why many incumbents fail to adapt. The trade-offs could entail the abandonment of the existing means of value creation, which the incumbent firms could have spent a lot of time and effort to develop and nurture. The reluctance to make these painful trade-offs gives rise to organizational inertia, which results in sub-optimal decision-making that precipitates a delayed response or lack of response (Lucas and Goh, 2009).

5. Managing Digital Transformation as Incumbents

Incumbents, in particular larger organizations such as the ones in the Fortune 500 rankings, contribute a high share of GDP, but they also suffer high mortality rates and greater difficulty in transforming themselves. For example, of the original Fortune 500 companies that were named in 1955, only 52 remain in the 2019 list. Examples of companies such as Kodak, Blockbuster, Borders, and A&P are all sobering reminders of the difficulties in transforming and sustaining the business of these organizations (Lucas, 2012; Mithas, 2015). The recent break-ups of General Electric (GE), Johnson & Johnson, and Siemens are the latest examples of incumbents facing challenges in transforming themselves (Gryta, 2021; Kantchev, 2021; Rockoff and Loftus, 2021).

IT has made managing disruptive technologies even more difficult by blurring the distinction between "atoms and bits," breaking with the need to trade-off between reach and range, informing physical and information processes and value chains, and making conventional value chains irrelevant. This has been exacerbated, especially over the last two decades, with digitalization and the emergence of the networked economy (Van Alstyne *et al.*, 2016). If emerging technologies are a fundamental threat for the incumbents, how should incumbents approach emerging technologies, and what are some of the critical questions they must ask in order to harness their potential? Proponents of disruptive innovation offer some prescriptions. First, determine whether the technology is competence-enhancing versus competence-destroying, or what Christensen refers to as "sustaining versus disruptive" innovations. This can be done by considering the performance trajectories of technologies and the absorptive capacity of the market. One clue, according to some, is that marketing and finance personnel rarely support disruptive technologies because their incentives are more closely aligned with the success of existing businesses, while technical personnel do. Disagreements between these two groups can alert managers to the disruptive potential of a technology (Young and Grant, 2003).

Second, incumbents should determine the strategic significance of a disruptive technology by asking the right questions of the right people. According to Christensen, the right question is whether the slope of improvement in a disruptive technology will overtake the slope of performance improvement demanded by the mainstream market — not whether the slope of improvement in a disruptive technology will overtake the slope of sustaining innovations in an existing technology. The right people are customers in fringe markets, not lead customers. These customers may be located currently in emerging markets such as China and India, and/or may be at the bottom of the pyramid and beyond the radar screens of managers. Although serving these customers can be challenging, it can provide opportunities for creating disruptive innovations for developed markets.

One example of a firm currently doing this is Alibaba, which has been investing heavily in developing what it terms "rural e-commerce" for close to a decade (Leong *et al.*, 2015). By bringing e-commerce to rural agricultural villages across China, Alibaba was able to cultivate its ecosystem of suppliers and customers and develop the infrastructure in some of the more remote areas of the country. Beyond the immense social benefits of catering to this fringe market, such as increased incomes and standards of living, Alibaba was able to expand its potential market by increasing the pool of potential suppliers and customers, while avoiding the stagnation that many e-commerce firms tend to encounter in developed economies.

Third, the initial market for an emerging technology must be located. Market research is sometimes not helpful for new products; for example, Polaroid instant cameras were projected at a mere 100,000 in total demand over its life cycle. Similarly, AT&T did not recognize the full significance of mobile phones because of a McKinsey report that predicted fewer than 1 million wireless users by 2000. The report was remarkably off, and there were about 740 million actual wireless users in 2000 (*The Economist*, 2005). Instead of relying on market research alone, one should locate and create the initial market for an emerging technology and then experiment rapidly, iteratively, and inexpensively with both the product and the market, as TikTok did. TikTok, owned by Chinese tech firm ByteDance, was launched just over five years ago in 2016 as Douyin in China. But it did not achieve mainstream acceptance until it decided to explicitly target teenage consumers, especially by making its services available to this customer segment worldwide with its merger with another Chinese social media service, Musical.ly, in 2018. The latter, in particular, was immensely popular among school-age children and provided TikTok with the foothold it needed. TikTok is currently the fourth largest social media platform in the world with around 1.6 billion users by the end of 2021, just over 5 years of its inception.

Finally, some argue that an independent organization should be used to build a business based on a disruptive technology. Note that it is not necessary to have a separate organization if the new technology is a sustaining technology or is so financially attractive that the current organization will support it anyway. A separate organization may be necessary when the disruptive technology has a lower profit margin than the mainstream business and serves the unique needs of a new set of customers. But it is important to note that the extent of disruptiveness may vary for different entities, even if they are within the same business network. For instance, as digital books are more profitable than physical copies, some argue that online book publishing is not disruptive for publishers, although it may be disruptive for brick-and-mortar retailers who may be disintermediated, as happened in the music industry. Establishing a new entity for a disruptive offering may help create excitement in spite of smaller orders and lower profits initially, while at the parent firm big orders and profit margins may be needed to turn heads. A new organization also avoids other problems. For example, Kodak, before George Fisher, kept electronic imaging dispersed and mixed with chemical imaging, and its policies did not allow the hiring of better-paid IT employees because they would need larger salaries than the "chemical" employees, who held sway at the time (Day and Schoemaker, 2000b; Day *et al.*, 2000).

Too much organizational separation should also be avoided, however, because separation would not allow the new organization to benefit from the strengths of its parent, as the example of Xerox's PARC lab proves. IBM's personal computer division is another example of where there may have been too much separation (Day and Schoemaker, 2000b). It may be worthwhile to keep the disruptive organization independent even if it becomes successful at what it does. While reintegrating a unit back into the company may work for sustaining technologies because of scale and scope logic, it often fails for disruptive technologies because of arguments about which groups get certain resources. As Bower and Christensen (1995) argue, "For the corporation to live, it must be willing to see the business units die. If the corporation doesn't kill them off itself, competitors will."

As we noted earlier, there remain fundamental questions about the very notion of "disruptive" innovations and its underlying definitions, about the unit of analysis, rigor of research, and predictive or prescriptive power. Hence, caution is necessary to avoid over-interpreting recommendations or prescriptions coming from proponents of disruptive innovation. Regardless of the validity of the ideas related to disruption, managers should monitor new technologies and think carefully about developing new capabilities, while also creating new organizational structures and incentives to make informed decisions on pilot programs or seed investments to avoid surprises.

A literature review and analyses of some real-world cases suggest that established firms suffer from at least four traps when they face emerging technologies (Day and Schoemaker, 2000a): (1) delayed participation, (2) sticking with the familiar, (3) a reluctance to fully commit, and (4) a lack of persistence. The trajectories of companies such as Kodak, Borders, Blockbuster, and Barnes & Noble lend credence to these suggestions. For example, Borders and Blockbuster delayed investments in technologies and websites to compete with the threat from Amazon.com and Netflix, respectively. As indicated earlier, Kodak had a hard time imagining a filmless future, even though it invented the first digital camera in 1975. It stuck to its existing business model for far too long and failed to commit to new business models. Similarly, Barnes & Noble did not show persistence and exited the e-reader business prematurely, only to reenter again, even though it had invested in that business before Amazon.com did.

But how should firms avoid or deal with these traps? Day and Schoemaker (2000b) suggest a number of solutions. First, firms should invest in widening their peripheral vision and creating a learning culture. This will require scanning emerging technologies, assessing their significance, and launching pilot projects to be familiar with them. Second, firms should stay flexible in pursuing new strategies and be prepared to abandon obsolete strategies and business models. However, these decisions should be data driven and not based on superficial analyses or driven by fads such as the pursuit of outsourcing due to mimetic tendencies or blindly following the advice of consultants with a narrow view. Finally, providing organizational autonomy to new businesses based on emerging technologies may be a sensible idea if such ideas are hard to nurture within the enterprise because of turf wars or a lack of incentive alignment.

6. Managing Digital Transformation as New Entrants

Many incumbents may have a difficult time managing and leveraging disruptive technologies, but then so do the new entrants challenging them. And what makes it worse for the new entrants is that they tend to be resource-constrained start-ups, which means that they can ill afford missteps in terms of their business decisions (Xiao *et al.*, 2020). For these firms, there is a need to decide between two ways of framing how they approach the use of digital technologies: technical framing and market framing.

Technical framing involves improving the features of an existing product or service with digital technologies such that the product or service becomes more acceptable or attractive to mainstream customers. The emergence of sharing economy platforms, such as Uber and Airbnb, is a perfect illustration of technical framing at work, because the new consumption paradigm is only made possible by the increasing bandwidth of mobile networks, advances in GPS technology, and the proliferation of smartphones globally (Geissinger *et al.*, 2020). New entrants tend to be inherently more flexible in the adoption of digital technologies. Their biggest challenge, however, is that they tend to have limited resources to experiment with a broad range of technologies (Starr and MacMillan, 1990), and even if their initial business ideas prove successful, they would be subject to the responses of the incumbents and/or imitation from other new entrants (Tan *et al.*, 2010). To increase the effectiveness of technical framing, we recommend that new entrants must think ahead and try to anticipate the competitive actions of incumbent firms and imitators before their ideas arrive at fruition. This could entail the protection of their innovation and intellectual property (Makadok, 1998), as well as a relentless pursuit of continuous innovation so that they can continuously disrupt the competitive equilibrium to establish a constant stream of temporary competitive advantages (Sambamurthy *et al.*, 2003).

Market framing, on the other hand, would involve taking technology as a given and focusing instead on finding the relevant unserved or underserved customer segments that are not catered to by the incumbents. For instance, bottom-of-the-pyramid markets in not only emerging economies but also in developed economies are especially well suited as a target for initiatives aligned with market framing. GE, Panasonic, Alibaba, Tata Motors, and 3M are among some of the prominent companies across the globe that are trying to use reverse or frugal innovations to target bottom-of-the-pyramid markets. The emergence of the global fintech movement is another example of the workings of market framing. To illustrate, let us consider the case of Ppdai.com, the first online peer-to-peer (P2P) lending platform in China that was established in 2007. Ppdai's four founders were a mix of experienced professionals from finance and IT backgrounds who were motivated to set up the business to extend the benefits of micro-lending services to the segment of customers that have been traditionally excluded by the existing banks and financial institutions in China. This segment — which may include those living in rural or remote areas, young adults, and proprietors of cash-based microbusinesses — typically borrowed from family, friends, or even illegal loan sharks who charge exorbitant interest rates when they were unable to obtain loans. The founders of Ppdai realized that the unmet need for loan services among this customer segment was significant, and sought to match individual borrowers to individual lenders with its platform-based business model to provide safer, fairer, and more transparent access to loans for the former and investments for the latter.

Nonetheless, there are formidable challenges that new entrants pursuing market framing have to overcome, the foremost of which is the need to deal with the "liability of newness" (Singh *et al.*, 1986). If a market segment has been neglected by the incumbent firms, there is typically a good reason for them to do so. For example, the segment may be too risky or simply economically unviable to serve (Tynan and Drayton, 1987). While technological advances may mean that serving these previously neglected segments is now feasible, the new entrants would face a greater need for legitimacy (Deephouse and Suchman, 2008). For instance, regulatory authorities will have to ensure that the new entrants are not exploiting vulnerable groups in society, while investors will have to have confidence in the new entrants' business viability. To overcome the liability of newness and attain legitimacy, we recommend that new entrants be hypersensitive to environmental changes and the sentiment of their stakeholders. They will have to carefully consider the social pressures that will confront them as they attempt to serve a new customer segment, and adopt an appropriate response to the pressures (see Oliver, 1991) so as to maintain access to the resources required for their survival.

Making the right choice between technical and market framing is crucial for the competitive success of new entrants. In fact, some people argue that the main reason for Kodak's failure was that it erroneously framed its issue as a technology problem to make digital camera performance similar to that of silver halide film, as opposed to a market problem that creates a demand for a new product that they invented. In contrast, entrants such as Canon were trying to sell what they had, and thus framed the issue as a market problem. Similarly, Apple's Newton failed because of technology framing, whereas Palm Computing succeeded initially because of its market framing, which emphasized making do with simple, low-end applications.

7. Conclusion

This chapter has defined digital transformation and distinguished it from evolutionary change and other digitalization processes that have captured the attention of IS academia and practice over the last five years. We discussed the role of technology, particularly emerging technologies, in digital transformations, and why both incumbents and new entrants have a difficult time dealing with "competence destroying" or "disruptive" innovations, a particular class of emerging technologies.

We focused on how incumbents should think about digital transformations, and in particular, should seek to avoid traps such as delayed participation and sticking with the familiar, a reluctance to fully commit, and lack of persistence. Some of the key prescriptions we offered are to stay curious and keep abreast of new technologies, calibrate responses to them carefully, launch pilot projects or "dabble" in new technologies to reduce technical uncertainties, and pay attention to timing because it is sometimes possible for a technology to be ahead of the market. In such cases, waiting may be appropriate until the necessary complements or "killer apps" emerge (Tiwana, 2014).

We then turned our attention to discussing how new entrants should approach digital transformation, and we framed this as a careful choice between technical or market framing. The former refers to the enhancement of an existing product or service with digital technologies to increase their value or attractiveness, while the latter entails identifying and catering to customer segments that have been previously neglected through the use of digital technologies. Our recommendations for new entrants in relation to technical framing emphasize staying ahead of the competition by defending against imitation (Makadok, 1998) and relentlessly innovating to establish a continuous stream of temporary competitive advantages (Sambamurthy *et al.*, 2003). On the other hand, our prescriptions for effective market framing are centered on overcoming the "liability of newness" (Singh *et al.*, 1986, p. 171) and adopting the appropriate response to social pressures (Oliver, 1991) for the attainment of legitimacy (Deephouse and Suchman, 2008).

While this chapter provides some useful concepts to work with when it comes to considering emerging technologies and making sense of digital transformation, an important caveat to note is that no two digital transformations are alike, and heuristics based on the past or from a different context may not hold in the future. As such, managers should be prepared to navigate new waters and learn as they go along. It may be worth remembering that in the end, technologies themselves rarely change or transform anything; it is thoughtful leadership and managerial actions that drive positive change (Tabrizi *et al.*, 2019). It may require some "craziness" and determination. Apple's "Think Different" commercial in 1997 is a particularly apt reminder: "The people who are crazy enough to think they can change the world are the ones who do."

References

Ajao, E. (2021). A look at Honeywell's digital transformation strategy. https://www.techtarget.com/searchenterpriseai/feature/252510464/A-look-at-Honeywells-digital-transformation-strategy.

Anand, D. and Mantrala, M. (2019). Responding to disruptive business model innovations: The case of traditional banks facing fintech entrants. *Journal of Banking and Financial Technology*, 3(1), 19–31.

Ansari, S. and Krop, P. (2012). Incumbent performance in the face of a radical innovation: Towards a framework for incumbent challenger dynamics. *Research Policy*, 41(8), 1357–1374.

Argyres, N., Mahoney, J.T., and Nickerson, J. (2019). Strategic responses to shocks: Comparative adjustment costs, transaction costs, and opportunity costs. *Strategic Management Journal*, 40(3), 357–376.

Baiyere, A., Avital, M., Berente, N., Henfridsson, O., Hinings, C. B., Tuertscher, P., and Yoo, Y. (2019). Digital "X": In need of new theories or do prior theories suffice? In *79th Academy of Management (AOM) Proceedings*, 9–13.

Bharadwaj, A., El Sawy, O.A., Pavlou, P.A., and Venkatraman, N. (2013). Digital business strategy: Toward a next generation of insights. *MIS Quarterly*, 37(2), 471–482.

Bockshecker, A., Hackstein, S., and Baumöl, U. (2018). Systematization of the term digital transformation and its phenomena from a socio-technical perspective — A literature review. *Proceedings of the European Conference on Information Systems (ECIS) 2018*, Portsmouth. Research Papers 43. https://aisel.aisnet.org/ecis2018_rp/43.

Boston Consulting Group (2016). *Transformation: Delivering and Sustaining Breakthrough Performance*, Fæste, F. and Hemerling, J. (eds.). Boston Consulting Group. https://media-publications.bcg.com/transformation-ebook/BCG-Transformation-Nov-2016.pdf.

Bower, J.L. and Christensen, C.M. (1995). Disruptive technologies: Catching the wave. *Harvard Business Review*, January–February, pp. 43–53.

Catlin, T., Lorenz, J.T., Sternfels, B., and Willmott, P. (2017). A roadmap for a digital transformation. https://www.mckinsey.com/industries/financial-services/our-insights/a-roadmap-for-a-digital-transformation.

Chandler, A.D. (1977). *The Visible Hand: The Managerial Revolution in American Business*. Cambridge, MA: Harvard University Press.

Chang, H.H. and Sokol, D.D. (2022). How incumbents respond to competition from innovative disruptors in the sharing economy — The impact of Airbnb on hotel performance. *Strategic Management Journal*, 43(3), 425–446.

Chanias, S., Myers, M.D., and Hess, T. (2019). Digital transformation strategy making in pre-digital organizations: The case of a financial services provider. *Journal of Strategic Information Systems*, 28(1), 17–33.

Chen, M.A., Wu, Q., and Yang, B. (2019). How valuable is FinTech innovation? *The Review of Financial Studies*, 32(5), 2062–2106.

Cramer, J. and Krueger, A.B. (2016). Disruptive change in the taxi business: The case of Uber. *American Economic Review*, 106(5), 177–182.

Day, G.S. and Schoemaker, P.J.H. (2000a). Avoiding the pitfalls of emerging technologies. *California Management Review*, 42(2), 8–33.

Day, G.S. and Schoemaker, P.J.H. (2000b). A different game. In Day, G.S., Schoemaker, P.J.H., and Gunther, R.E. (eds.), *Wharton on Managing Emerging Technologies* (pp. 1–23). Hoboken, NJ: Wiley.

Day, G.S., Schoemaker, P.J.H., and Gunther, R.E. (eds.) (2000). *Wharton on Managing Emerging Technologies*. Hoboken, NJ: Wiley.

Deephouse, D.L. and Suchman, M.C. (2008). Legitimacy in organizational institutionalism. In Greenwood, R. Oliver, C., Sahlin, K., and Suddaby, R. (eds.), *The Sage Handbook of Organizational Institutionalism* (pp. 49–77). Thousand Oaks, CA, USA: Sage.

Dranev, Y., Frolova, K., and Ochirova, E. (2019). The impact of fintech M&A on stock returns. *Research in International Business and Finance*, 48, 353–364.

Elsworth, J., Ferguson, K., Kirca, A., Miller, J., Yildiz, H., Whipple, J., Beck, J., and McNamara, G. (2020). *The Home Depot Inc.: A Digital Transformation for Customer Experience*. London, ON: Ivey Publishing, 10. Available from

Ivey Publishing, product no. W20385. https://hbsp.harvard.edu/product/W20385-PDF-ENG.

Eriksson, M., Fleischer, R., Johansson, A., Snickars, P., and Vonderau, P. (2019). *Spotify Teardown: Inside the Black Box of Streaming Music*. Cambridge, MA, MIT Press.

Geissinger, A., Laurell, C., and Sandström, C. (2020). Digital disruption beyond Uber and Airbnb — Tracking the long tail of the sharing economy. *Technological Forecasting and Social Change*, 155, 119323.

Gersick, C.J.G. (1991). Revolutionary change theories: A multilevel exploration of the punctuated equilibrium paradigm. *Academy of Management Review*, 16(1), 10–36.

Gryta, T. (2021). "The end of the GE we knew": Breakup turns a page in modern business history. *Wall Street Journal*, 9 Nov 2021. https://www.wsj.com/articles/the-end-of-the-ge-we-knew-breakup-turns-a-page-in-modern-business-history-11636509385.

Guth, R.A. (2009). Microsoft bid to beat Google Builds on a history of misses. *Wall Street Journal*, 16 Jan 2009, A1, A8. http://www.wsj.com/articles/SB123207131111388507.

Hanelt, A., Bohnsack, R., Marz, D., and Antunes Marante, C. (2021). A systematic review of the literature on digital transformation: Insights and implications for strategy and organizational change. *Journal of Management Studies*, 58(5), 1159–1197.

Hund, A., Wagner, H.-T., Beimborn, D., and Weitzel, T. (2021). Digital innovation: Review and novel perspective. *Journal of Strategic Information Systems*, 30(4), 101695.

Iansiti, M. and Levien, R. (2004). *The Keystone Advantage: What the New Dynamics of Business Ecosystems Mean for Strategy, Innovation and Sustainability*. Brighton, MA, USA: Harvard Business School Press.

Kane, G.C., Palmer, D., Phillips, A.N., Kiron, D., and Buckley, N. (2015). Strategy, not technology, drives digital transformation. *MIT Sloan Management Review*, 14, 1–25.

Kantchev, G. (2021). GE was once a model for Siemens but now follows its rival's path. *Wall Street Journal*, 11 Nov 2021. https://www.wsj.com/articles/ge-was-once-a-model-for-siemens-but-now-follows-its-rivals-path-11636656545.

King, A.A. and Baatartogtokh, B. (2015). How useful is the theory of disruptive innovation? *MIT Sloan Management Review*, Fall, 77–90. http://sloanreview.mit.edu/article/how-useful-is-the-theory-of-disruptive-innovation/.

Landes, D.S. (2005). *The Unbound Prometheus: Technological Change and Industrial Development in Western Europe from 1750 to the Present*, 2nd edn. Cambridge, England: Cambridge University Press.

Leong, C.M.L., Pan, S.L., Ratcham, P., and Kaewkitipong, L. (2015). ICT-enabled community empowerment in crisis response: Social media in

Thailand Flooding 2011. *Journal of the Association for Information Systems*, 16(3), 174–212.

Lepore, J. (2014). The disruption machine. *The New Yorker*, June 23, 2014. http://www.newyorker.com/reporting/2014/06/23/140623fa_fact_lepore.

Lucas, H.C. (2012). *The Search for Survival: Lessons from Disruptive Technologies*. Santa Barbara, CA: ABC-CLIO.

Lucas, H.C., Jr. and Goh, J.M. (2009). Disruptive technology: How Kodak missed the digital photography revolution. *Journal of Strategic Information Systems*, 18(1), 46–55.

Lyytinen, K. and Yoo, Y. (2002). Research commentary: The next wave of nomadic computing. *Information Systems Research*, 13(4), 377–388.

Makadok, R. (1998). Can first-mover and early-mover advantages be sustained in an industry with low barriers to entry/imitation? *Strategic Management Journal*, 19(7), 683–696.

Mithas, S. (2015). *Making the Elephant Dance: The Tata Way to Innovate, Transform and Globalize.* Penguin Portfolio. http://www.amazon.in/dp/B012G9MSCA.

Mithas, S. (2016). *Digital Intelligence: What Every Smart Manager Must Have for Success in an Information Age*. Finerplanet. http://a.co/hxsPEJv.

Mithas, S., Chen, Z.-L., Saldanha, T., and De Oliveira Silveira, A. (2022). How will artificial intelligence and industry 4.0 emerging technologies transform operations management? *Production and Operations Management*, 31(12), 4475–4487.

Muthukannan, P. and Gozman, D.P. (2019, January 21, 2021). Meeting the challenge of fintech startups: The development of dynamic capabilities at incumbent banks. *Proceedings of the International Conference on Information Systems (ICIS) 2019*. Paper 6. https://aisel.aisnet.org/icis2019/blockchain_fintech/blockchain_fintech/6.

Muthukannan, P., Tan, B., Gozman, D., and Johnson, L. (2020). The emergence of a Fintech ecosystem: A case study of the Vizag Fintech Valley in India. *Information & Management*, 57(8), 103385.

Nambisan, S., Wright, M., and Feldman, M. (2019). The digital transformation of innovation and entrepreneurship: Progress, challenges and key themes. *Research Policy*, 48(8), 103773.

Oliver, C. (1991). Strategic responses to institutional processes. *Academy of Management Review*, 16(1), 145–179.

Parker, G.G., Van Alstyne, M.W., and Choudary, S.P. (2016). *Platform Revolution: How Networked Markets are Transforming the Economy and How to Make Them Work for You*. New York, USA: Norton.

Pierce, L. (2009). Big losses in ecosystem niches: How core firm decisions drive complementary product shakeouts. *Strategic Management Journal*, 30(3), 323–347.

Porter, M.E. (1985). Technology and Competitive Advantage. *Journal of Business Strategy*, 5(3), 60–78.

Porter, M.E. and Rivkin, J.W. (2000). *Industry Transformation*. Boston, MA: Harvard Business School Publishing, 14. Available from Harvard Business Publishing, product no. 9-701-008. https://hbsp.harvard.edu/product/701008-PDF-ENG.

Riemer, K. and Johnston, R.B. (2019). Disruption as worldview change: A Kuhnian analysis of the digital music revolution. *Journal of Information Technology*, 34(4), 350–370.

Rockoff, J.D. and Loftus, P. (2021). Johnson & Johnson's breakup: What to know. *Wall Street Journal*, 12 Nov 2021. https://www.wsj.com/articles/johnson-johnsons-breakup-what-to-know-11636715701.

Saldanha, T.J., Lee, D., and Mithas, S. (2020). Aligning information technology and business: The differential effects of alignment during investment planning, delivery, and change. *Information Systems Research*, 31(4), 1260–1281.

Sambamurthy, V., Bharadwaj, A., and Grover, V. (2003). Shaping agility through digital options: Reconceptualizing the role of information technology in contemporary firms. *MIS Quarterly*, 27(2), 237–263.

Singh, J.V., Tucker, D.J., and House, R.J. (1986). Organizational legitimacy and the liability of newness. *Administrative Science Quarterly*, 31(2), 171–193.

Starr, J.A. and MacMillan, I.C. (1990). Resource cooptation via social contracting: Resource acquisition strategies for new ventures. *Strategic Management Journal*, 11, 79–92.

Tabrizi, B., Lam, E., Girard, K., and Irvin, V. (2019). Digital transformation is not about technology. *Harvard Business Review*, 13. Retrieved January 6, 2022, from https://hbr.org/2019/03/digital-transformation-is-not-about-technology.

Tan, B., Pan, S.L., and Hackney, R. (2010). The strategic implications of web technologies: A process model of how web technologies enhance organizational performance. *IEEE Transactions on Engineering Management*, 57(2), 181–197.

Tan, B., Pan, S.L., Lu, X., and Huang, L. (2015). The role of IS capabilities in the development of multi-sided platforms: The digital ecosystem strategy of Alibaba.com. *Journal of the Association for Information Systems*, 16(4), 248–280.

The Economist (2005). The fall of a corporate queen. *The Economist*, 3 Feb. http://www.economist.com/node/3632638.

The Economist (2012). Technological change: The last Kodak moment? *The Economist*, 14 Jan 2012, pp. 63–64.

Tilson, D., Lyytinen, K., and Sørensen, C. (2010). Research commentary — Digital infrastructures: The missing IS research agenda. *Information Systems Research*, 21(4), 748–759. http://www.economist.com/node/21542796.

Tiwana, A. (2014). Separating signal from noise: Evaluating emerging technologies. *MIS Quarterly Executive*, 13(1), 45–61.

Tushman, M. and Anderson, P. (1986). Technological discontinuities and organizational environments. *Administrative Science Quarterly*, 32, 439–465.

Tynan, A.C. and Drayton, J. (1987). Market segmentation. *Journal of Marketing Management*, 2(3), 301–335.

Van Alstyne, M.W., Parker, G.G., and Choudary, S.P. (2016). Pipelines, platforms, and the new rules of strategy. *Harvard Business Review*, 94(4), 54–62.

Verhoef, P.C., Broekhuizen, T., Bart, Y., Bhattacharya, A., Qi Dong, J., Fabian, N., and Haenlein, M. (2021). Digital transformation: A multidisciplinary reflection and research agenda. *Journal of Business Research*, 122, 889–901.

Vial, G. (2019). Understanding digital transformation: A review and a research agenda. *Journal of Strategic Information Systems*, 28(2), 118–144.

Wessel, L., Baiyere, A., Ologeanu-Taddei, R., Cha, J., and Blegind-Jensen, T. (2021). Unpacking the difference between digital transformation and IT-enabled organizational transformation. *Journal of the Association for Information Systems*, 22(1), 102–129.

Westerman, G., Calméjane, C., Bonnet, D., Ferraris, P., and McAfee, A. (2011). *Digital Transformation: A Roadmap for Billion-Dollar Organizations*, pp. 1–68. MIT Sloan Management, MIT Center for Digital Business and Capgemini Consulting. https://www.capgemini.com/it-it/wp-content/uploads/sites/13/2017/07/Digital_Transformation__A_Road-Map_for_Billion-Dollar_Organizations.pdf.

Wu, A. and Na, C. (2020). Microsoft Azure and the cloud wars. Boston, MA: Harvard Business School Publishing, 23. Available from Harvard Business Publishing, product no. 9-720-409. https://hbsp.harvard.edu/product/720409-PDF-ENG.

Xiao, X., Tan, B., Leong, C., and Tan, F.T.C. (2020). Powered by "Qinghuai": The melding of traditional values and digital entrepreneurship in contemporary China. *Information Systems Journal*, 31(6), 769–802.

Yoo, Y., Boland, R.J., Lyytinen, K., and Majchrzak, A. (2012). Organizing for innovation in the digitized world. *Organization Science*, 23(5), 1398–1408.

Young, S. and Grant, P. (2003). How phone firms lost to Cable. *Wall Street Journal*, 14 Mar, M8.

https://doi.org/10.1142/9789811271984_0004

Chapter 4

The Impact of Risk Perception on Cyber Insurance in the Era of Digital Transformation

Angelica Marotta

MIT Sloan School of Management, Cambridge, MA, USA
amarotta@mit.edu

Risk management entails various measures for lowering risks to a level deemed acceptable by an organization and enabling residual risk to be transferred to insurance providers. The effectiveness of these measures is heavily reliant on people's perceptions of the threats to which they are or may be exposed. However, little is known regarding the connection between risk perception and cyber insurance. Therefore, the purpose of the research in this chapter is to examine the role of risk perception in determining people's cyber risk-taking behaviors and the related implications for cyber insurance policies and dynamics. This study provides a high-level analysis of the existing risk perception literature through a detailed examination of social, demographic, economic, cultural, psychological, and performance factors. The findings suggest that the nature of the relationship between risk perceptions and cyber insurance benefits may be influenced primarily by an organization's ability to keep its risk profile stable over time. More specifically, the cultural dimension of risk perception has been identified as one of the areas where risk reduction strategies have the most significant potential for lowering cyber insurance costs. The findings of this study can assist businesses and insurance companies in directing training efforts and forecasting organizational reactions to cyber threats as they navigate digital transformation.

1. Introduction

Nowadays, businesses are rapidly discovering possibilities and capabilities for increasing competitive advantage and development. As the pandemic progressed, organizations began to differ significantly in how they responded to the challenges associated with the emergency, accelerating the adoption of new technologies. This shift represented an essential milestone in the advancement of digital transformation, which transitioned from being considered a long-term goal to being a reality. Any transformation, however, carries some risks with it, and those related to technology are among the most severe. Digital assets (i.e., digital content or resources) are an appealing target for fraud, theft, and cyberattacks due to their intangible nature.

As a result, various techniques have been developed to compromise digital assets or disrupt their underlying technology. For example, cybercriminals have increasingly targeted digital assets by performing the so-called "51% attack" over the past few years. Through this type of attack, an attacker may be capable of taking control over digital assets technology by acquiring more than 50% of all the network hashing power (Ye *et al.*, 2018). For a long time, performing this attack was hardly possible due to the high costs involved. However, attacks have become more advanced and, therefore, more frequent over the years, resulting in millions of dollars in cryptocurrency losses. A more common tactic causing severe harm to digital assets is the denial-of-service (DoS) attack.[1] Consequences may range from significant waiting periods to network congestion, during which the user may be unable to dispose of the essential digital assets or may suffer loss or damage (Ayala, 2016). One of the most pressing concerns emerging from this situation is recognizing the actual risk level that insecure digital assets pose.

[1]Through the DoS attack, an attacker can make digital assets network resources inaccessible by overwhelming it with service requests.

1.1 *Cyber risk management: An imperfect discipline*

Cyber risk represents one of the greatest dangers for all business activities. According to the National Institute of Standards and Technology (NIST), cyber risk is defined as "the risk of depending on cyber resources, that is, the risk of depending on a system or system elements which exist in or intermittently have a presence in cyberspace" (Ross *et al.*, 2021). This definition emphasizes the growing reliance on information technology systems, including cyber resources (e.g., computers, networks, and digital information). This aspect implies that cyber risk is a real risk that may cause damage to businesses in a variety of ways, and it must be tackled in a methodical and well-defined manner. The most common mathematical formula for representing risk in a quantitative manner is the following:

$$R = P \times M$$

where P is the probability or frequency of occurrence of a hazard, and M is the magnitude of the impact of that hazard. Though different risk models have different input variables for calculating risk, most experts agree that these two components represent the most significant ones. However, despite the high relevance of these variables, current cyber risk analysis methods have several limitations. One of the primary deficiencies is the inaccuracy of the risk metrics (i.e., the techniques for quantifying risk exposure) used to support risk decisions. In order to maintain the metrics used to perform up-to-date risk assessments, cyber threats and vulnerabilities must be evaluated and monitored regularly; rapid changes in the evaluation of risk may be a determinant in qualifying the seriousness of a cyber threat. However, keeping up with the constant changes in the threat landscape may require modifying the initial risk estimates. As a result, the accuracy of risk assessments may decrease, leading to an increase in incorrect evaluations over time. When uncertainty prevails, risk management can be dependent on the perception of the risk decision-maker. Risks, particularly complicated risks with a high human component, may be more subject to personal judgment than scientific processing and analysis. Generally, in formulating a risk judgment, it is necessary to consider all the available information to identify the best options and draw conclusions about a hazard or its characteristics. While this cognitive process may be a valuable ally for risk management in particular instances, it should also be noted that it may have drawbacks if not adequately handled. For example, in the cybersecurity industry, decision-makers may struggle to grasp the nature of the cyber risk while also weighing numerous perspectives to make the best decision in the time available. A key issue in the way companies perceive cyber risks occurs when it is necessary to foresee both tangible and intangible hazards. Tangible hazards, such as damages to computers and other equipment, are generally easy to perceive, and the evaluation of the impacts on physical assets is relatively predictable. Conversely, intangible risks stemming from a breach, such as the deletion of personal data or reputational harm, may be more difficult to perceive. Potential financial damage is another type of risk that usually bypasses the perception of the hazards involved with an attack. Financial implications, such as loss of revenue due to service outages or forensic investigation expenses, can be far reaching and hard to quantify. Therefore, as the value of intangible assets rises, so does the need for businesses to safeguard themselves against "intangible hazards." For example, in response to this need, cyber insurance[2] is evolving to meet these new challenges. Cyber insurance can assist businesses in improving their protection mechanisms by regularly analyzing their security posture and discovering weaknesses (Marotta *et al.*, 2017). To obtain reduced premiums, organizations are required to reduce their risks and implement solid cybersecurity safeguards. While most efforts to minimize cyber risk focus on improving technical approaches, recognizing the importance of human behavior in using those approaches can be a crucial component of improvement. Therefore, a necessary task is to investigate how risk perception influences cyber risk decisions and their consequent implications on cyber insurance requirements and costs. In particular, this work explores some of the risk factors connected with cyber risk reduction and investigates their role in influencing the cyber insurance space. Finally, this study provides a guideline for businesses and insurance companies to follow as they deal with the quick pace of digital transformation.

2. The Unifying Link between Risk Perception and Cyber Insurance

Cyber insurance can be an excellent way to provide financial security for businesses. However, it is a considerable investment that depends on

[2]Cyber insurance is a form of risk management strategy in which cyber risks are passed to an insurance company in exchange for an insurance premium (i.e., cost of insurance).

several elements that must be taken into account when pricing insurance policies. Some of these factors can be outside of an organization's control, while others specifically depend on the organization's ability to mitigate cyber threats. In this context, the impact of risk perception in influencing individuals' cyber risk-taking behaviors may be fundamental in determining cyber insurance policies. This assumption is the investigation's core premise, and it is defined in this study through the following hypotheses:

H1: Risk perceptions are significantly linked to the effectiveness of risk reduction measures in cybersecurity.

H2: An organization's ability to reduce risk is directly proportional to the possibility of obtaining insurance benefits.

H3: Risk perception determines whether risk management successfully reduces vulnerability and, consequently, increases insurance benefits.

These hypotheses are explained in detail in the following sections.

2.1 *The connection between risk perception and risk reduction*

The effectiveness of a risk management program in any organization is heavily reliant on human factors. Individuals' actions performed before, during, and shortly after a cyberattack can substantially impact an organization's recovery ability. One of the objectives of addressing human factors in relation to risk is to improve human performance and decrease human failures. In this context, risk perception is often considered to be an essential aspect driving preventative or mitigation actions. The relationship between individuals' perceptions of risks and their willingness or readiness to reduce risk has been the subject of substantial research in a variety of domains (Lepesteur *et al.*, 2008; Lindell and Prater, 2002; Wildavsky, 1991; Weinstein *et al.*, 1998). According to the risk literature, despite variances in how people perceive risk, the likelihood of participating in risk reduction actions is directly proportional to the amount of risk they perceive (Lepesteur *et al.*, 2008). Setbon *et al.* demonstrated a significant causal relationship between risk perceptions and actions (Setbon *et al.*, 2005).

Furthermore, McGee and Russell state that individualization of the risk is a critical link between hazard awareness and mitigation strategies

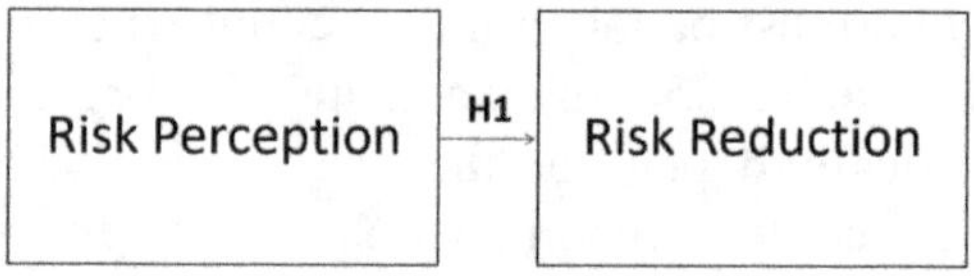

Fig. 1. First hypothesis.

(McGee and Russell, 2003). Thus, these perspectives suggest the first hypothesis in this study. *H1* considers risk perception as a critical driver of risk reduction efforts because it can shape how individuals respond to the occurrence of a cyber event. Therefore, this hypothesis focuses on risk as a cognitive means for determining future risks and enabling risk reduction efforts. Figure 1 shows a visual representation of this hypothesis, in which risk perception is directly related to the level of reduction achieved by individuals through positive or negative actions.

Individuals' actions may be inadequate or even harmful in circumstances when they have a poor perception of a specific cyber risk. In other circumstances, where risk perception is aligned with actual risk, risk perception is high, so the likelihood of reducing possible damages increases. Exploring this aspect may be beneficial in understanding how risk perception drives risk management and is effective in lowering exposure to cyber risk.

2.2 *The connection between risk reduction and cyber insurance*

Cyber insurance has become one of the fastest-growing insurance industry segments. The increasing relevance of this emerging market presents a considerable opportunity for the insurance sector to help companies better manage and minimize cyber risks. A significant part of the existing literature on risk management suggests that cyber insurance can incentivize risk reduction (Majuca *et al.*, 2006; Shetty *et al.*, 2010; Pal *et al.*, 2013; Marotta, 2015).

Cyber insurance companies generally require organizations to analyze their risk of attack, calculate potential damage, and establish suitable mitigation measures. Therefore, the result of this analysis is an important criterion to assist the insurer in measuring the organization's level of risk and establishing a contract. Thus, similar to purchasing health insurance, the "healthier" an organization is in terms of security, the cheaper the

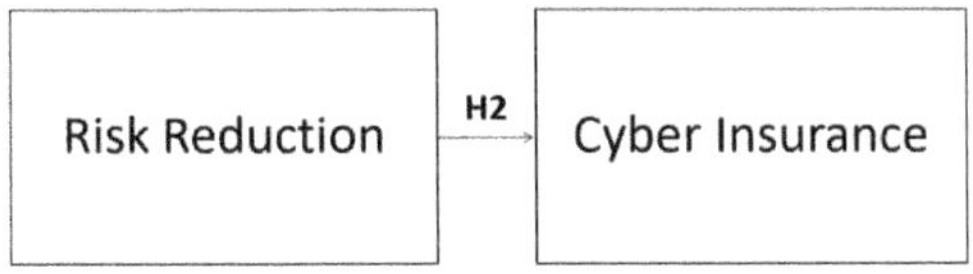

Fig. 2. Second hypothesis.

insurance premium is likely to be. As a result, businesses are not only pushed to address their security deficiencies to qualify for cheaper and better cyber insurance coverage but they are also incentivized to improve their risk profile. Along this line, a publication by the Department of Homeland Security (DHS) noted that cyber insurance "is designed to mitigate losses from a variety of cyber incidents including data breaches, business interruptions, and network damage" (US Department of Homeland Security, 2012). However, although insurance providers specify the degree of risk reduction necessary to obtain and retain a certain type of cyber insurance coverage, the actual achievement of that level is dependent on an organization's capacity to manage risks. Thus, relevant to this consideration is the hypothesis that an organization's ability to reduce risk is directly correlated to the possibility of obtaining insurance benefits (*H2*).

Figure 2 shows a visual representation of this hypothesis.

Implementing effective risk mitigation measures can also make the process for transferring risk to insurance companies more efficient. However, the benefits of enhanced risk reduction on cyber insurance are frequently connected to the company's long-term performance (Nash, 2017). As a result, this aspect needs to be included in the examination of this hypothesis.

2.3 *Risk reduction as a unifying factor between risk perception and cyber insurance*

Organizations are moving their risk perception from physical to digital, which is also affecting how they insure against risk. In accordance with this line of thought, De Smidt and Botzen surveyed business professionals involved in risk and insurance decision-making at large organizations (De Smidt and Botzen, 2018). The authors observed that these experts tend to overestimate the chance of a successful cyberattack and

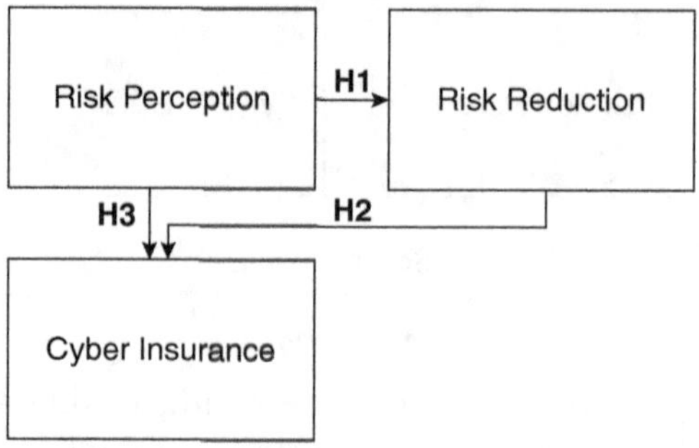

Fig. 3. Third hypothesis.

underestimate the related financial consequences. Some of the limiting elements influencing this incorrect estimation included the quality and availability of data on both cyberattacks and the resulting losses. Therefore, this perceptual distortion has been demonstrated to have a considerable influence on risk insurability.

Thus, following on from the initial hypotheses, it is reasonable to formulate that adequate risk perception management is a requirement for risk reduction and, therefore, necessary for obtaining enhanced insurance benefits (*H3*).

Figure 3 shows a visual representation of this hypothesis.

Thus, understanding the characteristics and nature of risk perception is essential for proper risk management. In turn, it also becomes critical for the provision of cyber insurance and the assessment of insurance coverage and rates.

These hypotheses set the foundation for exploring whether risk perceptions of cyber risk impact cyber insurance. The method utilized to validate the hypotheses included two main phases:

- ***Phase 1: Literature review*** — This phase involved a thorough review of academic research materials and documentation to identify the cybersecurity domain's primary risk perception elements. The list of documents examined included industry reports and academic papers. In particular, the review resulted in a selection of over 100 research endeavors over a time period of 50 years. These works were then chosen from the risk decision-making domains. This collection of studies reflected a solid interdisciplinary perspective of the subject, incorporating a total of 20 risk perception factors and 7 risk perception categories.

- ***Phase 2: Analysis and discussion*** — The resulting risk perception factors and categories identified in the literature review were then synthesized and examined in relation to risk reduction and cyber insurance implications. These investigations, in particular, assisted in the validation and development of the hypotheses and results presented in this work.

3. Review of the Literature about Cyber Risk Perception Factors

Risk perception is an important concept in the risk management literature that explores the decision-making process behind risk-taking behaviors. This topic has a solid historical academic foundation that includes many characteristics linked with the concept of multidisciplinarity across several domains, ranging from behavioral science to economics (Kahan *et al.*, 2011; Slovic *et al.*, 1991, 2016). For example, Slovic, one of the world's leading risk management experts, contributed to the psychometric paradigm of risk perception, a research technique used to explain how people perceive various threats (Slovic, 1987). The author outlined several social and cultural elements that may contribute to erroneous risk assessments in the general public. Slovic also underlined the critical distinction between experts' and laypeople's perspectives on risk. This work provided a preliminary examination of the growing concerns in the risk perception literature. Other researchers expanded on Slovic's work by demonstrating that different elements can affect human perceptions of risk (Sjöberg, 2000; Manika *et al.*, 2021). Examples include factors such as whether or not exposure to a hazard is regarded to be "familiar" (e.g., it frequently appears in the media) or "unfamiliar" (e.g., individuals do not know the causes and consequences of a certain hazard). Another similar distinction that has been observed in the literature is that between controllable and uncontrollable risks. Some authors argue that the perception of risk is likely to change depending on whether protection measures are available and can be put in place (i.e., risks are, in some ways, manageable) (Bada and Nurse, 2020). Additionally, Sjöberg also proposed that additional characteristics such as risk sensitivity, fear, and individual attitudes might be used to explain why people develop different perspectives about the dangerousness of risks (Sjöberg, 2000).

However, some studies on the topic have specifically been undertaken in the field of cybersecurity as well (Emami-Naeini *et al*., 2021; Johnston and Warkentin, 2008; Brender and Markov, 2013; Jackson and Rahman, 2019). Several scholars reviewed the psychology literature on the public perception of risk and extended their findings to perceptions of threats in cyberspace. Some academics, for example, used the Protection Motivation Theory (PMT)[3] to investigate the motivations for the implementation of specific cybersecurity safeguards (e.g., anti-spyware software), as well as the adoption of cyber-secure behaviors in general (Johnston and Warkentin, 2008; Herath *et al*., 2014; Vance *et al*., 2012).

Another theory used to investigate cyber risk perception is the Technology Threat Avoidance Theory (TTAT). The TTAT demonstrates how users avoid the risks of harmful effects that might result from information technology (Carpenter *et al*., 2019). An example can be found in the work conducted by Liang and Xue (2010). The authors utilized the TTAT to show how risk perception influences spyware threat avoidance. In a related line of research, other researchers applied the concept of perceived risk to the privacy field to explain individuals' willingness to divulge information about themselves online (Jarvenpaa *et al*., 1999; Xu *et al*., 2011). Similarly, other scholars further investigated how individuals use different metrics to judge online risks and use emotions for directing their actions toward risks (Manika *et al*., 2021; Bada and Nurse, 2020; Elena and Johnson, 2015).

3.1 *Summary*

Following a thorough assessment of the literature, it is important to note that risk perception is determined by a complex combination of social, demographic, economic, cultural, psychological, and performance factors (Slovic, 1987; Brooker, 1984; Dholakia, 2001; Grewal *et al*., 1994; Kaplan *et al*., 1974).

Figure 4 summarizes the risk perception categories and the related factors that comprise them.

These risk perception categories are described below in more detail.

---

[3]The Protection Motivation Theory (PMT) is a psychology theory that seeks to explain why individuals participate in harmful behaviors and suggests recommendations for improving those behaviors (Moody *et al*., 2018).

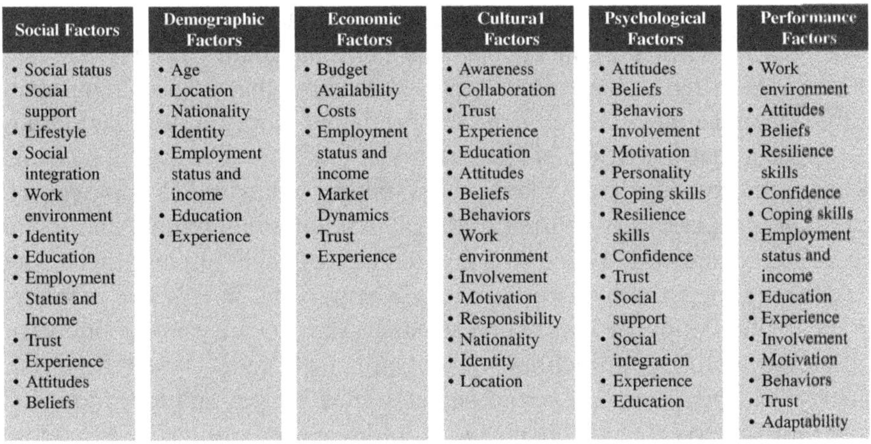

Fig. 4. Risk perception factors.

3.1.1 *Social factors*

As individuals are increasingly tasked with monitoring cyber threats and entrusted with averting catastrophic events, the social side of an individual's work environment is becoming a source of worry in terms of risk perception. In particular, people's understanding of cyber risk is likely to be influenced by a series of social factors. Individuals, for example, might indirectly impact risk perceptions by sharing knowledge about typical cyberattack strategies, risk variables, and security solutions. Furthermore, if the members of a social group are victims of a cyberattack, they may act as reminders of the threat's existence. Such direct social exposure to risks may enhance perceptions of vulnerability, presumably through the availability heuristic, a decision-making method in which individuals assess the likelihood of an occurrence based on the number of precedents they can quickly recall (De Smidt and Botzen, 2018; Folkes, 1988). Increased social exposure to a hazard may thus result in increased risk perceptions. In this context, there are several social factors at play. Various studies on the topic, for example, reveal that accepting responsibility for hazard risk prevention is impacted not only by personal experience but also by social forms of support and integration (Maidl *et al.*, 2021).

Another critical point is the interaction between social status and perceived risk. In the literature, social status is often described as a mechanism for accessing particular material and immaterial benefits, such as higher education levels, employment status, and income (Wachinger *et al.*, 2013). While the concept of social status has mainly been researched in the field of psychology, preliminary data show that it has a significant influence on people's risk choices and behaviors. For example, some studies suggest that lower social class status is linked to risk aversion, while others indicate that it is linked to risk-taking behaviors (Kish-Gephart, 2017). Regardless of the varied findings, it is important to note that social status is considered to be a powerful predictor of behavioral risks (i.e., the risks stemming from human behavior) (Zhang *et al.*, 2014). For example, in the context of cybersecurity, social status may impact the likelihood of following security guidelines or engaging in good cyber behavior. Therefore, it is clear that social status affects beliefs about individuals' susceptibility to external threats and attitudes toward mitigating behaviors (Kish-Gephart, 2017). In order to explain individuals' risky decision-making in a digital setting, several authors also extended the existing studies on risk to include trust as a determinant of "intention" to engage in secure behaviors (Gefen and Straub, 2000; Chung and Kim, 2009). For example, Ogbanufe and Kim investigated the concept of trust to understand its function in limiting or encouraging risk-based click-through decisions (Ogbanufe and Kim, 2018). In social networks, for example, trust may come from the ability of users to trust one another as well as the network provider (Albladi and Weir, 2020). However, these two dimensions of trust have also been found to increase the risk of exposing personal information (Houston *et al.*, 2019). As a result, the authors who examined this topic argue that individuals make "calculated" decisions to accept risks based on their level of trust in certain social contexts (Twigg, 2003).

However, it was also observed that lifestyle factors, especially those related to online patterns (e.g., online shopping habits), have a crucial role in changing risk perception (Herath *et al.*, 2014; Isaak and Hannah, 2018). These results suggest that consolidated online habits can be hard to remove and can trigger further recurrences of the same behavior.

The social factors illustrated above also reflect a person's social position in their digital environment. They, in particular, contribute to the building of their social identity — that is, any collection of information that characterizes an individual at the social level (Grobler *et al.*, 2021). A part of the literature on risk perception focuses on social identity as a critical player in cybersecurity-related user behavior. Some studies show that social identity is critical in virtual platforms, which are fundamental in cybersecurity activities. For example, Grobler *et al.* investigate behaviors associated with cybersecurity through the lens of a social identity context (Grobler *et al.*, 2021). The authors observed a correlation between an individual's social identity and their tendency to formulate stronger (or weaker) passwords. Therefore, developing a coherent sense of self can help support a consistent set of risk choices.

3.1.2 *Demographic factors*

Organizations are continuously putting in place advanced technical solutions to protect their information and technology resources, but they mainly rely on their employees to be their primary threat detectors. For this reason, previous studies on risk perception highlighted the importance of studying demographic differences among employees to see any underlying causes of insecure behaviors in cybersecurity (McCormac *et al.*, 2017).

In particular, Whitty *et al.* found that age is a critical demographic risk perception predictor in organizations (Whitty *et al.*, 2015). Younger individuals, for example, are far more likely to engage in the risky practice of password sharing. Other studies on the topic agree that older individuals are more willing to protect themselves than younger people (Choi *et al.*, 2016). However, they also observe that older people often lack proper IT support and, as a result, may underestimate risks (Morrison *et al.*, 2021).

Education is another demographic area that has a significant influence on risk perception. For example, Sheng *et al.* explored how users' security behavior is affected by their level of education and how their perception of risks is affected (Sheng *et al.*, 2010). The authors found that a higher level of education positively impacts security behavior. However, Pattinson and Anderson found opposite findings as they argued that a lower level of education could lead to better cybersecurity behaviors (Pattinson and Anderson, 2007). In some cases, individuals with lower education levels may be more willing to learn and acquire a broad picture of the risk environment.

Similar studies have moved the focus from education to employment status and income (Crete-Nishihata *et al.*, 2020). They observed that employment status influences the ability of individuals to perceive risks effectively, and therefore implement appropriate cybersecurity measures.

Most authors describe employment status as a key factor presenting contrasting effects on risk (Wachinger *et al.*, 2013). Salaried employees, for example, have greater access to resources but may also be more limited in making risk decisions and using resources to solve a problem. In this case, a lack of autonomy might be detrimental to risk perception since it reduces feelings of control (Lunardo and Saintives, 2019). Conversely, self-employed workers may have more autonomy but may not be able to access greater resources. The ability to dispose of resources may foster a fatalistic attitude among individuals who recognize risk but feel powerless to respond to cyber events as an individual or group (Covi, 2014). Employment status was also linked to higher incident experience with threats and, as a result, greater risk perception toward cyber threats (Sund *et al.*, 2017).

A limited but significant amount of research literature has been produced on variations in risk perception caused by location and nationality (Scalia, 2017). The authors that researched this issue argued that countries have varied concerns about cybersecurity due to differences in technical level, culture, tradition, and laws and regulations (Slovic *et al.*, 1986). A similar issue identified in the literature seems to involve disparities in privacy and security definitions (Barnett and Breakwell, 2001). Different countries may also have diverse levels of security technology. Some countries' technologies may be more sophisticated, while other countries' technology tools may fall behind. As a result, certain countries may face increased threats and lack sophisticated software to protect their computer systems (D'Antoni *et al.*, 2017). Other instances of nationality difficulties include security issues in foreign outsourcing and doing business with foreign companies. Thus, these studies suggest that nations not only differ in terms of risk categories but also in terms of the likelihood and severity of a security incident.

Finally, a subset of demographic factors impacting cyber risk perceptions may stem from a person's sense of identity (i.e., the characteristics or affiliations that identify a person) (Ogbanufe, 2020). According to the majority of authors, identity is often a powerful factor in self-determination (Bada and Nurse, 2020; Grobler *et al.*, 2021; Ogbanufe, 2020). People's drive to retain beliefs that are congruent with their identities may influence their risk perception, thus outweighing their willingness to consider alternatives. Therefore, people have distinct differences in their evaluations, expectations, interpretations, and behaviors depending on their identities. Modern cyberattacks exploit these distinctions by employing identity deception.[4] For this reason, existing studies suggest paying close attention to identity, as it is a foundational aspect that determines risk perceptions (Halevi *et al.*, 2017).

3.1.3 *Economic factors*

Risk perception issues are also caused by the uncertainty that organizations and individuals experience when they cannot forecast the outcomes of their financial actions (Araujo *et al.*, 2016). Studies on this aspect show that such uncertainties arise from global mechanisms and propagate to organizational levels (Emami-Naeini *et al.*, 2021).

Global economic situations often have a significant impact on cybersecurity investments and, therefore, on risk perception. The market for cybersecurity technologies, for example, is rapidly expanding and highly competitive. These market dynamics call for new approaches in managing expenditures to deal with a range of costs, especially those necessary to address vulnerabilities and digital transformation. As part of this process, executives and managers are tasked with identifying the appropriate spending amount based on the level of risk they are willing to accept. For this reason, budget availability can be a highly significant decision driver. While each organization is unique, generally, low-budget availability induces risk managers to be cautious and take fewer risks to ensure budget maintenance. In contrast, high-budget availability provides the flexibility to take more significant risks. Managers' risk perception is based on an assessment of what they can afford to lose or what amount of risk they consider acceptable (Markowska *et al.*, 2019). However, the calculation of affordable loss is often based on personal financial conditions (e.g., employment status and income) and their experience in evaluating the risk scenarios (Markowska *et al.*, 2019).

Another important component impacting economic variables of risk perception is trust. In the literature concerning the economic field, the study of trust refers to the examination of the trust factors established when risk or financial managers take investment or financing decisions. Some studies demonstrated that trust has a distinct impact on investing and financing decisions, depending on the associated perception levels.

[4]The attacker sends a message that appears to originate from a source that is associated with a certain identity, such as an individual, an organization, or a brand that the victim is likely to trust.

For example, according to Dalmolin *et al.*, when risk perception is high, trust has a greater impact on investment decisions, and when risk perception is low, trust impacts financing decisions (Dalmolin *et al.*, 2019). This observation is particularly important in the cybersecurity area. In unpredictable contexts such as those arising in the cybersecurity landscape, where information varies and competition is persistent, trust may play an essential role in risk decision-making (Burzynski and Burzynski, 2014).

3.1.4 *Cultural factors*

The current literature agrees that a well-defined culture, particularly the one centered on cybersecurity, impacts risk-based decisions and reinforces the perception that cybersecurity is an advantage rather than a burden (Marotta and Pearlson, 2019). However, the effects of culture on risk perception vary (Palm and Carroll, 2019; Rohrmann and Renn, 2000). Some studies, for example, have found disparities in risk perception among cultures with different levels of security awareness (Jarvenpaa *et al.*, 1999). For example, Nyblom *et al.* investigated this topic by examining attitudes, experience levels, beliefs, behaviors, trust in authorities, and involvement in training (Nyblom *et al.*, 2020). Their findings indicate that the level of security awareness is inherently subjective and highly dependent on human factors. Similarly, other works suggested that culture shapes the way responsibility is understood and applied (Walsh, 2004). Consequently, it determines the individual's capacity to discern what is safe or unsafe in cyberspace and how concerned employees are about certain risk situations (Gunleifsen, 2018).

This concept is the foundation of what scholars label as Cultural Theory (CT), which posits that culture influences the human mind and, consequently, management practices (Díaz, 2015). CT grew in importance in the field of risk research throughout the 1980s (Dake, 1991). Indeed, the CT theory became critical to understanding risk perception in cultural contexts as it provided a way of investigating the effects of culture-level factors on individual behavior. Some of these factors include collaboration among members of the same cultural group, education level, and motivation to adhere to cultural standards. In this context, especially noteworthy is the theory developed by Douglas and Wildavsky, the major proponents of the cultural perspective of risk (Douglas and Wildavsky, 1982). The authors proposed that risk perception is a collective phenomenon in which members of various cultures selectively respond to different categories of risk. These responses shape the work environment and set the cultural identity of an organization, which may, in turn, influence individuals in their attitudes to cyber risk decisions. For example, a company that does not have a clear risk-based cultural identity may fail to recognize the benefits of a functional risk management program, such as adequate internal sharing of practices, audit findings, or reports. Therefore, the significance of the CT theory to understanding risk perception in cultural contexts is that it provides a way of accounting for the effect of culture-level variables on the behavior of individuals. Other authors built on the CT theory to explore other cultural variables influencing the differences in risk perception. The literature exploring these concepts mainly investigated cultural variations in risk perception caused by differences in nationality and location (Bagchi *et al.*, 2004).

3.1.5 *Psychological factors*

Since the 1970s, several scholars have been studying the psychological aspects that influence risk perception in various areas. For example, some of them focused on health (e.g., smoking issues) and safety (e.g., injury prevention factors) (Slovic *et al.*, 1986; Reitsma *et al.*, 2017; Fiorenza, 2020). More recently, the literature has also drawn attention to the presence of psychological components in the evaluation of cyber risk. For example, Bada and Nurse examined how individuals perceive and engage with risk and how psychologically affected they are during and after a cyberattack (Bada and Nurse, 2020). However, a recurring observation in these studies is that, from a psychological perspective, risk perception is highly influenced by the emotional states of individuals. The main factors affecting the modulation of these emotional states involve personality traits (Bada and Nurse, 2020). Personality can be defined as a set of patterns that impact an individual's behaviors, beliefs, attitudes, and involvement (Hampson *et al.*, 2006). Personality not only determines how individuals respond to risky situations in their environment but it can also be a driver for motivating individuals to act (McCormac *et al.*, 2017; Hampson *et al.*, 2006). For example, when it comes to risk, one essential component influenced by an individual's personality is the ability to develop coping and resilience skills (Bada and Nurse, 2020). Coping mechanisms ensure that a person engages in a recommended preventative reaction (e.g., not opening emails from an unknown source). Similarly, resilience refers to a person's capacity to recover quickly from difficult and complex situations (Bartone, 2012). Studies have found associations between coping/resilience skills and risk perception. In particular, it was observed that both sets of skills influence individuals' response to stress and their ability to engage in protective behaviors (Howatt, 2015; Yıldırım and Arslan, 2020). Such factors can drive risk acceptance choices and significantly impact actions before, during, and after a cyber incident, especially in crisis response situations.

A portion of psychology research has also focused on the various benefits and disadvantages of trust and confidence in risk perception (Das and Teng, 2004). Several scholars argued that individuals' high self-confidence and trust levels can act as a psychological "buffer" toward perceived risk (Colquitt *et al.*, 2007). On the one hand, this buffer can positively deaden the impact of the stressful situations caused by critical or difficult risk decisions. On the other hand, it can act as a filter against prudent and preventive risk decisions. Trust can also serve as a psychological foundation for building forms of social support and integration (Phillips-Wren, 2012). When individuals have insufficient time, knowledge, or motivation to evaluate risks carefully, they tend to rely on the community into which they are integrated. According to Deline *et al.*, in a cybersecurity context, the number of operations to be handled and the potential technical challenges involved may cause individuals to rely heavily on teamwork for a more balanced distribution of work (Deline *et al.*, 2021). These team processes are the mechanisms through which individual knowledge structures are used and shared in establishing a realistic perception of risk. As a result, the individual's ability to demonstrate high levels of experience and education is often regarded as the most effective means of establishing authority within a community of risk decision-makers. To explain these psychological dynamics, some authors have theorized the concept of "interactive team cognition," which refers to the cognitive processes that generate the collective perception of risk in a given situation (Cooke *et al.*, 2005).

3.1.6 *Performance factors*

The work environment is often the most likely place for a cyber incident to occur because of the human component that makes it up. Human-enabled mistakes are commonly recognized to be responsible for a majority of cyberattacks, data breaches, and ransomware attacks (Nobles, 2018). For this reason, employees are frequently deemed as the "weakest link" in any organization because they are the most vulnerable access point for attackers. Assessing employees' risk perception can thus be highly significant in determining their behavioral outcomes, including their performance. For example, employees' reactions to risks may depend on various factors derived from different risk evaluations. These assessments rely on the clarity with which outcomes can be envisioned, which is critical for determining an individual's intention to accept, reject, or ignore the presence of risks. Some contributing factors can be the lack of experience with certain outcomes, education in probability computation, and individuals' attitudes toward risk. For instance, the ability to tolerate uncertainty (i.e., developing adaptability, coping, and resilience skills) is likely to be shaped by an individual's beliefs, involvement, and motivation (Vance *et al.*, 2012; D'Antoni *et al.*, 2017; Cellier and Ghernaouti, 2019). These factors may influence the likelihood of an individual performing inadequately and causing a cyber incident.

However, the risk-coping process can also be impacted by the fear of being laid off, which is regarded as a crucial external factor in risk perception. Thus, the fear of losing employment status and income may cause workers to place themselves in risky circumstances, even knowing the implications for their productivity. Furthermore, employees who have lost their jobs or had their income reduced may seek "revenge" against their company and act in ways they would not normally consider. These behaviors may generate insider threats (i.e., employees, former employees, or other organizational stakeholders who can introduce hazardous conditions within a company) (Ayala, 2016).

Finally, scholars found that enhancing confidence in employees and ensuring employee trust in supervisors can positively influence risk perception and, therefore, performance (Colquitt *et al.*, 2007). For example, mutual trust between employees and their managers is a critical factor that may either impede or accelerate the success process. With the presence of trust, a company's work environment becomes more comfortable for individuals, leading to positive performance outcomes and improved risk management.

4. A Conceptual Analysis of the Literature Review

Each of the categories mentioned above contains a set of risk perception factors that can influence individual behaviors toward risks. For example, forms of social support can lead individuals to adopt preventive measures

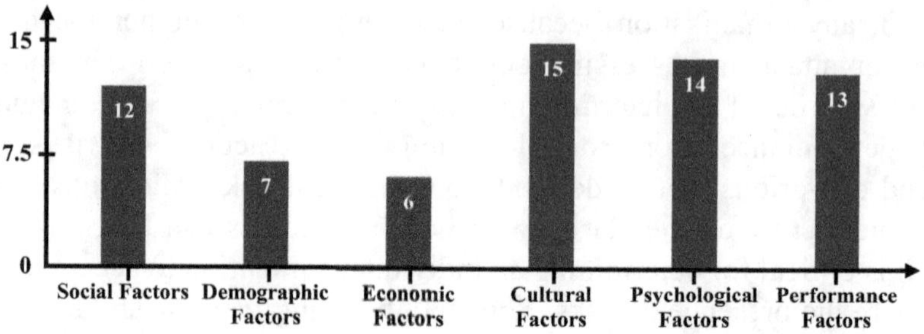

Fig. 5. Scoping analysis.

that may limit the consequences of a loss and its occurrence. Therefore, these factors may be key drivers of risk reduction, thereby supporting the first hypothesis (*H1*). To assess the validity of this concept, the following section provides an analysis of the most influential risk perception factors in risk reduction.

4.1 *Scoping analysis*

The first stage in analyzing the literature is to develop an assessment (scoping analysis[5]) of the size of each risk perception category (see Figure 5). The first observation is that cultural influences may have a higher impact on risk perception than other factors. This consideration shows that culture can be one of the areas where risk reduction actions may produce the highest benefits for organizations. Conversely, the analysis revealed that only a small number of economic factors are considered relevant toward risk perception in the literature. As a result, while further study is likely to be required in this area, economic factors may not significantly impact risk reduction.

4.2 *Intersection analysis*

The primary point of this analysis is that multiple risk perception categories share some risk perception factors. This interrelation seems to be primarily caused by the reliance of risk perception on the human element, which extends across all the categories. Figure 6 shows the intersections

[5]A method for determining the importance and scope of the literature (Tricco *et al.*, 2015; Munn *et al.*, 2018).

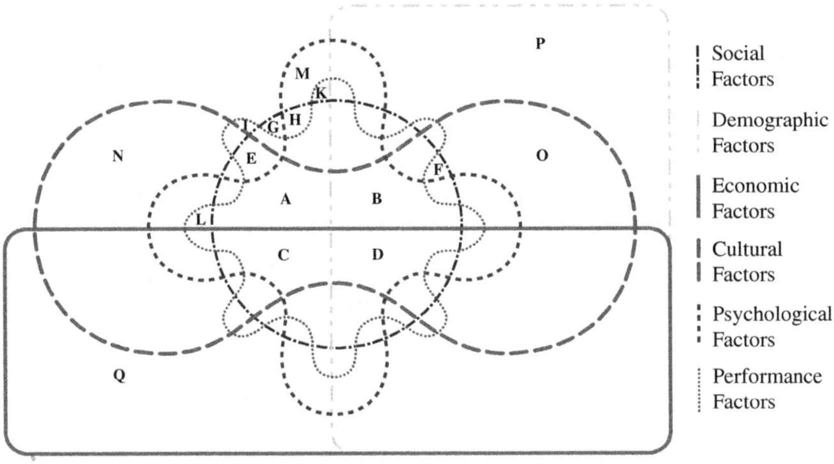

Fig. 6. Intersection analysis.

between the six risk perception categories (social, demographic, economic, cultural, psychological, and performance factors) represented in the form of an Edwards–Venn diagram. The elements (risk perception factors) resulting from each intersection are grouped in sets named with a letter between A and Q. For example, the intersection of psychological and performance factors is defined as a set named with the letter K containing three elements (coping skills, resilience skills, and confidence).

Table 1 lists the intersection sets resulting from Figure 6, their elements (i.e., the risk perception factors in common), and the corresponding risk perception categories. In addition, it is possible to observe that A, B, C, and D (highlighted in gray) are the emergent set of risk perception factors since they overlap in more than three areas of risk perception (risk perception categories).

As evidenced by the intersection analysis, risk perception is an inter- and transdisciplinary issue in which multiple elements converge across disciplines to bridge the gap between intention and actual behavior. As a result, the more common to a wide range of categories a risk perception factor is, the more significantly it impacts the occurrence (or non-occurrence) of a hazard. For example, attitudes and beliefs are two factors that fall under four categories (social factors, cultural factors, psychological factors, and performance factors). Thus, attitudes and beliefs can influence multiple areas of an individual's perception. For instance, people

Table 1. Intersection sets, set elements, and risk perception categories.

Intersection Set	Set Elements	Risk Perception Category
A	Attitudes, beliefs	Social factors, cultural factors, psychological factors, performance factors
B	Education	Social factors, demographic factors, cultural factors, psychological factors, performance factors
C	Trust	Social factors, economic factors, cultural factors, psychological factors, performance factors
D	Experience	Social factors, demographic factors, economic factors, cultural factors, psychological factors, performance factors
E	Work environment	Social factors, cultural factors, performance factors
F	Identity	Social factors, demographic factors, cultural factors
G	Social status, lifestyle	Social factors
H	Social support, social integration	Social factors, psychological factors
I	Employment status and income	Social factors, demographic factors, economic factors, performance factors
J	Adaptability	Performance factors
K	Coping skills, resilience skills, confidence	Psychological factors, performance factors
L	Behaviors, involvement, motivation	Cultural factors, psychological factors, performance factors
M	Personality	Psychological factors
N	Awareness, collaboration, responsibility	Cultural factors
O	Location, nationality	Demographic factors, cultural factors
P	Age	Demographic factors
Q	Budget availability, costs, market dynamics	Economic factors

may develop certain security attitudes to not only avoid security risks but also avoid social repercussions (e.g., peer pressure or criticism) and work problems (e.g., negligence issues or legal responsibilities). Therefore, attitudes are more likely to have a greater influence on the adoption of preventive measures than other factors, such as age, which falls only under one category (demographic factors). For this reason, the factors contained in A, B, C, and D have significant implications in the context of risk reduction (*H1*).

5. Implications on Cyber Insurance

The previous analysis sets the context for the connection between risk reduction and cyber insurance, thereby supporting the second hypothesis (*H2*). Indeed, managing the factors in A, B, C, and D can contribute to changing unacceptable risks to acceptable risks and enabling risk transfer of residual risk to an insurance company. This mechanism is often incentivized by insurance companies as well. Insurers often demand a certain level of risk reduction as a condition of coverage, and companies that employ better risk reduction strategies are likely to pay cheaper insurance rates. This incentive allows businesses to internalize the advantages of good security and offset the costs of recovering from cyberattacks, resulting in increased investment and enhancements in their cybersecurity posture. However, the degree to which these benefits are maintained over time may vary depending on the company's long-term capacity to maintain constant levels of risk reduction. Therefore, the longer a firm takes to reduce risk, the longer it may take to obtain cyber insurance advantages. In this case, possible benefits may lose their significance or turn into disadvantages in the long run. Each of the previously discussed factors has the potential to provide either advantages or disadvantages in the context of cyber insurance. An overall summary of these considerations is given in Table 2 and explained below.

5.1 *Attitudes and beliefs*

The existing literature suggests that risk perception research needs to take into account the attitudes and beliefs of individuals as they are equally fundamental to the perception and response to cyber risks (Slovic, 1987; Sund *et al.*, 2017; Van den Steen, 2010). In particular, attitudes represent

Table 2. Implications on cyber insurance.

Perception Factors	Risk Reduction Implications	Cyber Insurance Implications	
		Advantages	Disadvantages
Attitudes and beliefs	Reducing risk by minimizing human errors, recurrences, and deception-based attacks	Reducing premium costs by lowering the average expected damage Minimizing the likelihood of large cascading loss events	Difficult for insurers to obtain reliable information on the attitudes and beliefs of employees Difficult to measure the magnitude of the value created through attitude and belief management
Trust	Reducing risk by minimizing confidentiality issues	Reducing premium costs by lowering the average expected damage Improving information sharing Minimizing information asymmetry Reducing complexity	Hard to assess trust indicators Benefits can be limited by privacy and reputational concerns, budgetary restrictions, and fear
Experience	Reducing risk by minimizing unpreparedness and an unwillingness to engage in security behaviors	Reducing premium costs by lowering the average expected damage Minimizing lack of historical data	Experience may not be indicative of future exposure Experience cannot be used to assess cyber risk directly
Education	Reducing risk by minimizing skills gap	Reducing premium costs by lowering the average expected damage Long-term benefits for keeping evolving risk profiles	Education needs constant investment in training, thus delaying the efforts to reduce premiums

stable inclinations to respond to risks or related situations; beliefs are structured filters toward risks and may support, discourage, or change attitudes. For example, preventing staff from clicking on phishing emails is often a challenge for many businesses. While training programs can help shape employees' attitudes on cyber risk, they may not be sufficient to overcome resistance, especially among those who have little technical expertise. One of the most common reasons for this reluctance is that employees believe that cybersecurity is not their primary duty. As a result, failing to change this belief may be the missing link preventing employees from enacting the attitudes learned during the training. These considerations imply that attitudes and beliefs can be modified with a measurable impact on employees' engagement with cybersecurity. The resulting effect can considerably reduce risk by minimizing human errors (e.g., careless behaviors) and recurrences. Another benefit of adequately managing attitudes and beliefs is reducing the risk of human deception-based attacks, such as those that use social engineering techniques. These attacks are particularly damaging because they exploit human vulnerabilities, including those related to beliefs and attitudes, rather than flaws in software or operating systems. Addressing the organization's human aspect can help reduce these risks significantly.

These advantages may also reflect the adoption of cyber insurance in two ways. Firstly, implementing effective cybersecurity attitudes and beliefs can minimize the average expected damage and save insurance costs. Secondly, it can help minimize the likelihood of significant cascading loss events. Cyberattacks are highly scalable, which means that they can potentially affect thousands of companies concurrently, resulting in massive interconnected losses for insurers. An attack on a power grid is a common example of a cascading failure, in which the destruction of a key infrastructure component may cause breakdowns throughout the rest of the grid. A similar incident took place in 2017 when Russia targeted Ukraine with the NotPetya virus (Nakashima, 2018). The attack affected entire networks and caused more than $10 billion in damage worldwide (Nakashima, 2018). These types of cyber events pose several challenges to cyber insurers. For example, one possible issue arises when a critical service utilized by multiple policyholders (e.g., a large telecommunication platform or a cloud-based technology service) stops working. In this case, if a single component in a network is affected by an attack, then several other components are likely to be hit simultaneously. The insurer may thus be required to pay all its policyholders' claims at once. To avoid these issues, these types of incidents are generally not covered in an insurance policy or, in some cases, are subject to policy coverage limits[6] (Gu *et al.*, 2015). For this reason, insurance companies tend to encourage the adoption of preventive measures (e.g., through incentives) to avoid these incidents.

However, from a cyber insurance point of view, there may also be downsides to investing time and energy in managing employees' attitudes and beliefs. For example, individuals' attitudes to risk may not be regular or consistent enough to guarantee continuation over time. Furthermore, insurers may find it challenging to collect accurate information on employee attitudes. The same considerations may apply to beliefs; it may be hard for companies to define which beliefs are acceptable and which are not. As a result, it can be challenging to measure the magnitude of the value created by the handling of attitudes and beliefs, thus limiting or weakening the efforts to reduce premiums through these means.

5.2 *Trust*

The literature shows that trust is essential for successful information exchange and cooperative practices among employees and external stakeholders (Ghosh and Fedorowicz, 2008). Therefore, trust has been positioned as a critical factor in minimizing potential exposure of sensitive data and consequent confidentiality issues (Inkpen and Tsang, 2007). Confidentiality is one of the most critical concepts in cybersecurity as it reduces the possibility of disclosing personal information. Therefore, a breach of confidentiality may lead to unauthorized access to personal information or even total loss of privacy. An example may be a healthcare app being compromised in a way that health data are transferred to servers in another country without the data subject's consent. The application of trust to prevent confidentiality vulnerabilities is often achieved using encryption, digital signatures, and electronic certificates.

From a cyber insurance point of view, implementing correct trust management can involve several benefits. More specifically, in addition to reducing premium costs, it contributes to solving well-known cyber insurance problems, such as lack of information sharing and increasing information asymmetry. Sharing information on cyber threats and

[6]Maximum compensation available to businesses in the case of a claim.

vulnerabilities is critical to ensuring that cyber insurers are in the best position to address cybersecurity risks proactively and guarantee cyber risk insurability. However, policyholders are reluctant to reveal information about their incidents, expenditures, and losses, while insurers are cautious about sharing data from their customers. This hesitation stems from various factors, including concerns about privacy, legal ramifications, reputational harm, and the risk of showing vulnerabilities. Such a circumstance may also result in information asymmetry, which is another major issue impacting cyber insurance. The term "information asymmetry" refers to a scenario in which there is inadequate information about the market and its players (Marotta *et al.*, 2017). Nevertheless, developing forms of trust in risk management may entail a bilateral expectation that both parties proactively disclose helpful information in support of their mutual agreement. Finally, trust can help to reduce the complexity inherent in the cyber insurance process by alleviating organizations and insurance companies from the burden of verifying every piece of information.

One of the disadvantages of directing efforts toward trust management is that trust is hard to measure in the cybersecurity environment. Trust assessment necessitates the creation of a trust indicator that can aid an informed decision, such as the level of trustworthiness and credibility (Colquitt *et al.*, 2007). However, trust indicators may be subjective, and therefore challenging to use as insurance metrics. Another disadvantage is that the benefits generated by the introduction of trust initiatives may be limited by independent factors, such as legal and privacy concerns and budgetary restrictions. For this reason, it may be complex for insurers to base their policies on trust-based risk reduction measures and also reciprocate customers' trust.

5.3 *Experience*

Experience is the only risk perception factor that can be observed in all of the categories covered in the preceding analyses, making it the most influencing risk perception variable. According to the reviewed literature, personal experience with a threat is likely to induce people to consider hazards as more serious and perceive themselves as possible future victims (Barnett and Breakwell, 2021). As a result, this perception increases individual willingness to participate in risk-reduction actions and be more prepared to face risky situations.

Experience with threats is also valuable to cyber insurers as it provides access to historical data on cyber incidents. Therefore, lack of experience can be a major issue as it prevents insurers from building predictive models on which they rely to establish lower premiums and exposure models (Marotta *et al.*, 2017). The presence of this problem, in turn, affects insurance firms' willingness to offer considerable amounts of coverage. Instead, utilizing customers' experiences to acquire precise data on breaches may benefit insured organizations and provide helpful information to avoid future cyber events.

However, the extent to which experience effectively lowers risk is not only determined by how individuals learn from their observations and the consequences of their actions. In addition, due to the evolving nature of cybersecurity threats, previous experience may not be sufficient to respond dynamically to new risks. For example, if an attack is relatively infrequent, direct experience may offer a limited source of information. As a result, experience may not accurately prevent future exposure and may not be used to assess and price future cyber risks accurately.

5.4 *Education*

Education in the context of cyber risk seeks to provide people and groups with the information they need to minimize their exposure to cyber hazards (Sjöberg, 2000). The results of the studies discussed above provide consistent and substantial evidence on the beneficial influence of education on risk reduction. As a result, when confronted with cyber risks, highly educated individuals are considered to have better preparedness and response to risks. This aspect suggests that investing in improving capabilities via education may reduce vulnerability and build adaptive capability in the face of changing cybersecurity issues. Education can also contribute to skill gap prevention. Nowadays, the lack of qualified employees is one of the biggest threats to organizations as it generates two main problems (Van Niekerk and Solms, 2010). Firstly, it may lead to increasing vulnerabilities. Unskilled personnel may affect the quality of services delivered, thus leaving organizations exposed. Secondly, it may lead to an increase in cyberattacks. Due to their lack of security understanding, cybercriminals often intentionally use unskilled employees as an attack vector.

Hiring and retaining highly qualified professionals can also generate long-term benefits for cyber insurance policyholders. In addition, cybersecurity education initiatives, such as specific training and workforce development, imply maintaining relatively stable risk profiles, which is a highly desired condition in cyber insurance. Generally, the increasing frequency of sophisticated threats makes it difficult for insurers to determine the actual risk of a potential client being attacked. For this reason, insurance companies are more likely to reward companies that are able to withstand evolving cyber threats and wisely arrange strategies that last in the long term. In this case, organizations are considered to have a strong risk profile that is worth insuring.

However, implementing an effective education program is not an easy task. Delivering content and sharing information on cyber risk and ways to address it may not be enough. To execute a robust education strategy, all organizational stakeholders may need to be included from the beginning in the creation of cyber risk education and training. In addition, it may be necessary to devote a significant amount of time and money to improve specific cybersecurity behaviors that may put the company at risk. As a result of these extra efforts and investments, potential measures to minimize risk may be delayed, making it more difficult for organizations to obtain lower insurance rates.

6. Discussion and Results

The results of the previous analyses suggest that the category named "cultural factors" may have a higher impact influence on risk perception than others, making it one of the categories where risk reduction measures have the most beneficial impact on cyber insurance costs. Figure 7 shows how managing cultural factors in risk perception can result in cyber insurance benefits when directed to mitigate risk.

It is also interesting to note that, among the cultural factors, experience seems to be the most important variable for a successful risk reduction and cyber insurance strategy. The ability to use customers' experiences to obtain historical data on breaches may provide advantages to insured organizations. It is also true that prior experience with threats may not necessarily result in more accurate decisions due to the dynamic nature of cyber hazards. However, it is possible to argue that adopting educational

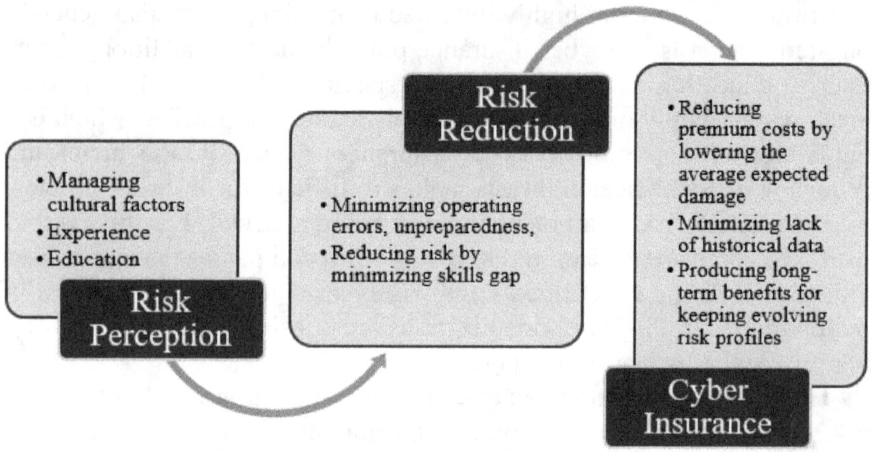

Fig. 7. Influence of risk perception on cyber insurance.

measures can compensate for this disadvantage. The integration of experience with education can maximize the effects on risk reduction and may, therefore, contribute to the stability of the organization's risk profile. Finally, it is important to note that this conclusion supports the third hypothesis of this study (*H3*) as it shows that adequate experience and education are essential requirements for risk mitigation and, therefore, necessary for obtaining insurance benefits.

7. Conclusion

As businesses of all sizes are trying to adapt to the new market realities produced by the effects of the coronavirus pandemic, the digital transformation trend is set to accelerate. This development will also contribute to the expansion of the cyber insurance industry, which is expected to expand in the coming years. However, while cyber insurance policies can help businesses cover the costs of data breaches and cyberattacks, the unpredictable nature of cybersecurity continues to affect how insurance companies operate. From the day insurance agents draft a policy through its validity period, there is often too much uncertainty to accurately quantify cyber risk (Marotta *et al.*, 2017). The findings that emerged in this study highlight the numerous challenges in insuring cyber risk, mainly due to a lack of data on cyber risk and difficulties in assessing unpredictable vulnerabilities and hazards. One way to address these issues is to adjust insurance prices based on a company's level of risk and its capacity to engage in secure behaviors. Human behavior in cybersecurity is generally driven by risk perception, which is fundamental in shaping decision-making under uncertainty. The analysis results explicated the strong influence of cultural factors on risk perceptions. In particular, experience and education appear to be the most prevalent cultural factors determining how individuals estimate the severity of hazards and how prepared they are to manage risk. The findings indeed reveal that both factors have a positive correlation and depend on each other to mitigate risk effectively. These observations represent the basic steps toward understanding the cognitive variations that may lead individuals to incorrectly assess risks, engage in risky actions, and fail to reduce risks. By uncovering these characteristics, it may be possible for insurance companies to better design policies that are more successful at providing organizations with the necessary solutions. However, one limitation of the current research is that it describes a "snapshot" in time. As highlighted in the previous sections, some influences on cyber risk perception may be dynamic, thus resulting in new patterns of behavior. Therefore, further studies may be needed to examine how cyber risk perception varies throughout risk events and contexts. Future works, for example, may use experimental methodologies and compare data before and after a cyber event to seek evidence on risk perception. Finally, this research may be a source of reference for risk managers, policy makers, and regulators who need to develop sound cybersecurity policies to deal with new risk realities.

References

Albladi, S.M. and Weir, G.R.S. (2020). Predicting individuals' vulnerability to social engineering in social networks. *Cybersecurity*, 3(1), 1–19. https://cybersecurity.springeropen.com/articles/10.1186/s42400-020-00047-5.

Araujo, C.F., Ladeira, W.J., Santini, F.O., and Sampaio, C.H. (2016). Domain-specific innovativeness: A meta-analysis in business and consumer. *RAI Revista Administração e Inovação*, 13(2), 99–106. https://www.elsevier.es/es-revista-revista-administracao-e-inovacao-239-articulo-domain-specific-innovativeness-meta-analysis-in-business-S1809203916300134.

Ayala, L. (2016). *Cybersecurity for Hospitals and Healthcare Facilities*. New York City: Apress.

Bada, M. and Nurse, J.R.C. (2020). The social and psychological impact of cyberattacks. *Emerging Cyber Threats and Cognitive Vulnerabilities*, 73–92.

Bagchi, K., Hart, P., and Peterson, M.F. (2004). National culture and information technology product adoption. *Journal of Global Information Technology Management*, 7(4), 29–46. https://www.researchgate.net/publication/280170907_National_Culture_and_Information_Technology_Product_Adoption.

Barnett, J. and Breakwell, G.M. (2001). Risk perception and experience: Hazard personality profiles and individual differences. *Risk Analysis*, 21(1), 171–178. https://doi.org/10.1111/0272-4332.211099.

Bartone, P.T. (2012). Social and organizational influences on psychological hardiness: How leaders can increase stress resilience. *Security Informatics*, 1(1). https://www.researchgate.net/publication/257885088_Social_and_organizational_influences_on_psychological_hardiness_How_leaders_can_increase_stress_resilience.

Brender, N. and Markov, I. (2013). Risk perception and risk management in cloud computing: Results from a case study of Swiss companies. *International Journal of Information Management*, 33(5), 726–733.

Brooker, G. (1984). An assessment of an expanded measure of perceived risk. *Advances in Consumer Research*, NA-11(1972), 439–442. http://www.acrwebsite.org/volumes/display.asp?id=6292.

Burzynski, J. and Burzynski, T. (2014). *Taming Risk: Uncertainty, Trust and the Sociological Discourse of Modernity*. UK: Cambridge Scholars Publishing.

Carpenter, D., Young, D.K., Barrett, P., and McLeod, A.J. (2019). Refining technology threat avoidance theory. *Communications of the Association for Information Systems*, 44(1), 380–407. https://doi.org/10.17705/1CAIS.04422.

Cellier, L. and Ghernaouti, S. (2019). An interdisciplinary approach for security, privacy and trust in the electronic medical record: A pragmatic legal perspective. *IEEE International Conference on E-Health Networking, Application and Services, HealthCom 2019*, Bogota, Colombia.

Choi, K.-S., Choo, K., and Sung, Y.-E. (2016). Demographic variables and risk factors in computer-crime: An empirical assessment. *Cluster Computing*, 19(1), 369–377. https://www.researchgate.net/publication/290478097_Demographic_variables_and_risk_factors_in_computer-crime_an_empirical_assessment.

Chung, J.B. and Kim, H.K. (2009). Competition, economic benefits, trust, and risk perception in siting a potentially hazardous facility. *Landscape and Urban Planning*, 91(1), 8–16. http://www.elsevier.com/copyright.

Colquitt, J.A., Scott, B.A., and LePine, J.A. (2007). Trust, trustworthiness, and trust propensity: A meta-analytic test of their unique relationships with risk taking and job performance. *Journal of Applied Psychology*, 92(4), 909–927.

Cooke, N.J., Salas, E., Kiekel, P.A., and Bell, B. (2005). Advances in measuring team cognition. In Salas, E. and Fiore, S.M. (eds.), *Team Cognition: Understanding the Factors That Drive Process Performance* (pp. 83–106). https://www.researchgate.net/publication/228392482.

Covi, M.P. (2014). Water's gonna rise: Sea-level rise risk perception, communication and policy-making in North Carolina. East Carolina University. https://core.ac.uk/download/pdf/71976116.pdf.

Crete-Nishihata, M., Oliver, J., Parsons, C., Walker, D., Tsui, L., and Deibert, R. (2020). The information security cultures of journalism. *Digital Journalism*, 8(8), 1068–1091. https://doi.org/101080/21670811202017777882.

D'Antoni, D., Smith, L., Auyeung, V., and Weinman, J. (2017). Psychosocial and demographic predictors of adherence and non-adherence to health advice accompanying air quality warning systems: A systematic review. *Environmental Health: A Global Access Science Source*, 16(1), 1–18. https://ehjournal.biomedcentral.com/articles/10.1186/s12940-017-0307-4.

Dake, K. (1991). Orienting dispositions in the perception of risk: An analysis of contemporary worldviews and cultural biases. *Journal of Cross-Cultural Psychology*, 22(1), 61–82. https://journals.sagepub.com/doi/10.1177/0022022191221006.

Dalmolin, D., Basso, K., Reck, D., Laimer, C.G., and Corte, V.F.D. (2019). Effect of risks perceived on trust and decisions of investment and financing. *Contab Gestão e Governança*, 22(2), 243–260.

Das, T.K. and Teng, B.S. (2004). The risk-based view of trust: A conceptual framework. *Journal of Business and Psychology*, 19(1), 85–116.

De Smidt, G. and Botzen, W. (2018). Perceptions of corporate cyber risks and insurance decision-making. *Geneva Papers on Risk and Insurance — Issues and Practice*, 43(2), 239–274. https://riskcenter.wharton.upenn.edu/.

Deline, S., Guillet, L., Rauffet, P., and Guérin, C. (2021). Team cognition in a cyber defense context: Focus on social support behaviors. *Cognition, Technology & Work*, 23(1), 51–63.

Dholakia, U.M. (2001). A motivational process model of product involvement and consumer risk perception. *European Journal of Marketing*, 35(11/12), 1340–1362.

Díaz, L. (2015). Cultural theory. In *Ubiquitous Computing, Complexity and Culture* (pp. 30–32). https://www.taylorfrancis.com/books/mono/10.4324/9780429501180/cultural-theory-michael-thompson-richard-ellis-aaron-wildavsky.

Douglas, M. and Wildavsky, A. (1982). Can we know the risks we face? *Risk and Culture: An Essay on the Selection of Technological and Environmental Dangers* (pp. 1–15). https://www.ucpress.edu/book/9780520050631/risk-and-culture.

Elena, G. and Johnson, C.W. (2015). Laypeople's and experts' risk perception of cloud computing services. *International Journal on Cloud Computing: Services and Architecture*, 5(4), 1–19.

Emami-Naeini, P., Dheenadhayalan, J., Agarwal, Y., and Cranor, L.F. (2021). Which privacy and security attributes most impact consumers' risk perception and willingness to purchase IoT Devices? *Proceedings of the IEEE Symposium on Security and Privacy*, May 2021, San Francisco, pp. 519–536.

Fiorenza, M. (2020). The importance of perception of occupational risk to reduce the accident phenomenon: An analysis of the variables. *Journal of Advanced Health Care*, 2.

Folkes, V.S. (1988). The availability heuristic and perceived risk. *Journal of Consumer Research*, 15(1), 13. https://academic.oup.com/jcr/article/15/1/13/1840928.

Gefen, D. and Straub, D. (2000). The relative importance of perceived ease of use in IS adoption: A study of E-commerce adoption. *Journal of the Association for Information Systems*, 1(1), 1–30.

Ghosh, A. and Fedorowicz, J. (2008). The role of trust in supply chain governance. *Business Process Management Journal*, 14(4), 453–470. http://dx.doi.org/10.1108/14637150810888019.

Grewal, D., Gotlieb, J., and Marmorstein, H. (1994). The moderating effects of message framing and source credibility on the price-perceived risk relationship. *Journal of Consumer Research*, 21(1), 145. http://jcr.oxfordjournals.org/.

Grobler, M., Chamikara, M.A.P., Abbott, J., Jeong, J.J., Nepal, S., and Paris, C. (2021). The importance of social identity on password formulations. *Personal and Ubiquitous Computing*, 25(5), 813–827. https://link.springer.com/article/10.1007/s00779-020-01477-1.

Gu, J.Q., Mei, S.E., and Zhong, W.J. (2015). Cyber insurance as an incentive for information system security. *Xitong Gongcheng Lilun yu Shijian/System Engineering Theory and Practice*, 35(4), 1057–1062. https://www.semanticscholar.org/paper/e2d83d529386147e25dcdb47423a30cf70adb4b1.

Gunleifsen, H. (2018). Cyber security awareness and culture in rural Norway. *NTNU*. https://ntnuopen.ntnu.no/ntnu-xmlui/handle/11250/2592269.

Halevi, T., Memon, N., Lewis, J., Kumaraguru, P., Arora, S., Dagar, N., *et al.* (2017). Cultural and psychological factors in cyber-security. *Journal of Mobile Multimedia*, 13(1–2), 43–56.

Hampson, S.E., Andrews, J.A., Barckley, M., Lichtenstein, E., and Lee, M.E. (2006). Personality traits, perceived risk, and risk-reduction behaviors: A further study of smoking and radon. *Health Psychology*, 25(4), 530–536. https://pmc/articles/PMC2409280/.

Herath, T., Chen, R., Wang, J., Banjara, K., Wilbur, J., and Rao, H.R. (2014). Security services as coping mechanisms: An investigation into user intention to adopt an email authentication service. *Information Systems Journal*, 24(1),

61–84. https://onlinelibrary.wiley.com/doi/full/10.1111/j.1365-2575.2012.00420.x.

Houston, D., Cheung, W., Basolo, V., Feldman, D., Matthew, R., Sanders, B.F., Karlin, B., Schubert, J.E., Goodrich, K.A., Contreras, S., and Luke. A. (2019). Influence of hazard maps and trust of flood controls on coastal flood spatial awareness and risk perception. *Environment and Behavior*, 51(4), 347–375. https://doi.org/10.1177/0013916517748711.

Howatt, W.A. (2015). *The Coping Crisis: Discover Why Coping Skills Are Required for a Healthy and Fulfilling Life*. Foreword by Gillian Livingston from *The Globe and Mail*. www.morneaushepell.com.

Inkpen, A.C. and Tsang, E.W.K. (2007). 10 learning and strategic alliances. *The Academy of Management Annals*, 1(1), 479–511. https://doi.org/105465/078559815.

Isaak, J. and Hanna, M.J. (2018). User data privacy: Facebook, Cambridge Analytica, and Privacy Protection. *Computer*, 51(8), 56–59.

Jackson, G.W. and Rahman, S.S.M. (2019). Exploring challenges and opportunities in cybersecurity risk and threat communications related to the medical Internet of Things (MIOT). *International Journal of Network Security & Its Applications*, 11(4), 12.

Jarvenpaa, S.L., Tractinsky, N., Saarinen, L., and Vitale, M. (1999). Consumer trust in an internet store: A cross-cultural validation. *Journal of Computer-Mediated Communication*, 5(2), 45–71. https://d1wqtxts1xzle7.cloudfront.net/52990493/00_slj_nt_mv-with-cover-page-v2.pdf?Expires=1643830060-&Signature=A7bFRvzculVkgcTBAwdU66k2wmdc-yiNtyWPoe84bK71GeopwfpA3prD66vDk5BwBuSNbDEv7GQmyWKxQiH9hicp3YnDCSKJbAuqIbB7SRJzUSZfKf0rNkWY3rFvdFwPfqGY63msx1kzdt7.

Johnston, A.C. and Warkentin, M. (2008). Information privacy compliance in the healthcare industry. *Information Management & Computer Security*, 16(1), 5–19.

Kahan, D.M., Jenkins-Smith, H., and Braman, D. (2011). Cultural cognition of scientific consensus. *Journal of Risk Research*, 14(2), 147–174. http://www.informaworld.com.

Kaplan, L.B., Szybillo, G.J., and Jacoby, J. (1974). Components of perceived risk in product purchase: A cross-validation. *Journal of Applied Psychology*, 59(3), 287–291. https://record/1974-32397-001.

Kish-Gephart, J.J. (2017). Social class & risk preferences and behavior. *Current Opinion in Psychology*, 18, 89–92.

Lepesteur, M., Wegner, A., Moore, S.A., and McComb, A. (2008). Importance of public information and perception for managing recreational activities in the Peel-Harvey estuary, Western Australia. *Journal of Environmental Management*, 87(3), 389–395. www.elsevier.com/locate/jenvman.

Liang, H. and Xue, Y. (2010). Understanding security behaviors in personal computer usage: A threat avoidance perspective. *Journal of the Association for Information Systems*, 11(7), 394–413. https://www.researchgate.net/publication/220580586.

Lindell, M.K. and Prater, C.S. (2002). Risk area residents' perceptions and adoption of seismic hazard adjustments. *Journal of Applied Social Psychology*, 32(11), 2377–2392.

Lunardo, R. and Saintives, C. (2019). How autonomy makes an experience pleasurable: The roles of risk perception and personal control. *Recherche et Applications en Marketing* (English edition), 35(1), 43–61. https://doi.org/101177/2051570719828674.

Maidl, E., Bresch, D.N., and Buchecker, M. (2021). Social integration matters: Factors influencing natural hazard risk preparedness — A survey of Swiss households. *Natural Hazards*, 105(2), 1861–1890. https://link.springer.com/article/10.1007/s11069-020-04381-2.

Majuca, R.P., Yurcik, W., and Kesan, J.P. (2006). The evolution of cyberinsurance. http://arxiv.org/abs/cs/0601020.

Manika, D., Dickert, S., and Golden, L.L. (2021). Check (it) yourself before you wreck yourself: The benefits of online health information exposure on risk perception and intentions to protect oneself. *Technological Forecasting and Social Change*, 173, 121098.

Markowska, M., Grichnik, D., Brinckmann, J., and Kapsa, D. (2019). Strategic orientations of nascent entrepreneurs: Antecedents of prediction and risk orientation. *Small Business Economics*, 53(4), 859–878. https://link.springer.com/article/10.1007/s11187-018-0107-4.

Marotta, A., Martinelli, F., Nanni, S., Orlando, A., and Yautsiukhin, A. (2017). Cyber-insurance survey. *Computer Science Review*, 24, 35–61.

Marotta, A. and Pearlson, K. (2019). A culture of cybersecurity at Banca popolare di sondrio. In *25th Am Conf Inf Syst AMCIS 2019*. https://aisel.aisnet.org/amcis2019/info_security_privacy/info_security_privacy/24.

Marotta, A. (2015). A survey on cyber insurance. In *Seminar. National Research Council (IIT-CNR)*, Pisa, Italy. https://www-old.iit.cnr.it/en/node/36232.

McCormac, A., Zwaans, T., Parsons, K., Calic, D., Butavicius, M., and Pattinson, M. (2017). Individual differences and information security awareness. *Computers in Human Behavior*, 69, 151–156.

McGee, T.K. and Russell, S. (2003). "It's just a natural way of life…" an investigation of wildfire preparedness in rural Australia. *Environmental Hazards*, 5(1), 1–12. https://www.researchgate.net/publication/223839832.

Moody, G.D., Siponen, M., and Pahnila, S. (2018). Toward a unified model of information security policy compliance. *MIS Quarterly: Management Information Systems*, 42(1), 285–311.

Morrison, B., Coventry, L., and Briggs, P. (2021). How do older adults feel about engaging with cyber-security? *Human Behavior and Emerging Technologies*, 3(5), 1033–1049. https://onlinelibrary.wiley.com/doi/full/10.1002/hbe2.291.

Munn, Z., Peters, M.D.J., Stern, C., Tufanaru, C., McArthur, A., and Aromataris, E. (2018). Systematic review or scoping review? Guidance for authors when choosing between a systematic or scoping review approach. *BMC Medical Research Methodology*, 18(1), 143. https://bmcmedresmethodol.biomedcentral.com/articles/10.1186/s12874-018-0611-x.

Nakashima, E. (2018). Russian military was behind 'NotPetya' cyberattack in Ukraine, CIA concludes. *The Washington Post*, p. 12. https://www.washingtonpost.com/world/national-security/russian-military-was-behind-notpetya-cyberattack-in-ukraine-cia-concludes/2018/01/12/048d8506-f7ca-11e7-b34a-b85626af34ef_story.html?noredirect=on.

Nash, K.S. (2017). Thomson Reuters CISO: Cybersecurity leadership brings personal, professional challenges. *The Wall Street Journal*. Available from: https://www.wsj.com/articles/BL-CIOB-11982.

Nobles, C. (2018). Botching human factors in cybersecurity in business organizations. *HOLISTICA — Journal of Business and Public Administration*, 9(3), 71–88.

Nyblom, P., Wangen, G., and Gkioulos, V. (2020). Risk perceptions on social media use in Norway. *Future Internet*, 12(12), 1–40. https://www.mdpi.com/1999-5903/12/12/211/htm.

Ogbanufe, O. (2020). "Information security is not really my job": Exploring information security role identity in end-users. In *Proc. Annual Hawaii International Conference on System Sciences 2020*, pp. 4256–4263. https://hdl.handle.net/10125/64263.

Ogbanufe, O. and Kim, D.J. (2018). "Just how risky is it anyway?" The role of risk perception and trust on click-through intention. *Information Systems Management*, 35(3), 182–200. https://www.tandfonline.com/doi/abs/10.1080/10580530.2018.1477292.

Pal, R., Golubchik, L., Psounis, K., and Hui, P. (2013). Improving network security via cyber-insurance: A market analysis, 1–12. https://www.semanticscholar.org/paper/af2dd038dfc21d7f2af75ef328df955e58161bec.

Palm, R. and Carroll, J. (2019). Culture and risk perception. *Illusions of Safety*, 57–68. https://www.taylorfrancis.com/chapters/mono/10.4324/9780429039713-6/culture-risk-perception-risa-palm-john-carroll.

Pattinson, M. and Anderson, G. (2007). How well are information risks being communicated to your computer end-users? In *Proceedings of the International Symposium on Human Aspects of Information Security & Assurance (HAISA 2007)*, pp. 25–36.

Phillips-Wren, G. (2012). AI tools in decision making support systems: A review. *International Journal on Artificial Intelligence Tools*, 21(2), 1240005.

Reitsma, M.B., Fullman, N., Ng, M., Salama, J.S., Abajobir, A., Abate, K.H., *et al.* (2017). Smoking prevalence and attributable disease burden in 195 countries and territories, 1990–2015: A systematic analysis from the global burden of disease study 2015. *Lancet*, 389(10082), 1885–1906.

Rohrmann, B. and Renn, O. (2000). Risk perception research. In Renn, O., and Rohrmann, B. (eds.), *Cross-Cultural Risk Perception*, 11–53. https://link.springer.com/chapter/10.1007/978-1-4757-4891-8_1.

Ross, R., Pillitteri, V., Graubart, R., Bodeau, D., and Mcquaid, R. (2021). Developing cyber-resilient systems: A systems security engineering approach. National Institute of Standards and Technology (NIST) Special Publication 800-160, 310. https://nvlpubs.nist.gov/nistpubs/SpecialPublications/NIST.SP.800-160v2.pdf.

Scalia, A.M. (2017). The influence of sociodemographic, location, and health characteristics on environmental risk perception. Clemson University Libraries, 77. https://tigerprints.clemson.edu/all_theses.

Setbon, M., Raude, J., Fischler, C., and Flahault, A. (2005). Risk perception of the "mad cow disease" in France: Determinants and consequences. *Risk Analysis*, 25(4), 813–826. https://onlinelibrary.wiley.com/doi/full/10.1111/j.1539-6924.2005.00634.x.

Sheng, S., Holbrook, M., Kumaraguru, P., Cranor, L.F., and Downs, J. (2010). Who falls for phish? A demographic analysis of phishing susceptibility and effectiveness of interventions. *Conference on Human Factors in Computing Systems — Proceedings*, 1, 373–382.

Shetty, N., Schwartz, G., and Walrand, J. (2010). Can competitive insurers improve network security? Lecture Notes in Computer Science (including Subseries Lecture Notes in Artificial Intelligence and Lecture Notes in Bioinformatics), 6101 LNCS, pp. 308–322. https://www.semanticscholar.org/paper/c9b5aced74e0d5b34b87f199717e941d15a3c704.

Sjöberg, L. (2000). The methodology of risk perception research. *Quality & Quantity*, 34(4), 407–418. https://link.springer.com/article/10.1023/A:1004838806793.

Slovic, P. (1987). Perception of risk. *Science*, 236(4799), 280–285. https://pubmed.ncbi.nlm.nih.gov/3563507/.

Slovic, P., Fischhoff, B., and Lichtenstein, S. (1986). The psychometric study of risk perception. *Risk Evaluation and Management*, 3–24. https://link.springer.com/chapter/10.1007/978-1-4613-2103-3_1.

Slovic, P., Flynn, J., and Layman, M. (2016). Perceived risk, trust and the politics of nuclear waste. In *The Perception of Risk* (pp. 275–284). London: Earthscan Publications, Ltd.

Slovic, P., Kraus, N., Lappe, H., and Major, M. (1991). Risk perception of prescription drugs: Report on a survey in Canada. *Canadian Journal of Public Health*, 82(3), S15–20, S38–44.

Sund, B., Svensson, M., and Andersson, H. (2017). Demographic determinants of incident experience and risk perception: Do high-risk groups accurately perceive themselves as high-risk? *Journal of Risk Research*, 20(1), 99–117. https://www.tandfonline.com/doi/abs/10.1080/13669877.2015.1042499.

Tricco, A.C., Antony, J., Zarin, W., Strifler, L., Ghassemi, M., Ivory, J., *et al.* (2015). A scoping review of rapid review methods. *BMC Medicine*, 13(1), 224. https://doi.org/10.1186/s12916-015-0465-6.

Twigg, J. (2003). The human factor in early warnings: Risk perception and appropriate communications. *Early Warning Systems for Natural Disaster Reduction*, 19–26. https://link.springer.com/chapter/10.1007/978-3-642-55903-7_4.

US Department of Homeland Security (2012). Cybersecurity Insurance Workshop Readout Report. CISA, 1–50. https://www.cisa.gov/sites/default/files/publications/November/2012/Cybersecurity/InsuranceWorkshop.pdf.

Van den Steen, E. (2010). On the origin of shared beliefs (and corporate culture). *RAND Journal of Economics*, 41, 617–648.

Van Niekerk, J.F. and Von Solms, R. (2010). Information security culture: A management perspective. *Computers & Security*, 29(4), 476–486.

Vance, A., Siponen, M., and Pahnila, S. (2012). Motivating IS security compliance: Insights from habit and protection motivation theory. *Information and Management*, 49(3–4), 190–198.

Wachinger, G., Renn, O., Begg, C., and Kuhlicke, C. (2013). The risk perception paradox-implications for governance and communication of natural hazards. *Risk Analysis*, 33(6), 1049–1065. https://onlinelibrary.wiley.com/doi/full/10.1111/j.1539-6924.2012.01942.x.

Walsh, K. (2004). Interpreting the impact of culture on structure: The role of change processes. *Journal of Applied Behavioral Science*, 40(3), 302–322. https://www.researchgate.net/publication/250959727_Interpreting_the_Impact_of_Culture_on_StructureThe_Role_of_Change_Processes.

Weinstein, N.D., Rothman, A.J., and Nicolich, M. (1998). Use of correlational data to examine the effects of risk perceptions on precautionary behavior. *Psychology & Health*, 13(3), 479–501. https://www.tandfonline.com/doi/abs/10.1080/08870449808407305.

Whitty, M., Doodson, J., Creese, S., and Hodges, D. (2015). Individual differences in cyber security behaviors: An examination of who is sharing passwords. *Cyberpsychology, Behavior, and Social Networking*, 18(1), 3–7.

Wildavsky, A. (1991). Risk perception. *Risk Analysis*, 11(1), 15–16. https://link.springer.com/chapter/10.1007/978-1-4684-5484-0_13.

Xu, H., Luo, X., Carroll, J.M., and Rosson, M.B. (2011). The personalization privacy paradox: An exploratory study of decision making process for location-aware marketing. *Decision Support Systems*, 51(1), 42–52. https://www.sciencedirect.com/science/article/abs/pii/S0167923610001983?via%3Dihub.

Ye, C., Li, G., Cai, H., Gu, Y., and Fukuda, A. (2018). Analysis of security in blockchain: Case study in 51%-attack detecting. In *Proceedings — 2018 5th International Conference on Dependable Systems and Their Applications (DSA 2018)*, September 22–23, 2018, Dalian, China, pp. 15–24.

Yıldırım, M. and Arslan, G. (2020). Exploring the associations between resilience, dispositional hope, preventive behaviours, subjective well-being, and psychological health among adults during early stage of COVID-19. *Current Psychology*, 41, 5712–5722. https://link.springer.com/article/10.1007/s12144-020-01177-2.

Zhang, R., Brennan, T.J., and Lo, A.W. (2014). The origin of risk aversion. *Proceedings of the National Academy of Sciences*, 111(50), 17777–17782.

https://doi.org/10.1142/9789811271984_0005

Chapter 5

The Perils and Promise of Digital Transformation: Incremental versus Disruptive Change

Stephen J. Andriole

Villanova University School of Business, Villanova, PA, USA
stephen.andriole@villanova.edu

Digital transformation comes in all shapes and sizes. Most digital transformation projects, however, are not really "transformative." They do not disrupt business processes or whole business models. Instead, they're "incremental," or just as often part of planned technology "modernization" initiatives. These kinds of projects are safer, less risky, less expensive, and "politically" protective of executive reputations, which is perhaps why a vast majority of digital transformation projects focus on incremental changes or modernization. But digital transformation projects that are truly transformative are targeted at replacing or automating business processes, or replacing or automating whole business models — which are riskier, more expensive, and more politically dangerous projects than incremental and modernization ones. Impact follows risk: incremental and modernization projects are easily less impactful than disruptive ones. The "perils" and "promise" of digital transformation are defined around a simple risk/impact ratio. Companies should decide how and where they want to "transform," acknowledging the likely return on their digital transformation investments. But eventually, because of the trajectories of technology and business, all companies will have to pursue more disruptive transformation.

1. Introduction

It's impossible to list all of the companies that have launched digital transformation projects over the past decade — or the number of companies that will launch digital transformation projects over the next decade. It's also impossible to overstate the importance of the failure rate of big technology projects expected to "transform" business processes, and in some cases whole business models. Digital transformation fails 70% of the time (Saldanha, 2019). McKinsey reports that only 30% of digital transformation projects result in improved corporate performance (Hjartar *et al.*, 2019). There's failure data everywhere (Kimberling, 2015; Lee, 2014; Lynch, 2015; Charette, 2012, 2018; Forrest, 2016; Florentine, 2016): Technology projects fail at an astounding rate at enormous cost to the companies — and executives — who support them. Perhaps the harshest finding is that "90% fail to deliver any measurable ROI" (Carlton, 2019).

2. Definitions

So, what is digital transformation? Digital transformation, according to *Salesforce.com* (2022), is as follows:

> ... the process of using digital technologies **to create new — or modify existing — business processes**, culture, and customer experiences to meet changing business and market requirements. **This reimagining of business in the digital age is digital transformation.**

Definitions vary according to the emphasis placed on business processes versus whole business models, or incremental versus disruptive transformation. Most digital transformation projects — in spite of their aspirations — are incremental or part of planned technology modernization efforts, as suggested by Figure 1: very few are truly disruptive.

As Figure 1 suggests, incremental and modernization digital transformation projects are by definition "safer" than ones targeted at disrupting

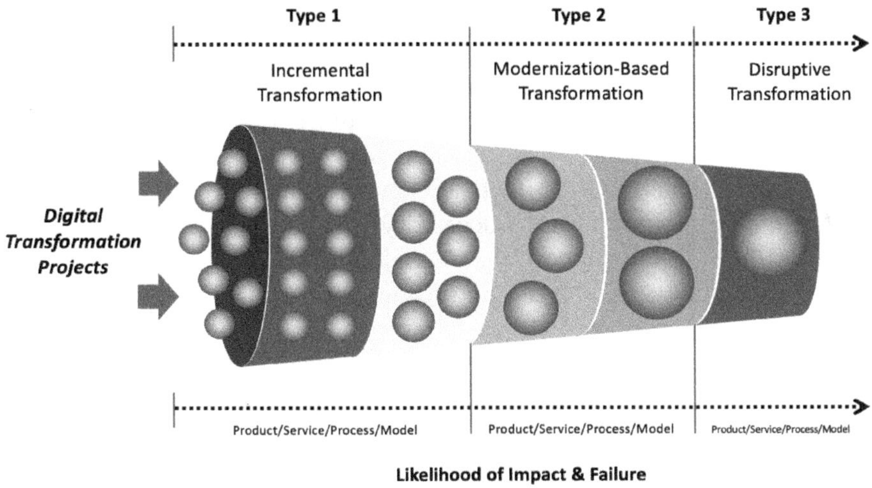

Fig. 1. The type, impact, and risks of digital transformation projects.

business processes and models. But incremental digital transformation projects have — also by definition — limited impact on a company's larger digital mission. So, the trade-off is straightforward: Stay with safer, simpler projects — or attempt to disrupt business processes and whole business models through riskier digital transformation projects. As the figure suggests via the size of the project balls, the farther one moves across the digital transformation continuum, the greater the impact. So while the impact of incremental projects is relatively small, so are the risks.

3. The Perils of Digital Transformation

Even if we only focus on enterprise resource planning (ERP) and big data incremental and modernization projects, there are tons of studies about why technology projects fail. The ERP business routinely experiences failure, and sometimes famously: The Gartner Group reports that 75% of ERP projects fail. Others report that CRM projects fail at nearly the same rate. Big data analytics projects also fail at an alarming rate. Innovation? None other than Clayton Christensen suggested that 95% of product innovation projects fail — regardless of their location on the incremental-disruption continuum (Christensen, 1996).

We know why these projects fail:

(1) Companies cannot define the problems they're trying to solve.
(2) Companies cannot identify the right requirements or manage scope creep.
(3) Companies cannot do project crisis management.
(4) Companies do not have the necessary talent.
(5) Executives fail to support big technology projects.
(6) Most corporate cultures are anti-technology.

But we also know that numbers 4 to 6 explain most of the failure of digital transformation and other technology projects. Since these causes of failure are "understood" at some level in most companies, is this why there's so much incrementalism and very little disruption across the range of digital transformation projects? It appears so. Executives, managers, and project managers should invest in the causes of numbers 1 to 3 (to reduce the number of failed digital transformation projects), but they should respect the difficulty of solving numbers 4 to 6. Unless companies are willing to actually "refresh" their talent pools (which they're usually unwilling to do), hire savvier executives who understand that project support is far more than a signature on a business case (which they're equally loath to do), and change their corporate cultures to truly believe in the short- and long-term power of digital (which they cannot do no matter how hard they try), they're doomed to repeat their failure histories.

Based on all this failure and the probability of success, many companies have decided that the best way to proceed — to address the perils of digital transformation — is to pursue smaller, less risky projects. While this may sound like capitulation, for the majority of companies the digital transformation race is a conscious race to the bottom — not to the disruptive top. Given the percentage of technology project failures, they have perfected the art of incrementalism. While everyone loves a good digital transformation story, they're resisted until they've been proven worthy (usually after the fact) or reconstituted as big wins in small packages.

Skilled CIOs and CTOs understand that a huge part of their job is managing digital transformation expectations downward, or — even smarter — setting expectations as low as possible while still generating project excitement. Is this a two-step process? Yes. When it comes to big technology project management, given the failure rates, everyone should learn how to dance in slow, small steps — not large ones. These are "the perils of best practices." But are they good enough, or should expectations about impact be increased? Can incremental and modernization-based digital transformation projects continue to be "sold" as real digital transformation, or will companies realize that the difference between incremental and modernization digital transformation is small and in fact no different from business as usual? Will incremental and modernization digital transformation keep companies competitive? Will it enable profitable growth? Is it responsive to the competition? Can companies respond slowly and deliberately to market trends, believing they always have time to pivot to more disruptive behavior? Or should they pivot now to disruptive digital transformation?

4. The Promise of Digital Transformation

The promise of digital transformation lies far from incremental or modernization projects. Digital transformation can transform business processes and whole business models if certain things are true.

First, digital transformation champions must assess the environment in which transformation will occur. Some verticals, like financial services and healthcare, are more likely to transform their processes than others, like accounting. Vested interests — like saving money by reducing fraud with intelligent systems — are powerful drivers. Transformation leaders must be open to change and have the willingness to "sell" transformation for its business value: Professional introverts need not apply. Nor should leaders be driven by panic. Support should also descend into business units (where resistance can be significant) by describing the business value of transformation at all levels, which should include the right incentives for the key players.

Second, data must be plentiful and high quality. Not just piles of structured and unstructured corporate data about customers, production, manufacturing, distribution, competitors, and processes, but high-quality data that's clean, consistent, and analytically accessible. Transformation projects that involve big data analytics and artificial intelligence are especially dependent upon quality data. Sometimes, companies must be told that their current data repositories will not enable digital transformation. Understandably, these are tough conversations, but sometimes necessary before spending a ton of money on projects that are destined to fail:

Honesty and transparency are still key to digital transformation project success.

Third, in addition to the right data and methodology, digital transformation projects require additional capabilities that companies need to exhibit internally and externally. The assumption is that companies — no matter how enthused they might be about digital transformation — cannot master all of the skills necessary to accomplish their goals. This is a significant acknowledgment and suggests that definitions of digital transformation "core competency" cannot be satisfied internally by most — if not all — companies. Vendors are necessary partners since they're far more likely to be tracking emerging technologies than their clients, who are deeply emerged in the domains of their business. For the same reasons that most companies are now in the cloud (and why most of us no longer fix our own cars), companies need partners and should not attempt to build out their own wide, deep, and expensive digital transformation teams. Instead, they should share capabilities with their partners.

Fourth, disruptive digital transformation is likely to be enabled by — and in many cases is dependent upon — emerging digital technology. Figure 2 lists the technologies that should be tracked. At the center are the disruptive business processes and models that define the essence of transformative digital transformation.

Figure 2 formalizes the role that emerging technologies must play in disruptive digital transformation, including a team whose job is to track emerging technologies and continuously assess their potential impact on disruptive digital transformation. Note that lists like these change all the time, so tracking emerging technologies is itself a discipline that needs talent, resources, and milestones, especially as they all relate to macro trends such as The Future of Work and the 4th Industrial Revolution.

Fifth, and most importantly, disruptive digital transformation must challenge executives and corporate cultures skeptical of big projects designed to change existing business processes and, in some cases, whole business models. As we know from the failure data, talent, the lack of executive support, and non-digital corporate cultures all contribute to digital transformation project failure. Those committed to disruptive digital transformation cannot avoid these challenges. Objective assessments about industries, companies, the executives who run them, and the employees who execute projects are necessary to gauge the likelihood of disruptive digital transformation projects.

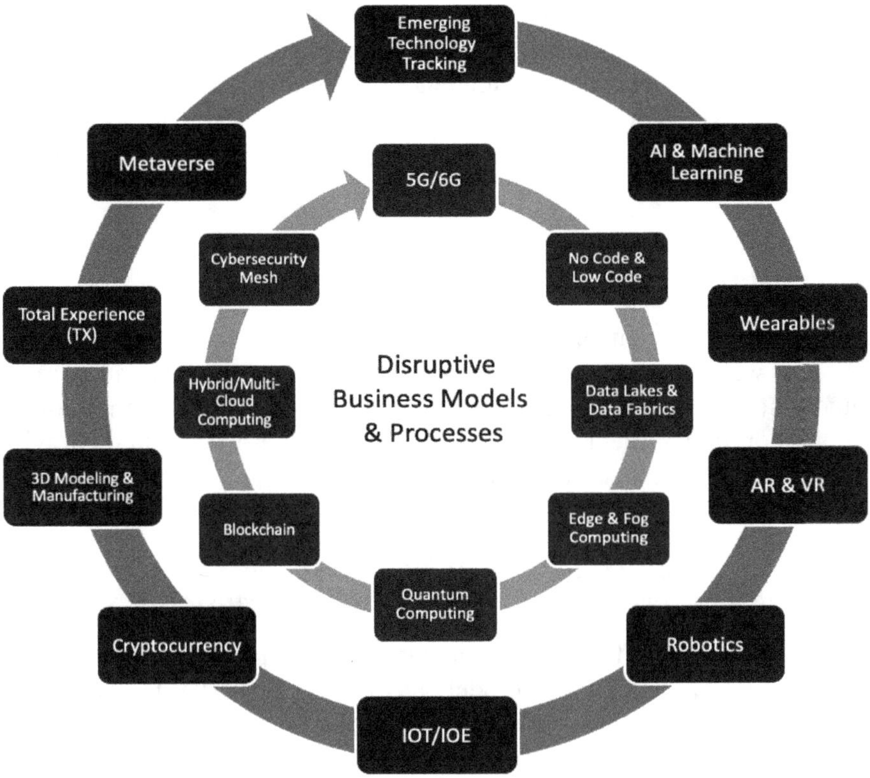

Fig. 2. Emerging technologies for disruptive digital transformation.

5. Decision Points

Companies must decide on the type of digital transformation they want to pursue. This is a difficult decision for some — but not most —companies. Most companies have already defaulted to incremental and modernization digital transformation projects. They've decided that the risks of disruptive digital transformation are just too great, that the cost is too high, and the political threats to executives who support disruptive digital transformation are too great. They also do not believe that their industry (or competitors) has committed to disruptive change in any serious way, so they have time to play "catch-up" if the competitive environment requires a more disruptive response.

But (relatively few) other companies see digital transformation as an opportunity to disrupt business processes and business models to become market leaders. These are the courageous companies led by executives willing to take risks for profitable growth. These companies satisfy the conditions described above, but are also — and especially — culturally prepared to change.

6. Digital Transformation in Perspective

Digital transformation has evolved over the years to become all-inclusive, which is why the distinctions among types, impact, and outcomes are so important. There are also myths surrounding digital transformation. I reported on five of them in 2017 (Andriole, 2017). Let's revisit them with some perspective gained after five more years of studying the perils and promise of digital transformation.

6.1 *Myth 1: Every company should digitally transform*

This is still a myth. The assumption that every company should transform their business processes and models has always been wrong. That said, every company must obviously still incrementally change the way it does business and modernize its aging systems. Longer term, however, companies that refuse to change will find themselves at a competitive disadvantage. So, yes, it's still a myth that every company needs to digitally transform itself, but we should note that continuous refusal to change will likely be listed by the business coroner as the most likely cause of death.

6.2 *Myth 2: Digital transformation leverages emerging or disruptive technologies*

Incremental and modernization-focused digital transformation often uses conventional, existing digital technology. There's often no need to adopt emerging technology to affect incremental changes or modernization projects, so this myth still stands. Incremental and modernization digital transformation can stick with tried-and-true technologies (until they can't).

6.3 *Myth 3: Profitable companies are the most likely to launch successful digital transformation projects*

This myth is still true! The assumption that market leaders are the most innovative has always been false (Christensen, 1996). Data suggests the opposite. "If it ain't broke, don't fix it" is the mantra. Companies doing well believe that doing well is the result of repetition processes and an unassailable business model. They do not believe their path to profitability should be disrupted in any way, shape, or form. I asked the following five years ago (Andriole, 2017):

> Where is there the least resistance to digital transformation efforts? At companies hemorrhaging customers and cash, and at start-ups with plenty of investor cash to burn. That's because digital transformations work well when you have money to spend and a high capacity — and rationale — for taking risks. By contrast, established companies are "established" for a reason: they've reached consistent levels of profitable revenue generation, driven by well-understood processes that, together, comprise an ongoing business model. They are therefore, typically, unwilling to upend those processes, as long as they continue winning in the marketplace.

This is all still true.

6.4 *Myth 4: We need to disrupt our industry before someone else does*

Market leaders do not usually sense disruptive competition, especially from new entrants. This is an extension of the "If it ain't broke, don't fix it" phenomenon. So, no, market leaders are not obsessed with vulnerability. Instead, they feel strong and powerful, even invulnerable to disruptors that impacted whole industries, like Airbnb (hospitality), Uber and Lyft (transportation), Amazon (books and retail), SelectQuote (insurance), Purple (sleep), and Netflix (entertainment), among others that have reinvented a broad range of vertical industries.

6.5 *Myth 5: Executives are hungry for digital transformation*

They're still not — unless their companies (and therefore themselves) are threatened by falling revenues and serious competition. But that doesn't stop executives from talking endlessly about digital transformation projects and goals (Andriole, 2017):

> In short, there's a widening gap between what executives say about digital transformation and what they actually do. It would be nice to think that executives are primarily motivated by what's best for the long-term health of the company, but their motives are often more complex.

7. Conclusion

Confirmed myths aside, we now know a lot more about digital transformation than we did even five years ago. We know that there are types of digital transformations. We know that there are digital transformation risks, and we know that a majority of digital transformation projects — in spite of how they're described to internal and external stakeholders — are focused on incremental change, or just part of scheduled maintenance and modernization. But we also know that competitive risks will eventually force companies to accept more risk, to become more disruptive. We know that digital transformation will inevitably migrate from incremental to disruptive. The velocity and trajectory of change will make this a certainty.

References

Andriole, S. (2017). Five myths about digital transformation. *MIT Sloan Management Review*. https://sloanreview.mit.edu/article/five-myths-about-digital-transformation/.

Carlton, R. (2019). Ten ERP failure statistics that highlight the importance of getting it right the first time round. *ERP Focus*. https://www.erpfocus.com/ten-erp-failure-statistics.html.

Charette, R.N. (2012). US Air Force blows $1 billion on failed ERP project. *IEEE Spectrum*. https://spectrum.ieee.org/us-air-force-blows-1-billion-on-failed-erp-project.

Charette, R.N. (2018). 2018's IT failures already have a familiar look. *IEEE Spectrum*. https://spectrum.ieee.org/2018s-it-failures-have-a-familiar-look-already.

Christensen, C. (1996). *The Innovator's Dilemma: When New Technologies Cause Great Firms to Fail*. Boston, MA: Harvard University Press.

Florentine, S. (2016). More than half of IT projects still failing. *CIO Magazine*. https://www.cio.com/article/241054/more-than-half-of-it-projects-still-failing.html.

Forrest, C. (2016). The 20 biggest tech disasters of all time. *TechRepublic*. https://www.techrepublic.com/pictures/the-20-biggest-tech-disasters-of-all-time/.

Kimberling, E. (2015). Key findings from the 2015 report. *Panorama Consulting*. https://www.panorama-consulting.com/wp-content/uploads/2016/07/2015-ERP-Report-3.pdf.

Hjartar, K., Krishnakanthan, K., Prieti-Munoz, P., Shenai, G., and Van Kuiken, S. (2019). The CEO's new technology agenda. *McKinsey Digital*. https://www.mckinsey.com/business-functions/mckinsey-digital/our-insights/the-ceos-new-technology-agenda.

Lee, J. (2014). 9 VERY scary ERP and ERP system implementation statistics. *ERP/VAR*. https://www.erpvar.com/blog/bid/108723/9-VERY-Scary-ERP-and-ERP-System-Implementation-Statistics.

Lynch, J. (2015). *The Chaos Report 2015*. The Standish Group. https://www.standishgroup.com/sample_research_files/CHAOSReport2015-Final.pdf.

Salesforce.com (2022). What is digital transformation? https://www.salesforce.com/products/platform/what-is-digital-transformation/?d=nav-prev.

Saldanha, T. (2019). *Why Digital Transformation Fails: The Surprising Disciplines of How to Take Off and Stay Ahead*. Oakland, CA: Berrett-Koehler Publishers.

https://doi.org/10.1142/9789811271984_0006

Chapter 6

Digital Transformation and Artificial Intelligence: Opportunities and Challenges

Frederic Lemieux

Georgetown University, Washington, DC, USA
fl409@georgetown.edu

The adoption of artificial intelligence (AI) is booming and was accelerated during the pandemic of 2020, directly impacting the pace of digital transformation across industry verticals. It is now critical to explore current and emerging challenges as well as opportunities offered by AI solutions to better understand how organizations and society could be affected. First, this chapter examines the evolution of computerization and its influence on AI. Second, we scrutinize how AI performance has been harnessed through digital solutions that are transforming for the better and the worse numerous industries. Third, we address fundamental ethical and moral challenges that derive from the application of AI in real life and its implications for human beings. Finally, we discuss the challenges of securing and protecting AI solutions against cyberattacks. The chapter concludes on the future of AI as it relates to technology convergence with cloud computing, Internet of Things, and eventually quantum computing.

1. Introduction

The concept of digital transformation appeared about 40 years ago with the adoption of computers by companies, governments, and households. The inception of computers led to a first important step: digitization, or the transition of analog content and processes to digital content and processes. Digitization is critical to the creation of an information-rich environment and the accessibility of data. The inception of the internet in the mid-1990s accelerated the digitization process in western societies. The availability and accessibility of data through multiple digital communication channels (email, websites, and forums) contributed directly to the transformation of modern business models as well as the ways governments deliver services. Digitization also includes the adoption of digital processes to enhance organizations' engagement with their customers, patients, employees, and constituents. More recently, the development and application of new technologies such as cloud computing, artificial intelligence (AI), and Internet of Things (IoT) have directly contributed to the expansion of the digitization of businesses and allowed for innovative digital transformation across industry verticals.

For the purposes of this chapter, our analysis focuses on the rise of AI in digital transformation and the challenges related to its use. It is now undeniable that AI is one of the main core technologies that is enabling digital transformation (McKendrick, 2021). More specifically, AI combined with digital transformation currently generates the most results or value in these three areas: (1) 360-degree view of customers; (2) dynamic analytics; and (3) AI-driven automation for customer service. To better understand the development of AI and its impact on digital transformation, this chapter will examine the following topics: (1) from computerization to artificial intelligence; (2) AI performance and digital solutions; (3) ethical challenges; (4) security challenges; and (5) protecting AI solutions.

2. From Computerization to Artificial Intelligence

In 1950, Alan Turing published an influential article in which he developed the concept of the electric digital computer and its universality through programming (Turing, 1950). The author also introduced the idea of a learning machine using the analogy of a "child-machine" that was able to learn through a logical process bound by a set of rules that constantly validate or invalidate the accuracy of the answer. Finally, Turing introduced the "imitation game," a test to assess whether a machine is intelligent and in which an interrogator wouldn't be able to distinguish the answers provided by both humans and computers. By the mid-1950s, researchers had already developed digital computers as well as programs enabling machines to solve problems and learn by themselves. In 1951, Nathaniel Rochester was the first scientist to design a commercial computer known as IBM 701, and a few years later Remington Rand built the UNIVAC 1103 in 1953. The computational power of these new commercial systems led to deeper exploration of problem-solving capabilities and military applications.

In 1955, John McCarthy coined the term "artificial intelligence," and the first conference on AI took place in 1956 at Dartmouth College in New Hampshire. During the 1960s, AI programs were able to simulate conversation through natural language processing and analytics. However, that decade corresponded to a slowdown of government investment in computational research and development, especially as it related to AI. However, in the 1970s and 1980s, the private sector started to commercialize digital computers and AI with the deployment of expert systems, machine vision, and automated assembly lines. The 1980s are also associated with the commercialization of personal computers, led by IBM and Apple with the famous talking Macintosh computer. However, one major issue preventing the expansion of AI was the lack of large datasets and computing power for more complex applications. To be effective and accurate, AI needs to learn and train regularly with a vast amount of quality data; this prevents the decay or drift of the AI decision process (algorithm modeling).

In 1995, the internet became a breakthrough in digital communication and accelerated the computerization and digitization of our society. For instance, computer penetration in U.S. households was 8.2% in 1984 and jumped to 37% in 1997, reaching 87% in 2020 (Statista, 2022a, 2022b). Computing power has also grown rapidly since the 1950s, increasing by at least 1 trillion-fold. For instance, consider that any laptop assembled in 2021 has far more computing power than the Apollo computer guidance system. Regarding data, a study conducted in 2016 shows that a single person is responsible for creating 1.7 MB of data each day, which amounts to an aggregated 1.145 trillion MB of data created every day worldwide (Statista, 2022c). Finally, data storage has also increased tremendously. In 2020, the installed base of storage capacity reached 6.7 zettabytes and is projected to grow by 19% each year between 2020 and 2025 (Statista, 2022c).

However, the interdependence of computerization and AI also has its downsides; one of the most important is the speed of computing power growth, which doubles every two years according to Moore's Law, compared to the growth of AI, which doubles every 3.4 months (Mack, 2011). While greater computing power leads to better predictability and accuracy of AI systems, the need for operating this technology creates an unsustainable "computation pressure." As a result, we could witness a slowdown in the growth of AI performance in the next few years unless there is a breakthrough in quantum computing that could lead AI to its next development phase: quantum AI. Indeed, AI powered by quantum computing is believed to be able to train faster machine-learning models and create optimized algorithms that ensure the stability of AI.

Today, AI is mostly known for machine learning and deep learning. Machine learning is basically all forms of automated functions that require math and coding to develop an algorithm that will process data, learn from the data (supervised learning), and apply what was learned to make a decision. A few examples of machine learning used in digital solutions are search engine result refining, email spam and malware filtering, facial recognition, and speech recognition. Deep learning is based on artificial neural networks that are designed similar to human biological networks of neurons. The learning process is continuous and the AI analyzes data with a logical structure, but it requires a significant amount of training to reduce errors and increase the confidence interval of deep-learning models. A few examples of deep learning used in digital solutions include virtual assistants, vision for driverless cars, and big data analytics. More recently, deep learning was used to identify synergistic drug combinations for treating COVID-19 (Shorten *et al.*, 2021).

3. AI Performance and Digital Solutions

With the rapid digitization of society, the access to large datasets is no longer a problem, which provides the required conditions for the deployment of AI solutions on a large scale. It is now undeniable: The AI revolution is well underway and is transforming several industry sectors. For instance, in the automobile industry, AI systems are used for collision detection, driving assistance, and maintenance planning. In retail, AI models are used to predict consumers' online shopping patterns and improve their shopping experience by offering more personalized services such as sales assistance (chat bots). In the banking sector, AI systems help identify fraud, detect money laundering patterns, and better understand customers' banking behaviors. Investment firms also use AI predictive models for trading on the stock exchange and investing in different markets. Finally, the manufacturing, warehouse, and supply chain sectors rely on AI systems to optimize manufacturing operations such as staffing, inventory control, energy consumption, and the supply of raw materials. AI is also used to create smarter robots for factories and warehouses.

Over the past 15 years, the field of AI has progressed exponentially, and AI is now better than humans at performing certain complex tasks. In general, there are three key areas in which AI outperforms humans, as discussed in the following.

3.1 *Analytical, strategic, and creative thinking*

The combination of computing power and AI modeling has allowed for the development of big data analytics, which refers to the use of advanced analytic techniques to examine very large and diverse datasets that include structured, semi-structured, and unstructured data from different sources and in different sizes. These advanced analytic techniques are used to uncover information such as hidden patterns, unknown correlations, market trends, and individuals' behaviors (customers' or employees' habits). Through big data analysis powered by AI, an organization can find new actionable insights to support decision-making processes, predict outcomes of business operations, and unify data from different sources and platforms to provide strategic understanding about the lifecycle of a product, service, or customer.

Regarding strategic thinking, AI performs better than humans at gaming. For instance, AI bots have been able to beat "human masters" in poker and chess (Gander, 2019). The complexity of these games requires strategy, intuition, and reasoning based on unknown information. The capabilities of AI to outperform human intelligence through adaptation do not make an interesting technology for gaming, but are also used to support training. For instance, AI is being used to develop simulation training programs to test human abilities with more realism and accuracy. AI simulators are used to train pilots, surgeons, soldiers, and police officers, to name a few. The use of AI to train the workforce is poised to grow rapidly with the deployment of the Metaverse.

Finally, AI is also evolving into the realm of creative thinking. In September 2020, *The Guardian* published an op-ed that was completely written by AI (*The Guardian*, 2020). The task was to write a 500-word essay on "why humans have nothing to fear from AI." The text was generated by GPT-3, an open-source AI language model that uses machine learning to produce human-like text. And in 2018, the music industry welcomed its first album that was fully composed and produced by AI: "Hello, World!" (Marshall, 2018). AI is no stranger to the music industry; for several years, musicians have been using software that improves sound harmonization (Auto-Tune) and composition. This breakthrough in creative intelligence raises the prospect of emotional AI that can connect feelings to words and behaviors. The commercial application of such creative and emotional intelligence is currently revolutionizing the industry of home assistants, medical and psychological care (detection of dementia and depression), and support for children and adults with autism.

3.2 *Speech transcription and translation*

AI models are faster than human beings in transcribing speech to text and translating different languages. However, the accuracy of transcription remains imperfect. Recent benchmarking showed that applications developed by Amazon had an accuracy of 83.12%, Microsoft was 81.01% accurate, Google came in at 84.46%, and Revai scored slightly better at 86.1%. In terms of translation accuracy, Facebook's translate feature shows a 90% accuracy rate over 100 languages. However, the accuracy of translation seems to vary tremendously from one industry to another, and the quality of the translation is better with text-based content than with speech. That explains why many websites use this feature to enhance accessibility for different languages and cultures.

Big tech companies have commercialized computer, car, and home assistants like Amazon's Alexa, Apple's Siri, Google's Now, and Microsoft's Cortana that can reach a high level of accuracy in human speech recognition. Consider Google's home assistant, which reached a 95% word accuracy rate for American English, the highest rate of accuracy of all voice assistants in 2021 (Glaser, 2017). In 2020, there were more than 4 billion digital voice assistants being used worldwide and more than 110 million virtual assistant users in the United States alone (Statista, 2022d).

3.3 *Medical diagnosis and assisted surgery*

AI programs have made important progress in healthcare, especially in medical diagnosis and surgery assistance. AI algorithms are 77% accurate regarding the diagnosis of regular disease compared to 71% for doctors. The precision rate increases significantly when it comes to cancer and rare disease detection, with a 91% accuracy level. These results have major implications, since more than 20% of misdiagnosed diseases are harmful to patients (Richens *et al.*, 2020). Regarding the use of surgery assistants, a recent study shows that an AI-powered surgical assistant system is expected to replace approximately 41% to 60% of the workforce (Park *et al.*, 2020). Moreover, a study of 379 orthopedic patients conducted in multiple surgical sites shows that an AI-assisted robotic technique resulted in a five-time reduction in surgical complications compared to when surgeons operated alone (Kalis *et al.*, 2018). In fact, AI robots exceed human accuracy on some surgical tasks, like placing a pin into a bone (such as for knee and hip replacements). The scientific community expects that the accuracy of medical robots will increase in accomplishing other medical tasks such as incisions or suturing (Metz, 2021). However, the role of medical robots is set to have a negative impact on healthcare jobs, raising some ethical challenges related to the implementation and expansion of AI in our society.

3.4 *Cybersecurity solutions*

The cybersecurity industry is increasingly impacted by the deployment of AI-supported solutions. AI is largely used to protect networks as well as increase data security and endpoint security, according to 850 senior IT executives surveyed in 2019 (Statista, 2022e). Moreover, the market of AI in cybersecurity is expected to grow at a compound annual growth rate of 23.6% from 2020 to 2027 to reach $46.3 billion by 2027 (Meticulous Research, 2020). This predicted growth is likely to increase when considering all the social changes that have been brought on by the COVID-19 pandemic, from a boost to the digital economy to the displacement of millions of workers who now work remotely. Add the exponential increase in the number of IoT-connected devices, the major shortage of skilled cybersecurity workers, and the rapidly growing internet attack surface, and the need to automate and use AI will become a market driver for years to come. Currently, machine learning supports cybersecurity professionals in three major functions: (1) network vulnerability surveillance and threat detection, (2) incident diagnosis and response, and (3) cyber threat intelligence reports (Lemieux and Brooks, 2021).

4. Ethical Challenges

The rise of AI poses several ethical challenges that touch key concepts in our society: economy, sociology, psychology, and power. Here are some of the challenges that our governments and social institutions have to consider in the face of a rapid expansion of AI.

4.1 *Job loss*

AI is becoming increasingly successful at performing repetitive actions, transcriptions, precision tasks, and complex problem management. For example, it is important to consider that up to 20 million manufacturing jobs worldwide will be lost to robots by 2030. In the U.S., displacement by automation will affect 512 counties, representing 20.3 million people, where more than 25% of workers could be displaced in search of new jobs. Low-skilled workers will be the most impacted by the expansion of AI. Women will be particularly impacted by this transformation due to the type of tasks AI can accomplish. It is expected that AI implementation will increase gender disparity in job loss, creating a disadvantage for women compared to men in certain job positions like administrative assistant and secretaries mostly occupied by women versus heavy assembly lines mostly occupied by men (Jones, 2018), not to mention gender disparity in the booming AI industry that is mainly composed of men (Martinho-Truswell, 2019). However, development of AI will not only impact low-skilled jobs, as currently there are programs powered by AI that write code and programs. Nonetheless, according to the World Economic Forum, AI automation would create 97 million new jobs by 2025 (World Economic Forum, 2020). The major issues with such a significant restructuring of the job market are that (1) automation will clearly impact a more economically vulnerable and less-educated workforce and

(2) it is unlikely that upskilling and reskilling programs will allow a direct transition of workers who were displaced by AI to high-paying technical jobs such as programmers, data scientists, data architects, and machine-learning engineers, to name a few. AI job displacement and the economic inequality it will create are pressing ethical challenges that need to be addressed.

4.2 *Redistribution of wealth*

Another important ethical dilemma related to the economic impact of AI is the redistribution of wealth created by automations and the replacement of low-skilled workers with machines. The argument here is fairly simple: Assuming the cost of the workforce is the primary expense for most organizations (hourly wages), then cutting the human capital will significantly reduce expenses and increase profits. This accumulation of money for AI-driven companies will exacerbate the problem of wealth inequality, and the profit surplus won't be redistributed into communities as it would be for human workers who spend their wages on lodging, products, and services. This situation could also jeopardize the economic vitality of disadvantaged communities and, to a certain extent, some industries servicing low-skilled workers.

4.3 *Human–machine interaction*

Another growing area of ethical challenge is the increasingly blurry line regarding the interaction between humans and machines. On the one hand, we are witnessing the deployment of smart assistants with voices that sound more and more like humans. Additionally, we have recently witnessed the commercialization of emotional AI through "artificial friends." Consider the application Replika, which offers a virtual friendship service through a bot powered by AI. Their website claims that Replika is "The AI companion who cares. Always here to listen and talk. Always on your side." The service could be extremely useful for a certain segment of the population, like elders who may be isolated and lonely.

On the other hand, the broad commercialization of such services raises the issue of biased interactions with a fake friend who agrees with you all the time, altering individual perceptions of what real human interaction is like: agreements and disagreements, competition and collaboration, likes and dislikes. All these binomial interactions are essential to balance our relationships with one another. It is important to mention that similar applications are now available to simulate romantic relationships (iGirl and Anima). In a less virtual world, Sophia is a social humanoid robot powered by AI and developed by the Hong Kong-based company Hanson Robotics. Sophia was activated in 2016 and is the first robot to receive full citizenship from a country (Saudi Arabia). The fact that we are offering fundamental rights that are normally reserved for humans to a machine alters the definition of humanity and introduces biases as it relates to roles and responsibilities of citizenry.

4.4 *Biased AI decisions*

In recent years, the media has been reporting on AI biases that directly affect people. For example, in 2018, Amazon deployed an AI tool to assist with its hiring process to improve the gender diversity of its workforce and develop a more objective recruiting process. However, instead of improving the gender diversity of the new pool of recruits, the AI algorithm learned to prefer males' resumes over females' resumes, mostly by negatively labeling any mention of the word "women" such as "women's clubs" or "women's association" and positively labeling words that tend to be used more frequently in males' resumes, like "captured" and "executed." In other words, the AI construed through the learning process that two different forms of language were present in the training data of male and female resumes. The AI learned to discriminate against women. This issue was detected and the project was abandoned (Dastin, 2018).

A second example is when the face recognition feature of Apple's iPhone X was not properly recognizing facial features based on race; specifically, it was not recognizing Asian iPhone users (Finley, 2017). More precisely, the algorithm had difficulty distinguishing two people of Asian descent. At that time, Apple claimed that "the probability that a random person in the population could look at your iPhone X and unlock it using Face ID is approximately 1 in 1,000,000 (versus 1 in 50,000 for Touch ID)." The issue was mainly caused by an insufficient number of pictures of Asian individuals in the dataset used to train the face recognition algorithm.

These two examples show that there are two main categories of biases with AI algorithms. First is cognitive bias; there are more than

100 different cognitive biases that have been identified by psychologists, and many of them can be replicated by AI by way of design and programming. In other words, programmers can unknowingly introduce biases into algorithm coding and make the machine learn through datasets with a biased lens. On the other hand, machine learning could learn to identify a discriminant feature already in the dataset without the programmers noticing it. These AI algorithm biases are illustrated in the Amazon hiring algorithm experiment. The second bias emanates from skewed analysis based on the lack of representation in the dataset used to train the AI. Incomplete datasets can lead to a lack of input on all the variations that can exist on a specific subject. This bias is illustrated by the iPhone facial recognition flaw based on racial diversity.

4.5 *False dilemma*

Finally, ethical debates have emerged over the years regarding the moral responsibility of AI in certain situations where human life is at stake. One of the most cited is what an AI-powered autonomous vehicle should do if a car accident with human casualties is unavoidable: swerve to avoid hitting pedestrians crossing the street, crashing and potentially killing the passengers in the car, or hit and kill the pedestrians. First, this very constraining scenario puts the AI in a situation that a vast majority of humans will never encounter. Second, humans make all sorts of split-second decisions in stressful and tense situations that rarely follow any logical or ethical reasoning. It is important to understand that AI is the imperfect product of the interaction between artificial neural networks, which we believe think like humans do, and a perceived reality that the interpretation is mostly subjective and composed of a myriad of perspectives. It is therefore questionable whether we should be discussing ethical AI or whether we should question the ethical use of AI. After all, when Amazon "fired" the gender-biased AI program, they did not fire the HR personnel who provided the dataset to train the algorithm, which was the source of the discrimination to begin with.

5. Security Challenges

Digital solutions powered by AI certainly provide a high degree of accuracy and performance, but some levels of error do exist, and AI technology can produce false positives or false negatives in its decision-making process. Also, AI can be a double-edged sword as it can be manipulated for nefarious purposes. Hackers can use AI as a tool to misdirect a program or application into thinking that activities are normal when they are not. Hackers do this via adversarial machine learning, a technique employed to exploit four critical security vulnerabilities:

(1) Poisoning attack: Injecting poison data in the training dataset to compromise the AI's learning process.
(2) Evasion attack: Designing data that maliciously look normal to a human but can be misclassified by AI (for instance, altering pixels on a picture that make a cat look like a dog).
(3) TrojAI attack: Unlike a broader data-poisoning attack that disrupts everything from the beginning, TrojAI inserts a trigger (malware) that will change a program's behavior only in certain circumstances (for instance, only when a certain activity occurs on a network).
(4) Model inversion attack: Hackers can reconstruct the training data by figuring out the model parameters to unveil sensitive information and identity (e.g., see the case of Netflix and IMBD (Al-Rubaie and Morris Chang, 2019)).

Hackers can also use AI for their own activities. A Forrester Research report notes that "there are already instances of threat actors and hackers using AI technologies to bolster their attacks and malware" (Cunningham and Blankenship, 2018). Nation-state or criminal enterprise actors can use malicious AI to hide malware in regular downloadable applications. Once downloaded, the malware is triggered by one or several factors after a certain amount of time. These delayed self-executing attacks provide the opportunity to collect information on users (authentication process/identity management features). Malicious AI can also support intelligent malware learning from unsuccessful and successful attacks (deep exploit). Then, smart malware can self-propagate by detecting and exploiting system vulnerabilities and adapt to mitigation measures by attempting new types of attacks. Malicious AI can also launch stealth attacks by learning from system maintenance and blending into an organization's security environment. These very sophisticated attacks using AI are not yet common, but they will certainly increase over time. Cybersecurity criminals are already automating their own attacks: They are systematically sharing tools available on the Dark Web and their attacks are now faster, more calculating, and more lethal with the help of AI.

6. Protecting AI Solutions

An integral part of injecting security into processes is for organizations to integrate security solutions at the onset of the deployment and development cycle of new software and technology. DevSecOps was created in response to security concerns generated by the DevOps timeline in which security considerations were left until the very end of the software development cycle. The idea was to resolve security problems by addressing security at every stage of the software development cycle. However, this approach was flawed because the security solutions were left in the hands of software developers who were poorly equipped to address these issues (lack of tools and knowledge). Then, another approach was recently developed: SecDevOps, which requires security to be at the forefront of every stage of the software development cycle by promoting secure coding and embedding security measures into the planning, analysis, design, and deployment stages in addition to traditional implementation and testing stages. In addition, changes in software application code are tied to security requirements related to deployment procedures.

7. Conclusion

This chapter examined the role AI played in digital transformation. First, it was established that the development of AI relied heavily on the digitization and computerization of society. With a significant increase in data and computer power, new applications of AI emerged, boosting digital solutions in many key industries. High-performing AI-driven solutions are slowly becoming the backbone of digital transformation and one of the preferred technologies used to support decision-making processes. This chapter also highlighted some of the downsides of AI, namely, ethical dilemmas and security challenges. Nonetheless, AI is poised to dominate the future of digital transformation due to its integration with other core transformative technologies such as cloud computing, IoT, and high-performance computing. The new frontier of AI will emerge with the development of quantum computing, which will significantly expand the capabilities of AI.

References

Al-Rubaie, M. and Morris Chang, J. (2019). Privacy preserving machine learning: Threats and solutions. *IEEE Security and Privacy Magazine*, 17(2), 49–58.

Cunningham, C. and Blankenship, J. (2018). Using AI for evil. A guide to how cybercriminals will weaponize and exploit AI to attack your business. https://www.forrester.com/report/Using-AI-For-Evil/RES143162.

Dastin, J. (2018). Amazon scraps secret AI recruiting tool that showed bias against women. https://www.reuters.com/article/us-amazon-com-jobs-automation-insight/amazon-scraps-secret-ai-recruiting-tool-that-showed-bias-against-women-idUSKCN1MK08G.

Finley, K. (2017). Can Apple's iPhone X beat facial recognition's bias problem? https://www.wired.com/story/can-apples-iphone-x-beat-facial-recognitions-bias-problem/.

Gander, K. (2019). AI vs. humans: Artificial intelligence beats 6 professional players at No-limit Texas Hold'em Poker. *Newsweek*. https://www.newsweek.com/ai-humans-artificial-beats-intelligence-humans-no-limit-texas-holdem-poker-1448488.

Glaser, A. (2017). Google's ability to understand language is nearly equivalent to humans. *Vox*. https://www.vox.com/2017/5/31/15720118/google-understand-language-speech-equivalent-humans-code-conference-mary-meeker.

Jones, B. (2018). When robots take over our jobs, it's women who will lose out most. *Futurism*. https://futurism.com/when-robots-take-over-our-jobs-women-lose-most.

Kalis, B., Collier, M., and Fu, R. (2018). 10 promising applications in health care. *Harvard Business Review*. https://hbr.org/2018/05/10-promising-ai-applications-in-health-care.

Lemieux, F. and Brooks, C. (2021). Three key artificial intelligence applications for cybersecurity. *Forbes*. https://www.forbes.com/sites/chuckbrooks/2021/09/24/three-key-artificial-intelligence-applications-for-cybersecurity/?sh=4bb937fd7b7e.

Mack, C.A. (2011). Fifty years of Moore's law. *IEEE Transactions on Semiconductors Manufacturing*, 24(2), 202–207.

Marshall, A. (2018). Is this the world's first good robot album? *BBC Culture*. https://www.bbc.com/culture/article/20180112-is-this-the-worlds-first-good-robot-album.

Martinho-Truswell, E. (2019). As jobs are automated, will men and women be affected equally? *Harvard Business Review*. https://hbr.org/2019/11/as-jobs-are-automated-will-men-and-women-be-affected-equally.

McCarthy, J., Minsky, M., Shannon, C.E., Rochester, N., and Dartmouth College (1955). A proposal for the Dartmouth Summer Research Project on Artificial Intelligence.

McKendrick, J. (2021). AI adoption skyrocketed in the last 18 months. *Harvard Business Review*. https://hbr.org/2021/09/ai-adoption-skyrocketed-over-the-last-18-months.

Meticulous Research (2020). Artificial intelligence in cybersecurity. https://www.meticulousresearch.com/product/artificial-intelligence-in-cybersecurity-market-5101#download-sample.

Metz, C. (2021). The robot surgeon will see you now. *New York Times*. https://www.nytimes.com/2021/04/30/technology/robot-surgery-surgeon.html.

Park, S.J., Lee, E.J., Kim, S.I., Kong, S.H., Jeong, C.W., and Kim, H.S. (2020). Clinical desire for an artificial intelligence-based surgical assistant system: Electronic survey-based study. *JMIR Medical Informatics*, 8(5), 238–251.

Richens, J.G., Lee, C.M., and Johri, S. (2020). Improving the accuracy of medical diagnosis with causal machine learning. *Nature Communication*, 1(3923), 1–9.

Shorten, C., Khoshgoftaar, T.M., and Furht, B. (2021). Deep learning applications for COVID-19. *Journal of Big Data*, 8, 18.

Statista (2022a). Percentage of households with a computer at home in the United States from 1984 to 2010. https://www.statista.com/statistics/184685/percentage-of-households-with-computer-in-the-united-states-since-1984/.

Statista (2022b). Share of households with a computer at home worldwide from 2005 to 2019. https://www.statista.com/statistics/748551/worldwide-house holds-with-computer/.

Statista (2022c). Volume of data/information created, captured, copied, and consumed worldwide from 2010 to 2025. https://www.statista.com/statistics/871513/worldwide-data-created/.

Statista (2022d). Number of digital voice assistants in use worldwide from 2019 to 2024 (in billions). https://www.statista.com/statistics/973815/worldwide-digital-voice-assistant-in-use/.

Statista (2022e). Top artificial intelligence (AI) use cases for cybersecurity in organizations in selected countries as of 2019. https://www.statista.com/statistics/1028823/ai-security-use-cases-in-organizations/#statisticContainer.

The Guardian (2020). A robot wrote this entire article. Are you scared yet, human? https://www.theguardian.com/commentisfree/2020/sep/08/robot-wrote-this-article-gpt-3.

Turing, A.M. (1950). Computing machinery and intelligence. *Mind*, LIX(236), 433–460.

World Economic Forum (2020). Recession and automation changes our future of work, but there are jobs coming, report says. https://www.weforum.org/press/2020/10/recession-and-automation-changes-our-future-of-work-but-there-are-jobs-coming-report-says-52c5162fce/.

https://doi.org/10.1142/9789811271984_0007

Chapter 7

Agile Digital Transformation: A Seven-Step Conceptual Model

John Palfreyman* **and Josh Morton†**

Leeds University Business School, University of Leeds, Leeds, UK
**j.palfreyman@leeds.ac.uk*
†j.morton1@leeds.ac.uk

Digital transformation drives sustained business value through the use of digital technology. However, there is often confusion regarding what steps organizations should follow to achieve this. In this chapter, we outline seven steps in a conceptual process model, the digital transformation loop, which organizations can adopt for what we call "agile digital transformation." Our aim is to offer a compelling and comprehensive conceptualization which illustrates challenges faced by organizations and poses questions that they need to reflect upon to realize value from the agile use of digital technology. We argue that agile digital transformation must be part of achieving a clear strategic vision and should drive sustained and demonstrable business value.

1. Introduction

Digital transformation has emerged as an important phenomenon in the academic domains of strategy and technology, and for practitioners who are involved in business and technology teams as part of strategy and transformation processes. The term digital transformation captures *a process that aims to improve an entity by triggering significant changes to its properties through combinations of information, computing, communication, and connectivity technologies* (Vial, 2019, p. 118). We argue that an agile approach is required for digital transformation, especially given the propensity for uncertainty in organizational and institutional environments, as has been demonstrated in recent times within major economies with, for example, radical political events including Brexit and the rise of the Trump administration, and with the worldwide disruptions such as the COVID-19 pandemic.

In our pursuit of unpacking an agile approach to digital transformation, we devise the following research question to motivate this chapter: *What steps are required for an agile approach to digital transformation in organizations?*

In response to this question, we outline seven steps in a conceptual process model which we call the "digital transformation loop" (these steps being *prepare*, *scan*, *prioritize*, *learn*, *experiment*, *plan*, and *build*). Collectively, these distinct steps coalesce to form a structured, agile approach to digital transformation. We illustrate the aforementioned steps with several reflective questions for all organizations to consider in navigating the transformation loop and their own transformation challenges. We start with an overview of literature on digital transformation and the role of strategic agility, before we move onto a detailed outline of our model, and then end the chapter with some brief concluding remarks and reflections.

2. Digital Transformation and the Role of Strategic Agility

The fourth industrial revolution (or Industry 4.0) drives organizational efficiencies through the integration of digital technologies with organizational processes and people. The term Industry 4.0 was first used in 2011 in the German manufacturing industry, and its goals continue to challenge both manufacturing and service organizations alike, across various industries. There are three concepts at the heart of Industry 4.0 (Palfreyman, 2020):

1. Ubiquitous connectivity through the availability of high-speed networking.
2. The Internet of Things (IoT), connecting small, embedded devices together which are usually sensors, actuators, or a combination of the two.
3. Cyber-physical systems which bring together modern digital technology with physical systems and processes.

With the prevalence of Industry 4.0 in today's business environment considered, there is need to unpack the role of digital transformation, which has been defined as *a process that aims to improve an entity by triggering significant changes to its properties through combi- nations of information, computing, communication, and connectivity technologies* (Vial, 2019, p. 118). Digital transformation is critical for organizations wishing to embrace Industry 4.0 and reap the opportunities and rewards, which include heightened efficiencies, productivity, flexibility, decentralization, and growth (Palfreyman, 2020; Vial, 2020). A 2019 survey of directors, CEOs, and other senior executives published in the *Harvard Business Review* found that digital transformation and its associated risks were their primary concern (Tabrizi *et al.*, 2019). Such transformation is driven by three factors: (i) developments in digital technology, (ii) changes in competition through digital technology, and (iii) changes in consumer behavior as a result of the prevalence and widespread availability of digital technologies (Verhoef *et al.*, 2021).

In addition to drivers, there are also many important enablers of digital transformation which include having a collaborative and innovative organizational culture, digital wisdom and skills, and transformation experience and knowledge. Additionally, there are also nascent explorations of the role that agility has in enabling (effective) digital transformation processes. For instance, such agility concerns the ability to sense and seize market opportunities provided by digital technologies (e.g., Tallon and Pinsonneault, 2011; Verhoef *et al.*, 2021). We liken this to extant literature on strategic agility which has also explored the role of digital technologies in strategically agile organizations (e.g., Morton *et al.*, 2018), and in (successful and unsuccessful) transformation over time (Doz and Wilson, 2018). Strategic agility represents the continuous adjustment and adaption of strategic direction in organizations, and acts as a function of strategic ambitions and changing circumstances

(Doz and Kosonen, 2010). The internal and external demands on organizations in the market (such as from shareholders, customers, and the media) and the ever-growing levels of competition in business suggest that as a result of rapid changes and growth in many industries and their complex nature, the tried and tested approach of sustainable advantage will no longer suffice (Tarba and Weber, 2014; Tarba *et al.*, 2018). Those involved in organizational change initiatives, such as those seen through digital transformation, must adapt strategically agile leadership skills (Lewis *et al.*, 2014) to embrace digital evolutions and drive success where agility is not only built but also maintained (Morton *et al.*, 2018). In this vein, strategic agility is important for organizations and managers in guiding their know-how and actions when responding to changes in the environment and quickly adjusting their strategies and approaches to transformation (Doz and Kosonen, 2008b; Franken and Thomsett, 2013).

There are three widely recognized capabilities of strategic agility which organizations must endeavor to develop: strategic sensitivity, resource fluidity, and leadership unity (Doz and Kosonen, 2008a, 2008b). Indeed, while building strategic agility is an ongoing challenge for organizations, so is maintaining strategic agility once achieved, particularly to avoid potential "toxic" side effects which cause organizations to lose sight of the environment, struggle to redeploy resources effectively, experience conflict among management (Doz and Kosonen, 2008b; Morton *et al.*, 2018). This ultimately leads to the failure of change initiatives as seen in organizations in today's business environment where there is increased emphasis on digital transformation (Palfreyman, 2020).

Strategic sensitivity is the ability and sharpness to connect to an organization's surroundings, particularly the perceptiveness of incipient trends in the organization's internal and external environment (Doz and Kosonen, 2008a). This is achieved through organizations having collaborative mechanisms by which managers within and outside organizational boundaries can have strategic conversations to heighten alertness regarding trends in the business environment and enact experimentation of ideas through open discussions (Doz, 2011). The challenge of achieving and maintaining such processes over time effectively and with efficiency is, however, substantial (Morton *et al.*, 2018). For example, as new technologies are developed, contested, and disrupted, organizations must scan the environment and adopt high-quality dialogue to sense-make quickly in understanding these changes and responding accordingly (Franken and Thomsett, 2013).

Resource fluidity is an organization's ability to reallocate and reconfigure its resources quickly, applying them to areas that need them most or where they would be better served (Doz and Kosonen, 2010). This ability to redistribute resources quickly and effectively toward identified strategic opportunities is crucial but can be complex (Fourné *et al.*, 2014; Junni *et al.*, 2015). For example, resource fluidity allows the dissociation of strategy from structure to ensure resources are deployed rapidly, mobilizes people to enable the delivery of key strategic goals and transformation, and ensures that modular processes for resource allocation are targeted (Brueller *et al.*, 2014). However, challenges are presented as some resources have more mobility than others; for example, patents or even corporate reputation are more likely to be locked down in complex, existing systems and processes. Further, resources can become imprisoned in specific areas of organizations and are difficult to mobilize effectively (Doz and Kosonen, 2008b).

Leadership unity is described as the ability of executives and leaders to be united in decision-making, allowing for quick decisions to be made without hindrance of company politics (Lewis *et al.*, 2014). There are various benefits to ensuring leadership unity, including having mutual dependency in making strategic decisions and creating an inclusive and collaborative culture of leadership in organizations (Franken and Thomsett, 2013). This is also key to ensuring that there is a degree of alignment to current and future organizational activities and the strategic direction of organizations (Arbussa *et al.*, 2017). A challenge in enacting leadership unity, however, lies in the consistency of organizational leaders and managers in organizations having a collective commitment to strategic issues and not being drawn in by self-importance or debating divergent views (Doz and Kosonen, 2008b). The negative role of politics at the top in organizations can have a detrimental effect to organizational success, and in some cases their survival (Morton *et al.*, 2018).

These capabilities are summarized in Table 1 (adapted from Doz and Kosonen, 2008a, 2008b). We integrate consideration of these into our later seven-step digital transformation loop model and in discussing this at the end of this chapter.

As a consequence of the careful balancing act required to build and maintain these capabilities, strategic agility has become a challenging contradiction for organizations and senior managers alike (Lewis *et al.*, 2014). While building strategic agility may help companies gain momentum toward digital transformation, in contrast there is difficulty in maintaining a fast and flexible strategic outlook and this may lead

Table 1. Three capabilities for strategic agility in organizations.

Strategic Agility Capability and Outline	Steps to Realize Capability
Strategic Sensitivity — Sharpness of perception and intensity of awareness leading to the ability to quickly interpret changing internal and external business environments	1. Strategy formulation based on open discussions 2. Heightened alertness and willingness to experiment with business 3. Quality internal dialogue and connectivity between areas of organizations
Resource Fluidity — Capacity to reconfigure processes, systems, and resources rapidly to meet changing circumstances	1. Decoupling strategy and organizational structure 2. Mobilizing teams to deliver strategic goals quickly and efficiently 3. Modular processes for resources allocation, incentivizing collaboration at different levels of organizations
Leadership Unity — Ability of organizational leaders and managers to act with unity and urgency, without getting caught up in personal politics and agendas	1. Mutual dependency and collective responsibility 2. Top team works together making key decisions quickly and effectively 3. Inclusive and collaborative leadership style

organizations to develop inertia or become misguided amid technological disruptions, or when market circumstances change and unexpected competitors appear (Doz and Kosonen, 2010).

The following section introduces seven structured steps that organizations can (or indeed should) follow to effectively approach and benefit from digital transformation in an agile manner. We include reflective questions along the way so that our steps are compelling to executives, consultants, managers, budgetary decision makers, and those in business and technology teams in organizations. We then outline a conceptual process model, the digital transformation loop, containing these steps.

3. The Digital Transformation Loop: Seven Structured Steps for Agile Digital Transformation

Although it is industry standard terminology, the term digital transformation is confusing. It makes it sound like "digital" comes first, which we and others (e.g., Tabrizi *et al.*, 2019) argue could not be further from the case. The transformation process must be in a clear strategic context and represent a way that organizations can improve efficiencies or drive competitive advantage through the smart use of technology. A clear, well-communicated strategic vision must always come first, and the transformation is part of the plan to achieve the vision.

As organizations embark on a digital transformation journey, a journey that is complex, multi-faceted, and full of risk, an incremental and structured approach will help such organizations understand where it is, where to go next, and how to get to the destination. In an environment where the market forces and available technology are constantly changing, it is vital that the approach leverages agile best practice. This section describes a structured approach to digital transformation which also embeds the fundamentals of strategic agility (e.g., Doz and Kosonen, 2008a; Lewis *et al.*, 2014; Morton *et al.*, 2018). As discussed, strategic agility implies that organizations need to establish capabilities which allow them to be sensitive to changes in their internal and external environment, fluid in their resource allocation, and unified across management teams and senior leadership (Doz and Kosonen, 2008b). The approach and the steps we outline are built by combining such insights from research with cross-sector practice. The scope and order of the steps was determined through author participation in, and leadership of, many digital transformation projects with companies of different sizes and in diverse industries and geographies over a twenty-year period. This practical learning was informed by, and cross-validated against, theoretical models relevant to various domains such as strategic agility (e.g., Doz and Kosonen, 2008a) and strategy and technology (e.g., Porter and Millar, 1985). The steps are representative of practices in organizations, which broadly capture norms and routines which we posit are required for structured, agile digital transformation.

We work through each of the seven steps and offer example questions which organizations need to consider, and this helps to create a holistic story about digital transformation (O'Hara, 2014). This also helps us to articulate key concepts in our conceptualizing of agile digital transformation (Suddaby, 2010) and associated business value in understandable terms with background technical details and bring "what it feels like to use" to the fore (Palfreyman, 2020). In addition to providing conceptual clarity and example reflective questions, our model provides steps which are useful for managers and various types of organizations as is the key focus of this chapter. This is particularly valuable in guiding a clear and systematic overview of our proposed approach to digital transformation.

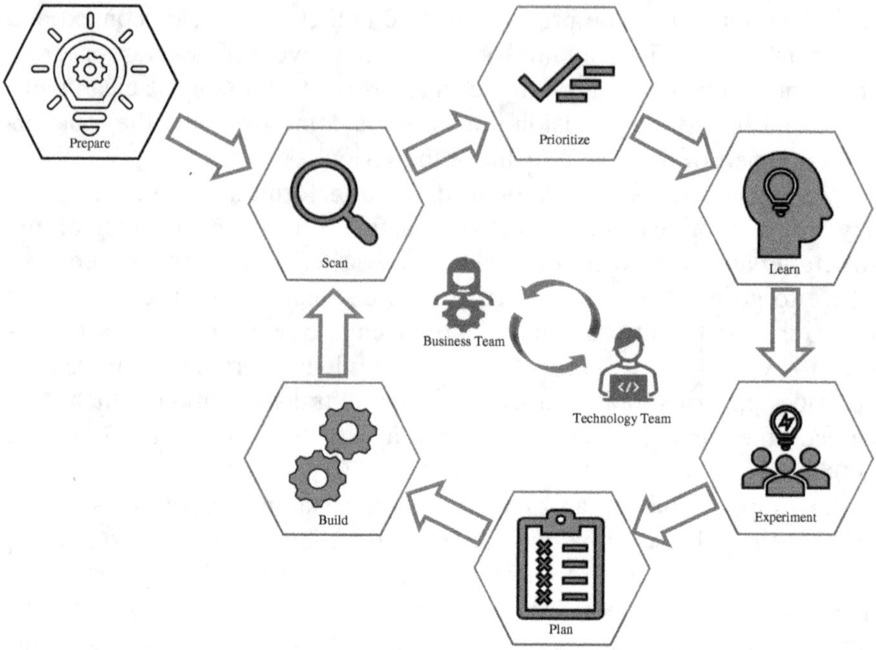

Fig. 1. The digital transformation loop: A conceptual process model showing seven structured steps for agile digital transformation.

Progress through the steps in transformation shown in Figure 1 is facilitated by the organization's business team and technology team working together. The business team brings first-hand knowledge of how the organization goes about their day-to-day business through detailed understanding of its process and information base. The technology team brings in-depth knowledge and ideally experience of the technologies which could be used for transformation within a number of sectors and industries.

A close, balanced collaboration between these two teams is needed for agile digital transformation to be successful. By balanced, we emphasize that each of these teams has something specialized to offer which ensures agile digital transformation projects make the most impact on the business and make best use of available technologies. This also means that the membership of each team needs to be balanced. For example, the business team must combine operations and lines of business with business services such as human resources, finance, and marketing. Equally, the technology team must include those responsible for systems and applications development in addition to infrastructure, end-user support, and security and privacy. These teams can then ensure close collaboration through process mapping techniques which capture relevant business and technology processes in an organization. Workshops can take place with business and technology teams to capture these maps. If using healthcare settings as an illustrative example, the business team would be able to share how operational patient data should be classified, stored, what the management practices are, while the technology team can advise on secure, reliable technological systems that meet this example requirement of the organization. Further, the technology team could research and guide on how similar problems are addressed in parallel or related industries and/or different geographies.

Step 1, the *prepare* step, ensures that the organization is ready to start the agile digital transformation process. It is a comprehensive starting point for organizations before they engage the main part of our outlined digital transformation loop. After checking that organizational strategy is up to date, well communicated, and stakeholders are aligned to key goals, the organization's information, business process, and cultural foundations are examined to understand how these must evolve to support the strategy. The step should ensure that the organization's culture and leadership are prepared to support the transformation process. This involves ensuring shared values and norms exist in the organization, and particularly between the business and technology teams central to agile digital transformation.

We propose that five key points are relevant here. First, organizational culture needs to be understood from the viewpoints of different leaders in the organization, and those leading digital transformation. Second, it needs to be considered if, and how, culture can be measured. There are also many value frameworks which can be used by organizations to assess organizational culture. Third, culture needs to be assessed directly in relation to digital transformation. Fourth, it can be assessed whether any changes are needed to support effective digital transformation. Lastly, the role of different leaders and other stakeholders needs to be clearly outlined as part of the digital transformation process. If leadership and culture are not well understood, any initiative to change the organization is likely to be sub-optimal. Should deficiencies be found in any of these five areas, corrective action must be taken so the organization can get the best

Table 2. The role of business and technology teams in the prepare step.

Business Team Role	Technology Team Role
1. "Hands on" expert in a specific area of the organization's business (e.g., supply, finance, operations, marketing) 2. Have alignment with organizational strategy and need for competitive differentiation and/or efficacy through the adoption and use of digital technology 3. Passionate about constant business improvement and tracking competitor activities in the market	1. Expert practitioner in specific technologies with a broad forward-looking technology interest 2. Committed to, and passionate about, business transformation and aligned with organizational strategy 3. Understands their organizations and processes/areas of operations but defers to expert business team knowledge 4. Constantly curious and always learning about how technology can transform their organization

return on their transformation investments. The role of each team and their balance to begin agile digital transformation are summarized in Table 2.

Now that the organization's culture and leadership are prepared to support the transformation process, and roles are clearly defined and understood, the business and technology teams can experiment with ideas inspired by the operating principles that define the organization's "to be" strategic vision. Such experimental ideas create a pathway toward design principles, which add a development or technology flavor to the experiment idea and use the style of "we will do X" as opposed to "we will do Y" format. For example, when building the design principle, "Y" will represent how the organization currently operates. Design principles can cover the application of new technology, the evolution of the organizational infrastructure, the optimization of processes (including adding new processes), or changes to an organization's information base. Once the design principles are complete and clear, the business and technology teams prioritize the list into a "transformation backlog." This backlog is then built by refining, prioritizing, and validating the experiment ideas which in turn will shape the digital transformation process. These important considerations as part of the prepare step are summarized with an illustrative example in Figure 2.

There are three key questions to reflect upon at this step which help organizations prepare for digital transformation:

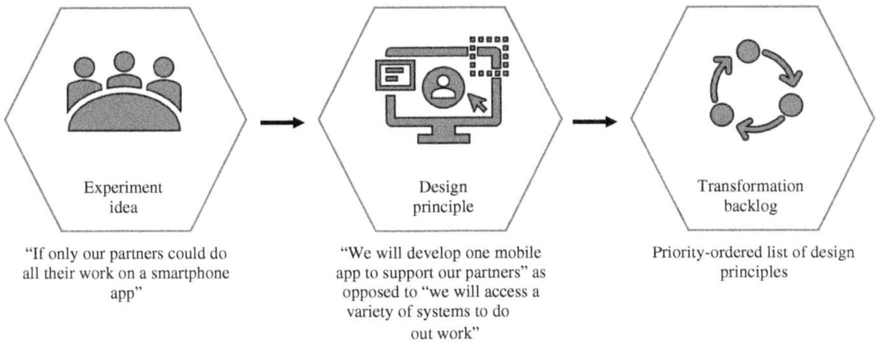

Figure 2. Experiment ideas, to design principles, and a transformation backlog.

- *Is the strategic vision clear and well communicated across the whole practitioner base?*
- *Are the current business processes well understood, including limitations (e.g., the over-reliance on paper-based system)?*
- *Is the organization's information base well understood, including the ability of care professionals to access patient information at the point of need?*

Following the prepare step, an organization can begin to progress through the main stages of the digital transformation loop. This progress is facilitated between the business and technology teams. Again, the close collaboration between these two teams is needed to achieve what we propose as an agile approach to digital transformation in this loop model. This is where **Step 2**, the *scan* step, comes in and where horizon-scanning techniques are used to find technologies which could help achieve desired digital transformation. This is referred to as a "search envelope." An organization and its teams learn more about the technologies in the search envelope, specifically their ability to solve the business problem at hand. An organization's technology team takes a lead in the search process, explaining the technology and expected business benefits to the business team, and the likely complexity of implementation efforts. When navigating the scan step, there are two key questions which need to be considered and get at the crux of selecting candidate technologies for adoption and considering specific points where business models may require innovation:

- *What technologies are driving efficiencies elsewhere in the sector, in different geographies or parallel industries?*
- *What innovative business models could be leveraged to address key sector challenges such as staff attrition or funding leakage?*

This projection of likely business benefit and implementation effort for each candidate technology is used in **Step 3**, the *prioritize* step, to put the candidate technologies into consideration order. This step also involves deliberation on interdependencies and conditionality between elements and comprises a series of structured discussions between the technology team that forms a view of implementation difficulty and the business team that estimates the expected business benefit. We have devised three questions which will guide such discussions for organizations:

- *Which candidate technologies can drive maximum organizational efficiencies in the near term?*
- *What capabilities can our organization leverage to realize these efficiencies through use of the candidate technologies?*
- *How can these capabilities be enhanced to support experimentation and potential rollout?*

A subset of candidate technologies is taken forward into **Step 4**, the *learn* step, where the teams acquire deeper knowledge and awareness of the technology to further calibrate the business potential and implementation difficulty. The goal is to refine these estimates and prepare for subsequent experimentation and potential delivery. This step draws on the extensive information available in open sources on candidate technologies. This includes but is not limited to vendor-furnished information. The step also assesses the organization's capability to deliver a project and business model innovation based on the candidate technology which will inform the later build step or inspire capability augmentation. There are two questions to be considered for this step for any type of organization, which zoom in on candidate technologies, implementation, and benefit:

- *What sources can be leveraged to gain enough information about the candidate technologies to decide whether an experiment would prove value?*
- *What organizational benefits (e.g., improved staff retention and enhanced care efficiencies) are expected from the experiment?*

Step 5, the *experiment* step, takes one candidate technology and further refines the difficulty and strategic value estimates by building a "proof of concept" solution that can be used by a pilot team (made up of business and technology personnel) in an organization. The step should combine industry best practices of design thinking with agile development to ensure that the proof of concept is centered on user need and is delivered in an efficient manner. During the experiment step, the technology team will lead the development and the business team will provide the "hands-on" expertise of how the organization operates to ensure maximum strategic benefit. The experiment step again focuses on two key questions which should be reflected upon by the organization, and this includes consideration on how those involved drive experimentation:

- *How can the candidate technologies be applied to the organization's business challenge to prove benefit prior to scale up/scale out?*
- *How will the stakeholders be involved in the experiment to provide first-hand information/process input?*

Step 6, the *plan* step, sets out the detailed project and architectural considerations for building the top-priority candidate technologies. This will include, but is not limited to, the construction of a detailed project plan to deliver the solution to time, quality, and budget. The step should analyze the pros and cons of extending the pilot system built at the experiment step versus building or buying a system from scratch. Irrespective of the chosen approach, the user must play a full and active role in the system realization. Too many initiatives have failed to realize their full potential by isolating the development from the users. Two questions require careful deliberation here:

- *What levels of investment will be needed to ensure the successful roll out of the system enhancement resulting from the experiment?*
- *How will the new/enhanced systems integrate with existing organizational infrastructure to add net agility?*

Last is arguably the most compelling part of the transformation, where managers and teams witness all the careful planning come to fruition and see the delivery of real benefit to the organization at **Step 7**, the *build* step. Following a full and successful plan step, the top priority elements are realized through a structured development process. Organizational change will be capacity limited, and the business and technology teams should take a measured approach to the transformation activities. Two final questions require reflection here:

- *How will the new systems be built and rolled out for maximum practitioner benefit?*
- *How will development risks be identified and successfully mitigated to maximize project success?*

We also reemphasize that a successful transformation must be highly inclusive, involving different groups of individuals as shown in Table 3. It is critical that key members of each of these groups are appropriately involved in the transformation as it progresses. Involvement should be through transparent, appropriate, and open communication supplemented by regular playbacks to check and validate progress.

The above reflection of steps, key questions, and groups is targeted at, and are malleable to, all organizations and might be adopted for consideration and benefit in different settings and situations. The examples shown in Table 3 can also be expanded in more detail and there is potential for further groups to be added (or some to be taken away).

Table 3. Groups and involvement in agile digital transformation.

Groups	**Involvement**
1. Customers	Customers can inspire change and need to advice on the transformation process and how it will affect interactions.
2. Board	The board supports sponsorship and funding of transformation. It is central to building and communicating strategy and removing barriers when they occur.
3. Operations	Operations have first-hand knowledge of how organizations deliver products/services. They guide the transformation in these aspects.
4. Business services	Business services have first-hand knowledge in critical supporting functions, and this guides transformation in these aspects.
5. Users	Users offer the detailed design of new systems and processes and guide the ultimate "acceptance" of new ways of working.
6. Supply chain	Key supply chain members will be involved in transformation as an extension of operations or business services.

We also stress again the importance of agility in our loop and refer back to our earlier review of strategic agility to explicate the relevance of the broad strategic capabilities outlined (Doz and Kosonen, 2008a, 2008b) as shown in Table 4.

Lastly, a key consideration here is that, although the steps outlined as part of our digital transformation loop are sequential, loop backs will be the norm as organizations progress around the planning loop. For example, the horizon scan may be revisited after the learn or experiment step if the technology does not do quite what was expected of it or is harder to work with than anticipated. Similarly, the prioritize step may be revisited as a result of the learn or experiment steps if organizations and those involved in transformation find technologies that add more or less business value than we originally thought.

Review points will be frequent as we progress around the planning loop. The purpose of these will be to ensure total business alignment and to improve the transformation process by constant — but constructive — peer group and stakeholder challenge. The business environment, both internally and externally, changes at great pace, and technology develops so quickly that organizations are increasingly turning to lessons learned from theories of agility to ensure their organizational change can navigate uncertainties and change. We conclude in the next section with some brief final remarks.

Table 4. The relevance of strategic agility in the digital transformation loop.

Strategic Agility Capability	**Implications for the Digital Transformation Loop**
Strategic Sensitivity	1. Horizon scanning monitors relevant technologies as they evolve. 2. Business and technology teams work together to interpret tech in the context of the organization's strategic plan(s).
Resource Fluidity	1. Processes and systems will evolve during transformation and culture must embrace these changes. 2. Business and technology team membership will change as transformation progresses, to maintain optimal progress.
Leadership Unity	1. The business and technology teams work together using appropriate collaborative methods (e.g., agile scrums) to engender unity and urgency. 2. Senior leaders and executives/boards must demonstrate similar unity in their transformation review activities.

4. Concluding Remarks

Our work has outlined the importance of an agile approach to digital transformation. The seven steps detailed in our work and conceptualized through the digital transformation loop provide a critical reflection on what is required for organizations and managers to be agile and approach digital transformation in simple terms. It also contributes to the growing literature on digital transformation (e.g., Vial, 2019), and its relevance to strategizing and maximizing strategic value in the digital age (e.g., Newell *et al.*, 2020; Morton *et al.*, 2022). We also hope that our seven steps and the conceptual model we have developed might inspire future research. For example, we encourage empirical studies that can expand, challenge, or validate these steps through varied methodological approaches and in different settings. We emphasize that the steps are not limited to, or drawn exclusively from insights within a specific context but rather come from the experience of working on several digital transformation projects over a number of years. Specific empirical work could be conducted, however, such as through explication of agile digital transformation in single case studies, or in wider studies which capture insights from across industry sectors. This would add richness and further validation to our conceptual loop model. Overall, our interpretation of seven distinct steps and a model incorporating examples, practices, and reflective questions relevant to agile digital transformation is, we hope, a valuable insight for extant literature, future research, and for a range of practitioners.

References

Arbussa, A., Bikfalvi, A., and Marques, P. (2017). Strategic agility-driven business model renewal: The case of an SME. *Management Decision*, 55(2), 271–293.

Brueller, N.N., Carmeli, A., and Drori, I. (2014). How do different types of mergers and acquisitions facilitate strategic agility? *California Management Review*, 56(3), 39–57.

Doz, Y. (2011). Qualitative research for international business. *Journal of International Business Studies*, 42(5), 582–590.

Doz, Y. and Kosonen, M. (2008a). *Fast Strategy*. Harlow: Pearson Education.

Doz, Y. and Kosonen, M. (2008b). The dynamics of strategic agility: Nokia's rollercoaster experience. *California Management Review*, 50(3), 95–118.

Doz, Y. and Kosonen, M. (2010). Embedding strategic agility: A leadership agenda for accelerating business model renewal. *Long Range Planning*, 43(2–3), 370–382.

Fourné, S.P.L., Jansen, J.J.P., and Mom, T.J.M. (2014). Strategic agility in MNEs: Managing tensions to capture opportunities across emerging and established markets. *California Management Review*, 56(3), 13–38.

Franken, A. and Thomsett, H. (2013). When it takes a network: Creating strategy and agility through wargaming. *California Management Review*, 55(3), 5–31.

Junni, P., Sarala, R., Tarba, S., and Weber, Y. (2015). The role of strategic agility in acquisitions. *British Journal of Management*, 26(4), 596–616.

Lewis, M.W., Andripoulos, C., and Smith, W.K. (2014). Paradoxical leadership to enable strategic agility. *California Management Review*, 56(3), 58–77.

Morton, J., Amrollahi, A., and Wilson, A.D. (2022). Digital strategizing: An assessing review, definition, and research agenda. *Journal of Strategic Information Systems*, 31(1), 101720.

Morton, J., Stacey, P., and Mohn, M. (2018). Building and maintaining strategic agility: An agenda and framework for executive IT-leaders. *California Management Review*, 61(1), 94–113.

Newell, S., Morton, J., Marabelli, M., and Galliers, R.D. (2020). *Managing Digital Innovation: A Knowledge Perspective*. London: Red Globe Press.

O'Hara, C. (2014). How to tell a great story. *Harvard Business Review*, July.

Palfreyman, J. (2020). *Digital Transformation Handbook: An Agile Approach to Maximise Value*. Seattle: Kindle Direct Publishing.

Porter, M.E. and Millar, V.E. (1985). How information gives you competitive advantage. *Harvard Business Review*, 63(4), 149–160.

Suddaby, R. (2010). Editor's comments: Construct clarity in theories of management and organization. *Academy of Management Review*, 35(3), 346–357.

Tabrizi, B., Lam, E., Girard, K., and Irvin, V. (2019). Digital transformation is not about technology. *Harvard Business Review*, 13 March.

Tallon, P.P. and Pinsonneault, A. (2011). Competing perspectives on the link between strategic information technology alignment and organizational agility: Insights from a mediation model. *MIS Quarterly*, 35(2), 463–486.

Verhoef, P.C., Broekhuizen, T., Bart, Y., Bhattacharya, A., Dong, J.Q., Fabian, N., and Haenlein, M. (2021). Digital transformation: A multidisciplinary reflection and research agenda. *Journal of Business Research*, 122, 889–901.

Vial, G. (2019). Understanding digital transformation: A review and a research agenda. *Journal of Strategic Information Systems*, 28(2), 118–144.

https://doi.org/10.1142/9789811271984_0008

Chapter 8

Digital Strategy, Machine Learning, and Industry Survey of MLOps

Robert Cohen

Seton Hall University, Stillman School of Business, South Orange, NJ, USA
robert.cohen1@shu.edu

As part of a digital strategy, machine learning (ML) has become a common toolset and capability across many businesses. However, the operational aspects of machine learning (MLOps) are often overlooked for ML projects until they are already installed and being executed in the business environment. This chapter provides a review of MLOps products and vendors to give data scientists the ability to set up the appropriate ML infrastructure in a proactive manner.

1. Introduction

MLOps is an emerging field that is focused on automating the life cycle for machine-learning (ML) applications. As firms begin to use ML as part of their digital strategy, the operational aspect of these models continues to grow in importance. In addition to documenting the MLOps life cycle, an industry survey of current products and platforms is reviewed.

Many businesses have begun to use ML as part of their overall digital strategy transformation. As firms continue with this approach, it requires a new way of managing technology, people, and organizations. It also requires transformation in many aspects of these firms' technology platforms. This chapter focuses on the operational aspects of using ML in large organizations and the tools and platforms that currently exist to manage ML environments.

It is useful to discuss terminology in this transformation — especially as related to ML, since it has become a key aspect in most digital strategy programs. For a while now, there has been a lot of "hype" around artificial intelligence (AI) and the potential benefits it can bring to the business community. ML is a subset of AI. It is used to provide the capability to develop systems for classification and/or prediction based on learning from data. This requires that significant time is spent analyzing a data source and engineering features of the data that will be useful for models of classification or prediction. Typically known as exploratory data analysis (EDA), this function can often take longer and be more complex than actually developing the learning model. This has caused a real paradigm shift in the time and cost spent on data analysis, as opposed to the time and cost of building models. This does not imply that modeling and learning algorithms are trivial or not important. In fact, the modeling component of ML is complex and crucial to gaining any benefits from this technology.

2. Why MLOps

The operational aspect of software development and the ability to efficiently manage the full software development life cycle has become a key part of rapidly building quality software. The functionality of DevOps is to provide the set of tools and practices that allow companies to build software quickly and to continuously deliver new enhancements effectively. Many capabilities of DevOps are consistent with agile software development and the associated rapid iterative process of continuous delivery. The DevOps life cycle is mature, and many standard platforms can provide the required tools and capabilities. As more companies gravitate to ML for a variety of applications, the need to manage the operational aspects of ML has also become evident. MLOps is a natural outgrowth of ML applications and modeling — however, it is an emerging field and continues to grow. Many new vendors have begun delivering platforms to automate the life cycle for ML.

3. MLOps Overview

The components of a robust operational platform for ML should contain most of the capabilities (Salama *et al.*, 2021) listed as follows:

(a) Model development and experimentation
(b) Operationalization of model training
(c) Continuous model training
(d) Deployment into a production platform
(e) Generating predictions or classifications as needed
(f) Continuous monitoring of model performance
(g) Dataset management and feature engineering

Note that all these components do not need to exist from day one in the MLOps platform. The entire operational platform can be built out over time. However, an ML system supporting real business decision-making should include the first several capabilities right out of the gate. Each of these capabilities will be discussed in more detail below.

A. *Model development and experimentation*: One of the first capabilities that is required in an ML operational platform is the ability to give data scientists and software developers the ability to develop models using multiple data sources and analyze the results. Data analysis, feature engineering, and ETL (extraction, translation, and loading) are performed in this step. Models are also built, reused, tweaked, and modified in this step. There needs to be a robust environment for creating, experimenting, documenting, and saving results. This capability is usually provided by a notebook environment where many of these functions are integrated into a common tool.

B. *Operationalization of model training*: Another life cycle component of MLOps is the ability to train models using various data sources. This includes the ability to split datasets into training and testing sections and to analyze various models and learning algorithms to determine the best choice for a given application. Using predefined configurations, software engineers need to be able to perform testing on a repeatable training pipeline (Salama *et al.*, 2021). After training is performed, the operational process needs to include the ability to deploy the trained model into a target (stage or production) environment.

C. ***Continuous model training*****:** The continuous training component is about the automated frequency of retraining the model as more data (or new data) become available. Since there is a true cost for retraining, the automated training frequency depends on a cost–benefit analysis (CBA) of the specific business situation. In general, retraining can be triggered by several methods including scheduled runs, event-driven runs (such as % new data or % changed data), ad hoc runs based on the preferences of data scientists or software engineers, and runs required based on model degradation. Tracking ML artifacts for each of the training runs is an important aspect of this MLOps phase.

D. ***Deployment into a production platform*****:** The deployment phase of MLOps includes packaging and testing the model, and then delivering the output to a target-serving environment (Salama *et al.*, 2021). In many cases, the deployment will move from a test environment into a production environment. However, larger firms may have one or more staging environments between test and production to ensure more thorough testing of models.

E. ***Generating predictions or classifications as needed*****:** In this phase of the MLOps life cycle, requests are accepted, and the model generates predictions or classifications to respond to these requests. Based on the business or application needs, the predictions can be generated based on real-time requests or batch requests. Interpretation and explanation of predictions and classifications are important parts of the capability delivered in this MLOps component.

F. ***Continuous monitoring of model performance*****:** Another important phase in the MLOps life cycle is monitoring the performance of models. Both the effectiveness and the efficiency need continual monitoring. It is important to assess model drift and model degradation. Based on a threshold related to accuracy, the monitoring facility should be able to alert software and ML engineers to retrain and/or reassess the current model (Salama *et al.*, 2021). Similarly, the performance of model runs needs to be continuously monitored to ensure the current model can run in the time required for the business use case.

G. ***Dataset management and feature engineering*****:** Finally, data management is an MLOps component that goes across all aspects of the MLOps life cycle. Analyzing data and managing datasets along with work required to deliver high-quality data are often time-consuming efforts. This capability in the MLOps platform is required in order to deliver properly trained models and to generate valid predictions or classifications. It is also an important aspect of the ability to reuse data across various models and projects. As an analogy, consider the paradigm of using framework libraries to leverage reuse of objects in an object-oriented programming (OOP) environment. For this to work properly, the OOP software developers must trust the framework library and have enough documentation to use it productively. In the same manner, the ML engineer needs to have the ability to access processed data and the feature engineering that was previously performed on it. They need to be able to access the documentation associated with prior data management efforts and to determine whether it is possible to reuse prior data or feature engineering to train newer models for new or enhanced applications.

4. Industry Survey of MLOps Tools and Platforms

There are a growing number of products and tools currently available to build robust platforms for MLOps. Listed in Table 1 are many of the

Table 1. Popular MLOps platforms and products, and associated vendors.

Platform/Product	Vendor
1. MLflow	MLflow
2. Google Cloud AI	Google
3. Kaggle	Kaggle
4. SageMaker	Amazon
5. IBM MLOps Starter Kit	IBM
6. Iguazio	Iguazio
7. Azure Machine Learning	Microsoft
8. Huawei Cloud ModelArts	Huawei
9. Darwin Automated ML Platform	SparkCognition
10. Comet	Comet
11. Grid.AI	Grid.AI
12. Modzy ModelOps Platform	Modzy
13. Valohai MLOps Platform	Valohai
14. HPE Ezmeral ML Ops	Hewlett Packard Enterprise
15. Domino Enterprise MLOps Platform	Domino

most popular platforms and products, along with their associated vendor names.

As reviewed in the following, some of the tools provide the full gamut of operational capabilities, while others provide only one or a few functions in the overall MLOps life cycle. Additional details about each of these MLOps tools are presented in the following:

1. *MLflow*: MLflow is an open-source platform for automating various phases of the ML life cycle. These phases include experimentation, reproducibility, deployment, and a central registry for models. MLflow currently offers four specific life cycle components: tracking, projects, models, and registry (MLflow, 2021). Each of these components can be used on their own for a given phase in the ML life cycle, but they are designed to be easily integrated into a more fully functioning MLOps platform. The tracking component of MLflow contains an API and a user interface for logging capability when running ML code. It provides the ability to log parameters, version of code runs, output files created, and metrics. The data from these logging functions can then be used to help visualize the results. The tracking API is available for common ML coding languages including Python, R, and Java. The project component of MLflow provides the ability to use a format for packaging ML code in a reusable way. It also provides the ability, through standard conventions, to make the package reproducible. The project component also provides the ability to chain projects together into larger workflows using an API and command line tools. The modeling component of MLflow provides a standard format for packaging ML models. These packages can then be used to run the models in many environments (online or in batch processing). The modeling format uses a standard convention that provides the ability to save multiple versions for use in different environments. Finally, the registry component is a centralized data store for models. It contains a set of APIs and a user interface to help manage several aspects of the ML life cycle. Specifically, the registry can store information on "which experiment and run produced the model" (MLflow, 2021). It can also store various model attributes including versions, stages (test versus production), and notes or annotations.

2. *Google Cloud AI*: The Google Cloud AI platform is a full-function ML platform containing all the components needed to build a robust life cycle for MLOps (Google Cloud, 2020). In the initial phase of ML development, Google Cloud provides tools for experimentation and support for data preparation and feature engineering. It also provides support for prototyping and validating models. In the second MLOps life cycle phase, the Google Cloud AI platform supports model training and operationalization. This platform provides the capability to build repeatable training and testing pipelines. The third life cycle phase in Google's platform provides the ability to do continuous training of models. "How frequently you retrain your model depends on your use case and on the business value and cost of doing so" (Google Cloud, 2020). Retraining models can be triggered based on scheduled runs, various events, or ad hoc runs. The fourth life cycle phase in this platform is model deployment. In this phase, "the model is packaged, tested and deployed to a target serving environment" (Google Cloud, 2020). In the fifth platform phase — prediction serving — the application and model provide predictions or classifications based on requests. The sixth phase of Google's platform is continuous monitoring. This phase determines the effectiveness of a production model and ensures the model performance does not decay. Finally, data and model management is provided on the Google platform including management of features, datasets, metadata, and model governance.

3. *Kaggle*: The Kaggle platform is primarily known for data science competitions. However, it also provides the capability to perform robust experimentation and can be used for the development step of the ML life cycle. While it is not really an MLOps life cycle platform, Kaggle does provide a notebook capability to store both code and documentation, and it also has the standard ability to load modeling libraries as needed (Kaggle, 2021). Kaggle can also maintain versioning for models. While this platform only handles one (experimentation) of the seven phases typically found in the ML life cycle, the Kaggle platform capabilities are continuing to grow. Kaggle has recently released the ability to do the following:

- Schedule notebooks to run at user-defined frequencies.
- Trigger notebooks to run when one of their data sources is updated.
- Sync models and their output by creating new dataset versions each time a given notebook runs.

The Kaggle platform may not be a full-function MLOps environment, but it can be used as a low-cost entry point into the operational management of ML applications.

4. *SageMaker*: Amazon's SageMaker platform provides several components to standardize processes and automate the ML life cycle. This platform delivers the ability to build, train, and deploy ML models. Management of the models is also provided, and this capability is scalable to very large numbers of models. SageMaker not only contains various tools to help manage models but it also provides the ability to integrate the ML process with other AWS services. SageMaker has the following broad capabilities (SageMaker, 2021):

- Building ML pipelines with both continuous integration (CI) and continuous delivery (CD) processing.
- Automating ML workflows for preparing data, developing models, training models, and overall experimentation.
- Monitoring the quality of models through analysis of bias and drift.
- Tracking of artifacts (code, models, and datasets) through each step of the ML life cycle.

The ability of SageMaker to provide CI/CD processes in the ML environment helps platform users create standards for model deployment. These CI/CD processes also provide version control, automated testing, and the ability to automatically migrate artifacts between development and production environments.

5. *IBM MLOps Starter Kit*: The MLOps Starter Kit is a framework that can be used on IBM's Cloud architecture to provide companies with the ability to operationalize various ML processes. This platform breaks down MLOps processes into modules that include data provisioning and preparation, model development, model monitoring, continuous integration, and continuous delivery. This kit also includes a use case with instructions, sample code, and sample data (IBM, n.d.). The template for this sample application can be used to extend MLOps capabilities for other applications based on specific user requirements.

6. *Iguazio*: Iguazio provides a data science environment using the platform as a service (PaaS) architecture model. Iguazio's platform provides many components to facilitate the operational aspects of ML (Iguazio, n.d.). For development, a workbench tool provides notebooks for code, integrating Python packages, and creating documentation. Model management is delivered with an open-source MLOps framework that provides the ability to track experiments and automate the model pipeline. The platform also provides a data layer that supports traditional SQL database sources as well as time series databases, streaming options, and integration with third-party data sources (Iguazio, n.d.).

7. ***Azure Machine Learning***: Microsoft's Azure platform provides an enterprise-level ML service for the full ML life cycle. The development tool consists of an integrated development environment (IDE) studio to access various model libraries and open-source frameworks. The Azure MLOps platform provides a straightforward set of mechanisms to deploy models and to manage them at scale. It provides the ability to score models and to manage endpoints for both batch and real-time model predictions and classifications. Both continuous integration and continuous delivery (CI/CD) functions are included on the platform. Workflows can be automated for repeatable pipeline management (Azure Machine Learning, n.d.). Machine learning pipelines typically consist of multiple steps that perform data extraction, preprocessing, model training, and model deployment. The Azure platform also has the ability to monitor model performance, detect drift, and automatically generate model retraining when required (Azure Machine Learning, n.d.). Finally, throughout the MLOps life cycle, tracking is available on various ML artifacts for auditing and governance.

8. ***Huawei's ModelArts***: Huawei's ModelArts development platform was created with the mission to be a one-stop shop for AI developers and data scientists. It contains several MLOps features including data preparation and labeling, model building and training, and deployment on various platforms (local and cloud). The platform is composed of several components (Huawei Cloud, n.d.). The data management component provides data preparation including collecting, translating, filtering, versioning, and labeling. The model training component provides a deep learning framework, and the product can perform automatic hyperparameter tuning of models. Most model algorithms or libraries provide the ability to set parameters for use during the model learning phase. These hyperparameters are used to train the model but they are not part of the resulting model

(Towards Data Science, 2020). ModelArts has the capability to deploy models in both local production environments as well as to the cloud. Finally, the product supports the MLOps life cycle and ML development workflows through a visual graphics engine. This visual interface provides the ability to track and manage data and model versions.

9. *Darwin Automated ML Platform*: The Darwin product contains various components for operationalization of ML models (SparkCognition, n.d.). In the data preparation component, the tool helps to uncover data issues and suggests approaches to fix data problems. Darwin's data cleaning component uses the prior preparation feature to convert/translate data into a usable form for model building. Then, Darwin helps perform feature engineering/generation to provide appropriate data selection for modeling. The algorithmic search component of Darwin has the ability to build multiple models and to determine the best solution for the specific problem domain. Finally, the model deployment component of Darwin places models into the production environment with the appropriate data sources. It also has the capability to monitor model health and detect model drift.

10. *Comet*: The Comet platform has several important MLOps functions including experiment management, artifact tracking, model production monitoring, user workspaces with reporting, and panels (Comet, n.d.). Comet provides the ability to track multiple ML assets including experimentation history, dataset usage, and models. Beyond tracking, the platform also provides a visualization suite, model debugging features, notebooks and scripting support, and a model registry. Comet positions its platform as foundational for ML and MLOps. The firm uses the analogy that "Comet is doing for ML what Github did for code" (Comet, n.d.). The main functions of Github include management of source code (all types of code) along with versioning and branching. The functions provided by Comet are also broad. The Comet platform provides functions across the ML environment, and it compares broadly with most of the products discussed here.

11. *Grid.AI*: The Grid.AI platform provides the ability to manage and train hundreds of ML models on the cloud through the use of a local device. Grid.AI's product breaks the ML process into "runs" and has the ability to scale runs to many computing processors and model configurations with minimal coding changes (Grid.AI, n.d.). Grid runs support many of the standard ML frameworks. They enable full sweeps for hyperparameter tuning of models. They also enable logging and asset management throughout the MLOps life cycle. Grid.AI has also implemented datastores to provide the ability to train models with large volumes of data from the cloud.

12. ***Modzy ModelOps Platform*:** Modzy's platform includes several capabilities for supporting MLOps. The platform handles model deployment, model, data scaling, and the overall management of ML models (Modzy ModelOps Platform, 2022). The platform is delivered through three different options that scale from basic (cloud) to enterprise (on premise or cloud). There is also an option for edge capability. The Edge support includes multi-cloud, connected edge, and mobile functionality. Experimentation and model training can be managed using external standard training frameworks and then imported as a pipeline into Modzy projects (Modzy ModelOps Platform, 2022). Modzy ModelOps can then provide full MLOps capability for these projects.

13. ***Valohai MLOps*:** The Valohai MLOps platform contains many features including version control, zero setup infrastructure, pipeline management, and team management. Together, these features cover each component of the MLOps life cycle (Valohai, n.d.). The version control feature automatically versions model runs. It also creates a data dictionary of all inputs and outputs to these model runs and a full audit trail. This component also provides model traceability and experiment comparison. The Valohai infrastructure capability provides "MLOps out of the box" (Valohai, n.d.). It provides the ability to perform infrastructure setup and maintenance from a single place and also provides the capability to automate machine start/stop to manage process costs. The platform allows the ability to use various languages and frameworks and to use code from notebooks, scripts, and Git projects. It provides the potential to perform parallel tuning runs and analyze hyperparameter tuning using distributed learning runs. The platform is also hardware agnostic and supports AWS, Azure, on-premises hardware, and other vendor/hardware options (Valohai, n.d.). The Valohai pipeline management component supports workflow automation, large dataset streaming, deployment, and the ability to use both structured and unstructured data. Finally, the Valohai team management component provides the ability to standardize workflows across a full team and allows projects to be shared between teams.

14. *HPE Ezmeral MLOps*: HPE Ezmeral MLOps allows large enterprise organizations to overcome the challenges in deploying and operationalizing ML across companies (Hewlett Packard Enterprise, 2021). The platform delivers several phases in the MLOps life cycle including data preparation, model building, model training, and model deployment and monitoring (Hewlett Packard Enterprise, 2021). HPE Ezmeral MLOps is a full life cycle platform with the ability to run on premises, on clouds (multiple), or a hybrid model. The platform's model-building component includes self-service sandbox environments with the ability to use several third-party modeling libraries. The model training component provides scalable training capability along with access to relational databases and big data. The deployment component provides a model registry for tracking versions and manages updates from the development environment to the production environment. The monitoring component provides visibility throughout each phase of the MLOps life cycle and provides resource tracking and model performance. The collaboration component provides source control, a project repository, and integration with Github. Finally, the platform runs on the major large public cloud environments including Google Cloud, Amazon Web Services, and Microsoft Azure.

15. *Domino*: The Domino platform supports data science and modeling at an enterprise-scale level. It allows data scientists and software engineers to collaborate and use their preference of tools and languages (Domino Data Lab, Inc., 2022). The platform's knowledge center component provides users with the ability to "find, reproduce, reuse, and manage" assets across the ML life cycle. The workbench component provides the ability to run, track, and compare modeling experiments. The launchpad component allows scheduling of data refreshes. Finally, the model monitoring component automates the analysis of data drift and model quality over time.

5. Conclusion

Many of the tools and platforms reviewed in this chapter contain robust automation for part, or all, of the MLOps life cycle. However, there are primarily three categories of vendors providing this capability.

The first category is made up of the large cloud computing vendors (Google, Amazon, and Microsoft). These vendors provide full life cycle functionality, support, and services. Large enterprise-level corporations often already use one of these vendors as their primary general computing partner and that naturally extends to using their MLOps platform as well.

The second category of platforms is delivered by software vendors including IBM, HP, MLflow, Iguazio, Huawei, SparkCognition, Comet, GRID.AI, Modzy, Valohai, and Domino. Each of these vendor platforms has advantages and disadvantages. Many support the full MLOps life cycle and are also good candidates for large-scale enterprise companies. However, most of these vendors also provide modular capability and life cycle components that can be purchased as needed by smaller firms just beginning to implement MLOps. These companies can then add modules as they need them, in order to perform additional automation of their ML systems.

Finally, the third category, for companies just beginning to transition into the ML landscape, consists of platforms like Kaggle with tools to provide the capability to experiment and generate models along with a few of the beginning features needed to automate the operational aspect of ML. However, since MLOps is not the goal of Kaggle, many of the major features of MLOps are not available and will likely not become available on this platform.

Overall, the operational aspects of ML are still in the early stages of adoption by most businesses. But, as reviewed in this chapter, there are already several quality platforms and products available to automate the needed operational capability. This includes both the capability to provide the infrastructure and to provide automation of common ML processes and operations. Many firms have begun creating, and will continue to grow, in their development ML applications and models. This competency will become a core part of their digital strategy. As firms continue to transition to ML, they need to choose an MLOps platform that will provide the capabilities they need now and in the future.

References

Azure Machine Learning (n.d.). https://azure.microsoft.com/en-us/services/machine-learning/#product-overview.

Comet (n.d.). Drive business impact from AI. https://www.comet.ml/site/enterprise/.

Domino Data Lab, Inc. (2022). The leading enterprise MLOps platform. https://www.dominodatalab.com/.

Google Cloud (2020). Setting up an MLOps environment on Google Cloud. https://cloud.google.com/architecture/setting-up-an-mlops-environment.

Grid.AI (n.d.). https://www.grid.ai/gridplatform/.

Hewlett Packard Enterprise (2021). HPE Ezmeral ML Ops solution brief. https://www.hpe.com/us/en/collaterals/collateral.a50000137enw.html.

Huawei Cloud (n.d.). https://www.huaweicloud.com/en-us/product/modelarts.html.

IBM (n.d.). Drive business results from your machine learning models by using the MLOps starter kit. https://www.ibm.com/cloud/architecture/architectures/machine-learning-ops-solution/.

Iguazio (n.d.). Welcome to the Iguazio data science platform. https://www.iguazio.com/docs/latest-release/intro/introduction/.

Kaggle (2021). State of machine learning and data science 2021. https://www.kaggle.com/kaggle-survey-2021.

MLflow (2021). An open source platform for the machine learning lifecycle. https://mlflow.org/.

Modzy ModelOps Platform (2022). ModelOps & MLOps platform. https://www.modzy.com/platform/.

SageMaker (2021). Amazon SageMaker for MLOps engineers. https://aws.amazon.com/sagemaker/mlops/.

Salama, K., Kazmierczak, J., and Schut, D. (2021). Practitioners guide to MLOps: A framework for continuous delivery and automation of machine learning. https://services.google.com/fh/files/misc/practitioners_guide_to_mlops_whitepaper.pdf.

SparkCognition (n.d.). Darwin®. https://www.sparkcognition.com/products/darwin.

Towards Data Science (2020). Parameters and hyperparameters in machine learning and deep learning. https://towardsdatascience.com/parameters-and-hyperparameters-aa609601a9ac.

Valohai (n.d.). The MLOps platform. https://valohai.com/product/.

https://doi.org/10.1142/9789811271984_0009

Chapter 9

Digital Technology in Changing Social Relations — The Social Internet of Things: Developing a New Method for Leveraging the Friendships between IoT Devices

Javad Abed

Johns Hopkins University, Baltimore, MD, USA
abedj@jhu.edu

Advancements in technology allow humans to add many interesting features to everyday devices. As humans, we can tackle many problems in complex societies and manage the complexity of networked social systems. Sociability is a vital human capability that improves our social lives and manages social interactions. Adding this feature to smart devices can facilitate the management of complex and networked Internet of Things (IoT) settings. We can improve the relationship between social and smart devices in different ways. Nowadays, researchers are investigating the future generations of IoT, namely, social IoT. This study aims to develop a new method for updating and leveraging the friendships between IoT devices by using social IoT and social networking principles. We utilize a design science approach to propose a novel friendship management method for social IoT that is able to effectively evaluate and manage the relationships between devices. The new friendship development and updating models use the basic concepts of Knapp's relational stage theory. In this chapter, a new simulation tool for evaluating the new friendship mechanism is proposed. The evaluation results show that the proposed method performs effectively and can enhance network navigability, service composition, and service discovery.

1. Introduction

Internet of Things (IoT) technology is growing quickly; according to Gartner, Inc., a research and advisory firm, the number of IoT devices will be more than 30 billion in 2025 (Middleton *et al.*, 2021). The overpopulated, large network of IoT devices presents many opportunities and challenges. Currently, researchers aim to explore the potential of IoT devices and try to develop effective IoT frameworks that can serve a complex human society.

The Social Internet of Things (SIoT) is one of the proposed frameworks for a future generation of IoT. SIoT uses social networking concepts for defining relationships and interactions between objects ("things"). In the SIoT framework, objects can interact with each other autonomously, discover services and information in the complex IoT environment, and provide services and information to other objects. They can start, update, and terminate friendships with other objects.

SIoT is an emerging trend in IoT literature. It considers smart objects ("things") as social objects that have social-like capabilities (Atzori *et al.*, 2014). SIoT is important because it considers handling both inherent requirements of IoT and users' needs, such as privacy and trust.

SIoT can increase the sociality, connectivity, pervasiveness, and availability of IoT systems (Ortiz *et al.*, 2014). In addition, it can create many capabilities such as object discovery functionalities, evaluation of trustworthiness of objects and the information provided by them, and deployment of value-added services. SIoT also enhances the network navigability by creating short links between friend devices.

The important goal of SIoT is to manage complexity in IoT networks. This complexity is increasing due to the rapidly growing number of devices and interactions between them. The other important goal of SIoT is providing high-quality services for humans.

Managing friendships and relationships is very important in SIoT. Smart objects can socialize with each other. The friendship and relationship between objects can create short links in the SIoT network and can increase network navigability and decrease network latency. Reviewing the literature shows that SIoT architecture and frameworks heavily focus on friendship initiation and termination. In other words, they focus on friendship selection and different types of relationships that objects can establish. However, updating the relationship and differentiating levels of friendship are rarely considered in the literature.

Similar to social networks, the level of friendship is very important for assessing trust and social interaction capabilities. In real life, humans have acquaintances, close friends, best friends, and maybe enemies. For each category, we have a different level of trust and a different level of communication. We do not share our private and personal information with acquaintances or strangers. We might need to interact more often with our best friends and have a high level of commitment to our relationship.

The main objective of this chapter is to develop a new friendship updating mechanism and a friendship leveraging method based on social networking concepts such as friendship development. To achieve this goal, this study will use friendship development factors and Knapp's relational stage model to define the relationships and interactions between IoT objects and to update the relationship level continuously and effectively. The Complex Social Internet of Things (CSIoT) is a new mechanism for friendship development and updating that we propose in this study.

2. Research Background

Currently, researchers in the IoT field have two important objectives. They aim to explore the potential of IoT devices and to develop more effective models of IoT that can serve the complex and networked human society (Atzori *et al.*, 2014). IoT encompasses many objects in a complex setting, which can create many opportunities as well as many threats. In terms of complexity, IoT is similar to complex social systems by having a large number of smart objects and a networked system.

In social and biological systems, humans can address the complexity of social systems and manage potential opportunities and threats like network navigability and privacy. Therefore, we can utilize the concepts of social systems to make the same capabilities in IoT devices. That's why for managing emergent opportunities and threats in complex IoT settings, it is necessary to develop and improve new IoT models that utilize networked social system concepts. In SIoT, objects can interact with each other autonomously, discover services and information in the complex IoT environment, and provide services and information to other objects.

According to Atzori *et al.*, SIoT is a future generation of IoT that can create many capabilities such as object discovery functionalities, evaluation of trustworthiness of objects and their provided information, and deployment of value-added services (Atzori *et al.*, 2014). Defining inter-object relationships is one of the important open research issues in SIoT.

There are four features of SIoT: finding server providers, publishing information, evaluating trustworthiness, and getting filtered information. The first feature is the capability of crawling networks of friends to find other objects that can provide useful services. The second feature is the capability of publishing information through friendship paths and limiting message exchanges for optimized consumption. The third feature is the evaluation of trustworthiness of services and information provided by other objects. Finally, the fourth feature is the collaboration of a community of objects with a common view to improve the accuracy of information.

To develop SIoT, the relationships between objects should be defined. After coding these relationships, an effective SIoT architecture can be developed. Then, we can analyze the social network structure of SIoT. Atzori utilizes several social network concepts and relationship types for defining and coding the relationships between objects in SIoT (Atzori *et al.*, 2012). The parent–object relationship (POR) is for objects that are created in the same period by the same producer. The co-location object relationship (C-LOR) is for objects that are in the same location (e.g., a smart home). The co-work object relationship (C-WOR) is for objects that work together to provide an IoT application. Finally, the social–object relationship (SOR) is for objects that continuously or occasionally are in contact with each other because their owners are contacting each other. Aztori develops a SIoT structure that contains three layers, that is, sensing, networking, and application layers. According to the authors, the main components of SIoT such as relationship management, service discovery (SD), service composition, and trustworthiness management are in the application layer.

IoT devices should be socialized to easily interact with humans. SIoT can increase the sociality/connectivity and pervasiveness/availability of IoT systems (Ortiz *et al.*, 2014). According to Ortiz *et al.*, there are several research issues in SIoT that can be categorized in three perspectives: interactivity, collaboration, and handled data. Interactivity is about interactions between objects or interactions between humans and objects. Most of the SIoT studies consider only one type of interaction. Collaborative perspective is related to collaboration of all types of SIoT components, especially human–object collaboration, to increase the quality of information (QoI). Finally, handled data is about using different data acquisition and processing techniques in SIoT (Ortiz *et al.*, 2014).

According to Ortiz *et al.*, social roles, intelligence, and socialized devices are key features of the SIoT paradigm. Social role refers to using social networking concepts and basics to develop a social structure in IoT objects. Intelligence can be defined as decision-making tools and methods that enable IoT objects to understand each other's services or manage their friendships. Finally, socialized objects can interact and communicate with humans or other objects (Ortiz *et al.*, 2014).

Kasnesis *et al.* integrate cognitive and social aspects in IoT objects by considering friendship management and goal management mechanisms. Friendship management is a smart component that considers trust, quality of data (QoD), QoI, and network structure. Goal management is also a smart component that includes SD, service orchestration (SO), and service binding (SB) (Kasnesis *et al.*, 2017).

A review of the SIoT literature shows two important factors that are the main motivations for this research. First, there is a need to investigate SIoT in the information systems (IS) field because the IS field has not broadly investigated IoT and future generations of IoT, such as SIoT and cognitive IoT. Obviously, IoT is a very important information system that has a considerable impact on our lives. We believe that more design science and behavioral studies are needed in the IS discipline about different aspects of IoT.

Second, in SIoT studies, there is no effective mechanism for updating and leveraging the friendships between devices. Updating friendships is very important because it has a major impact on privacy, network navigability, service quality, SD, and information quality.

Leveraging friendships means examining the trustworthiness of the friend devices and determining the level of friendship. Friendship updating or leveraging in SIoT is not investigated enough in the literature.

For instance, in the SIoT architecture proposed by Atzori *et al.*, the only factor for leveraging friendship between devices is trustworthiness, which is determined by network centrality and prestige (Atzori *et al.*, 2012). These factors are important, but other important factors (such as QoI) should also be considered in leveraging friendship. In addition, the authors do not consider time in this process. Suppose that a device has high trustworthiness at a certain point of time t_1 but a low trustworthiness at t_2. There is no effective mechanism in SIoT studies to monitor the variation of trustworthiness over time and leveraging friendship based on that.

Kasnesis *et al.* consider different factors like QoI, QoD, and network structure for leveraging different devices. They divide devices into low importance, medium importance, and high importance categories based on a game theory approach (Kasnesis *et al.*, 2017). However, they do not actually leverage the friend devices and just use this leveraging process in friend selection, friendship termination, and accepting friendship requests. In other words, they leverage the importance of non-friend devices. In addition, they do not provide a mechanism for considering time and utilizing friendship levels in SIoT. The importance level of friendship is not subject to update in their study.

3. Friendship Development in CSIoT

3.1 *Friendship evolution factors*

The evolution of friendship has been studied in different disciplines including social science, psychology, and communication. There are two questions that are very important for understanding friendship networks:

- What are the main factors in friend selection?
- What are the main reasons for friendship evolution and maintaining the relationship?

As mentioned earlier, the SIoT paradigm tries to apply social networking concepts in IoT settings to create new capabilities and manage some problems like network navigability. One of the vital factors in social networks is friendship evolution. In the SIoT literature, researchers propose new methods to make human-like capabilities (such as socialization and cognition) in connected devices (objects). Therefore, friendship management is very important in the SIoT architecture. Objects should be able to initiate, update, and terminate relationships with other objects.

In the SIoT literature, we can find different mechanisms for friendship management. These mechanisms are based on predefined and independent relationships that objects can establish in an IoT setting. In this study, the focus is instead on the mixture of factors that can initiate and maintain a friendship between objects.

This study tries to investigate the main friendship evolution factors in SIoT. We want to use these factors in friendship selection and in the updating or terminating of friendship.

This study proposes four important factors for friendship evolution: physical proximity, similarity, reciprocity, and competence. We believe that using these factors in friendship development provides a broader view of the friendship management process. The main idea here is that instead of having predefined and independent relationship types, we can manage the object's socialization by investigating the main causes for friendship and socialization. In addition, this study investigates the role of these factors in maintaining and updating friendship in SIoT. The descriptions of the friendship evolution factors are provided in the following.

3.1.1 *Proximity*

In several studies, proximity has been identified as an important factor for friendship development among humans (Schutte and Light, 1978; Sias and Cahill, 1997; Clark and Pataki, 1995). The basic idea here is that we choose our friends mostly from the people who are physically near us. Physical proximity makes interactions among people easy. Frequent interactions in same environment (e.g., workplace, gym, and school) increase the chance of friendship.

Proximity is also an important factor of friendship development in social networks. According to Backstrom *et al.*, physical proximity makes people interact more on Facebook (Backstrom *et al.*, 2010). In a review article, Rivera *et al.* show that proximity has a high impact on people's attachment and friendship development in social networks (Rivera *et al.*, 2010).

Physical proximity is also used as a co-location relationship, which is one of the device friendship factors in SIoT (Atzori *et al.*, 2012; Kasnesis *et al.*, 2017). In the SIoT framework developed by Atzori *et al.*, a co-location relationship is one of the relationship types that devices can establish in close distances. The proximity range can be defined in one room, a smart home, or even a smart city. Indeed, some devices located in the same area might not interact with each other. But physical proximity is still a useful factor for friendship selection and creating short links in a network.

Physical proximity is one of the friendship initiation factors in this study. Similar to co-location friendship in SIoT, objects can select friends located in close distances. The locality (L) can be determined by user preferences and the context. We can consider a room, a home, or even a city as the locality range. The user (device owner) can set the locality to any range considering the device technology and the device context. Obviously, the locality for a smart home is different from a smart city. In other words, for a device, a close distance range or locality (L) can be 100 m^2 and for other devices it can be 200 m^2. To initiate a friendship, two devices must be in the same local area. Therefore, we can formulate the physical proximity factor as follows:

If $L \geq d = \sqrt{((x2 - x1)^2 + (y2 - y1)^2)}$, then initiate the friendship, where L is the locality, d is the distance between two objects, and (x, y) is the device's location information.

3.1.2 *Similarity*

Similarity is one of the key factors in friend selection and initiating relationships between people. Several articles (Kandel, 1978; De Klepper *et al.*, 2010; Aboud and Mendelson, 1996) show that similarity makes mutual understanding easy and can attract and attach people to each other. Having a similar car, job, personality, interests, and other factors can initiate relationships among people in social networks. Obviously, not all people with similar factors become friends, but similarity is a good starting point for relationships.

The similarity concept in the SIoT literature can be found as POR, ownership–object relationship, C-LOR, and C-WOR. In other words, objects with the same production company, owner, location, and applications can establish a friendship in CSIoT.

In CSIoT, we use similarity in two forms: owner similarity and product similarity. Two devices are considered similar when they have the same owner or the owners are trusted friends. Two devices are also considered similar when they are produced by the same company in the same period of time.

Owner similarity is similar to the ownership–object relationship. However, we extend this relationship to friend owners. In other words, when the owners of two devices are trusted friends, they can initiate a friendship. Devices with the same owner can establish a strong friendship because they might interact with each other frequently to satisfy the owner's need. In addition, any device owner can consider trusted friends' devices to be friends with their own devices. There is a high possibility for the owner to interact with their friends frequently. Therefore, the owner's devices and the owner's friends' devices might interact frequently.

One of the device friendship factors in CSIoT is the owner and the owner's friends. The important point here is that the strength of the friendship between the owner and their friends affects the strength of the friendship in devices.

We consider three levels of friendship between the owner and their friends: highly trusted friends (best friends), average trusted friends (close friends), and lowly trusted friends (acquaintances). These levels are subjective and are based on the owner's opinion. Two devices with best friend owners can initiate a friendship and their friendship score (strength) will be the highest at the beginning. Two devices with close friend owners can initiate a friendship with an average score, and finally, two devices with lowly trusted friends can initiate a friendship with a low friendship score.

The product similarity is similar to the POR. This factor is useful for software problems and sharing information processes because smart objects with the same batch number are compatible and homogeneous (Atzori *et al.*, 2012; Kasnesis *et al.*, 2017).

3.1.3 *Reciprocity*

Reciprocity is a well-established factor for initiating or continuing a friendship. Reciprocity is defined as tendency to reciprocate a relationship. According to Selfhout *et al.*, reciprocity significantly increases the friendship selection (Selfhout *et al.*, 2010). In addition, reciprocity is important in friendship influence and continuing or maintaining the relationship (Leider *et al.*, 2009).

In the SIoT literature, reciprocity is considered in friendship initiation. A device sends the friendship request to other devices. If the request is accepted by a device, that device will be added to the friend list. By reviewing the SIoT literature, we can see that in SIoT friendship management, the role of reciprocity in friendship influence and friendship updating has not been studied.

Reciprocity is important in initiating the friendship as well as maintaining the friendship in CSIoT. If device 1 sends a friendship request to device 2, then device 2 accepts or rejects the friendship. In case of acceptance, both devices can add the other one to their friend list. We also consider reciprocity as one of the factors of friendship updating.

Suppose that device 1 and device 2 are friends. After a while, device 2 rarely responds to device 1 for different possible reasons (e.g., malfunction or busy node). Thus, device 1 should decrease the strength of the friendship because there is no satisfying number of responses or services from device 1. So, the accessibility of friend devices and the number of appropriate and useful responses and services during a certain amount of time are the main components of reciprocity. The link between two devices with low reciprocity will not be useful most of the time. However, high reciprocity between two devices can increase the friendship's strength. We can formulate reciprocity as follows:

$$R = n/t$$

where R is reciprocity, n is the number of appropriate responses (in terms of messages and services), and t represents time. The reciprocity factor will affect the friendship's strength in SIoT.

3.1.4 *Competence*

There are different definitions for social competence, but it generally refers to effectiveness in social interactions (Rose-Krasnor, 2006). Competence can be also defined as having set of skills (e.g., communication, problem-solving, and cognition) to manage everyday life. Several research works show that people have a high tendency to be friends with socially skilled people. Therefore, competence is very important in initiating and maintaining friendships (Pinquart and Sörensen, 2000; Cause, 1986; Buhmester, 1998).

In the SIoT literature, competence is not considered one of the factors in friend selection or updating. Rather, SIoT studies have applied some factors for leveraging and updating friendship. Atzori *et al.* (2012)

use trustworthiness for leveraging friendship in SIoT. Kasnesis *et al.* (2017) use QoD and QoI for leveraging friendship in SIoT.

We define competence as a set of factors that are socially important for smart objects in selecting and maintaining friends. These factors are QoD (Karkouch *et al.*, 2016), QoI (Wu *et al.*, 2014), and network structure (Nitti *et al.*, 2015). These factors are very important in communication between nodes and friendship selection. We believe that the social effectiveness of nodes is highly dependent on these factors.

In the CSIoT setting, nodes are equipped with sensors that can exchange data among each other. The quality of the sensed data is a very important measure for node performance. Assume that a person has a heart problem and his average heart rate should be monitored regularly. This person has a wearable device and a smart phone application that report two different values for average heart rate during a day. Here, data quality evaluation can find the most reliable value for average heart rate. Sometimes sensed data might be noisy, corrupted, or incomplete. Therefore, a node that provides high-quality data is more popular among the other nodes.

There are different criteria for evaluating QoD in IoT settings, but we chose the most important factors including interpretability, accuracy, completeness, timeliness, and reliability (Karkouch *et al.*, 2016). The comprehensive QoD evaluation is out of scope of this study. Interpretability refers to data clearness in terms of format and meaning. Accuracy represents data precision, and completeness is the ratio of non-interpolated items to all items available. Timeliness shows how up to date the data are. And finally, reliability represents the consistency of data.

QoI represents the importance of the information received from each node. Objects in CSIoT have different decision-making processes (e.g., friend selection). It is very important for each node to evaluate the information received from other nodes for decision-making. QoI is represented as follows:

$$\text{QoI} = Q * P * R * A * D * T * V$$

where Q is quantity and shows how much useful information is received for a specific task. If a node receives all required information, then $Q = 1$. P represents the precision and is the proportion of relevant information to all information received. So, if half of the information is relevant, then

$P = 0.5$. R denotes recall and represents the proportion of the relevant information to the number of all relevant information. A represents the accuracy of information for decision-making. D denotes the complete degree of information received for decision-making, and T represents the timeliness of information. Finally, V denotes validity and represents the trueness of information. If the received information is completely false, then $V = 0$. All of the QoI factors should be normalized in the (0, 1) range.

Each object in CSIoT has a computational limit and needs time to cope with a large number of connections and service searches. That's why this study adopts the heuristic proposed by Nitti *et al.* for friend selection in CSIoT (Nitti *et al.*, 2015). First, we define the maximum number of connections allowed (N_{max}). Then, a node utilizes the minimum local clustering strategy to manage any further friendship requests. Based on this strategy, a node ranks its friends based on the number of common friends. Then, it compares the node sending the friendship request with its friends. If this node has more common friends compared to other friend nodes, then it rejects the friendship request.

4. Leveraging Friendships

Although friendships between smart objects seem different from friendships between people, they are similar in different ways. In SIoT, objects have socialization capabilities. This makes them human-like things. The more human-like objects are, the more capabilities they have to serve humans. That's why considering the important factors in human friendships and applying them to object relationships can be useful and valuable.

One of the important factors in human relationships and friendships is leveraging. In real life, we consider different values and strengths for our friendships. Leveraging friendships is a process that develops based on different factors including time, commitment, reliability, and trust. Several other factors such as privacy, communication, and interaction are important in leveraging friendships.

We believe that leveraging friendships is also important in smart objects' communication, and that we should have an effective mechanism for that in SIoT. The information and services that would be exchanged between devices have different values and different levels of importance. That's why we should have different levels of communication between devices. Leveraging friendships can set boundaries for communication between devices.

Suppose that device 1 has three friends (device 2, device 3, and device 4). Leveraging friendship can show the level of friendship for each of these friend devices and the strength of the friendship link between device 1 and friend devices. Device 1 can use this information to manage the communication between itself and its friend devices. It can share sensitive and private information only with high-level friends. It can expect to receive vital and high-quality services from high-level friends. It can commit more or less based on the level of friendship. Finally, device 1 has a clear level of trust for each of the friend devices based on the friendship level.

This study takes a continuous and comprehensive approach to leveraging friendship between devices. In CSIoT, friendship can grow and end based on several factors including similarity, competence, reciprocity, and proximity. We believe that these factors can affect friendship initiation as well as friendship growth or termination. In CSIoT, friendship is not a linear relationship. It can grow and end gradually based on different factors.

Knapp's relational stage model inspires our model of friendship in CSIoT. This model gives us a good understanding of friendship development and termination. We believe that it is useful to apply the basic concepts of this model to SIoT friendship management.

4.1 *Knapp's relational stage model*

Knapp's relational stage model is a well-known theory about interpersonal communication and friendship development. This model is like a dual staircase that shows how a relationship can grow and how it can end. Figure 1 depicts Knapp's relational stage model (Knapp, 1978).

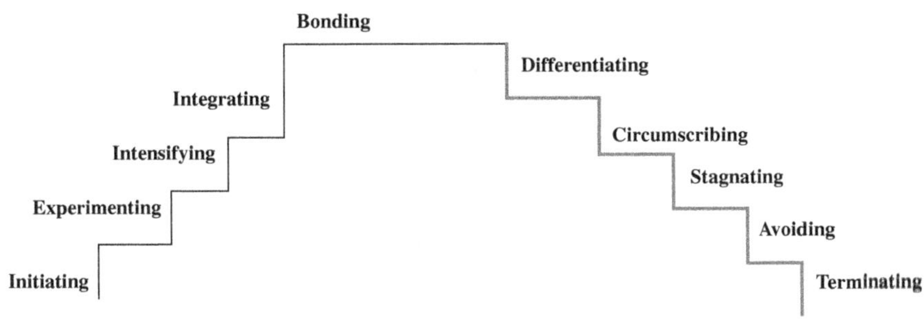

Fig. 1. Knapp's relational stage model (Knapp, 1978).

This model consists of two interrelated sets of stages (depicted in black and gray). These two sets are relationship escalation and relationship termination models. The important factor in this model is that the speed of growth and time for changing scales can vary in different relationships. Some of the stages can even be skipped in some relationships. This model shows that relationships between people generally grow and end through different stages. Obviously, time is an important factor here.

Each stage in this model has some unique characteristics (Fox *et al.*, 2013). The initiating stage includes first impressions and uncertainty. Two people have a willingness to meet each other and start a relationship, but they do not know each other well.

In the experimenting stage, people will explore each other to find commonalities or interesting factors that make them want to continue the relationship. In this stage, self-disclosure is low and people usually don't share sensitive information about themselves.

After experimenting, people start sharing their personal information to have an impact on the relationship's growth (intensifying). In this stage, participating parties have commitment expectation. They will find different ways to strengthen the relationship (e.g., gifts).

Oneness is an important characteristic of the integrating stage. In this stage, participating people call themselves "we" or "us." They are considered best friends and have a private commitment to the relationship. For two people to reach this stage, they need to know each other very well during this time.

The last stage in relationship growth is bonding. In this stage, two people have a shared identity and a public commitment. In business relationships, partnership and durable relationships for lowering costs and increasing benefits can be considered the bonding stage.

Differentiating is the first stage of relationship termination. Because of different reasons including different attitudes, different interests, and different personalities, participating parties may start fighting and having conflicts, and the relationship will start to fade.

In circumscribing, partners will limit their conversations. They may still hope to continue the relationship but set boundaries in their communications.

In the stagnating stage, partners limit the conversations even further. In this stage, partners may want to end the relationship but for some reason cannot yet terminate the relationship.

Partners in the avoiding stage intentionally avoid any conversation and contact. They are always too busy to see each other. After this stage, partners end the relationship in the terminating stage.

4.2 *Friendship model in CSIoT*

Obviously, in some aspects, the friendship between devices is different from the friendship between humans. Smart objects in SIoT are human-like in some aspects but they are not human. They do not have emotions, attitudes, and other complicated human features. However, the basics of friendship development and termination can be applied in smart objects in SIoT to create new capabilities and useful features in SIoT settings.

To model friendship, this study utilizes the basic elements of Knapp's model such as growth or termination in different stages. Friendship in CSIoT has three main components: initiating, growth, and terminating. Several factors such as time, similarity, proximity, reciprocity, and competence can affect the stage change in friendship.

Proximity, similarity, reciprocity, and competence are important factors for initiating a friendship and friend selection. The friendship initiation has two parts. In the first part, a device checks the friendship initiation criteria; in the case of satisfactory conditions, it sends the friendship request. In the second part, if this device receives the acceptance message from any device, it adds that device to its friend list and calculates the friendship score.

We define α as a threshold for the overall competency score for initiating friendship, and it can change based on user rules and context. We also define reciprocity I, which is a part of reciprocity criteria that are important in initiating friendship, and it has acceptance/rejection values.

In the second part, devices do not check reciprocity I. In the second part of the friendship initiation, a device receives a friendship request. It evaluates the sender based on the same criteria and if the sender satisfies the criteria, then it accepts the friendship request, adds that device into its friend list, and assigns a friendship score.

To leverage friendships in CSIoT, this study considers different friendship scores which show different stages of friendship. In Knapp's model, each friendship stage has some unique characteristics. Some of these characteristics, like public commitment, are special features of

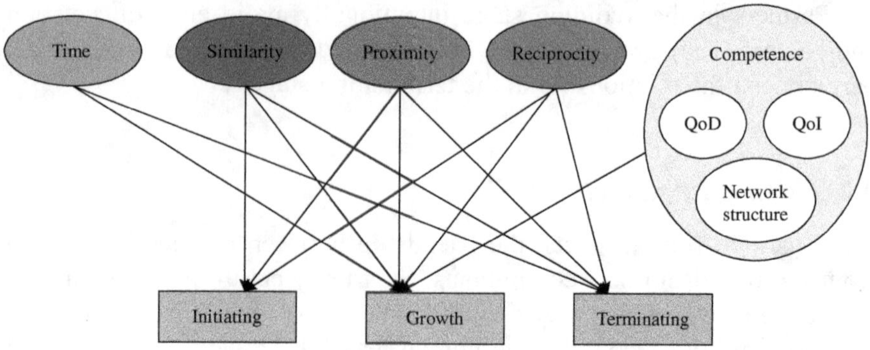

Fig. 2. Relationship model in the CSIoT.

human relationships. This study aims to mimic Knapp's relational stage model by considering different stages and characteristics that are suitable for smart devices and SIoT settings. Figure 2 shows the friendship leveraging model in SIoT.

This study considers five levels of friendship with five different scores. Score 1 is for the lowest level of friendship and score 5 is for highest level of friendship. Several factors including time, competence, reciprocity, proximity, and similarity can level up and level down the friendship between devices. Except level 1, which is the initiating level, all levels are dependent on a cumulative score of time, similarity, proximity, competence, and reciprocity. This is the main process of updating friendships in CSIoT.

The scores for similarity, proximity, reciprocity, competence, and time are normalized in the (0, 10) range. We define GMS_i as the minimum cumulative score for each level. We also define T_i as the friendship duration, and T_m denotes the minimum time tolerable for a low cumulative score in each friendship level.

CSIoT continuously checks the friendship criteria and considers time in increasing or decreasing the level of friendship. There are some exceptional cases (e.g., devices with the same owners) in which some levels can be skipped. The cumulative score and minimum time scores can be changed based on context and user rules.

5. Evaluation

5.1 *Fuzzy ontology*

This study extends the relationship types that Atzori *et al.* use in their SIoT structure (Atzori *et al.*, 2011). These relationships are POR, C-LOR, C-WOR, and ownership–object relationship. The difference between the relationships in this chapter and Atzori *et al.*'s relationships is that all of them are nonlinear here. To define nonlinear relationships, this study uses fuzzy ontology. A fuzzy ontology can be defined by a set of five elements (Calegari and Ciucci, 2007):

$$\mathrm{Of} = \{I, C, R, F, A\}$$

where I is the set of individuals, C is the set of concepts, R is the set of relationships, F is the set of fuzzy relations, and A is the set of axioms. The fuzzy ontology can be developed on Web Ontology Language (OWL) and can be generated by Protégé (Morente-Molinera *et al.*, 2016). The fuzzy ontology can help add nonlinearity and uncertainty to the relationships mentioned above.

The fuzzy ontology for CSIoT contains different entities such as object and social friend agents. This ontology also has several classes based on friendship types and complexity concepts. Figure 3 shows the fuzzy ontology generated for CSIoT.

In the CSIoT platform, all devices can interact with each other. The small-world phenomenon is used for exploring the required services. The heterogeneous nature of devices causes interoperability issues. To manage interoperability, this study uses semantic web technologies including Resource Description Framework (RDF) and OWL. These tools are used to explain the services and data exchanged between different devices. Because of the nonlinearity and uncertain nature of the relationship between devices, we developed a fuzzy ontology. This fuzzy ontology is used in all framework modules (social, cognitive, and service).

CSIoT fuzzy ontology includes two types of agents: human agents and device agents. The human agent represents the owners of the devices. Each owner might have several friends with different trust levels.

Each device has a friend list, which is continuously updated by the device agents. The friendship level has an impact on socialization and

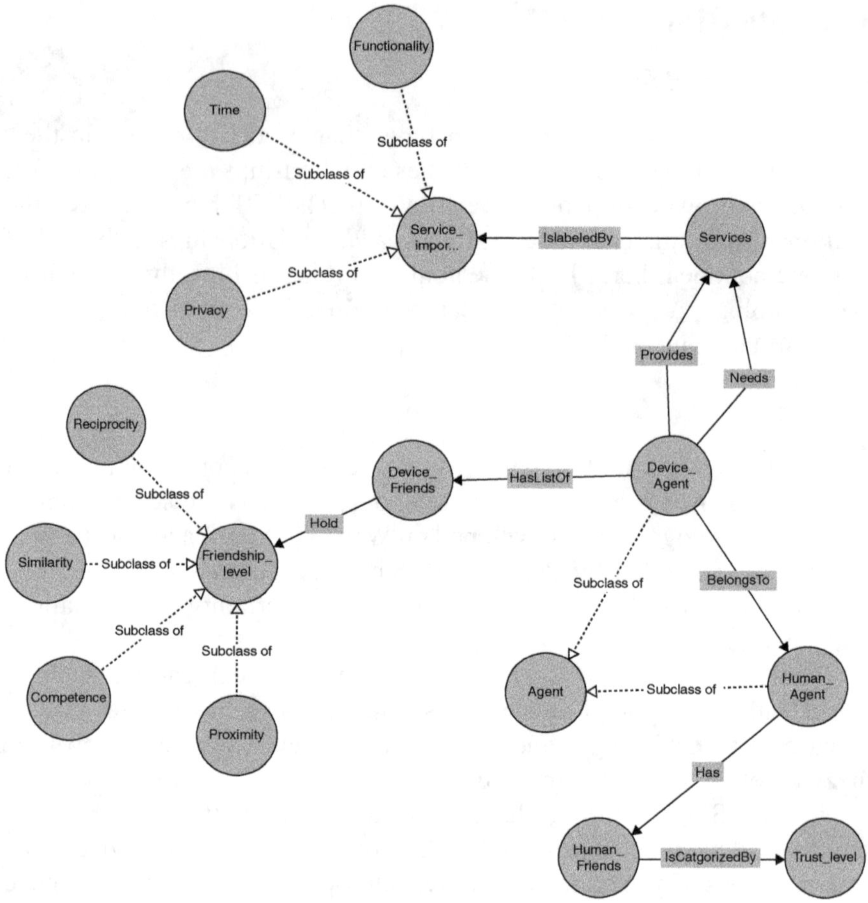

Fig. 3. CSIoT fuzzy ontology.

service management. There are four factors affecting the friendship levels: proximity, similarity, competence, and reciprocity.

There are two types of services in this ontology: services provided and services needed. Each device can provide services for other devices and each device will need services from other devices. Each service has an importance level. Functionality, time, and privacy affect the importance level of the services.

5.2 *Simulation*

To evaluate the CSIoT framework, this study conducts multi-agent system modeling. Each agent represents a smart device. The virtualization technique is used to manage heterogeneity of devices. CSIoT is web-based and developed with the Python language.

For CSIoT GUI, this study utilizes Cytoscape 3.6.1. Cytoscape is open-source software for visualization and analysis of complex networks. This platform helps to visualize the CSIoT network. Each node in this network represents an agent and each agent represents a device. To create a new agent, the following information is required: agent ID, owner ID, batch ID, locality location (x, y), highly trusted friend IDs, medium trusted friend IDs, and lowly trusted friend IDs.

Figure 4 shows the "new agent" component in CSIoT for creating a new agent and registering a new device.

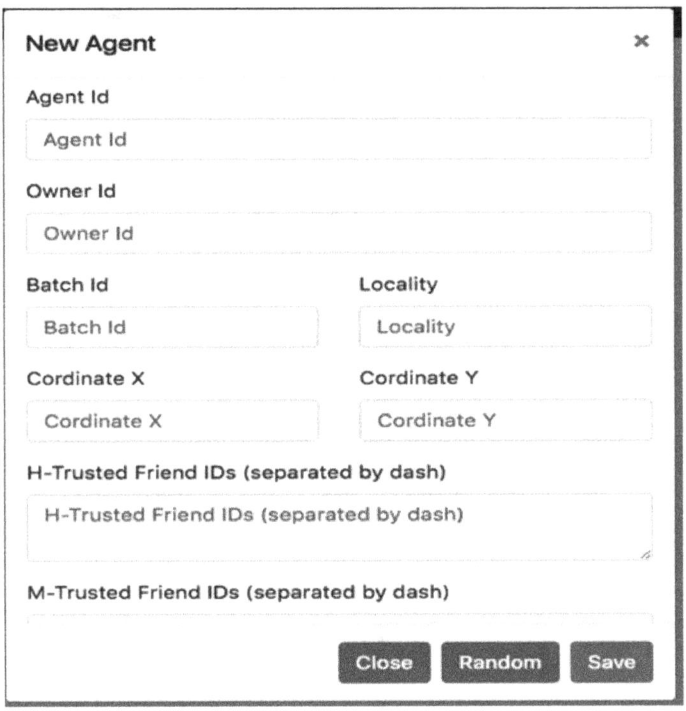

Fig. 4. Creating a new agent.

One of the important factors in CSIoT is the connection between human friendship and device friendship. Each device can recognize friends of its owner and their devices. Based on the trust level, they can establish different levels of friendship with them. Figure 5 shows an example of new agents.

After creating agents, we can run the CSIoT simulator. The simulation includes different steps. Each step represents a certain time slot. The "start simulation" option takes the number of steps and time slots for the simulation. "Simulation step 1" includes the main function of simulation. In this step, agents will start sending or receiving two types of messages.

The first type is related to friendship. Agents will send and receive friendship requests based on the criteria mentioned earlier. They can also accept or reject friendship requests based on the criteria mentioned earlier.

Fig. 5. New agents.

The second type of message is about services. Each agent has two lists of services including "services needed" and "services provided." Based on the criteria mentioned earlier, agents will start SD and service composition. SD, service composition, and service acquisitions are all dependent on the friendship management mechanism in CSIoT.

At the end of step one, the CSIoT simulator will visualize the friendship network of agents. The important factor in this network is the link between agents. This link represents the friendship strength between agents. Please note that two friend devices can have two different friendship scores for each other. The average of two agents' friendship scores is used to show the friendship strength (link weight) in the CSIoT network. Figure 6 shows an example of a friendship link. In this figure, you can see a link between agent 100 and agent 34. The friendship strength is 1, which is the average of friendship scores in both agents.

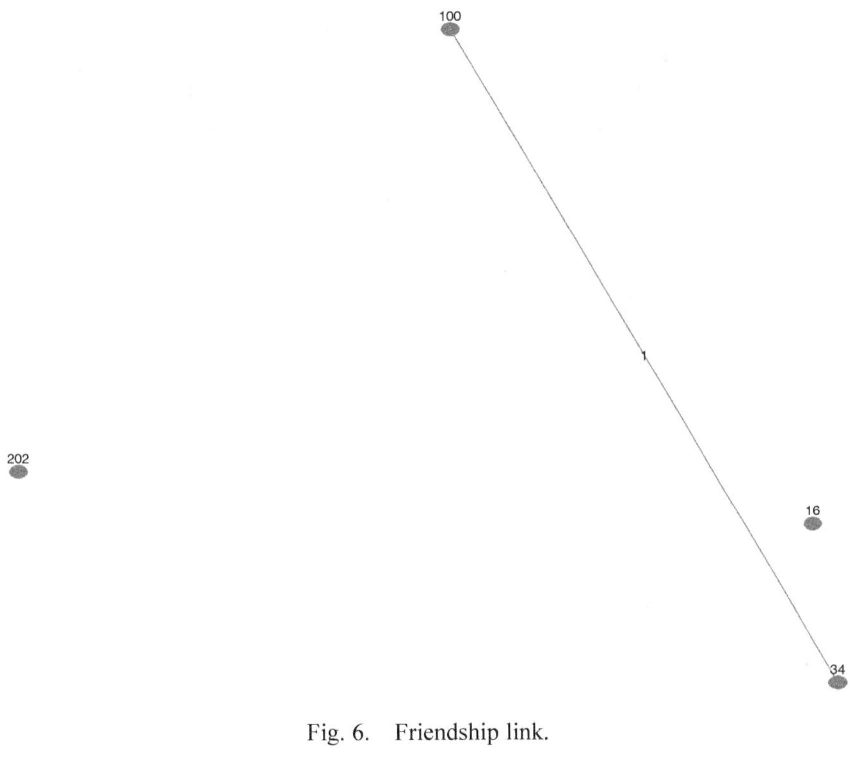

Fig. 6. Friendship link.

After running the simulator for any number of steps, we can use the weighted graph of the CSIoT network to apply social network analysis. The simulation log will be used in the semantic engine and learning process in both friendship management and service management.

6. Results

To evaluate the CSIoT framework, we simulated the SIoT setting by adding 500,000 device agents and 200,000 human agents. The agents were randomly created using the random button in the "creating a new agent" tab. As mentioned earlier, the simulation includes different steps and each step represents a different time slot. In each simulation step, the device agents can interact with each other for an hour. Between simulation steps, the device agents can perform decision-making, friendship updates, and service evaluation.

We ran the simulation step 15 times. During the simulation steps, the agent devices can parse the "services provided," "services needed," and "service importance" files for exchanging the services. In the simulation, the time stamp information for service exchange and friendship updating is recorded.

The first important factor that we evaluated after the simulation is latency. The latency factor represents the average delay of SD and service composition. We compared the average latency of conventional SIoT with the average latency of CSIoT. The conventional SIoT does not utilize the new mechanism for leveraging friendship and services. In addition, the conventional SIoT does not consider nonlinearity and uncertainty in relationships and concepts.

Figure 7 shows that in small populations, the conventional SIoT performs better than CSIoT. This is because CSIoT runs several queries for semantic reasoning and for leveraging friendship and services. In large populations, CSIoT outperforms the conventional SIoT in terms of latency. This is because CSIoT can find the smallest and most efficient paths in the network.

The second important factor for evaluating the CSIoT framework is the probability distribution in different path lengths. This factor represents the probability distribution of the minimum path length between a pair of

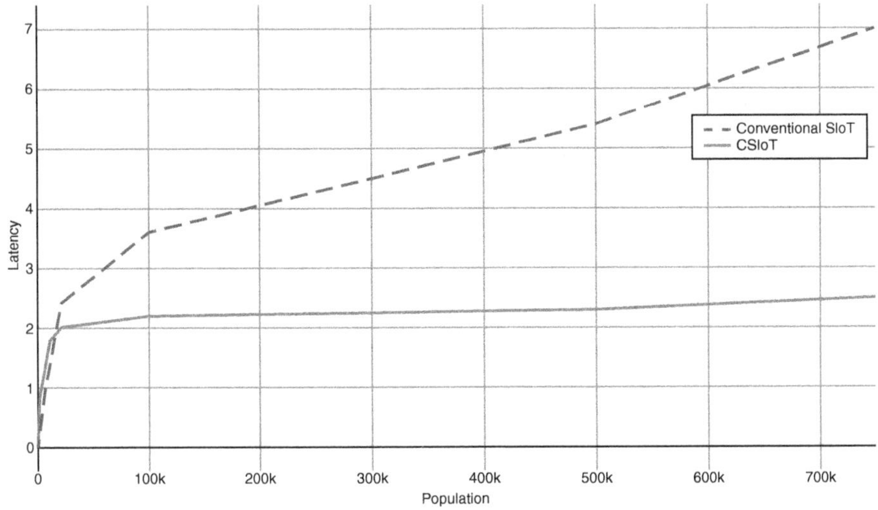

Fig. 7. Average latency distribution in different population sizes.

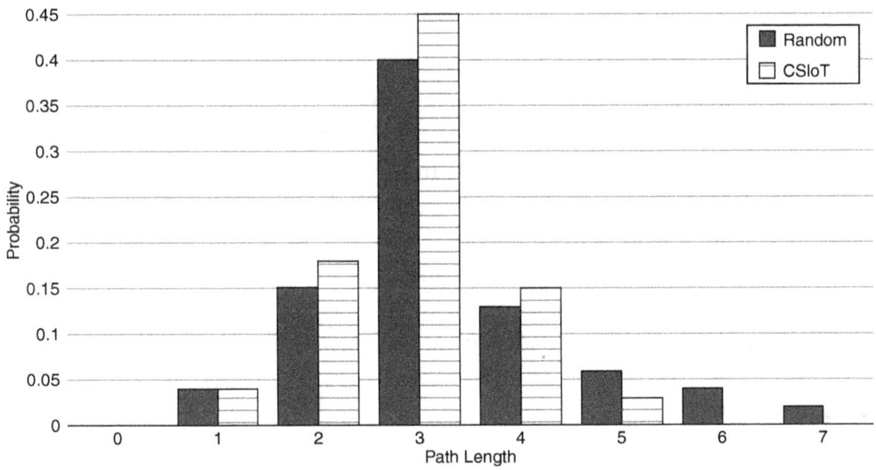

Fig. 8. Probability distribution in different path lengths.

randomly selected devices in CSIoT. Figure 8 shows that the network diameter is 6 and the average path length is 2.57.

We compared the probability distribution of a random IoT network and the probability distribution of CSIoT. The average path length for the random network is 3.45. In addition, the diameter of the random network

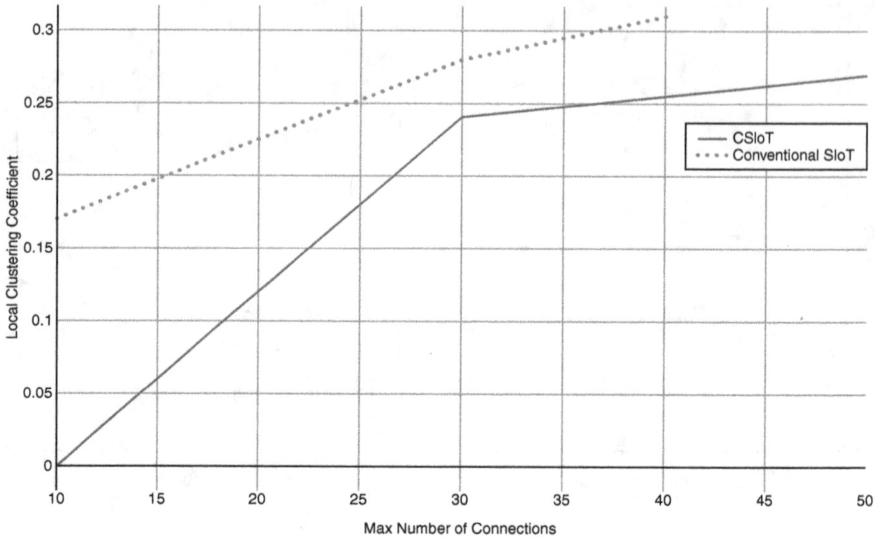

Fig. 9. Local clustering coefficient for different max number of connections.

is 9 and 2% of the devices are isolated. Figure 8 shows that CSIoT performs well in terms of average path length.

The last factor for evaluating the CSIoT framework is the local clustering coefficient for different max number of connections. This factor shows the network's navigability performance. Figure 9 shows that CSIoT performs very well and is effective in network navigability and managing the friendships and paths among them.

The evaluation results show that the CSIoT framework performs well in service management, friendship management, and network navigability. CSIoT can find the most efficient, shortest paths for SD and service acquisition.

7. Conclusion

IoT technology is growing very fast, and its growth is a transformative force across all modern organizations. According to the Business Insider, the IoT market is on pace to grow to over $2.4 trillion annually by 2027 (Newman, 2020). Technology advancement in IoT creates new opportunities and threats, and scientists are trying to explore and manage these new IoT challenges.

The growing number of connected smart devices enhances the complexity of IoT settings. This complexity can create new security and privacy concerns, and can also create new features that are useful for humans. Nowadays, researchers are investigating new models and future-generation frameworks for IoT. SIoT is one of the future-generation IoT frameworks that utilizes social networking concepts for defining the relationships and interactions between smart objects. SIoT can create new capabilities including object discovery functionalities, evaluation of trustworthiness of objects and the information provided by objects, network navigability, and deployment of value-added services.

One of the important factors in SIoT is the friendship management mechanism. There should be effective methods and criteria for defining the relationship between objects and leveraging friendships during the time when objects exchange information and services. The literature review shows that there is no effective method that uses a comprehensive view for friendship development and updating in SIoT settings.

This study proposes a new friendship management mechanism for SIoT settings. CSIoT utilizes a new friendship management model for continuously updating the friendships between devices. The results of simulation and evaluation of CSIoT show that leveraging friendships and services can improve the SIoT framework from different aspects. First, it enhances the SD and service composition in the SIoT setting. This means that devices can acquire appropriate services in a shorter time. Second, leveraging friendships and services can improve the network navigability in the SIoT network.

This study uses a fuzzy ontology for semantic reasoning and decision-making in the SIoT environment. The results show that CSIoT outperforms the conventional SIoT frameworks that have been proposed before.

In future work, we will investigate the performance of CSIoT in enhancing IoT privacy. We believe CSIoT can also improve the privacy in IoT settings by continuous friendship leveraging. Effective friendship updating can create useful trust criteria for smart IoT objects. Therefore, they can share information with different levels of privacy with friends with different levels of trust.

References

Aboud, F.E. and Mendelson, M.J. (1996). Determinants of friendship selection and quality: Developmental perspectives. In Bukowski, W.M., Newcomb, A.F., and Hartup, W.W. (eds.), *Cambridge Studies in Social and Emotional Development. The Company They Keep: Friendship in Childhood and Adolescence* (pp. 87–112). New York: Cambridge University Press.

Atzori, L., Antoniom I., and Morabito, G. (2011). Making thing socialize in the Internet — Does it help our lives? *ITU-T Kaleidoscope Academic Conference.*

Atzori, L., Antoniom I., and Morabito, G. (2014). From "smart objects" to "social objects": The next evolutionary step of the Internet of Things. *IEEE Communications Magazine*, January 2014, pp. 97–105.

Atzori, L., Antoniom, I., Morabito, G., and Nitti, M. (2012). The Social Internet of Things (SIoT) — When social networks meet the Internet of Things: Concept, architecture and network characterization. *Computer Networks*, 56(2012), 3594–3608.

Backstrom, L., Sun, E., and Marlow, C. (2010). Find me if you can: Improving geographical prediction with social and spatial proximity. *Proceedings of the 19th International Conference on World Wide Web*, April 26, 2010–30, 2010 Raleigh, USA, pp. 61–70.

Calegari, S. and Ciucci, D. (2007). Fuzzy ontology, fuzzy description logics and fuzzy-owl. *Applications of Fuzzy Sets Theory*, 4578, 118–126.

Clark, M. and Pataki, S. (1995). Interpersonal processes influencing attraction and relationships. In Tesser, A. (ed.), *Advanced Social Psychology* (pp. 283–331). St. Louis, MO: McGraw Hill.

De Klepper, M., Sleebos, E., van de Bunt, G., and Agneessens, F. (2010). Similarity in friendship networks: Selection or influence? The effect of constraining contexts and non-visible individual attributes. *Social Networks*, 32, 82–90. (Please see Section 3.1.2. Similarity.)

Fox, J., Warber, K.M., and Makstaller, D.C. (2013). The role of Facebook in romantic relationship development: An exploration of Knapp's relational stage model. *Journal of Social and Personal Relationships*, 30(6), 771–794.

Kandel, D.B. (1978). Homophily, selection, and socialization in adolescent friendships. *American Journal of Sociology*, 84(2), 427–436.

Kasnesis, P., Patrikakis, C.Z., Kogias, D., Toumanidis, L., and Venieris, I.S. (2017). Cognitive friendship and goal management for the social IoT. *Computers and Electrical Engineering*, 58, 412–428.

Knapp, M.L. (1978). *Social Intercourse: From Greeting to Goodbye*. Needham Heights, MA: Allyn & Bacon.

Karkouch, A., Mousannif, H., Al Moatassime, H., and Noel, T. (2016). Data quality in Internet of Things: A state-of-the-art survey. *Journal of Network and Computer Applications*, 73, 57–81.

Leider, S., Möbius, M.M., Rosenblat, T., and Do, Q.-A. (2009). Directed altruism and enforced reciprocity in social networks. *The Quarterly Journal of Economics*, 124(4), 1815–1851.

Middleton, P., Graham, C., Blackmore, D., Sharpington, K., Singh, H., Velosa, A., and Lheureux, B. (2021). *Forecast: IT services for IoT. Worldwide, 2019–2025*. Stamford, CN, USA: Gartner Research.

Morente-Molinera, J.A., Wikström, R., Herrera-Viedma, E., and Carlsson, C. (2016). A linguistic mobile decision support system based on fuzzy ontology to facilitate knowledge mobilization. *Decision Support Systems*, 81, 66–75.

Newman, P. (2020). The Internet of Things 2020: Here's what over 400 IoT decision-makers say about the future of enterprise connectivity and how IoT companies can use it to grow revenue. Business Insider.

Nitti, M., Atzori, L., and Cvijikj, I.P. (2015). Friendship selection in the Social Internet of Things: Challenges and possible strategies. *IEEE Internet of Things Journal*, 2(3), 240–247.

Ortiz, A.M., Hussein, D., Park, S., Han, S.N., and Crespi, N. (2014). The cluster between Internet of Things and social networks: Review and research challenges. *IEEE Internet of Things Journal*, 1(3), 206–215.

Pinquart, M. and Sörensen, S. (2000). Influences of socioeconomic status, social network, and competence on subjective well-being in later life: A meta-analysis. *Psychology and Aging*, 15(2), 187–224.

Rivera, M.T., Soderstrom, S.B., and Uzzi, B. (2010). Dynamics of dyads in social networks: Assortative, relational, and proximity mechanisms. *Annual Review of Sociology*, 36, 91–115.

Rose-Krasnor, L. (2006). The nature of social competence: A theoretical review. *Social Development*, 6(1), 111–135.

Schutte, J.G. and Light, J.M. (1978). The relative importance of proximity and status for friendship choices in social hierarchies. *Social Psychology*, 41, 260–264.

Selfhout, M., Burk, W., Branje, S., Denissen, J., Van Aken, M., and Meeus, W. (2010). Emerging late adolescent friendship networks and big five personality traits: A social network approach. *Journal of Personality*, 78(2), 509–538.

Sias, P.M. and Cahill, D.J. (1997). From coworkers to friends: The development of peer friendships in the workplace. *Western Journal of Communication*, 62, 273–299.

Wu, Q., Ding, G., Xu, Y., Feng, S., Du, Z., Wang, J., and Long, K. (2014). Cognitive Internet of Things: A new paradigm beyond connection. *IEEE Internet of Things Journal*, 1(2), 129–143.

https://doi.org/10.1142/9789811271984_0010

Chapter 10

No Fight. No Flight. Just Innovation! How the Most Pressing Need in Cybersecurity Today Could Propel the Development of Quantum Computing

Hector Santiago

Johns Hopkins University,
Baltimore, MD, USA
hsantia5@jh.edu

This work proffers that the biggest ongoing challenge currently facing cybersecurity professionals — namely ransomware — can be potentially mitigated by the expected benefits of quantum computing, a technology still in the nascent stages of demonstrating reliable and repeatable network defense support to broader commercial industries, particularly industries based in the United States. The author demonstrates that, counter to estimates of any public applications only appearing in the distant future, the commercial losses from ransomware — both incurred and expected — by US entities may be enough to justify the need for a concerted near-term "sprint" by US stakeholders to develop a quantum-based mitigation capability with all deliberate speed. The work highlights the competition among leaders in the quantum computing development space, the consequences to US national defense and business network's health of not having mitigatory quantum computing capabilities, and the global shifts in political and commercial influence which would likely result depending on which nation-state eventually establishes dominance in the quantum computing space. Scientific and economic challenges to the development of quantum computing capabilities in the current environment are also explored alongside benefits of investing at certain points along the innovation cycle of quantum computing technology.

1. Introduction

This work was written to address what the author believes is the most urgent application for a branch of computer science which still boasts most of its usefulness in the conceptual and theoretical spheres of knowledge. Continual breakthroughs and mastery of the science supporting quantum computing will provide stakeholders with both previously unimaginable near- and long-term positive opportunities. One would think that such opportunities would garner innumerable competitors willing to reallocate highly prized (and limited) resources for the chance at much greater returns, in terms of both financial wealth and security. Unfortunately, as the reader will learn, this is more perception than truth. It will be argued that what may prompt global "players" such as the United States to increase their focus on developments in the quantum computing space are not actually advantages to be gained but great, irrevocable losses in the spheres of wealth preservation, national security, and foreign policy influence which must be avoided at all costs.

Further, throughout this work, there are examples used to demonstrate activities and environments rooted in the financial and technology sectors, particularly those found in the United States and China, and to some extent in Russia. In no way do these choices lessen the potential value to the reader of the information aggregated or the thinking conveyed to argue points made. The author has worked diligently to ensure that lessons and views offered in this work, regardless of their origins, may serve the reader by being applied irrespective of the reader's particular global location and industry.

Lastly, although the work is rooted in the developments occurring in a highly technical scientific field, the ideas put forward are mainly those often found pondered at a strategic level of thinking and planning within organizations of all kinds. Therefore, the work should be useful to non-technical leadership and management, and not just to those readers who normally "reside" in the digital or quantum technology space.

2. A Dynamic Environment

The difficulty with forecasting is having a true understanding of the extent to which independent variables can overtake dependent variables upon which forecasted outcomes are based. In common parlance, it is hard to assess (exactly) when and how "big waves" will overtake and influence "smaller waves." However, approximating how and when these events will occur is where fortunes are lost and made. Regarding the formulation of any strategy and the management of organizational change, considerations for how to navigate today's global, dynamic environment to advance one's situation would surely include leveraging some of the following digital technologies: artificial intelligence (AI); the Internet of Things (IoT); cloud computing; distributed ledger technology (DLT); and big data storage, to name a few key fields. However, these may well be the "smaller waves," which act as notable and exciting enhancements or evolutions to standards of performance expected by broad users of information technologies. A "bigger wave," in this case, is arguably IT network defense. Such defenses are used by core IT network infrastructure through which all digital technologies interface and which are leveraged to provide all users ever-greater data confidentiality and integrity as data transacting continues to explode. Therefore, it stands that even a modest change in the heightening of the defensive postures of core networks would be highly impactful to all digital technologies relying upon this backbone. Enter quantum computing.

Before going any further, some context is required to ensure that key technical distinctions discussed throughout this work can be fully understood.

3. What Is a Quantum Computer?

According to a 2018 report by the *National Academies of Sciences, Engineering, and Medicine*, "A quantum computer utilizes the unusual characteristics of quantum mechanics — the non-intuitive behavior of very small particles — to perform computation, unlike current computers." This feature of the technology enables a quantum computer to span, and even exceed, the possible states of a classical computer and resultant calculations made by such machines (National Academies, 2018).

The key to quantum computing's power is what is known as a qubit, analogous to a bit in classical computers. However, bits work strictly on a binary system, meaning they can only be a value of either one or zero based on the presence or absence of electricity, light, or radio waves. Qubits, however, can be one, zero, or a linear combination of both values at the same time. This quantum behavior is known as superposition (IBM Quantum Composer (2), 2021; Narayanan, 2019). Furthermore, multiple qubits can also be "entangled," which means their quantum states can become linked together, regardless of the physical distance between each qubit (IBM Quantum Composer (1), 2021). Such a characteristic is important when needing to verify, in a different location than its final destination, that a value of a qubit remains unchanged during transmission. Another vital concept — although most challenging to fully internalize — is quantum interference, a seemingly impossible state where an individual particle such as a photon (a light particle) can cross its own trajectory and interfere with the direction of its [own] path (IBM Quantum Composer (2), 2021). This attribute is useful as it allows researchers to bias (or direct) the measurement of a qubit toward a desired state (or value). Superposition, entanglement, and (quantum) interference allow quantum computers to explore a vast set of possibilities using much greater amounts of data exponentially faster than today's classical computers (IBM Quantum Composer (1), 2021; IBM Quantum Composer (2), 2021; see also Savoie, 2021).

The remainder of this chapter promises not to be as conceptually complex as the reader learns about the potential cybersecurity applications derived from such a highly intricate field as quantum computing. These insights will be coupled with information on the "dance" done by players at the national and supra-national levels to effect advantageous outcomes — within geopolitical circles — using cyber- and quantum-related means.

4. The Most Pressing Need for Advancement in Quantum Computing

Potential applications being imagined for quantum computing include predicting fluctuations in stock markets, designing AI machines, and weather forecasting, with other applications to be named later in this work (CISOMAG, 2020). However, the focus of this work is one application in particular which could actually drive the race to construct the most dependable and error-free machines fueled by quantum computing processes. That application is reliable and repeatable quantum decryption — a foremost achievement to reach on the global stage. Such an innovation would tilt the scales of sovereign (nation-state) security, military confrontations in the cyber arena, and, most urgently, allow all victims of the exploding threat of ransomware to have a solution when — not if — these types of attacks occur.

A large body of literature touts US-based entities, including Google, Intel, IBM, Honeywell, and Microsoft, as the leading tech giants in this space. Such corporate entities already have tiny quantum computers that are continually and incrementally packed with more quantum bits to enhance their performance over time. Other (non-US) vendors with leadership stakes in this technology include Toshiba, NTT, D-Wave Solutions, and Alibaba Quantum Computing (CISOMAG, 2020). Some of the more reliable sources of literature espouse a view that, despite the determination demonstrated by all of these (and other) technology leaders, a completely robust quantum computer is unlikely to exist for another decade or more. This view can be well supported under what might otherwise be "normal" circumstances that surround innovation (i.e., business S-curves).[1] However, the author proffers that our current global circumstances are anything but normal. This view is based mainly on one ever-growing and unavoidable variable potentially affecting all information networking around the world. That variable is the unabated proliferation of ransomware. In the author's view, addressing this situation could drive the need to develop quantum computing decryption applications to the extent that doing so may push many other quantum computing-based applications to the fore quicker and much earlier than analysts of this particular technology sector are currently touting.

Traditional digital ciphers depend upon very complex mathematical formulas to convert data into encrypted messages for the sake of security during storage and transmission. A digital key (or two) is (are) used to encrypt and decrypt the data (Microsoft "Description," 2021).[2] However,

---

[1]The S-curve for business is a concept embodied as a logistic function which demonstrates the various growth phases of an enterprise. Initially, there is slow growth as early adopters try the product/service. Then, there is growing mass acceptance of the enterprise's offering. Lastly, a leveling off occurs as market saturation is reached (Future Business Tech, 2021).

[2]There are two basic techniques for encrypting information: symmetric encryption (also called secret key encryption) and asymmetric encryption (also called public key

a malicious cyber actor attempts to steal, modify, (re)encrypt, and ransom the previously protected information. The encryption key used (or a number of them used in a specific series) by the attacker is completely foreign to the victim enterprise. This situation limits the likelihood of that enterprise recovering the data using in-house methods. Regardless of the apparent futility, some victimized enterprises still have attempted to decrypt the data held hostage. These attempts leveraged processes using conventional computers, which (if successful, still) required a huge effort in processing power and an abundance of time. Moreover, great levels of assistance from the few entities with the necessary resources and intellectual capital to help were also required (Abrams, 2021; Filiz *et al.*, 2021).

Unfortunately, the time and effort required for such an endeavor are currently elements that work against a victim of a ransomware attack who, more times than not, is faced with the immediate need to access their very own data coupled with the knowledge that a return to access of their data — via the correct decryption key held by the malicious actor — is just one ransom payment away. In cases where healthcare facilities are targeted, for example, every second the administrators of a victimized network stall to find a solution to their dilemma could mean a higher likelihood of realizing (immediate or long-term) mortal outcomes among a patient population (Simpson, 2020; *HIPAA Journal*, 2021). Further, as the number of ransomware cases continues to explode year over year, the variety of victimized industries and organizations has also expanded with no evidence of the ransomware attacks abating, much less stopping.

At this point, a reader may presume one digital strategy for ensuring the health of an information network is to increase their defenses so that their network appears less appealing to attackers when compared to other networks. Perhaps transference of risk via cyber threat insurance is the key? Unfortunately, trends observed over time, especially against specific sectors such as the financial sector, do not demonstrate a positive correlation between the abundance of resources spent on network defense and

encryption). In symmetric encryption, the same secret key is used to encrypt and then decrypt all messages that use that key. In asymmetric encryption, there are two related keys: a key pair. A public key is made freely available to a sender of a file or message. A second, private key is kept secret so that only those authorized can decrypt the file or message sent (Microsoft "Description," 2021).

those well-resourced networks now being totally impervious to even older, known hacks. Further, anecdotally, cybersecurity professionals everywhere continue to wrestle with the open secret of "it's not a matter of if, but when you will get hit!"

5. The Destruction Left in Ransomware's Wake

The statistics demonstrating the trajectory and impacts of ransomware alone — outside of all other types of malicious information network compromise — are staggering. Outcomes collected from within the US finance and banking sector, for example, demonstrate the experiences of just one subset of victims from this crime and the costs incurred. According to ransomware trend analysis performed by the US Treasury's Financial Crimes Enforcement Network (FINCEN), published in October 2021, in the first six months of 2021 alone, ransomware-related Suspicious Activity Reports (SARs) worth approximately $590 million were recorded. This represented a 42% increase when compared to the total of $416 million for the entirety of 2020 [US (OCC), 2021].[3] Further, if that trend in the first half of 2021 continued, the transaction value for ransomware-related SARs expected for all of 2021 alone would have exceeded that of SARs filed over the previous 10 years combined (US Treasury, 2021).[4]

To those paying attention, the aforementioned milestones in record-setting ransoms — likely to be temporary — are the realization of trends which continue to paralyze all US-based stakeholders responsible for trying to mitigate the growing flurry of ransomware threats. Since 2016, over 4,000 ransomware attacks have happened daily in the United States (US Gov./How to Protect, n.d.). Given the ease with which a growing number of would-be malefactors could gain support from ransomware-as-a-service

[3]According to the US Office of the Comptroller of the Currency (OCC), as of April 1, 2013, under the Bank Secrecy Act of 1970, US financial institutions are required to assist US government agencies by reporting suspicious activity that might signal criminal activity, such as money laundering or cyber-based threats to networks [US (OCC), 2021].

[4]This trend potentially reflects the increasing overall prevalence of ransomware-related incidents as well as improved detection and reporting of incidents by covered financial institutions. Further, results may also be related to increased awareness of reporting obligations pertaining to ransomware and, subsequently, more of a willingness to report events [US Treasury (FINCEN), 2021].

(RaaS) vendors, the number of potential attacks is almost certain to grow, even if the impacts of these attempts might be minimal due to the lack of experience among those new recruits using the newly acquired tools (Vamosi, 2020). According to Russia-based cybersecurity firm Group-IB (2021), almost two-thirds of all ransomware attacks analyzed by the firm against US and non-US victims during 2020 came from criminal enterprises operating RaaS programs.

Arguably, there is no area that has been impacted by ransomware more than insurance companies, specifically those that offer cyber threat insurance. The impacts from such malicious and, unfortunately, highly lucrative activities have included thresholds exceeded in ransoms paid and damage wrought, which may prove continually to be surpassed quickly and often. For example, in 2021, the largest ransomware payout — at $40 million — was made by an insurance company to settle the CNA Financial ransomware attack, setting a world record at the time (Chang, B., 2021; Mehrotra and Turton, 2021). While coverage has remained available, insurers have scaled back ransomware-related offerings and have even withdrawn coverage completely for clients judged to have weak risk controls (Marsh McLennan, 2021). Regarding other shortcomings in needed coverage, according to cybersecurity firm Cybereason, in 2021, 42% of companies with cyber insurance policies in place indicated that insurance only covered a small part of damages resulting from a ransomware attack (Sobers, 2021).

6. The Broader Implications of Ransomware Outside of Financial Outcomes

Of course, both destructive and disruptive ends from ransomware have been felt in areas other than in the healthcare and financial sectors, which can often be found on the very top of lists of targeted industries (Beek *et al.*, 2021). The deleterious national security impacts, for example, from disruptive cyber activity such as ransomware — specifically against critical infrastructure within the United States — cannot be overstated. The perception is that relatively recent cyber events (i.e., the SolarWinds and Kaseya attacks) have had the effect of keeping the United States and other nation-state governments at bay regarding their responses to threatening situations on the world stage (i.e., the 2022 Russia–Ukraine Crisis)

(Jibilian and Canales, 2021; see also Roth *et al.*, 2021).[5,6] These likely concerns are justifiable, as no nation-state's leadership wants to appear to invite the defenseless victimization of their domestic critical infrastructure networks by highly disruptive cyberattacks, including ransomware. The ransomware attack of the US-based Colonial Pipeline in May 2021, for example, showed how embarrassingly vulnerable critical infrastructure within the US Homeland actually was to a cyberattack and is believed by the author to have acted as a major warning by Russia to North Atlantic Treaty Organization (NATO) countries, including the US.

7. The Threat of Ransomware as a Diplomatic Tool

On May 6–7, 2021, the US-based Colonial Pipeline was the target of a ransomware attack which was thought to be conducted by Russia-associated RaaS actors (Panettierri, 2021). The pipeline was responsible

[5]In early 2020, hackers secretly broke into Texas-based SolarWind's systems and added malicious code into the company's software system, which was used to manage other companies via software updates. Around March 2020, SolarWinds unwittingly sent out compromised software updates to its customers — including the US government — that allowed for use of backdoors to customers' information technology systems. Hackers then used these accesses to install even more malware that helped them spy on companies and organizations (Jibilian and Canales, 2021). A ransomware attack in July 2021 paralyzed as many as 1,500 organizations by compromising tech management software from a company called Kaseya. Knowledge of the compromise had set off a race among criminals looking for similar vulnerabilities. An affiliate of a top Russian-speaking ransomware gang known as REvil used two gaping flaws in software from Florida-based Kaseya to break into about 50 managed services providers (MSPs) that used Kaseya's products. Attacks multiplied before Kaseya could warn everyone, with hackers rapidly encrypting data and demanding ransoms of as much as $5 million per victim [US Cybersecurity (CISA), 2021 (c)].

[6]As of December 2021, Russia had forward-deployed hundreds of tanks, artillery, and short-range ballistic missiles from as far away as Siberia to within striking range of Ukraine's borders. Russia's goal was to secure legal guarantees that Ukraine would never join the North Atlantic Treaty Organization (NATO) or host NATO's missile strike systems. A 2015 peace deal established a line of demarcation and called on both sides to make concessions. Since then, low-level fighting has continued along the Russia–Ukraine border. Both sides had accused the other of violating the agreement, which observers said (at the time) was close to collapse (Roth *et al.*, 2021).

for approximately 40% of all gasoline and jet fuel distribution throughout the entire Eastern seaboard of the continental United States. Pipeline operations were reinstated in less than a week. Yet, the cascading effects were felt locally by Americans for extended periods of time as gas prices at service stations fluctuated greatly helping to temporarily destabilize local economies. These conditions created a sense among Americans that critical infrastructure within the United States could be attacked easily and compromised at any time (Greenberg, 2021; Panettierri, 2021).

Denials by Russian President Vladimir Putin regarding Russian state sponsorship of the malicious cyber actors did not diminish the view held by officials in the United States that Russia — or Eastern Europeans with strong ties to Russia — had influence over the event (Jasper, 2021). Supporting this view of Russian control over the actors was the observation that the Colonial attack occurred around the same time the RaaS actor who committed the attack — DarkSide — tried to recruit hackers on Russian language-based online fora. This active recruitment appeared coupled with the purposeful avoidance of targeting networks in former Soviet Union countries where these recruits were assumed to reside.

Discussions in Geneva, Switzerland, between US President Joe Biden and Putin about a month later, on June 16, saw Biden asking Putin to intervene in the activities of Russia-based malicious cyber actors. Less than a month after that discussion, Russian hackers allegedly compromised the network of the US Republican National Committee and a Russian cybercriminal network conducted a large-scale ransomware attack targeting approximately 1,500 businesses globally, some located in the United States (Bennett, 2021). It did not appear that the US president's appeal was successful.

During the remaining days of December 2021, tensions increased between Russia and the United States as Russia continued to amass troops along its own border against a US ally, Ukraine. At the time, Russia threatened military action in support of plans to annex eastern Ukrainian territories that allegedly wished to join Russia (Miller, 2021). One of the open concerns held by NATO partners, including the United States, was that Russia would not only occupy Ukrainian ground but also turn to hacking operations to put pressure on both NATO allies and Ukraine. Such concerns have long been validated by massive hacking efforts (attributed to Russia) against Ukraine over the past few years leading up to 2021. NATO partners, including the United States, have also been seriously plagued by ransomware activity (attributed to Russia-sponsored actors) over that time. Concerns were elevated even more recently when a highly destructive wiper malware attack (also attributed to Russia) struck dozens of Ukrainian government information systems in January 2022, making the data on affected systems irretrievable (Bracken, 2022).

8. The Need for a Decryption Countermeasure

Although President Biden openly made pushing back against Russian cyber aggression a priority, it is difficult to view any US actions against Russia as not being constrained by Russia's strategic dominance through its use of cyber operations.[7] Further, according to the head of the venerated IT company VMware in an interview with the US political publication *The Hill*, "Ever since the meeting in Geneva, [Russian actors] have dramatically, dramatically [sic] escalated systemic attacks against critical infrastructure and the technology community, period" (Miller, 2021). An objective viewer could come to the initial conclusion that Russia's in-house ransomware capabilities have rendered US tactics feckless in the cyber domain.

The relatively recent introduction of the universal LOG4J vulnerability (which will be explained later) has network defenders everywhere scrambling to patch everything they can as quickly as possible. This vulnerability will also likely be a consideration in calculating the potential reach of Russia-based cyber actors focused on countering — if not preempting — any US-based cyber or physical activity meant to disrupt Russian plans.

It is the author's view that it would be less advantageous to Russia-sponsored actors (or any actors, supported by any country) if victimized countries, including the United States, could credibly counter ransomware activities with dependable decryption processes done at blinding speeds through quantum computing (Shankland, 2021). Further, such an effective countermeasure could hinder aggressive governments from believing they could act unilaterally behind the threat of using cyber weapons such as ransomware. Governments which have assessed they would be victimized could move forward with the stewardship of their nations knowing that

[7]In game theory, strategic dominance occurs when one strategy is better than another strategy for one player, no matter how that player's opponents may play (Corporate Finance Institute, 2021).

critical infrastructure systems targeted by ransomware would not be permanently destroyed and only disrupted temporarily, all while allowing victimized networks' administrators the option to confidently deny ransom requests.

9. Drivers of Increased Ransomware Activity and the Inability to Operate in Such an Environment

Although ransomware is the component of a compromise which will eventually encrypt the data to be held ransom, entry onto a targeted system is another facet of a hack best executed by code or a process that no one knows exists: a zero-day vulnerability.[8]

The *MIT Technology Review* Zero-day Tracking Project stated that at least 87 zero-day exploits were found in 2021 alone — a large spike that was more than double the total amounts for 2020 (37) and 2019 (28), and which had exceeded observed zero-day vulnerabilities in any other year on record for the project (O'Neill, 2021). China-supported actors alone were suspected of committing nine of the exploits, according to cybersecurity firm Mandiant. The overarching zero-day trend explosion has no appearance of waning. According to participants of the *MIT Technology Review* project, it is easier than ever to buy zero-day exploits from the growing exploit industry. Once prohibitively expensive, high-end exploits are now more widely accessible to the layman via RaaS (Check Point, 2021; see also Group-IB, 2021; O'Neill, 2021). It must be remembered that every single unauthorized access method onto a victimized network increases the total number of potential compromises possible against a network geometrically, not arithmetically. This is the result of taking the total number of access methods available and multiplying that value times the number of all ransomware strains known; these values cannot simply be added together. Consequently, each new vulnerability discovered raises the total number of complete malicious processes available for use by a magnitude of one.

As alluded to earlier, a recent and notable zero-day exploit labeled LOG4J/LOG4Shell — high-severity vulnerability enabling attackers to

[8]A zero-day vulnerability is, at its core, a flaw. It is an unknown exploit in the wild that exposes a vulnerability in software or hardware and can create complicated problems well before anyone realizes something is wrong (FireEye, 2022).

run any code and access all data on a system — is likely to have long-term impacts on the integrity of and confidence in information networks everywhere (Crowley, 2021). The speed with which the zero-day was adopted and evolved by malicious cyber actors, including those known to be supported by nation-states, prompted one notable cybersecurity firm to call the event "a true cyber-pandemic" (Lakshmanan, 2021). Efforts by the US government, in particular, to address the LOG4J zero-day exploit underscored the urgency of building software securely from the start, as announced by the US Cybersecurity and Infrastructure Security Agency (CISA) on December 11, 2021 [US Cybersecurity (CISA), 2021 (a), 2021 (b)].[9] Before this announcement, a more widespread use of a Software Bill of Materials (SBOM) was directed by US President Biden in his Executive Order issued in May 2021 (Temple-Raston, 2021).[10,11] However, these best practices (and other measures) would only assist information network owners and defenders in the helpful step of knowing exactly what was in their software, and where entry vectors onto improperly defended networks could be located, while still not actively presenting a direct counter or mitigation (i.e., dependable decryption) to ransomware itself (US White House, 2021).[12]

Of all the possible access methods malicious actors have chosen to use to compromise a targeted network, supply chain vulnerabilities (or risks from third-party operations) have dominated the attention of IT network defenders. Stakeholders in this space continually attempt to serve end customers while trying to assess susceptibility to cyberattack via every partner with whom they are integrated. Such an environment was punctuated in early 2021 by public announcements of the SolarWinds attack, where both

[9]The US Cybersecurity and Infrastructure Security Agency (CISA) leads the national effort to understand, manage, and reduce risk to [US] cyber and physical infrastructure [US Cybersecurity (CISA), 2021 (b)].

[10]A Software Bill of Materials (SBOM) is an inventory of all the code used within a software application which would provide end users with the transparency they require to know if their products rely on vulnerable software libraries [US National Telecommunications (NTIA), 2021].

[11]Executive Order (EO) 14028 on Improving the Nation's Cybersecurity, issued May 12, 2021.

[12]Broad cybersecurity guidance issued by the White House, on October 13, 2021, focused on collaboration between allied nation-states to disrupt ransomware infrastructures (US White House, 2021).

the scale and scope of impacts to the US government and US commercial entities prompted the US Executive Branch to mandate sweeping changes to then-existing US software supply chain protocols and guidelines (Jibilian and Canales, 2021; Temple-Raston, 2021). The US Executive Branch also made open claims that the attack had nation-state sponsorship, namely, from Russia. While recovering from the Solarwinds attack, the Kaseya attack — announced in July 2021 — demonstrated continued determination by Russia-based ransomware actors (i.e., REvil). Hundreds of organizations worldwide had their operations disrupted due to having their managed service providers (MSPs) victimized [US Cybersecurity (CISA), 2021 (c)]. These manmade, logic-based disruptions to information network operations likely had been exacerbated by the knock-on effects of isolation and workflow protocols used to assuage the COVID-19 global pandemic. One of the most acute of these unintended outcomes was rising unemployment and underemployment among a tech-savvy (US, and likely global) citizenry potentially susceptible to insider threat recruitment after enviously watching ransomware actors continually succeed [Barth, 2021; see also US Cybersecurity (CISA), 2021 (d); US Bureau (BLS), 2021].[13]

Collectively, these threats and vulnerabilities, in their current or some other evolved form, are all expected to continue well beyond 2022. Given the uncertainty addressed earlier regarding backstops (like cyber insurance) which may no longer offer sufficient levels of risk transference, protection, or resilience needed in the face of exploding ransomware attacks, every single internet-facing enterprise is confronted with the prospect of engaging with a catastrophic ransomware attack from which they cannot recover. If only a technology existed which could turn such an existential event into a minor inconvenience and inconsequential disruption.

[13]In 2020, the Office of the Comptroller of the Currency (OCC), Federal Reserve Board (FRB), and Federal Deposit Insurance Corporation (FDIC) released the guidance document "Sound Practices to Strengthen Operational Resilience," which sought to provide stakeholders with ways to strengthen enterprise resiliency against both internal and external risks which would otherwise lead to broader systemic disorder. This seminal guidance document successfully aligned with the joint Cybersecurity and Infrastructure Security Agency (CISA)–National Institute for Standards and Technology (NIST) publication "Defending Against Software Supply Chain Attacks," which was made publicly available 6 months later, in April 2021, in response to the SolarWinds attack [US Cybersecurity (CISA), 2021 (d); US (OCC), 2020].

It is inconceivable that any type of security strategy — using evolved versions of current, classical technologies — would be able to provide any protracted level of positive return on investment (RoI) against the aforementioned threats, although vendors of short-term solutions will surely continue to find the space lucrative. The amounts being spent on cyber defenses — at least in the United States — have only ballooned and will continue to do so, all while proposed defensive measures appear to be penetrated in less time than expected and as cybersecurity professionals and tools take longer to actually detect a breach (Braue, 2021; see also Savoie, 2021; Statista, 2022).

10. Challenges to and Costs of Implementing Quantum Infrastructure

According to the US Government Accountability Office (GAO) in an October 2021 report, quantum networks will not be able to exist in isolation from classical networks, but will rely on them for tasks such as exchanging control information and the coordination of network operations. To support the development of quantum technology, the existing (classical) communications infrastructure will need to be upgraded or maybe even replaced entirely. Such infrastructure enhancements would likely require a new quantum-updated network stack with multiple hardware layers. This integration would include one layer for creating entanglement between quantum nodes and one for transporting qubits in coexistence with classical networks (US (GAO), 2021).[14]

Current global competitors in the space — including nations, companies, and academics — have demonstrated experimental, noisy intermediate-scale quantum computers designed to answer specific demonstration questions faster than a classical computer. The GAO report highlights that

[14] One logical expansion of the quantum network is a quantum internet. A quantum internet is a concept where quantum communications platforms connect many quantum devices — such as quantum computers — globally. A quantum internet could fully integrate classical and quantum networking technologies, as described previously. Such technologies would include quantum error correction, quantum repeaters, transducers, and memories — devices or systems that could store a quantum state for long periods of time [US (GAO), 2021]. It must be emphasized that as likely as it is that these innovations will eventually occur, the world must remain patient for this level of scientific breakthroughs, significant hardware improvements, and cost-effective applications to be realized.

a full-scale quantum computer, which is both scalable and dependable, is many years away. Dependability is defined here as free of "noise" and high in error correction (a.k.a. fault tolerance). The next major step — after achieving some semblance of a repeatable and dependable process — would likely be full-scale quantum computers, which would mitigate any system noise, including unintended qubit degradation or environmental interactions, and which could scale on demand in an environment that could hold thousands of logical qubits [US (GAO), 2021].

As could be expected in the nascent stages of development of a highly complex technology, costs to develop quantum communications technologies are very uncertain. According to one expert, one of the biggest quantum communications technology development cost drivers is the cost of fabricating quantum components, as there is no dedicated foundry that supports scalable quantum component development at this time. City-sized prototype networks could be developed within 10 years at a cost of $50 to $100 million, according to US Department of Energy laboratory officials. Further, systems extending beyond a 100-mile radius could also be possible in a decade [US (GAO), 2021]. One enterprise conceived plans to build a prototype one-million physical qubit quantum computer by 2030. However, the plan would require a $2 billion to $3 billion investment and 1,000 doctoral-level scientists and engineers.

However, early for-profit investment into such projects would likely cement an early stakeholder into the group of "first movers," who would continue to benefit from subsequent market branch-offs that were unthinkable when initial applications of the technologies were first made available to potential customers. Early investment or adoption may also allow winnings to be applied to other developments as they are discovered in nascent stages (prior to commercialization), thus acting as a force multiplier to build wealth and enterprise stability over time.

11. Determination Demonstrated by Major Stakeholders to Advance Quantum Computing

The United States continues to make public proclamations of an unyielding focus on the development of emerging and semi-established technologies which will be vital for the sake of being competitive in future markets and arenas. However, observations of recent relevant activity would paint a different picture. For example, the US government's adoption of Internet Protocol version 6 (IPv6) technology needed to ensure the effective and efficient use of internetworking addressing schemes — the basis of the entire internet — has been questionable throughout a number of recent US presidential administrations. It could be argued that this situation is particularly unnerving as Internet Protocol version 4 (IPv4) was developed in 1983 and ran out of readily available addresses in 2015. This "exhaustion" of IPv4 addresses necessitated action by nation-states to adopt IPv6 as to hinder disruptions to the health of a nation's own networks, as well as to the internet as a whole (Nyczepir, 2020). However, the US record for progressing toward its planned, complete transition to IPv6 has been dismal to say the least.

In August 2005, a memorandum from the US Office of Management and Budget required US agencies to enable IPv6 on their backbone networks by June 2008 (EOP/OMB, 2005, 2021).[15,16] A second memo, issued in September 2010, required agencies to upgrade servers, and web and email services, to IPv6 by the end of fiscal year 2012 (EOP/OMB, 2010).[17] Client applications communicating with the public internet and their supporting networks were also all scheduled for transition by fiscal year 2014 (Nyczepir, 2020). The US government missed every single deadline. The Biden administration has pushed new, seemingly lofty goals for the full transition to this necessary adoption, staggered by rates of completion until 2025.[18] In no area of this most recent US Office of Management and Budget (OMB) memorandum are the variables of seemingly untenable global supply chain disruptions and the constantly changing guidance on lockdowns due to the COVID-19 pandemic addressed by the US government as challenges to achieving these near-term goals (EOP/OMB, 2020).

---

[15]US Office of Management and Budget (OMB) Memorandum for the Chief Information Officers: Transition Planning for Internet Protocol Version 6 (IPv6); issued August 2, 2005.

[16]OMB serves the President of the United States in overseeing the implementation of his or her vision across the Executive Branch. OMB's mission is to assist the President in meeting policy, budget, management, and regulatory objectives and to fulfill the agency's statutory responsibilities (EOP/OMB, 2021).

[17]OMB Memorandum for the Chief Information Officers of Executive Departments and Agencies: Transition to IPv6; issued September 28, 2010.

[18]OMB Memorandum (M-21-07) for Heads of Executive Departments and Agencies: Completing the Transition to Internet Protocol Version 6 (1Pv6); issued November 19, 2020.

Although it was not the author's intent to disparage any enterprise (US-based or otherwise) working on technologies which could bring the standard of living up for everyone on the planet, it remains very difficult to see how a competitor such as the United States will achieve dominance in this "long race" as the country depends solely on commercial interests to drive "native" entities to push further than previously thought possible in the quantum computing space. Moreover, the US record for supporting recent efforts of technological advancement (like IPv6) appears indecisive at best, prompting the following open-ended question: What is it that allows US leadership to believe the United States could ever keep up with, much less gain supremacy over, competitors in the quantum space such as China? The answer certainly cannot be derived from observed budget allocations made by both countries toward achieving progress in this scientific field.

The failed bipartisan US bill — Quantum User Expansion for Science & Technology (QUEST) Act — would have directed $340 million over a 5-year time period to US-based, quantum-related research and development (R&D) helping to forge those ties between US industry and government likely to propel US-based achievements in this scientific space much further and faster than could otherwise have occurred (Taylor and Bahrami, 2022). It is not known whether the bill will be reintroduced or if any other attempt by Congress at making a substantial allocation to quantum R&D will occur (Guterl, 2020).[19] In contrast, it was reported in May 2021 that China had dedicated $10 billion to quantum R&D, including the continued building of a laboratory facility solely for quantum studies (Goled, 2021). It was at this Chinese laboratory that the Jiuzhang 2 (113-qubit) — an advancement over China's Zuchongzhi 2 (66-qubit) — was developed (Chang, Y., 2021; Choi, 2021). As the reader will discover, there are enterprises and entities (e.g., both nation-states and commercial companies) who are players in "the game." However, there are already indicators as to which players are simply representing respectable research efforts in the space and which ones are sacrificing major resources in the present, playing unapologetically to win.

[19] Since 2020, numerous news outlets announced the budgeting of about $1 billion by the US government — over a number of years — toward the development of quantum computing. However, it is unknown whether the related appropriations resulting in the dissemination of these funds to affected agencies has actually occurred (Goled, 2021; Guterl, 2020).

12. Leaders in the Quantum Computing Space and Achievements Made (So Far)

In any industry, there is always a leader. With regard to quantum computing, as of February 2022, the leader would appear to be IBM, on behalf of the United States. However, some sector analysts believe the eventual "prize" will go to China-based enterprises (Chen, 2021; Irving, 2021). There is strong evidence to support this forecast, although, at this time, the outcome is by no means definitive.

In October 2021, China announced the creation of Zuchongzhi 2, a supercomputer that was 1 million times more powerful than US-based Google's Sycamore, its nearest competitor on the planet, which set a performance record in 2019 (Chen, 2021; Garisto, 2021).[20,21] A supplement to that announcement was the creation of Jiuzhang 2, another China-based quantum computer, with a narrower field of applications but which could reach a speed of 100 sextillion (one followed by 23 zeroes) times faster than the largest conventional computer systems in the world (Chen, 2021). Unfortunately for China, these machines were neither durable nor dependable enough to use for greater than very short periods of time and only on highly specific tasks. One of the country's leading researchers, Pan

---

[20] Practical applications for the Zuchongzhi 2 include predicting the valuations of securities such as stocks, calculating deformities and mutations in genes, the formation of new materials, and even air flows in hypersonic flight at Mach 5 and higher. The limits of the machine range of applications, at this time, are the result of the current model used for making its calculation known as a random walk, based on the possible movements of pieces on a chess board. According to a leading Chinese scientist working on the project, Lu Chaoyang, Jiuzhang 2 can perform a task known as boson sampling. This task simulates the activity of light particles as they pass through a maze of crystals and mirrors. According to Lu, some studies have suggested that boson sampling could have some applications in cryptography (Choi, 2021).

[21] The Google scientist who led the team that created Sycamore, Dr. John Martinis, claimed to be very excited about the Chinese achievement as it appeared to be the first time any other party reproduced (and confirmed) the successful results of Sycamore's 2019 methodology and performance achievement (Garisto, 2021). In 2019, Google argued that it displayed quantum primacy with its 53-qubit Sycamore processor, executing a calculation in 200 seconds that the company estimated would take Summit, the world's most powerful supercomputer at that time, 10,000 years. However, researchers at IBM later called that quantum advantage claim into question, arguing that with better classical algorithms, Summit could readily solve that problem in 2.5 days (Choi, 2021).

Jianwei, has gone so far as to declare the next major milestone being quantum error correction, but only after a four- or five-year period of focused research (Chen, 2021; Q-CTRL, 2022).[22] This statement would seem modest as the first-generation Jiuzhang demonstrated quantum advantage in 2020, conducting a certain calculation in a few minutes that would have taken a conventional supercomputer 2.5 billion years to execute (Irving, 2021).

In November 2021, just one month after China's announcement of Jiuzhang 2's achievement, US-based IBM announced what it deemed to be the world's most powerful quantum processor, the Eagle. Boasting 127 qubits, the Eagle appeared to take the mantle as the most powerful quantum processor in the world, far surpassing China's 113-qubit Jiuzhang 2, Google's 72-qubit Bristlecone, and IBM's own 65-qubit Hummingbird processor. According to IBM, "... recreating one of the Eagle's [quantum] states on a regular computer would require more classical bits than there are total atoms in every single person on Earth" (Irving, 2021). Eagle is now available on the IBM Cloud to some members of the IBM Quantum Network, and such an achievement appears to be just the beginning for the organization. The company has already outlined its roadmap for future quantum processors. The company's plans included releasing the 433-qubit IBM Quantum Osprey in 2022, followed by the Quantum Condor in 2023, which is expected to use an astounding 1,121 qubits (Irving, 2021).

Critics of researchers who would tout their own short-term achievements claim that applications for the technology currently remain limited for civilian uses, and that it may take at least a decade to realize the full benefits and healthy profits. However, this has not stopped the Chinese military from making advances with the technology (Chen, 2021). According to open-source information, the Chinese military currently uses quantum technology for ultra-secure communications, radar that can reportedly detect stealth aircraft, and navigation for nuclear submarines. One Canadian scholar in the field of quantum computing wrote in an online scientific journal that the performance of these China-innovated machines suggests the achievement of quantum primacy, or the point where it is demonstrated that a quantum computer can outperform the best

[22]Quantum error correction (QEC) is an algorithm known to identify and fix errors in quantum computers (Q-CTRL, 2022).

possible conventional computer (Chen, 2021; Sanders, 2021).[23] This would not be surprising given the country's observed pace of innovation. In 2016, China launched the world's first quantum satellite, and then in 2019, deployed the world's largest land-based quantum communications network. In September 2021, work started on the country's first industrial park geared specifically to quantum computing technology in Hefei, the capital city of Anhui Province (Chen, 2021).

There should be little doubt that despite continuous jockeying for the lead position by determined organizations, the race for a reliable quantum computing capability will be decided over the long term by the competitor willing to dedicate and sacrifice the most to the cause while innovating on as many fronts as possible.

13. The Race to Set Global Standards and What It Means for Quantum Computing

Through previous sections of this work, the reader has been exposed to the impetus for a victimized stakeholder to act (i.e., ransomware proliferation), some of the areas of sovereign management at stake (i.e., commercial and diplomatic interests, as well as those areas connected to security), and the costs and efforts involved in making a credible push into quantum computing R&D. However, there is one more aspect of competition in this space which, if overlooked, would cede control of quantum-based infrastructure to very few who could dictate how others leverage the technology. That arena is the setting of global telecommunications standards in information technologies.

[23] In 2017, Chinese scientists were able to beam photons from the country's Micius satellite to conduct the world's first quantum-secured video call, which is when some experts declared China had taken the lead position in quantum communications development in the world. Arguably, this lead has been extended to quantum computing and other applications. In one study published by the University of Science and Technology of China (USTC), researchers reliably transmitted a single photon over 300 kilometers of fiber — well over 100 times farther than previous attempts. In another study, researchers improved their quantum computer by the number of qubits — the basic unit of quantum computing — from 76 to 113, demonstrating a marked upgrade to the machine's quantum advantage, or how much faster it is at a single task than conventional computers. In spite of the achievement, Chinese physicist Lu Chaoyang is quick to claim that "the current state of the art is that no experiments have demonstrated quantum advantage for practical tasks yet" (Garisto, 2021).

Chinese President Xi Jinping's repeated claims regarding his goal of making China a "cyber great power" should not be underestimated by Western powers, especially since his overarching design for doing so is fixed on enabling Chinese indigenous technology to "catch up and surpass" the West's technologies. However, it would appear the twofold strategy driving Xi's vision includes the shaping of international technology standards as well as growing native Chinese technological capability (Russel and Berger, 2021). Ostensibly, China has not hidden its deliberate push to gain influence in the international technical standards-setting bodies (also known as standards developing organizations, or SDOs), where industry and technical experts can participate freely. However, over time, the country has worked diligently to place Chinese nationals in key leadership positions of these SDOs to chair important technical committees and working groups, and to get Chinese companies to vote as a bloc on proposals that originated in China (Russel and Berger, 2021).

Processes developed for negotiating and approving technical standards were primarily the products of historical leaders in technology: the US and Europe. For the Chinese government, however, the dictating of technical standards is and will be critical to the country's national strategy to promote international norms that favor Beijing's interests. Chinese industry operates in SDOs in a manner which aligns with progress of nationally defined objectives: goals which are of both commercial and strategic importance, such as Beijing's concept of "cyber-sovereignty." This desired end state promotes the creation of national boundaries in cyberspace that allow total control over the free flow of information (Russel and Berger, 2021).

One other avenue China is leveraging to ensure its position as the global standards-setting lead in critical technologies is through its "Digital Silk Road" initiative, which allows the country to set de facto standards from the ground up through the export of its technologies. "Path dependency," or locking in a customer base by making it difficult and expensive to switch to an alternative product with different specifications, is also a tactic used by China, which was actually a tactic first seen among Western companies. The "bundling" of technologies is another tactic, where emerging technologies that have few standards associated with them during their introduction into a market can be provided with other "mainstream" technologies with which they have already been integrated. China may then demonstrate widespread adoption of its technologies as indicators of a high-quality standard. This situation bolsters Chinese companies' case in international standards negotiations (Russel and Berger, 2021). The country has gone so far as to sign agreements with Digital Silk Road partners for the harmonization of standards, funding of local standards certification centers, and the translating of Chinese-developed standards into local languages.

China does not appear to be holding back on fulfilling the leadership's strategic plans or intentions. According to a mid-2020 report from the US television news agency CNBC, China was set to release an ambitious 15-year plan for setting global standards for the next generation of global technologies (Kharpal, 2020). Again, the country's designs have never been hidden and, as of this writing, continue to be explicit. This plan, "China Standards 2035," was set to be released in 2020 after two years of planning, focusing on the standards for those technologies that are seen as defining the next decade (assumed to be 2025–2035) and beyond (Kharpal, 2020).

What could compel an objective observer to believe that China has the resolve to accomplish this "standards" goal is the documented success of its previous goal labeled "Made in China 2025." Some may argue that the country of China is already (in 2023) the world's manufacturing basket, through which innumerable supply chains have some leg of a product's or service's journey to a final customer anywhere (Kapadia, 2021). This view has also been reinforced through the unfortunate circumstance of global lockdowns as a response to the COVID-19 pandemic, with many needed products being out of reach because they are manufactured mainly in China and transport from the country is fraught with complexity (Kharpal, 2020).

Within a section of the 2035 plan for standards, there is a focus on developing standards for such technologies as IoT, cloud computing, big data, 5G, and artificial intelligence (AI). These technologies may all be considered as crucial future technologies that could underpin critical infrastructure throughout the world (Kharpal, 2020). Quantum Information (i.e., quantum computing) was listed in China's most recent five-year plan (the 14th of such plans) as one of the seven technological fields where the country had to achieve dominance to ensure its national security (Kaja *et al.*, 2021).[24] It is likely that setting standards in the field

[24]China's five-year plans are the centerpiece of the Chinese system of industrial planning and policy. On March 13, 2021, China's National People's Congress (NPC) approved the outline of the country's 14th Five-Year Plan, covering the period of 2021–2025 (Kaja *et al.*, 2021).

of quantum computing is also included within the spirit of the country's 2035 standards campaign. It is difficult to see how such an established track record, unyielding focus, and willingness to continually reorganize entire governmental bodies (and associated budgets) can be outpaced over the long term by competitors composed of a handful of commercial entities incented by simple profit-making.

The author believes it can be argued successfully that China's already substantial and growing status as a global leader in various technologies should allow the monolith to play an expansive role in shaping those fields where these technologies are applied. Competition often depends on meeting standards (if not exceeding them to win customer loyalty). Consequently, it would appear an understatement to say that perhaps other (e.g., Western) entities that want to remain competitive should partake more aggressively in how standards are engineered and decided, especially if national security, commercial interests, and civil rights implications are involved and are thought truly to be at risk (Russel and Berger, 2021).

14. Conclusion

Given the views and supporting evidence provided in this work, right now, those pondering how they would invest the limited resources of an organization for both security (i.e., financial and operational) in future downturns as well as long-term gains — via market creation and expansion — may not have to think long about where to allocate those resources and with whom they would partner. However, this view falsely presupposes that a notoriously dynamic environment such as the quantum computing space — where science, technology, national security, cybersecurity, and commercialization all intertwine — had become, and then remained, static. If for no other reason, the growing threats from malicious cyber activity against nation-states' critical infrastructure dictate continuous vigilance on the part of those protecting civil harmony in their respective societies. This vigilance prompts adaptation through innovative responses, which themselves change the environment.

With the continually exploding threat of ransomware gripping infrastructure and business sectors in countries around the world, technological advances like IoT and AI that were innovated to heighten standards of living simply become an expansion of a highly vulnerable attack surface.

In some areas like the United States and other Western countries, these advancements may be seen more by adversaries as pressure points to be used to exert disproportionate influence over strategic competitors in ways otherwise out of reach. That said, the global citizenry's desire for services, content, and goods that are offered by businesses using ever-more complex applications of technology has not waned. Could an evolution in the type of infrastructure used to make these connections between stakeholders — at the same time — also hold the key to securing the information networks leveraged? It appears likely.

The more important question discussed in this work is whether the reciprocal is true: Can the need for securing vital nation-state assets — namely, the critical infrastructure victimized by relentless ransomware attacks — cause the revolution in technological achievement urgently needed in many other areas of telecommunications? In the author's view, it can, with enough impetus and time. The problem: We are all quickly catching up to the future! The hard reality is that true competitors — in any race — know that it is futile to blame obstacles for getting in their way, and simply do what is needed to prepare themselves for the unexpected and then simply endure. As demonstrated in this work, some competitors have done so while others have not. Consequently, those who are more focused will undoubtedly get to dictate rules governing the use of applied technologies to all others. In such a situation, one can only hope that their "champion" is the one who wins the race.

For those not as concerned with "the race" but more with the points of entry where opportunity may lie, it is important to be cognizant of where those entry points are along the S-curve of innovation, especially when coupled with the amount of time a stakeholder is willing to wait for developments before they are commercially offered. In such an investment, the timing, amounts ventured, and on whom the "wager" is made are entirely situational, with earlier investments translating into higher risk but also higher potential payouts. In contrast, those fixated on the science and requiring the immediate application of any research findings, first-mover advantage in semi-tested technologies (e.g., military applications), or the need to integrate findings incrementally (e.g., testing of telecommunications components locally to be scaled up over time), will find that there really is no choice but the earliest investment possible. Add global competitors bent on dictating technology standards for purposes of pure national interest, and achievements that would otherwise be celebrated as advancements must now be hurried just to be preemptive.

If these variables are not enough for a victim-nation in crisis to find focus, then perhaps it may take a "Sputnik Moment," harkening back to US fears of a then-Soviet Union which could launch the first satellite into space and have it orbit the Earth repeatedly as though claiming it. It is unclear, at this time, what that moment would look like given the complex natures of both quantum computing and human psychology. However, what is clear is that such a devastatingly shocking moment may simply occur with little fanfare, when a small group of scientists in a nondescript laboratory make a discovery that no one previously thought was possible. At that point, every physics textbook in the world must be rewritten. At that point, runners-up in the quantum computing race will experience a swell of regret for not having pushed harder and persevered when they knew better. At that point, everyone having their technology standards — and possibly their liberties — dictated to them will be haunted by the prophetic words of aeronautical engineer and famed science fiction author Robert A. Heinlein: "Everything is theoretically impossible, until it is done."

References

Abrams, L. (2021). BlackMatter ransomware victims quietly helped using secret decryptor. *Bleeping Computer*. https://www.bleepingcomputer.com/news/security/blackmatter-ransomware-victims-quietly-helped-using-secret-decryptor/ (Accessed Nov 28, 2021).

Barth, B. (2021). Are cybercriminals actively recruiting your employees to attack you with ransomware? *SC Magazine*. https://www.scmagazine.com/analysis/insider-threat/are-cybercriminals-actively-recruiting-your-employees-to-attack-you-with-ransomware (Accessed Dec 4, 2021).

Beek, C., Dolezal, A., Fokker, J., Gaffney, M., Holden, T., Hux, T., Laulheret, P., McKee, D., Munson, L., Palm, C., Polzer, T., Povolny, S., Samani, R., Solanki, P., and Velasco, L. (2021). Advanced Threat Research Report. *McAfee*, October 2021. https://www.mcafee.com/enterprise/en-us/lp/threats-reports/oct-2021.html (Accessed Dec 8, 2021).

Bennett, B. (2021). Biden administration says talks with Russia on cyber attacks are progressing. Privately, staffers are skeptical. *Time*. https://time.com/6078997/biden-cyber-attacks-putin/ (Accessed Nov 9, 2021).

Bracken, B. (2022). Destructive wiper targeting Ukraine aimed at eroding trust, experts say. *Threat Post*. https://threatpost.com/destructive-wiper-ukraine/177768/ (Accessed Jan 23, 2022).

Braue, D. (2021). Global cybersecurity spending to exceed $1.75 trillion from 2021–2025. *Cybercrime Magazine.* https://cybersecurityventures.com/cyber security-spending-2021-2025/#:~:text=The%20imperative%20to%20protect %20increasingly,2025%2C%20according%20to%20Cybersecurity%20 Ventures (Accessed Oct 28, 2021).

Chang, B. (2021). One of the biggest US insurance companies reportedly paid hackers $40 million ransom after a cyberattack. *Business Insider.* https://www.businessinsider.com/cna-financial-hackers-40-million-ransom-cyberattack-2021-5 (Accessed Dec 22, 2021).

Chang, Y. (2021). Quantum wars. *CKNSG.* https://english.ckgsb.edu.cn/knowledges/quantum-wars/ (Accessed Dec 10, 2021).

Check Point (2021). The ransomware as-a-service (RaaS) economy. https://www.checkpoint.com/cyber-hub/threat-prevention/ransomware/ransomware-as-a-service-raas/ (Accessed Dec 3, 2021).

Chen, S. (2021). China launches world's fastest programmable quantum computers. *South China Morning Post.* https://www.scmp.com/news/china/science/article/3153727/china-launches-worlds-fastest-programmable-quantum-computers (Accessed Nov 9, 2021).

Choi, C. Q. (2021). Two of world's biggest quantum computers made in China quantum: Computers Zuchongzi and Jiuzhang 2.0 may both display "quantum primacy" over classical computers. *IEEE Spectrum.* https://spectrum.ieee.org/quantum-computing-china (Accessed Dec 20, 2021).

CISOMAG (2020). Quantum computing: Threat to cybersecurity? *CISOMAG.* https://cisomag.eccouncil.org/quantum-computing/ (Accessed Dec 20, 2021).

Corporate Finance Institute (2021). What is dominant strategy? https://corporate financeinstitute.com/resources/knowledge/other/dominant-strategy/ (Accessed Dec 4, 2021).

Crowley, D. (2021). How Log4j vulnerability could impact you. *Security Intelligence.* https://securityintelligence.com/posts/apache-log4j-zero-day-vulnerability-update/ (Accessed Dec 22, 2021).

Filiz, B., Arief, B., Cetin, O., and Hernandez-Castro, J. (2021). On the effectiveness of ransomware decryption tools. *Computers & Security*, 111, 1–4.

FireEye (2022). What is a zero-day exploit? https://www.fireeye.com/current-threats/what-is-a-zero-day-exploit.html (Accessed Feb 1, 2021).

Future Business Tech (2021). The S-curve pattern of innovation: A full analysis. https://www.futurebusinesstech.com/blog/the-s-curve-pattern-of-innovation-a-full-analysis#:~:text=The%20S-Curve%20Pattern%20of%20Innovation %20highlights%20the%20fact,offerings%20in%20place%20to%20capture %20future%20profit%20opportunities (Accessed Nov 18, 2021).

Garisto, D. (2021). China is pulling ahead in global quantum race, new studies suggest. *Scientific American.* https://www.scientificamerican.com/article/

china-is-pulling-ahead-in-global-quantum-race-new-studies-suggest/ (Accessed Dec 10, 2021).

Goled, S. (2021). Top countries pumping money into quantum computing technology. *Analytics India Magazine.* https://analyticsindiamag.com/top-countries-pumping-money-into-quantum-computing-technology/ (Accessed Oct 28, 2021).

Greenberg, A. (2021). The colonial pipeline hack is a new extreme for ransomware. *Wired.* https://www.wired.com/story/colonial-pipeline-ransomware-attack/ (Accessed Nov 8, 2021).

Group-IB (2021). Ransomware uncovered 2020–2021 (Report). March 2021, 47. https://explore.group-ib.com/ransomware-reports/ransomware_uncovered_2020 (Accessed Dec 30, 2021).

Guterl, F. (2020). As China leads quantum computing race, US spies plan for a world with fewer secrets. *Newsweek.* https://www.newsweek.com/2020/12/25/china-leads-quantum-computing-race-us-spies-plan-world-fewer-secrets-1554439.html (Accessed Oct 31, 2021).

HIPAA Journal (2021). Fifth of healthcare providers report increase in patient mortality after a ransomware attack. *HIPAA Journal.* https://www.hipaajournal.com/fifth-of-healthcare-providers-report-increase-in-patient-mortality-after-a-ransomware-attack/ (Accessed Nov 20, 2021).

IBM Quantum Composer (1) (2021). Entanglement. *IBM.* https://quantum-computing.ibm.com/composer/docs/iqx/guide/entanglement (Accessed Dec 6, 2021).

IBM Quantum Composer (2) (2021). Creating superpositions and quantum interference. *IBM.* https://quantum-computing.ibm.com/composer/docs/iqx/guide/entanglement (Accessed Dec 6, 2021).

Irving, M. (2021). IBM unleashes the Eagle, the world's most powerful quantum processor. *New Atlas.* https://newatlas.com/quantum-computing/ibm-eagle-quantum-processor/ (Accessed Dec 4, 2021).

Jasper, S. (2021). Assessing Russia's role and responsibility in the colonial pipeline attack. *Atlantic Council.* https://www.atlanticcouncil.org/blogs/new-atlanticist/assessing-russias-role-and-responsibility-in-the-colonial-pipeline-attack/ (Accessed Nov 9, 2021).

Jibilian, I. and Canales, K. (2021). The US is readying sanctions against Russia over the SolarWinds cyber attack. Here's a simple explanation of how the massive hack happened and why it's such a big deal. *Business Insider.* https://www.businessinsider.com/solarwinds-hack-explained-government-agencies-cyber-security-2020-12 (Accessed Dec 27, 2021).

Kaja, A., Stein, S., and Xiang, T. (2021). China's 14th Five-Year Plan (2021–2025): Signposts for doing business in China. *Global Policy Watch.* https://www.globalpolicywatch.com/2021/04/chinas-14th-five-year-plan-2021-2025-signposts-for-doing-business-in-china/ (Accessed Oct 28, 2021).

Kapadia, S. (2021). After years of 'Made in China,' supply chains consider alternatives. *Supply Chain Dive*. https://www.supplychaindive.com/news/china-supply-chains-procurement-sourcing-resilience-vietnam/606321/ (Accessed Nov 3, 2021).

Kharpal, A. (2020). Power is 'up for grabs': Behind China's plan to shape the future of next-generation tech. *CNBC*. https://www.cnbc.com/2020/04/27/china-standards-2035-explained.html (Accessed Oct 28, 2021).

Lakshmanan, R. (2021). Hackers exploit Log4j vulnerability to infect computers with Khonsari ransomware. *The Hacker News*. https://thehackernews.com/2021/12/ hackers-exploit-log4j-vulnerability-to.html (Accessed Dec 22, 2021).

Marsh McLennan. (2021). The state of the US cyber insurance market. https://www.marsh.com/us/services/cyber-risk/insights/the-state-of-the-us-cyber-insurance-market.html (Accessed Nov 5, 2021).

Mehrotra, K. and Turton, W. (2021). CNA Financial paid $40 million in ransom after March cyberattack. *Bloomberg*. https://www.bloomberg.com/news/articles/2021-05-20/cna-financial-paid-40-million-in-ransom-after-march-cyberattack (Accessed Dec 4, 2021).

Microsoft (2021). Description of symmetric and asymmetric encryption. *Support*. https://support.microsoft.com/en-us/topic/a082a391-dee8-6265-9ce6-77c7f07c48dd (Accessed Nov 19, 2021).

Miller, M. (2021). US concerns grow over potential Russian cyber targeting of Ukraine amid troop buildup. *The Hill*. https://thehill.com/policy/cybersecurity/586033-us-concerns-grow-over-potential-russian-cyber-targeting-of-ukraine-amid?rl=1 (Accessed Jan 17, 2021).

Narayanan, A. (2019). Quantum Superposition and what that means to Quantum Computation. *Becoming Human AI*. https://becominghuman.ai/quantum-superposition-and-what-that-means-to-quantum-computation-3fbb5a711b9a (Accessed Jan 6, 2021).

National Academies of Sciences, Engineering, and Medicine (2018). News release: New cryptography must be developed and deployed now, even though a quantum computer that could compromise today's cryptography is likely at least a decade away, says new report. https://www.nationalacademies.org/news/2018/12/new-cryptography-must-be-developed-and-deployed-now-even-though-a-quantum-computer-that-could-compromise-todays-cryptography-is-likely-at-least-a-decade-away-says-new-report (Accessed Dec 14, 2021).

Nyczepir, D. (2020). IPv6 is now the standard for Federal Agencies' Internet traffic. *Fedscoop*. https://www.fedscoop.com/omb-finalizes-ipv6-memo/ (Accessed Nov 9, 2021).

O'Neill, P.H. (2021). 2021 has broken the record for zero-day hacking attacks. *MIT Technology Review*. https://www.technologyreview.com/2021/09/23/1036140/ 2021-record-zero-day-hacks-reasons/ (Accessed Nov 9, 2021).

Panettierri, J. (2021). Colonial pipeline cyberattack: Timeline and ransomware attack recovery details. *MSSP Alert*. https://www.msspalert.com/cyber security-breaches-and-attacks/ransomware/colonial-pipeline-investigation/ (Accessed Nov 14, 2021).

Q-CTRL (2022). What is quantum error correction? https://q-ctrl.com/learning-center/beginner-foundations/quantum-error-correction/ (Accessed Dec 3, 2021).

Roth, A., Sabbagh, D., Blood, D., and De Hoog, N. (2021). Russia-Ukraine crisis: Where are Putin's troops and what are his options? *The Guardian*. https://www.theguardian.com/world/2021/dec/17/russia-ukraine-crisis-putin-troops-visual-guide-explainer (Accessed Jan 1, 2022).

Russel, D. and Berger, B. (2021). Is China stacking the technology deck by setting international standards? *The Diplomat*. https://thediplomat.com/2021/12/is-china-stacking-the-technology-deck-by-setting-international-standards/ (Accessed Dec 18, 2021).

Sanders, B.C. (2021). Quantum leap for quantum primacy. *Physics*, 14, 147. https://physics.aps.org/articles/v14/147 (Accessed Nov 9, 2021).

Savoie, C. (2021). How quantum computers could cut millions of miles from supply chains and transform logistics. *Forbes*. https://www.forbes.com/sites/forbestechcouncil/2021/02/05/how-quantum-computers-could-cut-millions-of-miles-from-supply-chains-and-transform-logistics/?sh=1707c9f25a92 (Accessed Nov 17, 2021).

Shankland, S. (2021). Quantum computers could crack today's encrypted messages. That's a problem. *C|Net*. https://www.cnet.com/tech/computing/quantum-computers-could-crack-todays-encrypted-messages-thats-a-problem/ (Accessed Dec 6, 2021).

Simpson, C. (2020). Someone died because of ransomware: Time to give hospitals emergency security care. *The Hill*. https://thehill.com/opinion/cybersecurity/519267-someone-died-because-of-ransomware-hospitals-emergency-security (Accessed Dec 11, 2021).

Sobers, R. (2021). Sponsored: 81 Ransomware statistics, data, trends and facts for 2021. *AFCEA*. https://www.afcea.org/content/sponsored-81-ransomware-statistics-data-trends-and-facts-2021 (Accessed Nov 7, 2021).

Statista (2022). Spending on cybersecurity worldwide from 2017 to 2021 (COVID-19 adjusted). https://www.statista.com/statistics/991304/world wide-cybersecurity-spending/#:~:text=In%202019%2C%20spending%20in %20the,19)%20pandemic%20in%20to%20account (Accessed Jan 20, 2022).

Taylor, M. and Bahrami, D. (2022). A quantum failure. *Fortune*. https://fortune.com/2022/01/18/a-quantum-failure-us-china-tech-research-investing-congress-biden-xi-stimulus-international-politics/ (Accessed Jan 22, 2021).

Temple-Raston, D. (2021). Biden order to require new cybersecurity standards in response to SolarWinds attack. *National Public Radio (NPR)*. https://www.npr.org/2021/04/29/991333036/biden-order-to-require-new-cybersecurity-standards-in-response-to-solarwinds-att (Accessed Nov 9, 2021).

US Bureau of Labor Statistics (BLS) (2021). COVID-19 ends longest employment recovery and expansion in CES history, causing unprecedented job losses in 2020. https://www.bls.gov/opub/mlr/2021/article/covid-19-ends-longest-employment-expansion-in-ces-history.htm (Accessed Dec 3, 2021).

US Cybersecurity and Infrastructure Security Agency (CISA) (2021(a)). Statement from CISA Director Easterly on "Log4J" vulnerability. https://www.cisa.gov/news/2021/12/11/statement-cisa-director-easterly-log4j-vulnerability (Accessed Dec 22, 2021).

US Cybersecurity and Infrastructure Security Agency (CISA) (2021(b)). About CISA. https://www.cisa.gov/about-cisa (Accessed Nov 3, 2021).

US Cybersecurity and Infrastructure Security Agency (CISA). (2021(c)). CISA-FBI guidance for MSPs and their customers affected by the Kaseya VSA supply-chain ransomware attack. https://www.cisa.gov/uscert/ncas/current-activity/2021/07/04/cisa-fbi-guidance-msps-and-their-customers-affected-kaseya-vsa (Accessed Nov 9, 2021).

US Cybersecurity and Infrastructure Security Agency (CISA) (2021(d)). Defending against software supply chain attacks. https://www.cisa.gov/sites/default/files/publications/defending_against_software_supply_chain_attacks_508_1.pdf (Accessed Oct 30, 2021).

US Executive Office of the President (EOP) Office of Management and Budget (OMB) (2005). Memorandum: Transition planning for Internet Protocol Version 6 (IPv6). https://georgewbush-whitehouse.archives.gov/omb/memoranda/fy2005/m05-22.pdf (Accessed Oct 31, 2021).

US Executive Office of the President (EOP) Office of Management and Budget (OMB) (2010). Memorandum: Transition to IPv6. https://obamawhitehouse.archives.gov/sites/default/files/omb/assets/egov_docs/transition-to-ipv6.pdf (Accessed Nov 9, 2021).

US Executive Office of the President (EOP) Office of Management and Budget (OMB) (2020). Memorandum: Completing the transition to Internet Protocol Version 6 (IPv6). https://www.whitehouse.gov/wp-content/uploads/2020/11/M-21-07.pdf (Accessed Nov 9, 2021).

US Executive Office of the President (EOP) Office of Management and Budget (OMB) (2021). (about) Office of Management and Budget (OMB). https://www.whitehouse.gov/omb/ (Accessed Nov 9, 2021).

US Government. How to protect your networks from ransomware (n.d.). Guidance document for Chief Information Officer and Chief Information Security Officers at critical infrastructure entities. https://www.justice.gov/criminalccips/file/872771/download#:~:text=On%20average%2C%20

more%20than%204%2C000,risk%20posed%20to%20your%20organization (Accessed Dec 13, 2021).

US Government Accountability Office (GAO) (2021). Technology assessment: Quantum computing and communications status and prospects. October 2021. https://www.gao.gov/assets/gao-22-104422.pdf (Accessed Nov 9, 2021).

US National Telecommunications and Information Administration (NTIA) (2021). Software bill of materials. https://www.ntia.gov/SBOM (Accessed Nov 13, 2021).

US Office of the Comptroller of the Currency (OCC) (2020). Sound practices to strengthen operational resilience. https://www.occ.gov/news-issuances/news-releases/2020/nr-occ-2020-144a.pdf (Accessed Nov 9, 2021).

US Office of the Comptroller of the Currency (OCC) (2021). Suspicious activity reports (SAR). https://www.occ.treas.gov/topics/supervision-and-examination/bank-operations/financial-crime/suspicious-activity-reports/index-suspicious-activity-reports.html (Accessed Nov 3, 2021).

US Treasury Department's Financial Crimes Enforcement Network (FINCEN) (2021). Ransomware trends in bank secrecy act data between January 2021 and June 2021. *FINCEN Financial Trend Analysis*. https://www.fincen.gov/sites/default/files/2021-10/Financial%20Trend%20Analysis_Ransomware%20508%20FINAL.pdf (Accessed Nov 3, 2021).

US White House (2021). Fact sheet: Ongoing public US efforts to counter ransomware. *White House Briefing Room*. https://www.whitehouse.gov/briefing-room/statements-releases/2021/10/13/fact-sheet-ongoing-public-u-s-efforts-to-counter-ransomware/ (Accessed Dec 9, 2021).

Vamosi, R. (2020). The emerging ransomware-as-a-service economy. *Forbes*. https://www.forbes.com/sites/robertvamosi/2020/11/27/the-emerging-ransomware-as-a-service-economy/?sh=72f07d287450 (Accessed Dec 2, 2021).

https://doi.org/10.1142/9789811271984_0011

Chapter 11

Business Growth through Digital Disruption

Shahdrick Samson

Johns Hopkins University, Washington DC, USA
ssamson4@jh.edu

Digital disruption has been underway for more than a decade. Traditional methods no longer seem effective and are detrimental to survival. How well a business becomes digital and adapts to the rapidly changing market forces will to a great extent determine how much market share it will gain in comparison to its competitors.

While becoming digital is not an easy or an inexpensive journey, it is an essential one. It requires a firm commitment and dedication of resources to be truly successful. However, the rewards for undertaking such a journey are well worth the efforts and will determine the new set of market leaders.

1. Introduction

For the past several years, organizations have been undergoing some form of digital business transformation: the use of technology to enable business processes in a way that adapts quickly to changing market conditions such as customers' needs, regulatory requirements, social expectations, global competition, and technological and economic factors.

Businesses can no longer rely on traditional methods and operating models to be competitive. The progressive changes in the market to become digital are inevitable and necessary for survival. These changes will be more drastic for some businesses than others. For some, it may mean making minor adjustments to their operations, while for others it may mean reinventing how they conduct business and generate revenue. Bedi stated that "A few years ago, 'digital transformation' was just another business buzzword. Today it's a strategic imperative, as machine learning, process automation and other emerging technologies change business from the ground up" (Bedi, 2019).

2. Digital Disruption

The key drivers behind the need for digital disruption are the challenges that businesses continue to face across the organization: too many manual and labor-intensive processes; lack of clarity on roles and responsibility; poor integration between processes, digital technologies, groups, and individuals; replacing legacy systems and organizational structures; painful tracking of information using spreadsheets and reporting on data from fragmented systems; and inadequate use of multiple software applications requiring licenses and on-going maintenance. These hurdles slow down productivity and become very costly and risky, while preventing the business from achieving its desired business outcomes.

According to Herbert, "Digital is everywhere, but it becomes truly powerful when you extend its definition to the enterprise level. In this sense, 'digital' also includes every element of your company's entire IT Infrastructure — from product and inventory management and running the supply chain to every aspect of marketing, communications, and human resources. In fact, you'd be hard-pressed to find an element of your business that doesn't have a digital component integral to its operations" (Herbert, 2017).

Interestingly, these challenges are more operational than technological. They are associated with business processes, human capital, data use, governance and management, and adequate use of digital technology to enable business operations. As a business embarks on its journey to become digital, it is crucial that it begins with a digital transformation strategy and roadmap that is driven based on business objectives and priorities. Next, the business needs to make a firm commitment to sustainable organizational change that rewards high-performing culture. Organizations need to thoroughly examine, document, and continuously improve their operating model multi-dimensionally across the four areas discussed in the following sections.

2.1 *Business processes*

Business process management (BPM) is imperative for any business that wants to thrive in this age. Processes need to be focused on achieving operational excellence through process efficiency, automation, and customer outcome-based experiences. They should be well defined end to end with dependencies identified, documented, updated, continuously improved based on published and established service-level targets, and more importantly, driven by business value.

However, many businesses do not invest enough time to properly engineer and streamline their processes. On the contrary, they focus on acquiring new technology in the hopes that it will solve all their problems. The flaw with this train of thought is that it assumes that the commercial off-the-shelf (COTS) technology has fully built business processes and activities tailored to one's business and industry, which is generally not the case. The first step is to optimize all your business processes and then automate as many as possible to deliver the best customer experience:

- Organizations should take the time to identify the stakeholder(s) most familiar with and impacted by the process in question and engage them in group sessions to review and improve the process. They should use a maturity model to determine the level of process maturity and aim to become business value driven. The objective is to streamline the process by determining the least number of steps required to produce the desired output.
- It is imperative to determine what steps can be automated through conditions and assignment rules using a low-code or no-code enterprise system. The key is to look for areas that can benefit from standardization and process automation, starting from quick wins that have the greatest impact to longer-term solutions focused on improving the overall customer experience.

2.2 *Human capital*

People are one of the most critical assets for a business. However, that asset becomes a liability when responsibilities are not clearly defined and communicated, and further worsens when roles are misaligned with skill sets. Supervisors are sometimes forced to assign employees to certain roles without proper training and experience due to internal politics with the expectation to achieve full performance. The majority of employees do not have the expertise required to optimally perform their duties. This creates a recipe for disaster.

Businesses should hire and retain individuals that are best qualified for a specific role based on their education, training, relevant experience, and abilities, not simply to keep them around because of their availability. They should be tightly aligned and integrated with the business processes and technology they support. According to Roth, "In further discussion about the skill sets for executives, management and all employees, Westbrook opined that the pace of change is moving very rapidly in all areas — business models, business and consumer processes — which is resulting in corporate downsizing, new positions and new job requirements. These changes result in people being displaced and/or stymied in their career. This is contributing to the growing income and wealth divide. It is also one of the disruptions that need to be addressed as we have a growing shortage of workers who are qualified to meet current workplace requirements. This results in increased competition for those with the required skill sets and disenfranchisement of workers that do not have the needed skills" (Roth, 2020).

2.3 *Meaningful use and governance of data*

Data are a critical asset for any organization. Data should be managed and protected to maintain integrity, from collection and transformation to validation and reporting. The collection and use of data should be strictly governed and managed. Data quality and validation rules should be established in the system of record (SOR), cross-referenced, and reconciled to determine accuracy, consistency, and correctness for reporting and decision-making purposes.

Many organizations do not make enough effort to minimize manual data entry. Businesses should use technology such as self-service portals and mobile phones to empower users to directly input data into the system as well as establish real-time dashboards and scheduled automated reporting.

2.4 *Appropriate use of technology*

Technology, once considered a cost center, is now deemed a strategic partner to the business and the backbone of operations. It provides the tools a business needs to conduct its operations and become competitive. The purpose of technology is to make our jobs easier by automating redundant tasks, empowering employees through self-help, and engaging with customers. However, in order to turn opportunities into revenue, it is imperative that organizations consider the following leading practices to reduce costs and increase operational efficiency and effectiveness:

- Avoid using software applications inadequately for purposes other than for which it was developed. It is less expensive in the long run to purchase and implement the software that is best suited to support a business service rather than customize the wrong software.
- Avoid painful tracking of data using spreadsheets. Instead, use a ticketing system to capture, track, and report on data.
- Replace legacy systems with physical servers with COTS products.
- Fix poor integration between enterprise systems.
- Establish systems of record (SOR) for reporting on data.

According to Chowdhary *et al.*, "The technologies used to help drive an industrial digital transformation may include one or more from the Internet of Things (IoT), cloud and edge computing, Artificial Intelligence (AI), big data, analytics, blockchain, robotics, drones, 3D printing, Augmented Reality (AR) and Virtual Reality (VR) Robotic Process Automation (RPA), and mobile technologies. New technologies continue to emerge, so this list is not meant to be an exhaustive one. The main goal of these transformations is to gain a competitive advantage, drive new revenues, improve productivity and efficiency, as well as enhance customer and stakeholder engagement" (Chowdhary *et al.*, 2020).

Enterprise service management systems, through capabilities such as self-service, request management, and performance analytics, have changed and in some ways substantially transformed the way organizations interact with their internal stakeholders and customers: from allowing fulfillers to automate their business processes using rules and workflows, to enabling users to resolve their issues using self-service and knowledge bases, to empowering management through creation of custom dashboards and reports for informed decision-making.

Consequently, these systems have enabled organizations to realize significant cost savings while working efficiently using a single cloud platform that could replace multiple convoluted applications in the enterprise to log, track, manage, deliver, and report on enterprise services across customer service, finance, IT, and human resources departments, among others. ServiceNow stated that "Like many companies, U.S. Bank previously relied on multiple productivity tools to manually create monthly IT incident reports and distribute them among managers. With the new dashboard, 'we're on a journey toward making [that whole process] digital'" (ServiceNow, 2019).

3. Journey to Digital Transformation

The journey to digital transformation is not easy and businesses face many hurdles including not having specialized skilled labor, complexity of migration from legacy systems, executive sponsorship and commitment, and getting budgetary approvals.

Many organizations have heavily customized legacy systems in their environment for well over a decade, and the reliance on these systems for business operations is colossal. Management fears losing functionality, data, and security as they transition to cloud-based systems due to many factors including complexity of the system. Additionally, management fears the considerable costs and major risks associated with the transition, including not having employees with the required skills to implement and support the system in production. However, it is necessary to become competitive and pay dividends in the long run through an increase in productivity, resulting in higher profits and cost savings through efficiencies.

Competition is fierce for a greater share of the global market, and the difference between winners and losers is based on how effectively they can create a connection, a sense of loyalty between their brand and their consumer through social media and other avenues. The market is shifting from reacting to consumer demands to proactively predicting consumer behavior based on their online activities through cookies and other tracking mechanisms. Competition is no longer local or even national with other businesses in the same industry; it has become global. Companies from around the world with lower labor costs, cheaper raw materials, and fewer regulations are actively challenging the status quo in both the product and service industries. In such a market, it is imperative to develop a business model that can adapt to ongoing changes and be globally scalable, yet flexible enough to meet the specific needs of its geographically dispersed consumers.

The role of business in society is also shifting as technology advancement reaches new heights. Consumers no longer view their favorite brands as a business for goods and services, but rather as a representation of themselves and what they deem ideal values, enabling enterprises such as Amazon, Apple, Google, and Facebook to influence every major issue. Technology has given the world a lot of good by connecting people across borders, cultures, and languages and providing quick access to information, products, and services like never before in history.

Through an enormous amount of online data collected by companies, behavior-forecasting capabilities, and access to hundreds of millions of people around the world, a handful of these technology companies set and shape the global agenda. From political to social, their impact is immeasurable. According to the Pew Research Center, "The pessimists about democracy in this canvassing make several arguments and foresee several outcomes. A share believe that there will be not be adequate reform in the design and management of technology platforms; that government will not respond in the best interests of citizens; that the speed, scope and impact of digital tools all work in favor of bad actors; and that educational processes and growing citizen awareness of the flaws now emerging in tech systems will not significantly lessen the known harms that networked digital technologies can enable in the next decade" (Anderson and Rainie, 2020).

Today's business environment is unprecedented. Consumers are demanding higher value from their favorite brands relative to what competitors offer and are willing to pay a premium for consistent delivery of high-quality products and services that are conveniently and quickly accessible. For example, Apple iPhone users are generally loyal to the brand and are willing to pay more for an iPhone compared to other, less-expensive smart phones. This shows that competition is no longer based on the lowest price alone. Rather, it is a holistic perception of a brand based on the quality, ease of use, friendliness of service, and continuous improvement of its products and services. It is imperative for businesses to continue to excel in these areas and give their consumers and employees more, or else they will struggle to survive in a highly competitive global market. Let's examine the case study below to see how Lumière Business Solutions (LBS) transitioned to the virtual workspace.

4. Case Study: LBS's Journey to a Virtual Workspace on the Cloud

LBS was a small-to-medium-sized research and consulting firm founded in 1996. It supported business clients through various services including consulting, online and market research, and providing insight and innovative solutions. What differentiated Lumière from the competition was its vision to provide women professionals with opportunities to balance their personal life with their careers, which made sense since most of the workforce comprised women. To accomplish this vision, Lumière supported the idea of a virtual workspace on the cloud that would enable staff members and teams to collaborate remotely from different geographical locations within the country and abroad to support client service delivery, while reducing costs associated with office space. It seemed like a win–win for both the business and the employees.

Being a small business with a social cause that competed with large market research companies in the industry itself presented a number of challenges to the business, such as resource allocation and controlling cost margins. "The senior management at Lumière knew that this opportunity could not come at the cost of quality, and for that reason, Lumière had to overstaff its projects by 30 per cent (compared to the rest of the industry) in order to provide quality work and efficiency that equalled that of its competitors … To stay competitive, Lumière had to improve its cost margins in other places" (Ray and Subramanian, 2016).

Lumière aspired to convert its qualitative research capabilities into a structured, scientific method by building structures, standardizing across processes, and creating frameworks to provide better and more accelerated solutions for its customers. However, it faced many challenges, including existing technology being obsolete, the need for document management, knowledge management, infrastructure to support operations, creation of transparency in project data for employees and customers, constant changing demands, and overworked staff.

Lumière's solution to these problems was to develop enterprise capabilities in the cloud that would enable instant communication, exchange of data, and knowledge management that could be accessible from anywhere. "Lumière's international technology (IT) solutions were based on using traditional data centers, a practice that comes with additional price costs, like licensing fees and leased lines for connectivity. On an ongoing basis, Lumière built its own solutions to accommodate the changing needs and demands of the organization, but this approach resulted in some monstrous home-grown solutions that could not keep pace with the customers' changing demands in the effervescent and creative domain of market research. Milind knew the technology could be leveraged to reduce the firm's spending and improve its access to resources across geographies. He also knew that IT was not core to their business. Lumière needed to identify a way for IT to solve its problems without becoming resource-intensive" (Ray and Subramanian, 2016).

In 2011, Lumière began its journey to the public cloud. It started with a cloud-based email system, which was a major pain point, and then migrated other applications to the cloud to create a virtual workspace. Some of the benefits of cloud adoption included cost-effectiveness, ease of implementation and maintenance, scalability, flexibility, and a wider choice of business-ready solutions to access productivity tools, business applications, and documents remotely at higher performance. These are considered a significant benefit since it enabled the staff to work remotely and flexibly from anywhere, including their homes and client sites, at any time without the constraints of a given location and time frame. According to the case study, "The clients were very happy with the results and with the solutions that Soman and her team provided. Additionally, they were very impressed with the way Lumière had used technology to give 24/7 access to project progress and documentation. The clients appreciated the fact that, despite being a small firm, Lumière was as competitive and quick to respond as any other big market-research company" (Ray and Subramanian, 2016).

There are many types of clouds: private, public, and hybrid. A private cloud is an on-premise option — the most expensive of the three — and is usually selected by a large organization that has the resources to support it internally. A public cloud is managed externally by a service provider; it is a lower-cost option, but can be perceived by some as less secure. A hybrid cloud is a combination of private and public clouds. Organizations select this option to balance the cost and allocate resources to be hosted in the private and public clouds based on the sensitivity of the data. In other words, if the data are more sensitive, the same would be hosted in a private cloud; however, if the data are not critical, one could use a public cloud.

Many organizational factors led to successful cloud adoption at Lumière, including the Chief Information Officer's understanding of what the cloud could do for the organization, agility of leadership and staff to adapt to the cloud just like they did with the intranet, cost reduction, security of systems and data, and dependability of services. However, migrating to the cloud created several issues for the firm, including a struggle to keep up margins, over-staffing on projects, cost-cutting mode across the organization, and overall loss of productivity due to loss of customer requests, emails, and documents. Overall, the move to the cloud addressed many operational needs of the firm, but it also adversely impacted the business from a profitability standpoint in terms of meeting the needs of its clients.

Organizations have some concerns as they consider moving to the cloud, such as internet connectivity (which in the case of Lumière was not always available), security, lack of a legal understanding concerning data controls, and the need for restructuring of work processes because staff would come up with unacceptable excuses such as "already emailed it," "forgot about it," "did not see it," and so forth. To address these issues, Lumière had to put links into the work processes to connect with workflows to ensure that there was transparency. Additionally, Lumière moved many of the home-grown systems which were hosted in traditional data centers and could not keep up with clients' needs and demands to the cloud to reduce costs, meet the changing needs of clients, and provide better performance.

Lumière could have leveraged Porter's Five Forces Model to help better position itself in the market and increase its margins. Lumière was a new entrant in a market with big competitors with similar offerings, and its success was perceived as a potential threat to the profit of its large competitors. According to Porter, there are five forces that create a competition in the market, which he refers to as "rivalry." These five forces are (1) threats of new entrants, (2) bargaining power of buyers, (3) threat of substitute products and services, (4) bargaining power of suppliers, and (5) rivalry among existing competitors (Porter, 2008). The threat of new entrants refers to your organization's position in the market, which can be changed by new rivals or competitors entering the market with products and/or services similar to those offered by your company. The bargaining power of buyers to affect the prices of your organization is based on supply and demand. If the demand (buyers) for your services and/or products is higher than the supply (competitors) in the market, the prices will go up. However, as the supply of competitors increases, the prices go down. This gives the buyers the power to bargain and purchase at lower prices; however, buyers also have to consider the cost of switching from an existing supplier to your organization, which allows suppliers to develop a strategy that enables them to increase prices based on the tolerance level of their buyers. This is referred to as bargaining power of suppliers. There is also a threat of substitute products and services, which means that customers can look for alternative solutions. For example, instead of purchasing a car and having to pay for the costs associated with vehicle ownership and operation, they can use car services such as Uber or public transportation. Another force to consider is the rivalry among existing competitors, which suggests identifying your competitors and then examining their positioning in the market by examining their strengths, weaknesses, and variety of offerings compared to those of your organization.

5. Conclusion

In conclusion, digital transformation is inevitable for businesses. Traditional methods and operating models are detrimental to survival. How well a business becomes digital and adapts to the rapidly changing market will to a great extent determine how it performs. While becoming digital is not an easy or an inexpensive journey, it is one that is indispensable. It requires a firm commitment and dedication of resources to be truly successful. However, the rewards for undertaking such a journey are well worth the efforts and will determine the new set of leaders in the market.

References

Anderson, J. and Rainie, L. (2020). Themes about the digital disruption of democracy in the next decade. Pew Research Center. https://www.pewresearch.org/internet/2020/02/21/themes-about-the-digital-disruption-of-democracy-in-the-next-decade.

Bedi, C. (2019). Digital transformation starts with people. *The Wall Street Journal*. https://partners.wsj.com/servicenow/digital-transformation-starts-with-people/.

Chowdhary, M., Dunkin, A., Nath, S.V., and Patel, N. (2020). *Industrial Digital Transformation: Accelerate Digital Transformation with Business Optimization, AI, and Industry 4.0*. Birmingham, UK: Packt Publishing.

Herbert, L. (2017). *Digital Transformation: Build Your Organization's Future for the Innovation Age*. London, UK: Bloomsbury Publishing.

Porter, M.E. (2008). The five competitive forces that shape strategy. *Harvard Business Review*. https://hbr.org/2008/01/the-five-competitive-forces-that-shape-strategy.

Ray, D. and Subramanian, L.S. (2016). *Lumière: Supporting a Virtual Workspace on the Cloud*. London, Ontario, Canada: Ivey Publishing. https://www.hbsp.harvard.edu/product/W16084-PDF-ENG.

Roth, L.J. (2020). *Digital Transformation: An Executive Guide to Survive and Thrive in the New Economy*. Bloomington, IN, USA: Balboa Press.

ServiceNow (2019). How ServiceNow is helping U.S. Bank build a culture of IT self-service. https://blogs.servicenow.com/2019/how-usbank-builds-culture-of-it-service.html.

https://doi.org/10.1142/9789811271984_0012

Chapter 12

Deep-Learning Applications in Car Damage Detection

Tanush Sharanarthi*, Shreyas Iyer†, Hsueh-Yao Lu‡, and Xiaoyue Li§

Johns Hopkins University, Washington DC, USA
**tanush29@gmail.com*
†*shreyas.iyer11@gmail.com*
‡*steven06642@gmail.com*
§*xiaoyue9907@gmail.com*

This chapter proposes a car damage detection model using Convolutional Neural Networks. The automobile industry can utilize cameras to catch the defects in vehicles and provide better-quality inspection than manual methods. AI-based machines using computer vision will help make the entire supply chain process more efficient and reliable. The proposed model uses the VGG-16 Convolutional Neural Network that is optimized to provide the best accuracy and minimal loss. The model is trained and validated with a dataset containing images of vehicles that have no defects and ones that are damaged. Results show the potential of such a model being widely used in the industry since it can accurately detect damages for a diverse set of vehicles.

1. Introduction

Automotive machine learning can improve factory efficiency and the quality of its products. The robots and equipment used to build cars have sensors that send alerts about defective parts (Petzold, 2021). This can help manufacturers make repairs before they shut down assembly lines or cause damage. A study by Capgemini (2018) found that smart technology could add $160 billion annually to the global automotive industry by 2023, as productivity increases (Mejia, 2019). Quality control in factories is also improving thanks to machine learning. The workers who take on this job are at risk of human error; machine learning can improve the process by collecting feedback and updating the system.

Audi uses cameras that can detect cracks in sheet metal that are not visible to the human eye. Software based on a sophisticated artificial intelligence neural network runs under this innovative machine-learning program, which accurately detects the tiniest cracks in sheet metal parts and reliably marks their location (Cprime Studios, 2021).

General Motors uses sensors to monitor plant conditions (Cprime Studios, 2021). For example, if a painted area is too hot or too cold, the paint will not cure and the equipment may malfunction.

For quality control inspection work like checking painted car bodies, human workers manually perform the inspection. However, this method is highly prone to errors and is very tedious. The chances of getting false positives are quite high, even when using automated methods if factors such as lighting are not perfect or due to incorrect mounting of the product. By contrast, AI-enabled visual quality control can focus only on the defects by filtering out these issues (Luckow *et al.*, 2019). The AI system uses feedback to constantly learn to improve its analysis. Using these methods, AI-powered hardware can visually inspect and provide superior quality control on various products such as machine parts, painted car bodies, and textured metal surfaces (Singh, 2021).

Also, AI-based machines can detect defects up to 90% more accurately than humans (Krishna, 2021). Valuable insights can be drawn from AI-based quality testing, which can be used to analyze the root causes of the defects and enhance the prosecution processes. Productivity increases in visual quality inspection by up to 50% are possible (Krishna, 2021).

Furthermore, an AI-enabled damage recognition system is a set of deep-learning algorithms that utilizes computer vision. Based on deep learning, the algorithms automatically detect a vehicle's body and analyze the extent of the damage. Parallel machine learning and analytical pipelines speed the analysis process up to seconds.

The solution speeds up the insurance claim, saving the company's spending on human resources, defending from fraud (in 80% and more), and boosting the process of image data analysis in time. The system is used on site and guides a user on actions to meet photo requirements. By deploying car damage recognition, businesses replace a human-operated, time-consuming process of claims proceedings and approval with machine-learning algorithms and analytical systems (Qualitas Technologies, 2020).

A machine-learning system was developed to reduce the time and effort spent on human inspection and ensures smart decision-making for the following businesses:

- **Insurance companies:** Helps prevent fraud (in 80% of cases) and speeds up the underwriting process.
- **Car repair services:** Creates a collaborative environment that brings transparency to the repair process and costs.

2. Deep Learning in Defect Detections

Deep learning is a subset of machine learning in artificial intelligence that uses mathematical models to map the input to the output. These models can extract the relevant information or patterns from the data, and this enables them to form a relationship between the input and the output. This process of machine learning is called training (Baheti, 2022).

Deep-learning models use artificial neural networks or simply neural networks to extract information. Neural networks are the crux of deep-learning models, and they are designed in such a way that they resemble actual neurons in the human brain (Baheti, 2022).

These neural networks are made up of simple mathematical models that can be stacked on top of each other and arranged in the form of layers, giving them a sense of depth, hence the term "deep learning" (Baheti, 2022).

The main characteristic of deep learning that distinguishes it from other machine-learning models is that deep-learning models can process unstructured data. Unstructured data include text, image, and video data. However, this has its drawbacks as well, since high computation power is required to run deep-learning models, and it is more expensive (Donges, 2019).

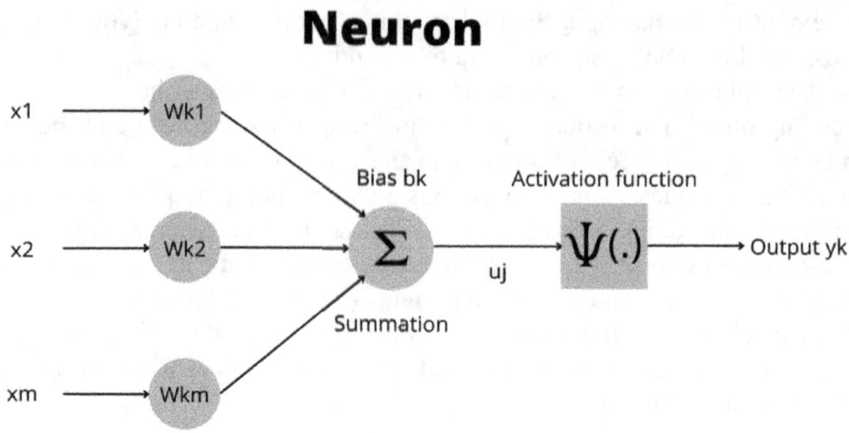

Fig. 1. Structure of a neuron in a neural network.

There are different types of neural networks, such as convolutional neural networks (CNNs), recurrent neural networks (RNNs), and long short-term memory (LSTMs). In our model to detect the defects in automobiles, we use a CNN to classify the images.

The components of a neural network are given in Figure 1.

Here, $x_1, x_2, \ldots, x_m$ are the inputs and multiplied by their respective weights $W_{k1}, W_{k2}, \ldots, W_{km}$, and then the overall weighted inputs are summed with a bias. The bias adds an element of unpredictability to our model, which helps it generalize and gives our model the flexibility to adapt to different unseen inputs when using testing data. This weighted sum is then pushed through a mathematical function known as an activation function. The activation function does some transformation on the nodes and then passes the result to the output so that it can be fed to the subsequent layer to be outputted as the final result.

3. Layers in Action

A neural network can comprise a large number of layers. These layers are of three types: an input layer, an output layer, and hidden layers (Figure 2). The data are fed into the input layer and each node in the input layer assimilates and passes the data to the next layers, which are the hidden layers. The hidden layers extract features from the input layer and transform them using a linear function (Bousqaoui *et al.*, 2018). Hidden layers

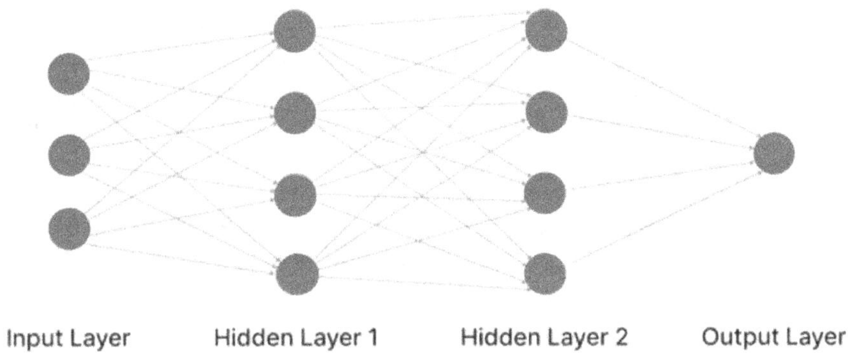

Fig. 2. Layers in a neural network.

are called this because the parameters (weights and bias) in the nodes are not known. Each output from these layers is different in that the layers add random parameters to transform the data (Krishna, 2021).

The output from these hidden layers is then passed on to the final layer, which is called the output layer. The output layer yields a result that can be used for a variety of tasks, such as prediction or classification based on the requirement. In our model, we perform a classification since we want the images of the vehicles to be classified as either damaged or whole cars. This process is called forward propagation.

There is another process called backward propagation, in which an algorithm such as gradient descent is used to calculate the errors by taking the difference between the predicted output and the original output.

By performing both forward propagation and backward propagation, the neural network can achieve high efficiency and accuracy, thereby reducing the error in a particular task. With each iteration, the algorithm gradually becomes more accurate. Therefore, we train the model on multiple epochs.

4. VGG-16 Convolutional Neural Network Model in Car Damage Detection

In our deep-learning model, we are using the VGG-16 (Visual Geometry Group) Convolutional Neural Network Model for detecting damages in cars. This model was originally developed by the Visual Geometry Group at the ILSVR 16 (ImageNet Large Scale Visual Recognition) competition in 2014 (Thaker, 2021). It has convolutional layers of 3×3 filter and stride 1 with padding and maxpool layers of 2×2 filter and a stride of 2. It focuses on these layers rather than having a large count of hyperparameters. The VGG-16 model contains an arrangement of alternating convolution and maxpool layers throughout the network. In the end, it consists of two fully connected layers with a softmax at the output. The model consists of 16 layers with weights associated with them (Krishna, 2021).

The network shown in Figure 3 is a representation of the VGG-16 model we used to build our car damage prediction system.

Layer (type)	Output Shape	Param #
input_1 (InputLayer)	[(None, 150, 150, 3)]	0
block1_conv1 (Conv2D)	(None, 150, 150, 64)	1792
block1_conv2 (Conv2D)	(None, 150, 150, 64)	36928
block1_pool (MaxPooling2D)	(None, 75, 75, 64)	0
block2_conv1 (Conv2D)	(None, 75, 75, 128)	73856
block2_conv2 (Conv2D)	(None, 75, 75, 128)	147584
block2_pool (MaxPooling2D)	(None, 37, 37, 128)	0
block3_conv1 (Conv2D)	(None, 37, 37, 256)	295168
block3_conv2 (Conv2D)	(None, 37, 37, 256)	590080
block3_conv3 (Conv2D)	(None, 37, 37, 256)	590080
block3_pool (MaxPooling2D)	(None, 18, 18, 256)	0
block4_conv1 (Conv2D)	(None, 18, 18, 512)	1180160
block4_conv2 (Conv2D)	(None, 18, 18, 512)	2359808
block4_conv3 (Conv2D)	(None, 18, 18, 512)	2359808
block4_pool (MaxPooling2D)	(None, 9, 9, 512)	0
block5_conv1 (Conv2D)	(None, 9, 9, 512)	2359808
block5_conv2 (Conv2D)	(None, 9, 9, 512)	2359808
block5_conv3 (Conv2D)	(None, 9, 9, 512)	2359808
block5_pool (MaxPooling2D)	(None, 4, 4, 512)	0
flatten (Flatten)	(None, 8192)	0
dense (Dense)	(None, 512)	4194816
dropout (Dropout)	(None, 512)	0
dense_1 (Dense)	(None, 1)	513

Total params: 18,910,017
Trainable params: 4,195,329
Non-trainable params: 14,714,688

Fig. 3. Representation of the VGG-16 model.

As we can see, there are a total of approximately 18 million parameters. At the input layer, images of dimension, 150 × 150 × 3 are used. Here, 150 × 150 is the size of the image and the 3 is used to represent the RGB color value.

The different layers have specific operations, which they will perform on the data. In the following, we have explained the use of each layer in the VGG-16 model.

4.1 *Convolutional layer*

A convolution is the application of a filter to an input that gives us an activation. Repeated application of the same filter to the input will result in a map of activations, which is called a feature map. The feature map will indicate the locations and strength of a detected feature in input, such as an image (Dumane, 2020) (Figure 4).

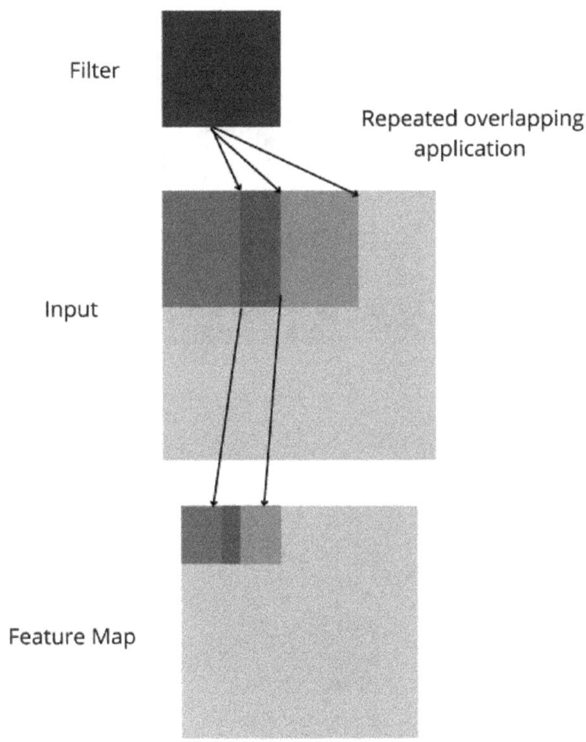

Fig. 4. Representation of convolutional layer.

4.2 *Maxpool layer*

In the maxpool layer, we select the maximum element from the region of the feature map that is covered by the filter. Hence, the output after a maxpool layer is a feature map that contains the most important features of the previous feature map (Dumane, 2020) (Figure 5).

4.3 *Dense layer*

The dense layer in a deep-learning model is a neural network that is deeply connected. This means every neuron in the dense layer is connected to all the neurons in the previous layer and receives inputs from them. Matrix-vector multiplication is performed in the dense layer and the values are the parameters that are trained and updated through backward propagation. The output from this layer is an *n*-dimensional vector. Hence, these layers are used to change the dimensions of a vector and also perform operations such as scaling, rotating, and translation on the vector (Dumane, 2020).

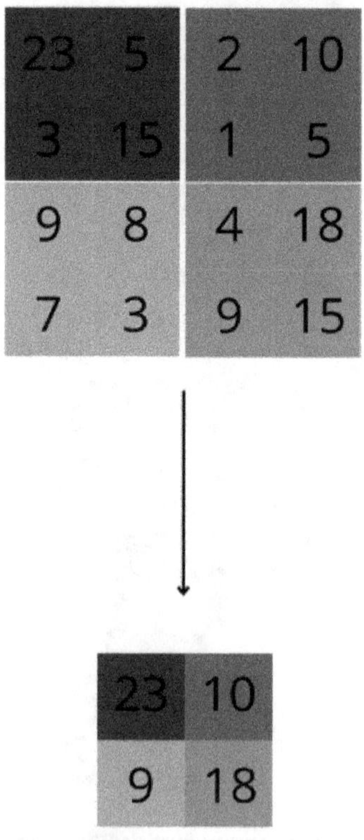

Fig. 5. Representation of maxpool layer.

4.4 *Flatten layer*

Flattening is used to convert data into a one-dimensional array for inputting it to the next layer. We flatten the output of the convolutional layers to create a single long feature vector. This is then connected to a fully connected layer that helps in classification (Dumane, 2020).

4.5 *Dropout layer*

The dropout layer will help reduce overfitting by dropping neurons in subsequent layers with particular probabilities. This is a form of regularization that we are using in our model (Dileep *et al.*, 2020).

5. Convolutional Neural Network Feature Map Visualization

Given in Figures 6 and 7 are feature map visualization outputs from two of the convolutional layers. We can see that in some of the images, the car as a whole is highlighted and in some places the background is

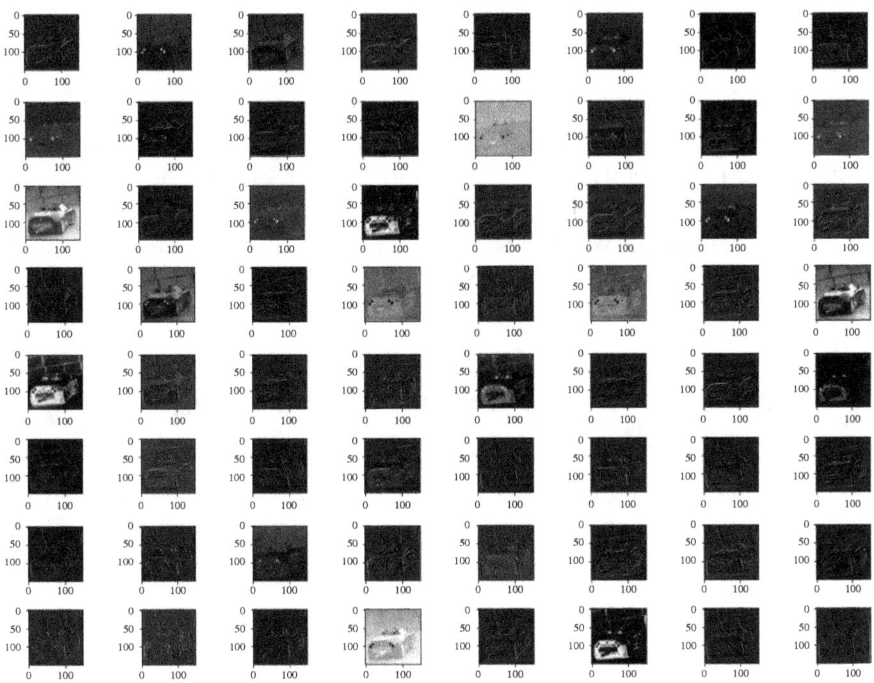

Fig. 6. Feature map visualization of first layer.

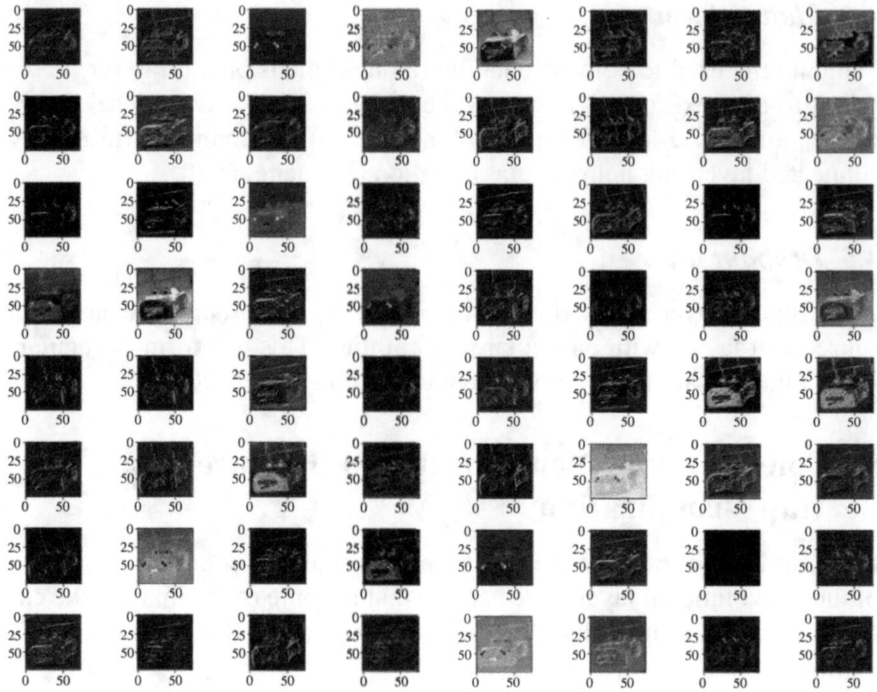

Fig. 7. Feature map visualization of third layer.

highlighted. In most places, we see that tiny features are being highlighted such as the car's door handles, wheels, and bumper, along with any of the damages. This is ideally what we are looking for, and as the images are passed through more and more layers, the features we are looking for become more evident. While it is not easy to visualize the features through this map, just like in any other CNN, we get a rough picture of how the model is working underneath (Khandelwal, 2020).

6. Training Damage Detection Model Using CNN

Now, we will use the deep-learning methods we just discussed to train a model and show the performance of our model in detecting damaged cars. The dataset we found was from Kaggle (Shah, 2019), which is an online data science community platform. It includes a set of training data and a set of validation data.

There are a total of 1,840 car images in the training data, where half of them are damaged cars and half of them are non-damaged cars. The validation data have 460 car images, where half of them are damaged cars and half of them are non-damaged cars. The following picture is a brief showcase of the images that are included in the datasets (Shah, 2019).

Given below is an example of a few images from the dataset that we have used for training our model. The first row contains cars that are damaged, and the second row contains a few images of cars that are whole and not damaged.

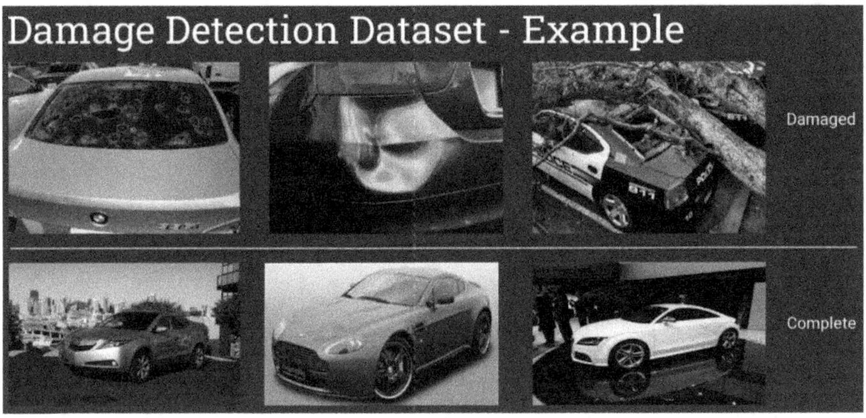

As explained earlier, we have used the VGG-16 Convolutional Neural Network to train our data and build the classifier for predicting whether cars are damaged or not.

7. Testing Accuracy

We use six epochs to train our model, and the validation accuracy and the validation loss for the final epoch are 88.67% and 30.07%, respectively. The accuracy and losses for each epoch are listed in Figures 8–10.

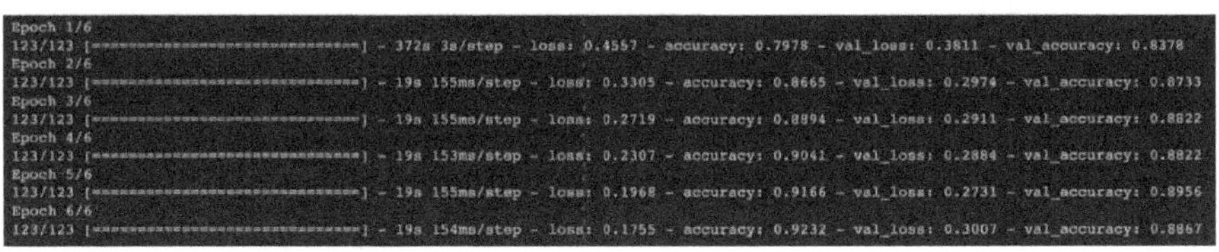

```
Epoch 1/6
123/123 [==============================] - 372s 3s/step - loss: 0.4557 - accuracy: 0.7978 - val_loss: 0.3811 - val_accuracy: 0.8378
Epoch 2/6
123/123 [==============================] - 19s 155ms/step - loss: 0.3305 - accuracy: 0.8665 - val_loss: 0.2974 - val_accuracy: 0.8733
Epoch 3/6
123/123 [==============================] - 19s 155ms/step - loss: 0.2719 - accuracy: 0.8894 - val_loss: 0.2911 - val_accuracy: 0.8822
Epoch 4/6
123/123 [==============================] - 19s 153ms/step - loss: 0.2307 - accuracy: 0.9041 - val_loss: 0.2884 - val_accuracy: 0.8822
Epoch 5/6
123/123 [==============================] - 19s 155ms/step - loss: 0.1968 - accuracy: 0.9166 - val_loss: 0.2731 - val_accuracy: 0.8956
Epoch 6/6
123/123 [==============================] - 19s 154ms/step - loss: 0.1755 - accuracy: 0.9232 - val_loss: 0.3007 - val_accuracy: 0.8867
```

Fig. 8. Training epochs.

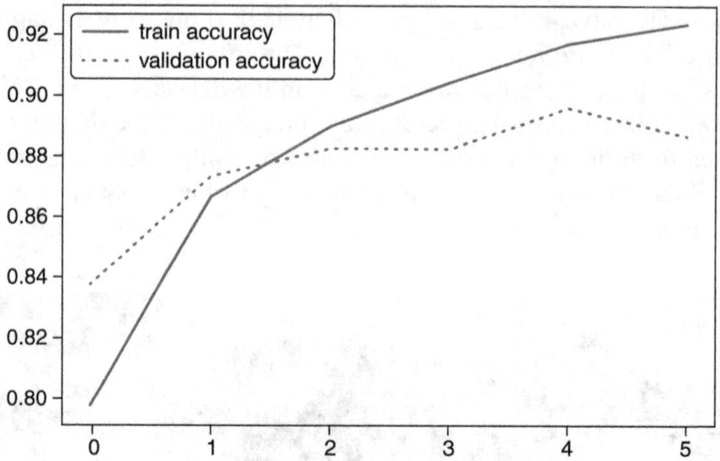

Fig. 9. Training and validation accuracy curves.

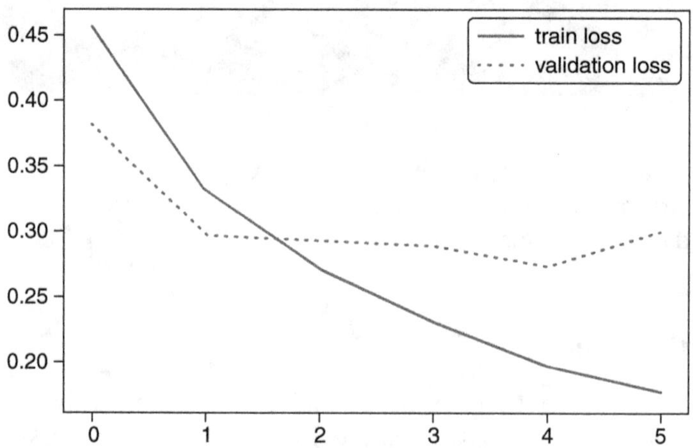

Fig. 10. Training and validation loss curves.

We can see that the validation accuracy lies around 90%, which is a good indication of the reliability of our model. Following are a few examples of the images detected (Shah, 2019):

Even small damages to the car would be detected, and some noise in the background would not affect the prediction. This indicates that our model is capable of making judgments like humans.

8. Drawbacks

Even though a neural network is very powerful and can save a lot of time and resources for auto companies, there are a few limitations and drawbacks.

First, the neural network process is a black box process. In other words, we do not know the process or reasons behind the output we are getting. This makes the model less convincing since we are not able to explain to the stakeholders why we are getting the results. Also, it makes it harder to improve the model since we would not know what part of the model is wrong if it does not give us a satisfactory result (Donges, 2019).

Second, the time and resources spent on the neural network process are huge. The company will need strong computational power computers, an enormous dataset, and enough time to run the results. These conditions will be hard for smaller companies to achieve; without them, a neural network model would not perform well, and it may even be worse than the traditional machine-learning model.

Lastly, neural network models have problems with overfitting, vanishing gradient, and local minima problems. All of these problems can make the model less accurate and less reliable.

9. Other AI Usage

Other than car damage detection, artificial intelligence can be used in many other areas in the automotive industry. For example, AI can be used in designing and developing new cars. By implementing AI, car manufacturers can develop a better design and eliminate possible errors in the first place. Volkswagen is already using the Generative Design method (Cprime Studios, 2021). Also, AI can be used in predictive maintenance. Automakers can find and eliminate malfunctioning parts beforehand instead of solving problems after they arise. It makes the manufacturing process go much more smoothly and saves unnecessary losses.

10. Conclusion

This chapter proposed an efficient AI-based model for the automotive supply chain that helps detect damage in cars using the VGG-16 Convolutional Neural Network model. Unlike the traditional manual processes of quality inspection, this method will help automate the operations, making the entire process more efficient. The results showed that the model was able to accurately detect any damage in cars irrespective of the automobile's type, color, and dimensions. It was observed that even automobiles with minor scratches and dents were classified as damaged, making this model highly reliable. There are many places this model can be used across the automotive supply chain, and the future scope is to determine how to integrate this technology into other industries such as insurance companies and car repair services.

References

Baheti, P. (2022). A gentle introduction to deep learning — The ELI5 way. *V7*, Mar 8, 2022. https://www.v7labs.com/blog/deep-learning-guide.

Bousqaoui, H., Achchab, S., and Kawtar, T. (2018). Machine learning applications in supply chains: An emphasis on neural network applications. *IEEE Xplore*, Feb 8, 2018. https://ieeexplore.ieee.org/document/8284722.

Capgemini (2018). New research from Capgemini shows the automotive industry could gain $160 billion through smart factory adoption by 2023 onwards, Apr 30, 2018. https://www.capgemini.com/pl-pl/news/new-research-from-capgemini-shows-the-automotive-industry-could-gain-160-billion-through-smart-factory-adoption-by-2023-onwards/.

Cprime Studios (2021). What are machine learning use cases in the automotive industry? Dec 17, 2021. https://cprimestudios.com/blog/what-are-machine-learning-use-cases-automotive-industry.

Dileep, P., Das, D., and Bora, P.K. (2020). Dense layer dropout based CNN architecture for automatic modulation classification. *2020 National Conference on Communications (NCC)*, Apr 6, 2020. https://ieeexplore.ieee.org/document/9055989.

Donges, N. (2019). 4 reasons why deep learning and neural networks aren't always the right choice, Jul. 24, 2019. https://builtin.com/data-science/disadvantages-neural-networks.

Dumane, G. (2022). Introduction to convolutional neural networks using tensorflow. *Medium, Towards Data Science*, Mar 2, 2022. https://towardsdatascience.com/introduction-to-convolutional-neural-network-cnn-de73f69c5b83.

Khandelwal, R. (2020). Convolutional neural network: Feature map and filter visualization. *Medium, Towards Data Science*, May 18, 2020. https://towardsdatascience.com/convolutional-neural-network-feature-map-and-filter-visualization-f75012a5a49c.

Krishna, D. (2021). The components of a neural network. *Medium, Towards Data Science*, Jan 5, 2021. https://towardsdatascience.com/the-components-of-a-neural-network-af6244493b5b.

Luckow, A., Kennedy, K., Ziolkowski, M., Djerekarov, E., Cook, M., Duffy, E., Schleiss, M., Vorster, B., Weill, E., Kulshrestha, A., and Smith, M.C. (2019). Artificial intelligence and deep learning applications for automotive manufacturing. *IEEE Xplore*, Jan 24, 2019. https://ieeexplore.ieee.org/document/8622357.

Mejia, N. (2019). AI in the automotive industry — An analysis of the space. *Emerj Artificial Intelligence Research, Emerj*, Feb 12, 2019. https://emerj.com/ai-sector-overviews/ai-in-the-automotive-industry-an-analysis-of-the-space.

Petzold, M. (2021). Use cases: Utilising IOT & AI in automotive. *Record Evolution*, Mar 31, 2021. https://www.record-evolution.de/en/blog/use-cases-utilising-iot-and-ai-in-automotive/.

Qualitas Technologies (2020). Machine vision in defect detection activities using AI and 3D, May 11, 2020. https://qualitastech.com/machine-vision-in-defect-detection-activities-using-ai-and-3d/.

Singh, K., Goyal, S.B., and Pradeep, B. (2021). The role of artificial intelligence and machine learning in supply chain management and its task model. *IEEE Xplore*, Jan 18, 2021. https://ieeexplore.ieee.org/document/9315890.

Shah, A. (2019). Car damage detection. *Kaggle*, Aug 28, 2022. https://www.kaggle.com/datasets/anujms/car-damage-detection.

Thaker, T. (2021). VGG 16 easiest explanation. *Medium*, Aug 8, 2021. https://medium.com/nerd-for-tech/vgg-16-easiest-explanation-12453b599526.

https://doi.org/10.1142/9789811271984_0013

Chapter 13

Digital Technology — AI-IoT in Transformation of Industrial Manufacturing

Xiangyu Lei*, Dian Huang†, Chuyun Zou‡, and Yumeng Zhuang§

Johns Hopkins University, Baltimore, MD, USA
**dhuang30@jh.edu*
†czou10@jh.edu
‡yzhuan10@jh.edu
§xlei7@jhu.edu

Starting with cloud computing, the foundation of the Internet of Things (IoT), combined it with artificial intelligence (AI), adds an essential capability to connected systems — action. In industrial scenes, AI-IoT is mainly used to achieve specific functions related to machine prediction and data processing, in addition to intelligent industrial robots, industrial vision detection, perception identification, and positioning.

We use Bosch's AIoT transformation example to illustrate how AIoT technologies can help a company in manufacturing and supply chain management in the real world and analyze four forces that drive the AIoT transformation. Finally, we conduct SWOT analysis to provide a comprehensive view of how AI-IoT can renovate smart manufacturing and where we should pay attention as we integrate it into manufacturing.

1. Introduction of AI-IoT

From a broad definition, AI-IoT is the integration of artificial intelligence (AI) technology and the Internet of Things (IoT) in practical applications. It is not a new form of IoT application, which differentiates itself from traditional IoT applications. If the IoT is to interconnect all ordinary objects that can perform independent functions, and use the network to connect all things, then AI-IoT is to give it more intelligent characteristics on this basis, to achieve the true interconnection of all things. With the rapid development of technologies such as AI, IoT, cloud computing, big data, and the application of vertical industries in many industries, the integration of AI and IoT in practical projects is becoming more common (Vinugayathri, 2022).

AI-IoT exists as a new form of IoT application. The difference between this and the traditional IoT is that the traditional IoT realizes the interconnection between things and things and people and things through wired and wireless networks. The interconnection between scenarios also needs to realize the interconnection of things–things, people–things, things–people, people–things–services, and data, as well as the empowerment of AI technology to the IoT, to achieve interconnection and interconnection between all "things" of mutual integration (Baidu Baike, 2017). In the vertical industry applications of many industries, the integration of AI and IoT in practical projects is also increasing.

Whether it is AI or the IoT, one keyword is inseparable — data. Data are the foundation of the Internet of Everything (IoE) and human–computer interaction. The intervention of AI gives IoT a connected "brain." Similarly, thanks to the development of current storage technology, data have basic "logistics support" (Vinugayathri, 2022). The rapid expansion of cloud services has given data a material basis for its value.

AI-IoT integrates AI technology and IoT technology, generates and collects massive amounts of data through the IoT, and stores it in the cloud and at the edge, and then through big data analysis and higher forms of AI to realize the digitization of everything, the intelligent connection of everything, the IoT technology. In fact, what the AI is pursuing is an intelligent ecosystem. In addition to the need for continuous technological innovation, the implementation and application of technology are the core issues that need to be broken through in the field of IoT and AI at this stage.

2. Manufacturing: From Past to Present

2.1 *Industrial revolution*

The first major transformation in manufacturing is known as the Industrial Revolution. This is a shift that took place in the 18th century, when objects were not produced by hand, but processes were invented that allowed machines to produce them. It started in England in 1760 and finally reached the United States in the late 18th century (Inventionland, 2018).

2.2 *Unified assembly line*

The next shift in manufacturing was the introduction of the assembly line, first patented in 1901 by car manufacturer Ransom E. Olds. Another important step was the creation of a unified assembly line for Buick (Inventionland, 2018). By creating a well-designed conveying system on a uniform line, costs can be cut drastically, and a high-quality product can be guaranteed.

2.3 *Lean manufacturing*

In 1948, the Toyota Motor Corporation developed what they called "Lean Manufacturing." This process was developed to improve production processes by identifying and eliminating waste (Inventionland, 2018). This system was a dramatic change from the previous system, as it required more persistent and detailed observations. By the 1970s, when the United Kingdom began to adopt its own lean manufacturing system, the concept of lean manufacturing began to spread beyond the automotive industry (Inventionland, 2018). It is now used in electronics, aerospace, healthcare, construction, and food manufacturing.

2.4 *Robotic*

By now, it has become commonplace for machines to dominate manufacturing. A company called Westinghouse first came up with the concept in 1926 (Inventionland, 2018). And today, robotics has reached a new level of innovation. Companies like Rethink Robotics are even trying to develop adaptive manufacturing robots that can work alongside humans. These robots will help increase efficiency and productivity while being low cost and user-friendly. The development process of robots is long, and we are at a critical point in the history of human manufacturing where anything is possible.

Therefore, the future development trend of the manufacturing industry — the combination of high technology and the improved level of manufacturing technology — depends largely on the digitization of equipment, and it has become a general consensus in the manufacturing industry to strengthen the automation of equipment and improve the degree of production automation. Digital technology including intelligent manufacturing technology accelerates the transformation and upgrading of the manufacturing industry, improves production efficiency and the technical level, and reduces energy and resource consumption. Green and sustainable development of manufacturing makes it sophisticated and eco-friendly, raises pollutant discharge standards, improves the standard system, and reduces pollutant discharge.

Moreover, in intelligent manufacturing, the intelligent manufacturing system is a human–machine integrated intelligent system composed of intelligent machines and human experts. It can simulate the intelligence of human experts with the help of computers in a highly flexible and low-integration manner during the manufacturing process, including activities such as analyzing, reasoning, judging, conceiving, and making decisions (Inventionland, 2018). For enterprises, lean production is the basis for realizing intelligent manufacturing, and intelligent manufacturing provides support for enterprises to achieve lean production. In the process of promoting intelligent manufacturing and intelligent factory construction, enterprises need to be lean first.

3. AI-IoT Enables Industrial Manufacturing

3.1 *Cloud-based AI-IoT*

An always-on architecture provides cloud computing with seamless connectivity between multiple devices. In addition to sending machine-to-machine (M2M) messages to each other, the devices also send telemetry data to the cloud, which are centrally received and stored. Computing services in the cloud process these large datasets, representing different devices' data to gain insight. Initially, data processing was based on big data architectures such as Hadoop and Spark (Janakiram, 2019). The IoT and big data help stakeholders understand the patterns and relationships between devices and sensors. The results are presented in insightful visualizations and charts that are part of the IoT dashboard (Janakiram, 2019).

However, combining AI with the IoT adds an essential capability to connected systems, that is, action. AI goes beyond visualization by acting on patterns and correlations in telemetry data. It fills critical gaps by taking appropriate actions based on data. Rather than just showing humans the facts so they can take action, AI completes the cycle by automatically taking action. It essentially becomes the brain that connects the systems (Janakiram, 2019).

4. Application of AI-IoT in Industrial Manufacturing

In the process of large-scale industrial production, the IoT, as an essential breakthrough in the industrial field to promote automation and information construction, can collect a large amount of complex machine data in real time through IoT sensing terminals. Furthermore, it can improve the monitoring and management of equipment, follow-up services based on data, and the adaptive and active intelligence capabilities of the equipment. At present, AI-IoT is mainly used in industrial scenes in the form of single-point applications to achieve specific functions related to machine prediction and data processing, in addition to intelligent industrial robots, industrial vision detection, perception identification, positioning, and other applications (Chen *et al.*, 2021).

4.1 *Digital scheduling*

The scheduling process in a factory is essential. The scheduling characteristics are small batches, multiple boundaries, and multiple constraints. However, the constraints considered manually are often imperfect, leading to low scheduling efficiency (Brillcapital, 2019). In the digital factory, the AI-IoT system can monitor and collect material data and production time data in the factory production; then model, simulate, and analyze the production process of the factory with the help of digital twin technology; and then generate the optimal scheduling plan (Brillcapital, 2019).

4.2 *Supply chain optimization*

Many of the products sold by manufacturing companies go through agents, making it difficult to get direct access to end users. AI-IoT can make raw material procurement and sales more predictable (Li, 2017) — optimizing supply chain selection, inventory management, allocation, and replenishment decisions. For example, Lenovo used the data held by the global data center to establish a sales forecasting system for steel in cooperation with Baosteel Group based on international market conditions, with a prediction accuracy of 92.2% and a 20% reduction in inventory turnaround time (Li, 2017).

4.3 *Device management*

AI-IoT can provide powerful, efficient, and visual batch device management. Managed devices include sensors, microcontrollers, and powerful gateways for routing device group communications (Chen *et al.*, 2021). Facing the massive amount of smart devices in the future, AI-IoT provides complete device access and management services. The communication between AI-IoT and devices is based on the UDP/COAP protocol, ensuring real-time controllability and low energy consumption of devices (Takyar, 2022). AI-IoT assigns private keys to each accessed device for encryption of link communication between the two sides, thereby ensuring communication security (Keyfactor, 2021).

4.4 *Predictive maintenance*

AI-IoT collects data from sensors installed in physical industrial equipment and then uses simulations to predict the future performance of the equipment. This preventive maintenance can be implemented to reduce the risk of downtime. This saves scheduled downtime and unscheduled maintenance costs (Record Evolution, 2022). You minimize emergencies and are better able to plan your resources. But more importantly, by creating optimal operating conditions for your assets, you can achieve overall operational efficiency and extend the life of your machine (Record Evolution, 2022).

4.5 *Industrial vision function*

AI-IoT can model critical equipment operating parameters based on machine vision and AI technology, thus realizing industrial vision detection, identification, and positioning functions (Chen *et al.*, 2021). Some new tools integrate with traditional visual systems, enabling end users to combine deep learning with traditional visual tools in the same application. This meets the requirements of industrial manufacturing where accurate measurement of scratches, contamination, and other defects is required, such as in medical devices and electronic manufacturing environments (Allie, 2022).

5. AI-IoT Application Example

5.1 *Bosch's AI-IoT transformation*

Bosch is an engineering and technology company headquartered in Germany. Its core operations include mobility solutions, industry technology, consumer goods, and energy and building technology. It has 270 plants and over 700 logistics centers worldwide (Bosch Industry 4.0 Solutions in Practice, Bosch, 27 Nov 2018). To improve the efficiency and performance of these plants and logistics centers, Bosch upgraded to the AI-IoT system which can connect the plants and the logistics centers to improve manufacturing.

The part of Bosch's AI-IoT system that is related to the manufacturing part is a software called Nexeed (Bosch, 2022). It connects individual lines, entire plants, plant networks, their intralogistics, and the external goods flow by gathering data and information from sensors.

Nexeed facilitates manufacturing in four ways. First, it can optimize production processes by collecting and harmonizing production and machine data from different sources in real time. Employees can see the data visualization and corresponding defined events so that they can react faster with the correct actions (Bosch Connected Industry, n.d.). According to information given by Bosch, the optimization can provide up to 15% machine availability and 5 to 10% higher production performance (Bosch Connected Industry, n.d.). Second, Nexeed makes maintenance easier and clearer (Bosch Connected Industry, n.d.). It bundles all necessary information and provided it to operators and maintenance personnel on mobile devices. It also enables remote maintenance and maximizes the security by sophisticated multi-stage authentication and release management. Third, Nexeed provides seamless transparency throughout the supply chain. Its track and trace solution provides a completely transparent view of material movements from the warehouse to the production line workstation which enables plant supervisors to steer all transport job orders throughout the plant (Bosch, 2022). Lastly, Nexeed AI solution can support decision-making. Nexeed has a data analytics feature that can intelligently draw important conclusions for optimization potential. This can help employees explore data regardless of their IT skill (Bosch Connected Industry, n.d.).

The implementation of Nexeed in Bosch's Oberallgäu plant illustrates its advantages. Sixty thousand sensors in this plant deliver the relevant information to employees in a timely manner which enables predictive maintenance (Bosch, 2022). For example, data can indicate that a caulking tool on the assembly line will soon need to be serviced. This can minimize the machine downtime. Also, employees can track the condition of machines either in-plant or remotely on a tablet.

5.2 *Forces drive Bosch's AI-IoT transformation*

Four forces drive the AI-IoT transformation of Bosch. First, the transformation is influenced by two major political forces. One political force is the energy policy of the European Union which aims to provide secure, sustainable, competitive, and affordable energy (Energy policy of the European Union — Wikipedia, 2022). Two of the five priorities of this policy are decarbonization and energy efficiency. According to Bosch, Nexeed helps it consume 40% less power by energy management. Another political force is the Industry 4.0 strategy (Fourth Industrial Revolution — Wikipedia, 2022). Its four themes of interconnection, information transparency, technical assistance, and decentralized decisions can be satisfied by the features of Nexeed and were shown in the example (Fourth Industrial Revolution — Wikipedia, 2022).

The second force is economic force. Labor cost in Germany has increased in recent years and it is above the average in Europe. AI-IoT transformation can help Bosch save labor cost by automation and improve productivity per labor by 24% according to its report. In addition, 40%

less power consumption helps Bosch face the increasing energy prices in Europe (Bosch, 2022).

The third force is social force. AI and IoT have become popular in recent years. More and more students choose AI-related majors and jobs. According to the AI index report 2021 from Stanford University, in just the last six years, the number of AI-related publications on an Xiv grew more than 6-fold (Zhang, 2021). This provides Bosch with a lot of AI-IoT-related human resources.

The last force is the technological force. Because of the development of AI and IoT technology, AI-IoT has become commercially useful and important. Companies leveraging AI-IoT can gain huge advantages against those who don't. Just as demonstrated in the Bosch example, Bosch gains advantages in cost efficiency, operation, and transparency (Bosch Connected Industry, n.d.).

6. Analysis for AIoT in Manufacturing

6.1 *Strengths*

One of the major strengths AI-IoT could provide manufacturers is to help them create synergies through real-time data collection and global transparency across functions. As customer needs are rapidly changing and evolving, how fast the smart manufacturers could fulfill these needs becomes the key to outperform competitors. The ideal way is to altogether streamline the process from data collection to analysis to implementation, enabling organization-wide fast decision-making based on as much up-to-date data as possible. That would require the manufacturer to have as much available production-related data from as many functions, in combination with sufficient data-analyzing capabilities (Record Evolution, 2022).

Another strength of employing AI-IoT in smart manufacturing is cost saving in the longer term. Extensive real-time analysis has a predictive nature if implemented appropriately for a period of time and could obtain regular results; therefore, it is less likely for emergencies to occur that will incur huge costs without any warning signs. Manufacturers can save costs from avoiding unexpected downtime in the production line and keep devices in ideal conditions, leading to better productivity (Record Evolution, 2022).

One counterintuitive strength of AI-IoT is its smooth integration with existing systems and easy scalability and flexibility (Record Evolution, 2022). Typically, implementation of a new IoT platform may be considered as a "big bang" that will incur much confusion. However, the AI-IoT platforms, such as Software as a Service (SaaS), allow test runs and corrections prior to deployment for the whole infrastructure, which offers sufficient flexibility to accommodate potential changes. For scalability and flexibility, once AI has been incorporated with the IoT, it can cross-compare data from different sources and establish a more holistic view from analytics, improving the quality and speed of production insight generation (Record Evolution, 2022).

6.2 *Weaknesses*

After identifying the strengths AI-IoT could bring to present manufacturers, we still need to realize that a lot of AI-IoT projects failed due to lack of compatibility for the following reasons. First, it is difficult to select an appropriate AI-IoT platform for manufacturers who have no previous experience in estimating the involved complexity (Record Evolution, 2022). In manufacturing, as the level of automation and compatibility across functions is different, each company would have different use cases that could be empowered by adoption of AI-IoT. Therefore, without a detailed top-down review of the need of AI-IoT and a thorough understanding of the organization's present production pain points, it would be relatively difficult to land on the most suitable AI-IoT solution.

Another type of bottleneck manufacturers face is a lack of strategy in dealing with different types of data sources altogether when incorporating IoT analytics. A common problem manufacturers encounter when deploying IoT and AI together is that their various existing systems do not comply with each other (Record Evolution, 2022). Extra costs may be spent on uniting different data sources, consuming resources that could have been spent on solving more crucial issues for overall implementation of the AI-IoT environment.

Given the above two points, it is difficult to manage costs if the objectives have not been clearly laid out. Nowadays, organizations may try to adopt IoT without adequately researching and consulting its unique implementation in the specific organization (Record Evolution, 2022). The increasing expenditure on pilot projects of AI-IoT in combination with insignificant improvement of production parameters would be a crucial concern for management.

6.3 *Opportunities*

One opportunity AI-IoT could take advantage of is condition monitoring; once the AI-IoT infrastructure has been established, production data both within and among different manufacturing sites are available for cross-analysis. Then, the insights generated by AI would be more in depth for analyzing parameters based on functions instead of just one site's production health (Record Evolution, 2022). Therefore, manufacturers could assess whether the key performance indicators are met at the organizational level and are more likely to detect trends and signs early on.

The adoption of smart manufacturing could also enable predictive maintenance. The previous point actually set the foundation for predictive maintenance — the trends shown in big data analytics could help manufacturers predict downtime needed in advance, so they can plan ahead and minimize its effect on production (Record Evolution, 2022). Therefore, operation efficiency is guaranteed.

6.4 *Threats*

A major threat AI-IoT is currently facing is the safety concerns of AI. For manufacturing businesses, in order to have cost advantage or differentiate themselves from competitors, adopting AI-IoT ahead of competitors and keeping insights to themselves would be crucial. Therefore, preventing production data breach would be one of the top priorities.

Another practical threat manufacturers face would be supply unable to match fragmented demand. As discussed in weaknesses, it is relatively hard for inexperienced manufacturers to decide on the right AI-IoT solution (Record Evolution, 2022). On the supply side, given their various use cases, the solution providers also face difficulties in suggesting the most suitable solutions for clients. Manufacturers may want to seek help from IT consulting companies for the extent of AI-IoT that they could integrate into businesses.

7. Conclusion

AI-IoT is the integration of AI technology and the IoT in practical applications. AI goes beyond visualization by acting on patterns and correlations in telemetry data. AI-IoT fills critical gaps by taking appropriate actions based on data. Rather than just showing humans the facts so they can take action, AI completes the cycle by automatically taking action and even becomes the brain that connects systems. In industrial manufacturing, AIoT grants manufacturers the power of automation and information construction, such as Digital Scheduling, Supply Chain Optimization, Device Management, Predictive Maintenance, and Industrial Vision Function. In Bosch's example, AIoT technology shows its ability to collect data and use data to improve productivity, facilitate maintenance, manage the supply chain, and conduct analysis. This example illustrates that AIoT transformation is feasible and it has a huge potential for manufacturers to discover. We should recognize the opportunities that AIoT brings while preparing for known and unknown concerns from different stakeholder groups.

References

Allie (2022, January). Four factors drive industrial AIoT to become the new favorite — 51CTO.com. Retrieved April 25, 2022, from https://www.51cto.com/article/698573.html.

Baidu Baike (2017). AIoT. https://baike.baidu.com/item/AIoT/23298459?fr=aladdin.

Bosch (2022). Nexeed — Welcome to the smart factory. Retrieved March 8, 2022, from https://www.bosch.com/stories/nexeed-smart-factory/.

Bosch Connected Industry (n.d.). NEXEED — Software and services. Retrieved March 20, 2022, from https://assets.bosch.com/media/en/global/products_and_solutions/connected_products_and_services/industy_40/bosch-connected-industry-brochure.pdf.

Brillcapital (2019). 2019 year-end roundup: AI into various industries. Retrieved April 25, 2022, from http://www.brillcapital.com/news/2019-12-28/74.html.

Chen, H., Peng, H., and Cheng, Q. (2021, July). CICC: AIoT series: AI-enabled IoT, Exploring new trends in AIoT development. Retrieved April 25, 2022, from https://mp.weixin.qq.com/s/ILwKzEsEYz-817w_sl4q9A.

Energy policy of the European Union — Wikipedia (2022). Retrieved March 8, 2022, from https://en.wikipedia.org/wiki/Energy_policy_of_the_European_Union#SET_Plan.

Fourth Industrial Revolution — Wikipedia (2022). Retrieved March 8, 2022, from https://en.wikipedia.org/wiki/Fourth_Industrial_Revolution#Key_themes.

Inventionland (2018, April 24). Manufacturing: From past to present. https://inventionland.com/blog/manufacturing-past-present/.

Janakiram, M.S.V. (2019, August 12). Why AIoT is emerging as the future of industry 4.0. Forbes. Retrieved April 25, 2022, from https://www.forbes.com/sites/janakirammsv/2019/08/12/why-aiot-is-emerging-as-the-future-of-industry-40/?sh=561835a0619b.

Keyfactor (2021, August 17). IoT device security + how to get started. Retrieved April 25, 2022, from https://www.keyfactor.com/resources/iot-device-security/.

Li, J. (2017, December). Industrial big data: Supply-side competitiveness to be cultivated-CCID. Retrieved April 25, 2022, from https://www.ccidgroup.com/info/1105/26865.htm.

Record Evolution (2022). Use cases: Utilizing AI and IoT in manufacturing. Retrieved March 8, 2022, from https://www.record-evolution.de/en/blog/use-cases-utilizing-iot-and-the-artificial-intelligence-of-things-aiot-in-manufacturing/.

Takyar, A. (2022, March 31). What is IoT device management and how it works? LeewayHertz. Retrieved April 25, 2022, from https://www.leewayhertz.com/iot-device-management/.

Vinugayathri (2022). AI and IoT blended — What it is and why it matters? Retrieved March 17, 2022, from https://www.clariontech.com/blog/ai-and-iot-blended-what-it-is-and-why-it-matters.

Zhang, D. (2021). Artificial Intelligence Index. Retrieved March 20, 2022, from https://aiindex.stanford.edu/wp-content/uploads/2021/11/2021-AI-Index-Report_Master.pdf.

https://doi.org/10.1142/9789811271984_0014

Chapter 14

Smart Organizational Learning with Digital Transformation

Jeffrey S. Ray[*,‡] **and Albert T. Mubako**[*,†,§,¶]

[*]*University of Maryland Baltimore County (UMBC), Baltimore, MD, USA*
[†]*Institute for Digital Business Strategy (IDBS), Cape Town, South Africa*
[‡]*jeffray@umbc.edu*
[§]*almubako@umbc.edu*
[¶]*albert.mubako@institutedbs.com*

This chapter presents a model for digitally transforming a business by first performing a digital maturity assessment of current capabilities, describing the maturity levels of the digital environment to define a starting point to base future modifications on, and then applying a Digital Business Strategy Model (DBSM) to ensure that required inputs and outputs for developing a Digital Business Strategy (DBS) will create and capture value for the firm from emerging digital technologies. A solution and cultural intelligence-driven approach is enabled through strategic alignment of a firm's organizational structure, infrastructure architecture, and the innovation strategy being pursued. The recommended digital transformation (DX) process will overcome sponsor hesitancy to make the investment required to modernize corporate infrastructures. Organizational learning must be part of a comprehensive DX effort.

An enhanced organizational learning model is presented with recommended practical implementation steps to ensure smart organizational transformation.

1. Introduction

With today's growing interest in digital business, it has become evident that digital disruption poses both opportunities and threats to institutions and individuals. Digital transformation (DX) occurs at two levels: individually (digital skills) and organizationally (organizational learning, digital business modeling, processes, and culture). As the risks in traditional markets lessened, the emergence of the digital economy created a modern battleground where those who are digitally skilled and savvy have utilized digital entrepreneurship to succeed in the marketplace. In the digital economy, both private and public sector organizations are taking transformational steps toward either digital business optimization or DX of their business processes. DX is the incorporation of emerging technology capabilities and innovative digital skills into the organization, which results in the incorporation of smart innovations into organizational operations.

2. Digital and Organizational Transformation

According to Hur *et al.* (2019), organizational transformation is the process of changing the existing corporate culture to achieve a competitive advantage or address a significant challenge. Organizational transformation intersects DX, as the first step includes adopting a digital vision and instituting a corporate digital culture to adapt to the rapidly changing technological and competitive environment. It is visible action taken by organizational leaders to move from the present to the future in order to achieve a specific outcome or benefit (Hur *et al.*, 2019). It goes without saying that an organization must have the capacity to learn and understand the disruptive technologies before those technologies can be leveraged to improve current products and services.

More and more companies are adopting DX and leveraging technology to improve every aspect of their business. It involves people, technology, and capabilities intersecting to execute modern processes. DX means applying emerging technologies to strategy, industry, business process, models, and culture with a clear commercial application.

DX for business organizations has been used to grow revenue and defend market position in disruptive industries. Businesses and governments have been forced to adopt emerging technologies and software, including intelligent and connected applications for operations. New analytical methods, data mining, and processing power have become available with emerging technologies such as big data analytics and robotic automation with artificial intelligence (AI).

Digital literacy remains the fastest-growing necessity for citizens, and organizations are quickly becoming dependent on their digital human resource skills, which are important for people to navigate daily work activities. In the workplace, digital skills are required for an ever-growing number of jobs, and digital applications are beginning to make inroads even in traditionally manual sectors like agriculture, with a corresponding requirement for some level of digital literacy. Developing a digitally skilled population calls for the involvement of different institutions: Universities need to undertake research and determine requirements, government institutions need to develop appropriate policies, training institutions need to deliver relevant digital skills training, and the private sector and civil society organizations need to support digital adoption and use. Therefore, it is necessary to have an organization-wide digital culture and assess both internal and external digital capabilities to have a successful DX journey and implementation.

3. Digital Transformation Maturity

Organizations need to use tools such as DX assessment, which is an investigative tool to determine an organization's strategic digital posture and knowledge of the current state of the customer experience, the workforce experience, and collaboration in the digital economy. To achieve this objective, a closer look at the influencing factors of the firm's operations can be carried out to establish the firm's DX maturity and where to go next in order to improve performance. The organization can be assessed in the five focus areas and the corresponding sub-areas indicated in Table 1 according to the relevance in their particular industry and sector.

Table 1. Digital transformation maturity assessment focus areas.

Focus Areas	
1. Infrastructure	1.1 Mobile Connectivity 1.2 Internet Access and Use 1.3 Physical Infrastructure
2. Policy and Regulation	2.1 Legal and Regulatory Environment 2.2 Legislation 2.3 Implementation
3. People and Skills	3.1 Basic Education 3.2 Digital Literacy 3.3 Digital Skills 3.4 Advanced Literacy
4. Digital Government and Governance	4.1 Financing 4.2 Digital Architecture 4.3 Services 4.4 Governance
5. Business and Innovation	5.1 Small and Medium-Sized Enterprises 5.2 Competition 5.3 Intellectual Property

Source: IDBS (2021).

The five focus areas are subject to their relevance in the sectors (private or public) and the industry in which the enterprise operates. For instance, the focus area of digital government is a more relevant focus area for public administration than it would be for the private retail sector. However, certain aspects can be taken into consideration in the assessment; the desired goal is to rightly position an enterprise's place on its DX journey. The scoring in each focus area will lead to the firm's digital maturity level, which reflects the digital business optimization and transformation required to improve performance levels. The results of a 360-degree look at digital capabilities include people and technical capabilities, which are the main drivers and can be used to begin mapping out the enterprise's digital journey. Figure 1 depicts what the five focus areas look like when a 360-degree assessment is envisioned around the DX maturity assessment.

After the DX maturity assessment and scoring, the firm will be able to ascertain its maturity and digital capabilities on a scale that ranges from

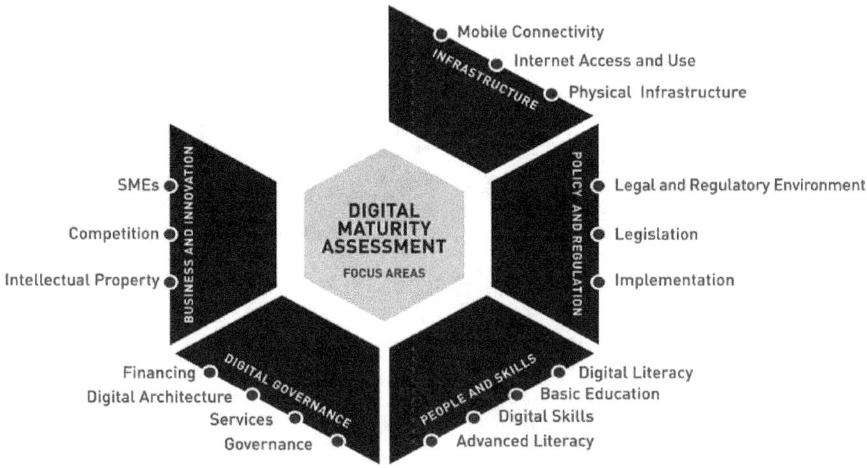

Fig. 1. Digital transformation maturity assessment.
Source: IDBS (2021).

nascent to transformed digital enterprise. From here, a corporation's key task is to learn how to enhance its digital performance.

Figure 2 identifies five DX levels that firms consecutively achieve as they become digitally transformed. Upon completion of the maturity assessment, the organizations will be equipped with information to use in the roadmap of their DX journeys, and to find their digital maturity level at any given moment. The roadmap is useful in choosing and implementing the changes to be made and highlighting benefits to the business's bottom line, ultimately increasing shareholder value. The digital maturity level indexes digital performance levels in industry, government, or public enterprises. The five digital performance and maturity levels are described as follows:

(1) **Nascent:** Digital performance capability is not implemented in industry or government. Economic activity has no clear vision for social media, mobility, analytics, cloud computing, or the Internet of Things (IoT). The capabilities are available but not monetized in the enterprise.
(2) **Functional:** Basic-level digital uses, including web and internet to extend relationships between people and businesses.

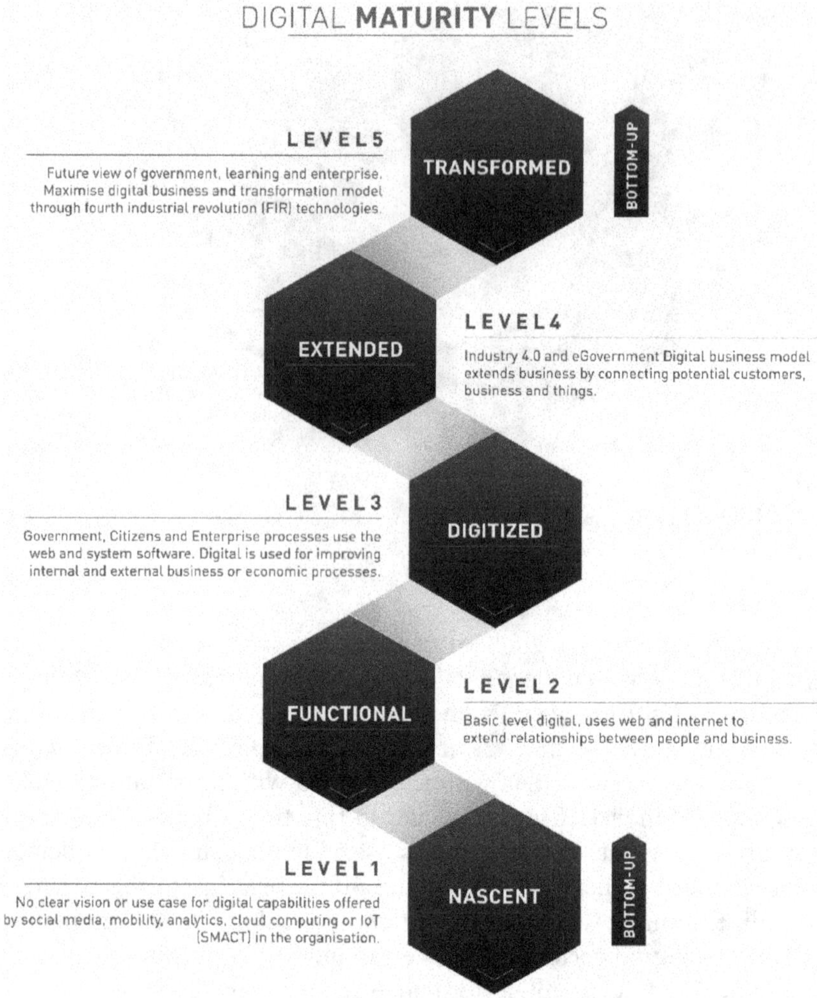

Fig. 2. IDBS Digital Business Strategy digital maturity levels.
Source: IDBS (2021).

(3) **Digitized:** Government, citizen, and enterprise processes use the web and system software. Digital is used for improving internal and external business or economic processes.
(4) **Extended:** Industry 4.0 and eGovernment digital business model extends businesses by connecting potential customers, businesses, and things.

(5) **Transformed:** Future view of government, learning, and enterprise. Maximizes the digital business and transformation model through Fourth Industrial Revolution (FIR) technologies.

The digital performance levels assist with planning and operations: how the organization will digitally plan, operate, monitor, and track the value captured. Executives need to pay careful attention to where they compete, and to closely monitor the return on their DX investments. Upon ascertaining their digital performance level and roadmap, the organization can begin to implement the transformative change using a step-by-step DX model approach that incorporates knowledge innovation and learning.

4. Digital Business Strategy (DBS) Model

As indicated in Figure 3, the DBS Model's foundation is that of a transformative digital culture of innovation and organizational learning. This allows for moderate risk-taking, speaking your mind, creativity, and solution-finding, and divergent thinking.

Digitalization is one of the forces driving industry change, and its impact will have a bearing on a competitive intensity and industry profitability (Mubako and Ray, 2020).

A DBS is a firm's business strategy incorporating the digital economy and ecosystems, which defines the business's objectives and goals (Bharadwaj *et al*., 2013). A DBS requires an enterprise-wide shift in culture and the identification of transient, competitive advantages in a disruptive digital economy (Mubako and Pavlou, 2017). The IDBS Digital Business Strategy Model (IDBSM) refers to the actionable, strategic steps that transform an organization to a digital enterprise with digital citizens (people) and digital accelerators (capabilities). This model breaks down how companies can develop a DBS with emerging technologies. IDBSM guidance includes implementing deliberate and actionable input steps to produce outputs for a successful DX. The model brings together elements from scholars of DBS for clarity and purpose, including three organizational value models for center-to-edge DX:

(1) In value chains by empowering choices easily in transactions and processes.
(2) In value shops through learning and knowledge creation.
(3) In value networks through sharing and engaging with a larger and more diverse network of people and resources (Gray *et al*., 2015).

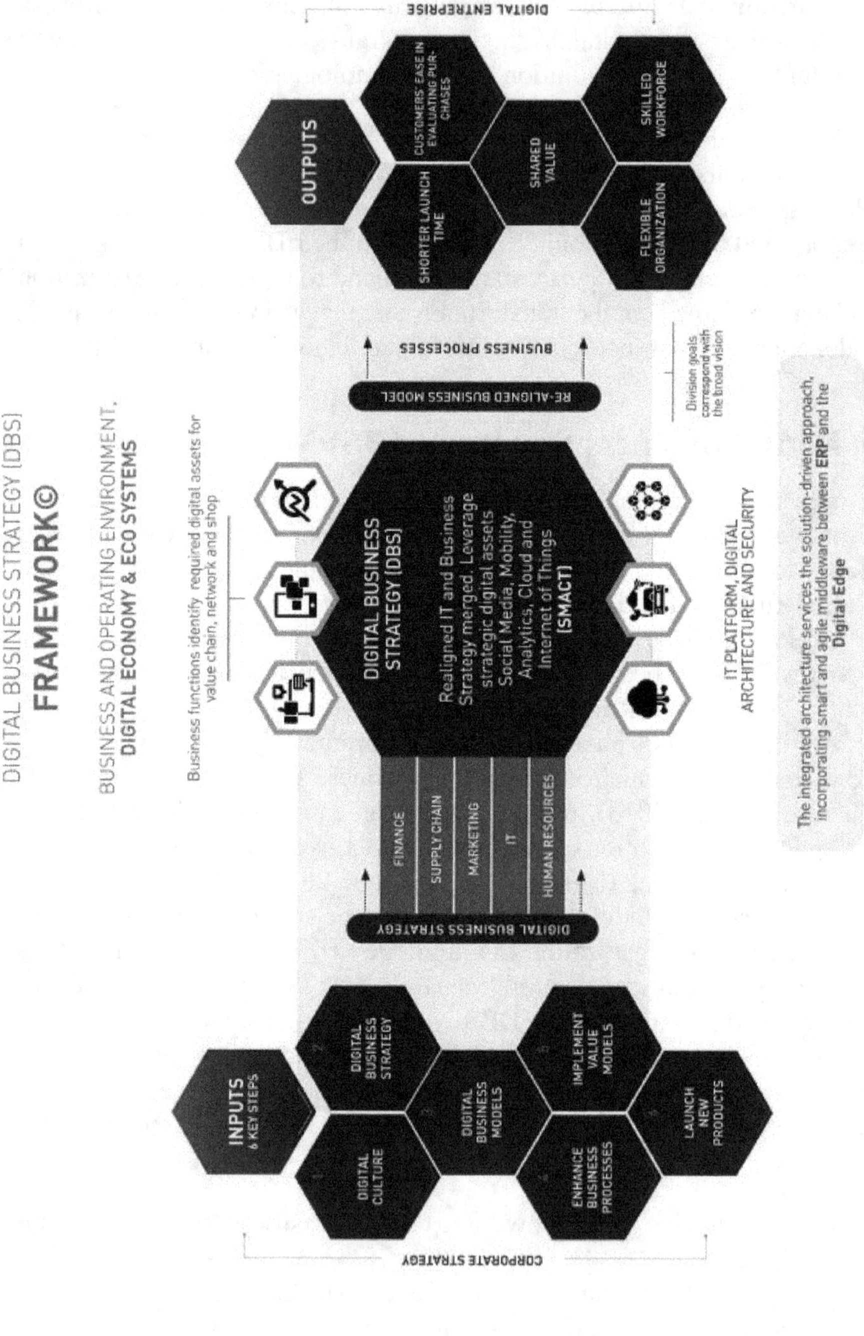

Fig. 3. IDBS Digital Business Strategy Model.

Inputs of the IDBSM include the following six key steps (Mubako and Ray, 2017, 2020):

(1) Adopt a digital vision, institute a digital culture, and seek to understand the rapidly changing technological and competitive environment.
(2) Implement a robust technology infrastructure and integrate the company's technology and business strategy. Realign IT and business strategies to include digital economy.
(3) Create a value proposition and develop business models based on the functionalities of new technologies coupled with existing company resources.
(4) Develop and employ the dynamic capability to transform and change by reconfiguring existing business processes to build new products and services.
(5) Create and capture differential value and build a competitive advantage with value models.
(6) Launch new products and accelerate products to market with shorter launch time.

Outputs of the IDBSM include the following:

- **Shorter launch time:** New products and new configurations of existing products become easier to launch in shorter time frames with the improved business model.
- **Customers' ease in evaluating purchases:** Processes that are based on outcomes will produce a better customer experience and reach different segments of consumers, improving the bottom line of the enterprises.
- **Shared value:** The digital economy is the modern-day environment in which public and private enterprises operate. The emergence of innovative technologies, along with the urgency of climate change clean tech, has created the need for shared value ecosystems between customers and providers and public and private partnerships alike.
- **Flexible organization:** The capabilities of the digital enterprise include agility and the ability to exploit the dynamic, plug-and-play nature of emerging technology to increase competitive and transient advantages. "To stay ahead, they need to constantly start new strategic initiatives, building and exploiting many transient competitive advantages at once" (McGrath, 2013a).

- **Skilled workforce:** Productivity and overall share value gains from the new digital operating models will be realized as the digital enterprises skillfully manage their workforce skills. As companies introduce software bots and digital self-service, and as they transform assembly lines, they must bring along their key employees, leaders, and customers as they redefine jobs, career paths, workforce management, and social contracts (Knoess *et al.*, 2016).

The following two infrastructure capabilities can increase the effectiveness of a firm's tailoring of the DBSM:

(1) Strategic alignment of the organization's existing capabilities, infrastructure, intended investment, and strategic business goals.
(2) Improved organizational learning postures that allow the firm to cognitively understand and comprehend the innovative and disruptive technologies about to impact their marketplaces.

Each of these capabilities is discussed in the following.

5. Strategic Alignment as an Element of Smart Organizational Transformation

The first infrastructure capability to facilitate smart organizational transformation is that of strategic alignment, which refers to strategic alignment of the organization's existing capabilities, infrastructure, intended investment, and strategic business goals, seeking to understand the rapidly changing technological and competitive environment (Mubako and Ray, 2017).

5.1 *Organizational alignment*

As firms are dealing with DX, the successful ones are improving their organizational alignment and reaping benefits such as increasing the speed of their decision-making, getting better employee engagement, wasting fewer resources, improving self-governance of staff, increasing leadership credibility, and getting better resource visibility (Deshler, 2016). Aligning the firm's cultural behaviors with its strategic business objectives will improve its product architectures through increased collaboration across the enterprise, which can require complementary changes to organizational structures. Organizational culture is "an elusively complex entity that survives and evolves mostly through gradual shifts in leadership, strategy, and other considerations" (Katzenbach *et al.*, 2016). Cultures are said to be deeply embedded and cannot be replaced en masse or swapped out in their entirety, like an operational system. Firms must work with their cultures effectively, understand them, and recognize the traits that are significant and consistent, and improve them across the enterprise (Katzenbach *et al.*, 2016). Now that cultural differences can be bridged, cultural skills such as empathetic understanding can be applied to support the effective operation of geographically dispersed teams. Armed with these benefits, firms can improve the alignment of their cultural behaviors with programmatic efforts and, in so doing, improve their performance.

5.2 *Innovation strategy alignment*

Due to the different types of innovation and the differing requirements associated with each, a firm's innovation strategy should specify how the different types of innovation being leveraged are aligned with the firm's strategic business plan and the resources being allocated to each strategic pursuit. Since the capabilities needed to support innovation initiatives depend on the type of innovation being pursued, firms should make defining their innovation strategy a primary focus so they can identify and acquire employees with the right skills. Firms tend to prioritize resource allocations for R&D initiatives based on sustaining innovation initiatives, but this tends to starve out disruptive innovation initiatives. According to Christensen and Overdorf, disruption is really just a continuous, ongoing alignment of the firm's price point with their customer's desires and product performance demands, which is related to their confidence level in the brand (Christensen and Overdorf, 2000). This makes brand management even more important, and firms should include alignment of price points within the disruption context in their strategic business planning.

Innovation strategy alignment consists of evaluating and assessing disruptive innovation in marketing; planning for and dealing with disruptive innovation; assessing whether or not to implement strategies that would make the firm a disruptor; and aligning the firm's innovation strategy with investment and strategic goals. The incumbents that solely focus on existing customers may become institutionalized, which makes them more vulnerable to disruption. A firm can counter this by recognizing disruption as a continuous, ongoing alignment of price points with their customer's desired end-product demands. As part of their strategic planning, firms should map their product price points over time and monitor the efforts of disruptors.

Innovation initiatives frequently fail, and even successful innovators have a hard time sustaining their performance with repeat successes (Pisano, 2015). The cause of these failures is attributed to not having a defined innovation strategy. Firms need to define an effective innovation strategy, which describes how to balance the different types of innovation initiatives, and then align the innovation pursuits within the context of the maturity of the firm's digital business transformation.

5.3 *Architectural alignment*

When disruptive technologies require that substantial architectural changes be made to a firm's current products, the firms lose their incumbent's advantage. These firms find it difficult to compete with upstart disrupter companies given their embedded infrastructure investments and entrenched organizational structures, which are based on old product lines. Such firms need to continuously align their organizational structure with the future architecture needs of the firms' products. Establishing cross-functional teams that are simultaneously responsible for both old and new technologies will ensure that embedded architectural knowledge from the staff is considered in future architectural design solutions. This is an element of smart organizational transformation, included as Step 2 in the IDBS Model (Mubako and Ray, 2017, 2020) by implementing a robust technology infrastructure and integrating the company's technology and business strategies, which realigns IT and business strategies to include a focus on the digital economy (Mubako and Ray, 2017).

As disruptive products improve along performance dimensions that are important to customers, and customers begin to embrace the disruptive products, the disruptors start to capture the incumbent's market share (Gans, 2016). Regarding defensive actions related to disruptive innovations, managers typically set up autonomous entrepreneurial units tasked with exploring disruptive technologies as defensive actions. Gans reports that firms are having trouble getting positive results from this approach and "find themselves unable to transfer the new technologies into their mainstream operations" (Gans, 2016). The difficulty in responding to new innovative technologies is attributed to a new form of disruption labeled "architectural disruption" (Gans, 2016). Architectural alignment is primarily focused on solving the architectural disruption problem and includes evaluating and assessing the firm's infrastructure for obsolescence; countering architectural disruption; selecting the correct architectural approach for firm initiatives, such as implementing product lines or platforms; exercising platform controls; and aligning the enterprise architecture with the firm's business strategy. By leveraging our cultural understanding across social distances and applying it to cross-functional teams with architectural knowledge, the enterprise architecture can be aligned with the evolving organizational structure needed to capture diverse cultures and capabilities across the enterprise.

5.4 *Knowledge alignment*

The outcome of DX is the ability to facilitate increased collaboration among employees, partners, suppliers, and customers. Some firms embrace collaboration through technology, management, training, culture, and workplace design, while others ignore such opportunities. Such firms need to align their knowledge management processes, particularly with regard to the continual supply of information collected by the firm about disruptive technologies and their applications, by updating their operational strategies to align organizational learning and knowledge creation modeling initiatives with the firm's strategic business plan. The focus should be on acquiring and processing the information related to innovative technologies that is needed to support the strategic plan.

Knowledge alignment includes advancing entrepreneurship and self-leadership qualities of the staff; implementing knowledge creation models to improve the organizational learning posture of the firm to support a continuous, constant learning capability related to innovative and disruptive technology concepts; receiving, gathering, tagging, improving, storing, mapping (to AI robot data structures), and processing information to make it meaningful so it can be retained more readily by the organization; leveraging implemented knowledge creation models to create effective learning environments; implementing knowledge management systems (KMSs) to handle and process new information as it is learned; and using the improved organizational learning infrastructure to self-tune the organization and speed up decision-making to make effective products and services faster and more efficiently.

Organizational learning involves knowledge conversion processes (KCPs) that transform knowledge states between individual and group focus, and between tacit and explicit forms, as the organization's core knowledge levels evolve iteratively to increasingly refined levels of accumulated base knowledge (Ray, 2014). Aligning the organization to continuous learning will create an effective organizational learning posture that can be used to conduct training that is aligned to the firm's ongoing operations, which, by definition, are aligned with capturing the firm's strategic objectives, and will create timely knowledge to be immediately used on the job to implement disruptive technology mitigation plans. Organizational learning and DX intersect with the outcomes to develop and employ the dynamic capability to transform and change by reconfiguring existing business processes to build new products and services, as indicated in Step 4 of the IDBS Model (Mubako and Ray, 2017, 2020).

Understanding the value of employees and their skill sets will allow the firm to plan their development paths to obtain the skills the firm will need to support the handling of near-term disruptive technologies. In order to initiate the transfer of tacit knowledge to explicit knowledge related to a specific job function, from within the context of a specific innovative technology, each staff member should so the following:

- Make a journal of their tasks.
- Define directions describing how tasks are completed.
- Seek out dependencies of the tasks in terms of other resources and people.
- Create some basic measurement metrics to compute how successfully the task is performed.
- Describe the anticipated self-impact to be expected when performing the task relative to stress levels, sense of accomplishment, and fatigue.
- Describe the relational impact regarding how people receiving the fruits of the completed task feel.
- Describe the learning impact specific to what the performer can be expected to learn from conducting the task.
- Place the task list and the corresponding directions into a folder structure and apply a revision system to track its configuration state (Sun, 2007).

This ensures the firm's acquisition of knowledge will be aligned to its evolving business strategy.

6. Organizational Learning Is the Essential Infrastructure Capability for Smart Organizational Transformation

The second infrastructure capability that can increase the effectiveness of the IDBS Model described above is an improved organizational learning posture that allows firms to cognitively understand and comprehend the innovative and disruptive technologies about to impact their business areas. This section describes the need for improved organizational learning and knowledge creation modeling, describes the foundational knowledge creation model as espoused by Nonaka (1991), and then introduces a new Enhanced Organizational Learning Model (EnOLM) to improve a firm's organizational learning postures.

6.1 *The need for improved organizational learning and knowledge creation modeling*

These are uncertain times for managers in large companies that have a global reach. Even before the internet and globalization, the track record for managers of large firms dealing with disruptive innovation cycles was disappointing. The numerous industries that were disrupted while firm managers sat and watched include hardbound encyclopedia sales (disrupted by digital encyclopedias), music CDs (disrupted by the iPod and iTunes), dial-up internet service (disrupted by hardwire cable modems), mini computers (disrupted by the personal computer), film-based cameras (disrupted by digital cameras), video rental stores (disrupted by streaming video services like Netflix), taxi services (disrupted by Uber), and brick and mortar stores (disrupted by Amazon), to name just a few.

With disruption as a backstop for the current economy, it becomes imperative that companies currently providing products and services assess their current status in the marketplace. Peter Drucker related the economic success of a corporation to its ability to create "core competencies" (Drucker, 1995). Jack Welch demanded that a firm's core competencies lead to market leadership positions (Ray, 2014). Most large companies have talented managers, competent digital technology subject matter experts, strong product portfolios, first-rate technological know-how, and funding. So, what are these firms missing that makes them vulnerable? Firms still try to maintain their leadership position in market areas by continuously making a number of incremental improvements to their core competency area products and services. These companies are more susceptible to disruption since they are getting increasingly locked into infrastructure investments that are focused on new, improved, and more expensive features for their current products. New entrants to the market can disrupt such products by using new technologies to offer less expensive versions of the products, which are intended to allow new customers to purchase products they previously could not afford.

When the magnitude of the potential contributions that can be anticipated from recent Industry 4.0 innovation technologies is considered, such as AI, the IoT, 3-D printing, machine learning, advanced robotics that emulates human motion, autonomous vehicles, and Bitcoin in the financial marketplace, one must wonder if any current businesses are safe from disruptive technologies. How products are used by consumers will likely change significantly when these manufacturing technologies are adapted to improve consumer products and services. Too many firms need to increase their cognitive understanding with respect to the disruptive technologies that are on the horizon. What the firms lack is a habit of thinking about their organizational capabilities as carefully as they think about individual staff member capabilities (Leonard-Barton, 1995). Both the individual and the corporation must have a plan for acquiring the skills and capabilities that will be required in future marketplaces. Independent of their staff's individual capabilities, organizations also have capabilities. To achieve good results continuously over time, managers need to be skilled not just in assessing their staff capabilities but also in assessing the capabilities and disabilities of their organization. What are the firms' strengths and weaknesses? A number of researchers have investigated how to answer this question.

Leonard-Barton reinforces the concern over a focus on core competencies and saw such core capabilities in another light: as compromising "core rigidities" attached to systems and processes that can inhibit growth (Leonard-Barton, 1995). Physical systems which once contributed to competitive advantage may later constrain the firm in its attempts at diversification or process change. Shared problem-solving approaches become limited, path-dependent, problem-solving processes, and may be tied to the existing physical infrastructure.

Christensen and Overdorf express another concern. In trying to transform an enterprise, managers can destroy the very capabilities that sustain it (Christensen and Overdorf, 2000). Managers must understand precisely what types of change the existing organization is capable and incapable of handling. Capabilities are said to reside in resources, processes, and values. In determining the capabilities an organization has, most managers look at its resources. Access to abundant, high-quality resources increases an organization's chances of coping with change, such as handling innovative technologies, but resource analysis doesn't come close to telling the whole story. An organization's processes and values must also be considered. Processes refer to the patterns of interaction, coordination, communication, and decision-making employees use to transform resources into products and services of greater worth (Christensen and Overdorf, 2000). Workflow processes are set up so that employees perform tasks in a consistent way. They are not meant to change; if they must change, they should change through tightly controlled procedures. If a process is used to do the task it was designed for, it is likely to perform efficiently. If the same process is used to tackle a very different task, it will result in some level of inefficiency (Christensen and Overdorf, 2000). For this reason, processes are where organizations experience serious disabilities for coping with change. The existing learning systems in these firms do not retain the causal knowledge regarding why the processes demand specific steps, only that if the steps are followed a product can be generated. As such, the learning system does not support reapplying firm processes to new problems. A new organizational learning approach must be stipulated that remembers why the process steps are conducted.

McGrath promoted a "competitive advantage" market analysis approach, which advised searching for opportunities where there is a change in the basis of competition that allows the potential for creating a customer lock-in, and a competitor lock-out, condition to create a competitive advantage (McGrath, 2005). Examining potential winner-take-all markets and determining whether there is an opportunity to create the customer lock-in and competitor lock-out conditions may allow the firm to grab a significant portion of the market (McGrath, 2005). The "winner take all" and "competitive advantage" were popular market strategies for almost a decade, but in 2013, McGrath updated her guidance in an attempt to better address the rapid changes that business models contend with in the dynamic marketplaces of today (McGrath, 2013a). She now informs us that long-term competitive advantages are a thing of the past, and that we must convert our companies into organizations with rapid organizational learning capabilities so they can target and create new competitive advantages by leveraging their increased capacity to learn, and cognitively understand the targeted technologies over a shorter length of time, repeatedly, over and over again. The focus now must be on instilling the rapid learning capability into the organization, as opposed to any specific skill mapped to an opportunity (McGrath, 2013b). In a later book, *The End of Competitive Advantage*, McGrath says the marketplace is so dynamic that achieving sustainable competitive advantage is not only impossible but a bad goal. The new goal should be for an organization to develop a learning capability and continuously apply it to identify business targets. Similarly, in *Transient Advantage*, McGrath concludes that corporate sustainability must now focus on developing organizational learning capabilities so that organizations can react quickly to changes in dynamic marketplaces and identify and pursue "waves" of opportunities (McGrath, 2013b). The transient advantages of McGrath (2013b) may be achieved by effectively applying digital business design models, like the IDBS Model, and learning to launch new strategic initiatives again and again, thus creating a portfolio of advantages via the various business functions that can be built quickly and abandoned just as rapidly with agility (Mubako and Ray, 2017).

6.2 *The Nonaka knowledge creation model*

Having just established a need for improved organizational learning capabilities, we can switch directions and investigate how to do it by describing and improving organizational knowledge creation models. The foundational knowledge creation model was contributed by Nonaka (1991), which consisted of four KCPs: socialization, externalization, combination, and internalization. Socialization refers to the sharing of individual tacit knowledge and experiences with other local group members. Tacit knowledge is deeply rooted in the individual and consists of a set of subjective perceptions, intuitions, rituals, mental models, beliefs, and insights that are difficult to express in a semantic auditory or visual way. Externalization involves the process of formalizing tacit knowledge into explicit concepts in transferrable forms that an organization can readily understand and distribute. Explicit knowledge is structured knowledge that is objective, rational, theoretical, and can be easily transferred. It can be expressed in a formal and systematic language (written, auditory, or visual) and can be shared as formulas, specifications, and manuals. Combination involves synthesizing explicit knowledge concepts with prior related knowledge into new superior forms and sharing them across the organization. Internalization includes the activities for absorbing explicit group knowledge in transferrable states and transforming it into organizational tacit knowledge. Collectively, these processes define the passive functional capabilities that firms must learn.

Industry has changed significantly since Nonaka introduced his knowledge-creation model 30 years ago. Due to its simplicity, the model has difficulty handling a new, complex, economic world. Specifically, Nonaka's organizational learning model is dated, too simplistic in scope, discussed in highly abstract terms, doesn't transition between learning cycles well, doesn't address the real-life complexity of today's organizational learning environments, doesn't provide industry executives with instructions for how to improve their organizational learning posture, and needs to be enhanced.

6.3 *Organizational learning via the Enhanced Organizational Learning Model*

Figure 4 depicts an Enhanced Organizational Learning Model (EnOLM) with added passive functional capabilities to handle today's complex economic forces.

As depicted in Figure 4, organizational learning involves knowledge conversion modes or processes that transform knowledge states between an individual and group, and between tacit and explicit forms, as the organization's core knowledge levels evolve iteratively into increasingly refined levels of accumulated base knowledge.

By depicting the states of knowledge and the modes of conversion processes, the figure provides perspective to the model elements and becomes useful since knowledge states, the conversion processes, and the modes of learning can be depicted in a single figure. These passive functions, or abstract uses, are equivalent to processes that represent the things we do to knowledge as it transforms into different states in support of the learning process. Interestingly, each passive function develops several successive states of knowledge as it transforms via the interaction of

Fig. 4. The Enhanced Organizational Learning Model (EnOLM).
Source: Ray (2014).

group members and the progression of intellect that naturally occurs through learning. The goal for each firm is to develop an organizational learning system that accomplishes each of the KCPs, tracks and maintains the knowledge states between each process, and defines where the transition of knowledge states occurs relative to each KCP. Each KCP is described below:

- **Acquisition:** The process of scanning, identifying, and selecting data to support propositions that become new knowledge.
- **Socialization:** One of Nonaka's four primary KCPs that represents the sharing of individual tacit knowledge and experience with other local group members.
- **Externalization:** One of Nonaka's four primary KCPs that represents the process of formalizing tacit knowledge into explicit concepts an organization can understand and distribute.

- **Assimilation:** The process of accumulating, analyzing, processing, and interpreting information so it can be analytically understood and processed accordingly.
- **Combination:** One of Nonaka's four primary KCPs that has been divided into two for the EnOLM, a new combination process with a reduced scope, and a new transformation process, which has been added to account for the fact the initial explicit knowledge can be combined with prior related knowledge and then transformed to new superior forms of explicit knowledge.
- **Transformation:** The process of developing and refining the routines that facilitate combining existing knowledge with newly acquired and assimilated knowledge.
- **Internalization:** One of Nonaka's four primary KCPs that represents the process of gathering explicit group knowledge in transferrable states into organizational synthesized explicit knowledge. Although Nonaka uses the term "absorption" to describe the internalization process, it has more to do with "gathering" in his model. It represents individuals internalizing knowledge by reading broadcast messages about the knowledge, but not within their personal context, and then viewing it from their personal perspective, background, capabilities, and context.
- **Absorption:** The process of translating explicit group knowledge in transferrable states and collecting it into organizational remembered tacit knowledge within specific contexts of interest. It equates to collecting the tacit perspectives of subject matter experts (SMEs) on the topic and involves translating an explicit group's organizationally remembered knowledge to promote its utilization by describing it within specific contexts of interest.
- **Utilization:** Applying organizationally remembered knowledge to new experiences to extend and leverage existing competencies.
- **Exploitation:** The process of creating new competencies by incorporating new transformed knowledge into operations and leveraging disruptive technologies to improve current products and services.

A common organizational learning use case occurs when individuals acquire some new tacit knowledge from external sources (acquisition) and share it with other individuals or small groups in their companies (socialization). As staff members take external training courses, attend conventions where competitors display their current products or services, or participate in an industry community of practice (CoP), they increase their individual knowledge base in areas deemed useful to the company via the acquisition KCP. Armed with this new knowledge, these employees then share this new tacit knowledge, along with their ideas of how it might be useful, with small project teams via the socialization KCP. The members of the small project team then collaborate and refine the idea as part of an informal vetting or improvement process. Next, the shared tacit knowledge is discussed and formalized into explicit concepts that are understandable by other members of the organization via the externalization KCP. The dialogs and deductive and inductive techniques such as metaphors, analogies, or constructed design solutions are shared to enable expression of the ideas in words, concepts, drawings, and models. Essentially, the tacit knowledge obtained from socialization is articulated and captured into an explicit form via externalization that can be combined with prior related knowledge and shared throughout the organization. The explicit knowledge acquired from externalization is synthesized with other concepts in the knowledge base through transfer processes normally conducted by the operating organization, such as presentations, staff meetings, emails, processing of documents, plans, reports, and market data as part of the assimilation KCP. The combination KCP takes the explicit concepts defined in externalization and analyzed and interpreted in assimilation, combines it with prior related knowledge that has been converted into current contexts of interest, and edits and integrates the knowledge in documents, databases, or by generating new knowledge applications via the Transformation KCP. The knowledge from transformation is shared within the organization, creating a new superior explicit knowledge. Next, the new superior explicit knowledge shared during transformation is gathered and collected into organizational memory and converted into organizationally synthesized superior explicit knowledge via the internalization KCP. This step includes learning through practice. As individual knowledge is explained in words and documented, it is translated and becomes part of the organization's consciousness in the form of organizationally remembered tacit knowledge during the absorption KCP. Each employee is granted access to the information through participation in the documentation effort, simulations, or role-playing activities. These individuals absorb the knowledge and extend their tacit knowledge in accordance with their own style, habits (Ramirez *et al.*, 2011), and contexts of interest (Ray, 2014).

When organizational explicit knowledge is absorbed into organizational memory during the absorption KCP and sent back to the individual staff members of the firm, and shared (organizationally remembered) as the next cycle's level of tacit knowledge, it is the same organizational explicit knowledge that is rendered in a transferrable state. These shared experiences facilitate the creation of common perspectives which "can be learned and shared by team members as part of their respective bodies of tacit knowledge" (Nonaka, 1991). During the utilization KCP, employees share time and space to work through and directly experience the interaction of the next cycle's tacit and explicit knowledge (Nonaka and Takcuchi, 1995) by applying the organizationally remembered knowledge to new experiences. Finally, the exploitation KCP converts the organizationally remembered utility knowledge to context-specific explicit knowledge by creating new competencies and applying the utility knowledge to new opportunities, thereby transforming the new transformed knowledge into new operational capabilities.

An effort is required by firms or projects to implement each one of the KCPs, and to collect knowledge in the states indicated in the model. After new technical knowledge is combined with prior related knowledge via the combination KCP, for example, the knowledge is transformed via the transformation KCP so that a cognitive understanding of the knowledge can assist with how it is integrated into the firm's KMS and distributed to relevant SMEs by the firm's organizational knowledge representatives (OKRs), who are scattered across operating units (OUs) and high-technology projects. Internalization involves gathering explicit knowledge and distributing it to relevant SMEs so it can be converted into tacit knowledge from a large number of contexts and backgrounds, and is similar to learning through practice (Ramirez *et al.*, 2011). Absorption would require collecting the tacit perspectives of SMEs on the topic after they have reviewed externalized forms of the knowledge and converted it to organizationally remembered tacit knowledge, for example, that collects the context from each SME's perspective. A project's knowledge management approach has to account for the states of knowledge at the beginning and end of each of the KCP to track how it evolves into organizational knowledge, and whether hypothesis-based assumptions turn out to be true or false. Staff must be trained on the knowledge management processes and how they lead to organizational learning.

When conducting project planning on complex, high-technology projects, the project manager needs to consider how to implement each element of the EnOLM in a way that reports essential aspects of the learning back to the firm's OU and ensure that the acquired knowledge interfaces with the organizational learning system implemented by the organization. These activities need to be incorporated into the plan and

Fig. 5. The EnOLM Implementing Activities Groups.

Source: Ray (2014).

funding profile. To map the required task into the EnOLM, another dimension of the model has been added, namely, the Implementing Activity Groups. Figure 5 depicts the Implementing Activities Group aspect of the EnOLM.

Figure 5 depicts how groups of implementing activities are positioned between KCPs in order to record the practical steps executive managers can take in order to implement all of the functional capabilities of the EnOLM.

The Implementing Activities Groups are designed to give managers practical recommendations on how to improve the organizational learning posture in their organizations and projects. These are the tasks that need to be incorporated into the program plan. Implementing Activity Groups allows the model to recommend definitive actions that corporate executives can take to improve organizational learning at their firms. Each of the Implementing Activities Groups shown in the figure is discussed in the following:

- **Searching activities:** Activities that an organization uses to scan external environments to find, identify, and select new knowledge sources.
- **Improving activities:** Activities for improving how a firm effectively uses knowledge during the learning process. Examples include improving defects of tacit knowledge and investing in research and development to improve a firm's absorptive capacity.
- **Abstracting activities:** Activities that transform knowledge situated in a specific context to a more generalized context.
- **Engaging activities:** Activities conducted by firms to encourage employees to participate in organizational learning.
- **Problem-solving activities:** Activities that solve problems important to the organization's operations by leveraging learning methodologies.
- **Confirming activities:** Activities (in the form of models and simulations) that verify the knowledge concepts being investigated as part of the learning process at the firm.
- **Codifying activities:** Activities that allow knowledge to be applied in new contexts; these are the main mechanisms for replicating knowledge and dispersing it to a larger community.
- **Planning activities:** Activities for organizing how new knowledge will be created and managed.
- **Impacting activities:** Activities that guide how a firm effectively uses knowledge during the learning process.
- **Diffusing activities:** Activities that result in the transmission of improved knowledge throughout the organization.

Each of the 10 implementing activity groups offered can have 5 to 10 implementing activity steps (100 maximum) that are recommended below as specific steps firms can take to implement effective organizational learning practices. Firms are offered the flexibility of tailoring these steps by modifying or supplementing them to match their specific business operations, or to just use the sample steps as indicated in Table 2.

To implement an effective EnOLM, organizations should consider the following actions:

- Implement the KCPs of the EnOLM.
- Tailor the list of implementing activities in the EnOLM to the project and then implement the tailored activities list.
- Implement social media communications methodologies across the project to improve collaboration.

Table 2. Example implementing activities mapped to Implementing Activity Groups.

Searching Activities	Improving Activities	Abstracting Activities	Engaging Activities	Problem-Solving Activities
1. Scan external environments for new technologies and knowledge related to key competency areas the firm currently has, or which the firm intends to pursue as defined in their strategic business plan.	1. Invest in R&D to improve the absorptive capacity of the organization, update priorities to increase the ratio of Realized Absorptive Capacity divided by Potential Absorptive Capacity (efficiency ratio) to create value from the firm's knowledge base.	1. Prepare a responsibility map to define and track key concepts that will apply to lower-level units. Categorize knowledge on a continuum of specific to general, with general knowledge concepts being applied at higher org. levels with a broader application.	1. Facilitate staff participation in the maintenance of CoP websites for key technology areas. Assign CoP management to appropriate SMEs. Require projects developing new design solutions to update CoP websites with new design data.	1. Match findings from completed research in relevant industries to the needs of knowledge users in the organization. Tailor knowledge handling processes to the type of knowledge (a posterior or a priori).
2. Identify new evolving technologies that could be of interest to the firm with regard to improving its current products and services and report these areas to operational unit (OU) directors, OKRs, and potential SMEs so plans can be initiated to access the firm's prior related knowledge, and identify a new list of designated knowledge receptors.	2. Use computed efficiency ratio (ER) to ensure the firm can not only understand the evolving technical concepts (i.e., has potential absorptive capacity) but can also implement the concepts into new products and services (i.e., has high realized absorptive capacity levels).	2. Define a Research Breakdown Structure (RBS) of key knowledge categories and concepts required to support the firm's operations. Define a communications plan that maps each knowledge concept to responsible organizations.	2. Engage staff in org. learning. Train SMEs. Give qualified employees an option to charge a % of their time to overhead for improving or managing knowledge, creating investment propositions, uploading content to CoP websites, and establishing concept demonstration labs for integration of products with evolving technologies.	2. Define a set of social networking tools that can be applied by the firm to encourage collaboration and optimize firm communication capabilities while facilitating socialization. Which digital technology can remove silo-type boundaries?
3. Meet with customers to identify their needs, to	3. Define mentoring programs that give	3. Transform knowledge situated in a specific	3. Establish contacts with technology firms and make	3. Invest in IRADs to develop new technologies,

socialize possible design solutions, and to develop a personal relationship (Solomonson, 2014).	high-potential employees the opportunity to be mentored by SMEs and create ways to ensure staff have access to SMEs.	context or application to a more generalized context and transfer it as existing knowledge to other parts of the organization.	strategic use of technological alliances to improve technological absorptive capacity. Strategic digital assets can create shared value ecosystems.	or to find new ways to use existing technologies.
4. Scan the competitive environment to increase awareness and competency levels of new knowledge that is available in industry, and maintain a list of appropriate knowledge sources. Assess the digital maturity level of the organization and transient competitive advantages.	4. Implement a process for assessing new tacit knowledge and determining the right amount of effort to expend to articulate the tacit information well enough for the SMEs to understand it.	4. Develop a plan for accumulating prior knowledge and assessing its relevancy to OUs.	4. Update the firm's communications infrastructure, capabilities, and practices. Ensure human aspects of comms are planned and implemented. Designate OKRs, SMEs, and designated knowledge receptors to support all required OL messaging threads.	4. Hire a Chief Engineer and team of SMEs to monitor new evolving technologies, propose design solutions to customer needs, and develop business strategies (Solomonson, 2014).
5. Put enabling mechanisms in place to encourage all staff members to adopt sensory roles wherein they monitor industry for evolving technologies.	5. Employ the use of Yammer themes to solicit input from staff on a topic of interest to the firm as a form of collaboration and interactive training.	5. Implement a knowledge mapping approach for managing critical information and ensuring the correct functional units have access to it.	5. Engage HR to share responsibility to instill innovation. Instruct HR to create synergy, ignite employee engagement, create business value, be a steward of the firm's brand, calculate the knowledge value of employees, leverage social media to improve collaboration, and acquire, manage, and retain clever, high-potential employees.	5. Develop solutions to problems by ensuring knowledge has the correct context, engaging the best SMEs, planning the response, dedicating resources, and articulating the problem solution. Conduct whiteboard sessions with technical SMEs and define candidate design solutions (Solomonson, 2014).

(*Continued*)

Table 2. (*Continued*)

Confirming Activities	Codifying Activities	Planning Activities	Impacting Activities	Diffusing Activities
1. Conduct confirming activities such as experimentation, modeling and simulation, prototyping, and user jury events to verify the technical concepts being considered.	1. Implement a modern CM tool and establish baseline control processes to baseline successive configurations of the knowledge being generated through organizational learning.	1. Assess core competency areas, identify new ones, and plan how to acquire market-leading capabilities. Continually plan how to acquire new competencies to support strategic plans.	1. Designate OKRs at appropriate levels of the organization and task them to assess, improve, manage, and distribute knowledge.	1. Use a common CM tool (with data structures and supporting processes) for file sharing at the OU level to encourage collaboration of data across projects.
2. Treat evolving innovations **and technologies as imperfect theories or hypotheses related to** propositions of knowledge which must be proven by scientific scrutiny. Be skeptical and verify that the underlying hypotheses and assumptions are correct. Apply rigorous testing to eliminate weaker theories, leaving only the strong theories to survive.	2. Verify the adequacy of **common knowledge across internal functional groups to facilitate** distribution of knowledge as new knowledge is acquired.	2. Continually assess the **existing knowledge base and whether it can support knowledge** translation in new areas. Develop flow charts and sequence diagrams defining improvement threads as knowledge evolves from one state to another in support of the org. learning and designate the handlers and improvers of knowledge.	2. Conduct knowledge **mapping, benchmarking a firm's core capabilities, and standing up a CoP website** for core competency areas to develop new configurations of knowledge to meet requirements not previously thought possible, and to share understanding of technologies yet to be developed.	2. Broadcast difficult external **technical information not related to ongoing organizational activities to** designated knowledge receptors throughout the firm since centralized gatekeepers may not be able to assimilate the knowledge due to a lack of absorptive capacity, which can result in random information flows.
3. Develop models and simulations to evaluate new innovative technologies and characterize the concepts	3. Mobilize the use of existing component architectures (for reuse across the org.) and import capabilities to	3. Hire a team of SMEs to support strategic planning, market creation, and new business development activities,	3. Have each manager define the decisions they make and the information they need to make decisions so the information can be captured	3. Diffuse knowledge across the organization and ensure knowledge is situated in the correct context before diffusion.

in accordance with metrics of interest in support of developing product improvements.	address new aspects of enterprise or system-level architectures.	while monitoring evolving technologies and warning the firm when disrupting technologies are approaching (Solomonson, 2014).	to support effective decision-making.	Provide higher-quality (rich) information and more of it in multiple channel modes of communications.
4. Conduct a substantial advocacy process on new knowledge propositions related to innovation cycles to strengthen the interpreted meaning of the underlying theories, which, in turn, will increase understanding of the concepts.	4. Use systems engineering interface control techniques to create boundary objects (drawings, trade studies, prototypes) to ensure that a common vocabulary can represent the differences and dependencies of knowledge at boundaries.	4. Designate the OKRs, SMEs, and designated knowledge receptors responsible for evaluating the firm's prior related knowledge in new technology areas of interest to ensure that the firm has the requisite absorptive capacity. Hire new SMEs as necessary to address skill gaps.	4. Task the OKR and Chief Engineer to provide a reference framework indicating how research contributions fit within the firm's projected product lines and services as an impacting activity. Construct an RBS to organize and map knowledge and learning concepts.	4. Identify knowledge gatekeepers for each organizational unit which OKRs can interface with to facilitate exploitation of new information. Train staff on how to store information in the CM folder structure to facilitate collaboration across functional areas.
5. Conduct feasibility studies to prove proposed technical solutions. Standup an integration and test (I&T) lab to prove the feasibility of proposed design solutions.	5. Standup CoP websites in core competency areas to publish new configurations of codified knowledge to meet requirements once thought impossible to meet, and to share understanding of technologies yet to be developed.	5. Assess the path dependencies of new technology areas and ensure that the organization has the prior related knowledge and absorptive capacity to support it. Develop plans to invest in R&D to increase the firm's prior knowledge levels in key areas.	5. Connect knowledge producers with potential knowledge users to predispose users to changed behavior by raising their awareness about the opportunity for a change.	5. Incentivize key technologists with bonus potential for reusing shared corporate knowledge for additional products and services (VanOrmer, 2014).

- Upgrade KMS features to address elements of EnOLM.
- Distribute OKRs throughout the project, OUs, and selected executive management locations.

To date, researchers have defined knowledge creation and transfer in theoretical terms. With the advent of AI, automation capabilities can be built into an organization's KMS. In the real world, knowledge goes from individuals to small teams, from these small teams to a project KMS of some kind, and then is generally stored, but rarely converted, into actionable information and reused. The problem is that OUs and the organizations they support are successfully internalizing only a small amount of the knowledge related to disruptive technologies (Ray, 2014).

The expectation is that knowledge would be sent to a firm's OUs and then to corporate headquarters, where it would be internalized and distributed back out to all the employees of the firm. The related SMEs assigned to projects must receive these communications and assess opportunities to leverage new knowledge in ways that benefit the project, and in ways that exploit other opportunities to apply the technologies. Assessing the information flows in a typical company, one quickly recognizes that there is a shortage of information being transferred to the organization, or to the organization's KMS for that matter. Implementing the EnOLM, therefore, should take advantage of the related SMEs assigned to projects that must receive these communications and assess opportunities to leverage new knowledge in ways that benefit the project, and in ways that exploit other opportunities to apply the technologies. Implementing the EnOLM should also take advantage of the practical steps executive managers can take to improve their firm's organizational learning posture to ensure the model is implemented with a practical focus on supporting firm operations, and not merely a theoretical exercise in learning.

7. Digital Transformation Dividends

According to Morgan (2019) in a *Forbes* article, DX involves more than just updating technology and processes because revenue and shareholders are impacted. Many companies are hesitant to invest in DX without knowing if the investment will have a positive return for their business. DX that is implemented carefully and methodically with strategy, and as an

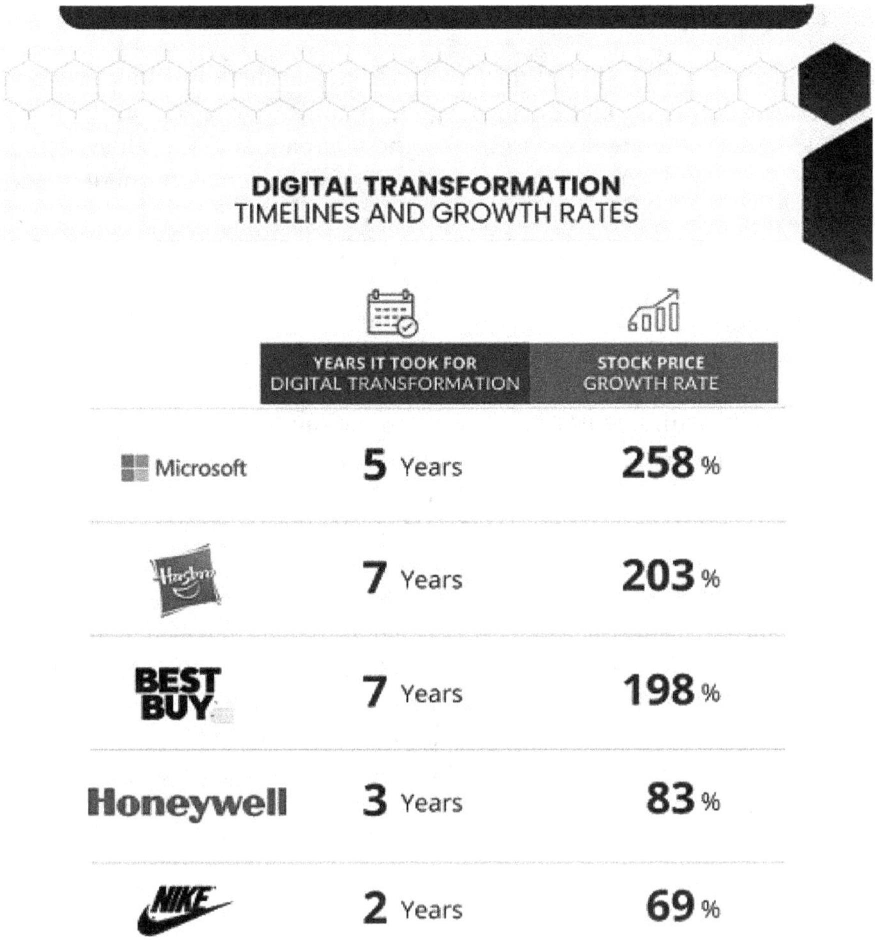

Fig. 6. Stock price growth rates for firms conducting digital transformation.
Source: Adapted from Morgan (2019).

element of smart organizational transformation, can improve share prices and revenue and thereby the future of a company. As indicated in Figure 6, there are examples of this value return in stock prices, and it is important to note some big companies that have benefited from applying DX to their processes and organizations.

8. Conclusion

It is evident from the studies described above that there is a link between emerging technology and business value outputs. Business leaders must be able to demonstrate the tangible business impact of DX to their teams, stakeholders, and customers through organization transformation and growth.

Top companies are prioritizing organizational learning, emerging technology, and digital innovation capabilities to increase their bottom line, and thus Industry 4.0 and Agriculture 4.0 processes and advanced capabilities are emerging even in the developing world. According to Morgan's 2019 stock price growth rate graphic of businesses that grew exponentially while exploiting digital technology capabilities, Microsoft tops the list (Morgan, 2019). The software company transformed its organization and products over 5 years, and the benefit was exponential as the share price went up 258%. The transformation saw Microsoft turn its products to digital products, software bought and sold online, from new subscription to upgrades. In 2014, the stock price of Microsoft US was approximately USD \$42; after the DX in 2021, it is around USD \$300 (Microsoft US Corporation, 2021). According to Denning, Microsoft's 2004 investment in the Nokia phone was disastrous and Microsoft's share price was stagnant. With the DX initiative, Microsoft exploited two main areas of opportunity: mobility and the cloud. While Microsoft's competitors defined their products as mobile, Microsoft's emphasis was on the mobility of human experiences, experiences made possible by Microsoft's cloud technologies (Denning, 2021).

References

Bharadwaj, A., El Sawy, O.A., Pavlou, P.A., and Venkatraman, N. (2013). Digital business strategy: Toward a next generation of insights. *MIS Quarterly*, 37(2), 471–482.

Christensen, C. and Overdorf, M. (2000). Meeting the challenge of disruptive change. *Harvard Business Review*, 78(2), 66–76.

Denning, S. (2021). How Microsoft's digital transformation created a trillion dollar gain. *Forbes*. https://www.forbes.com/sites/stevedenning/2021/06/20/how-microsofts-digital-transformation-created-a-trillion-dollar-gain/?sh=5dcaeff2625b.

Deshler, R. (2016). 10 benefits of an aligned organization. AlignOrg Solutions. http://alignorg.com/10-benefits-of-an-aligned-organization/.

Drucker, P.F. (1995). The information executives truly need. *Harvard Business Review*, 73(1), 54–62.

Gans, J. (2016). The other disruption: When innovations threaten the organizational model. *Harvard Business Review*, 94(3), 78–84.

Gray, P., El Sawy, O.A., Asper, G., and Thordarson, M. (2015). Realizing strategic value through center-edge digital transformation in consumer-centric industries. *Revista do CEAM*, 3(1), 37.

Hur, J.Y., Cho, W., Lee, G., and Bickerton, S.H. (2019). The "smart work" myth: How bureaucratic inertia and workplace culture stymied digital transformation in the relocation of South Korea's capital. *Asian Studies Review*, 43(4), 691–709.

Katzenbach, J., Oelschlegel, C., and Thomas, J. (2016). 10 principles of organizational culture. *Strategy + Business*, 82(2), 22–28.

Knoess, C., Harbour, R., and Scemama, S. (2016). Prepare your workforce for the automation age. *Harvard Business Review*.

Leonard-Barton, D. (1995). *Wellsprings of Knowledge*. Boston, MA: Harvard Business Review Press.

Pisano, G. (2015). You need an innovation strategy. *Harvard Business Review*, 93(6), 44–54.

McGrath, R. (2005). And the winner takes all? Necessary conditions and entry strategies in winner take all markets. In Galvan, R., Murray, J., and Markides, C. (eds.), *Strategy, Innovation and Change — Challenges for Management* (pp. 203–220). New York: Oxford University Press.

McGrath, R.G. (2013a). *The End of Competitive Advantage*. Boston, MA: Harvard Business Review Press.

McGrath, R.G. (2013b). Transient advantage. *Harvard Business Review*, 91(6), 62–70.

Microsoft US Corporation (2021). Microsoft historical annual stock price data. https://www.microsoft.com/en-us/investor/stock-lookup.aspx.

Morgan, B. (2019). 7 examples of how digital transformation impacted business performance. https://www.forbes.com/sites/blakemorgan/2019/07/21/7-examples-of-how-digital-transformation-impacted-business-performance/.

Mubako, A.T. and Pavlou, P. (2017). *Digital Business Strategy: Leveraging Emerging Technologies (IOT, AI and AR)*. Cape Town: IDBS Press.

Mubako, A.T. and Ray, J.S. (2017). *Digital Transformation. The Realignment of Information Technology and Business Strategies for Retailers in South Africa*. Hamburg: Anchor Publishing.

Mubako, A.T. and Ray, J.S. (2020). *The Definitive Guide to a Digital Business Strategy — Get Your Business Off the Ground, Disrupt a Big Digital Market*. Cape Town: IDBS Press.

Nonaka, I. (1991). The knowledge-creating company. *Harvard Business Review*, 69(6), 96–104.

Nonaka, I. and Takeuchi, H. (1995). *The Knowledge-Creating Company: How Japanese Companies Create the Dynamics of Innovation.* Oxford: Oxford University Press.

Ramirez, A., Morales, V., and Rojas, R. (2011). Knowledge creation, organizational learning, and their effects on organizational performance. *Inzinerine Ekonomika-Engineering Economics*, 22(3), 309–318.

Ray, J.S. (2014). Advancing knowledge creation modelling through improved organizational communications. SMC University, Zug, Switzerland.

Solomonson, D. (2014). Personal interview conducted by J. Ray on May 22, 2014.

Sun, T. (2007). *Survival Tactics: The Top 11 Behaviors of Successful Entrepreneurs*. Westport, CT: Praeger Publishers.

VanOrmer, J. (2014). Personal interview conducted by J. Ray on May 27, 2014.

https://doi.org/10.1142/9789811271984_0015

Chapter 15

Digital Transformation and Organizational Change: An Experiential Case

Ruchin Kansal

Department of Management, Stillman School of Business, Seton Hall University, South Orange, NJ, USA
Kansal & Company, Newtown, CT, USA
ruchin.kansal@shu.edu
ruchin@kansal3c.com

When it comes to digital transformation, the healthcare industry remains a laggard. The lack of adoption of digital products, services, and business models highlights the case. Despite the evidence that the rate of change is accelerating, such as in the hospital sector, true transformation will happen once digital skill sets are fully incorporated in the training and development of the healthcare workforce and its leadership. In the meantime, healthcare leaders should take pragmatic steps to enable the digital transformation of their respective organizations.

1. Introduction

It is 2022. How many times have you opened an app to order something? Food, clothes, groceries? And how many times have you picked up your phone and used an app to attend to your health?

Digital transformation is everywhere. We are now exploring new frontiers of digital life. Amidst this evolution, why is the healthcare industry still a laggard when it comes to adopting technology that seems so prevalent all around us?

2. Digital Transformation: A Fait Accompli?

Digital transformation entered the broad vernacular sometime in the late 1990s, before the dot-com boom. While e-commerce was in its early days, traditional businesses looked at digital models with curiosity. Some disdainfully regarded them as futureless. It was not "human" to transact digitally. For the early adopters, the business case was about cost savings primarily: contact centers, business process outsourcing, knowledge process outsourcing, data analytics, and process optimization. Digital business models were a far cry and left best to the non-threatening digital start-ups. Nowadays, digital presence and online business models have become a professional necessity: if you don't offer consumers the choice to interact with you digitally, you may as well close the shop. Even my barber allows me to make appointments online, pay, shop, and leave reviews — all through a fun-to-navigate app. And we have all seen the revenue-generating capabilities of digital business models — look at Google and Facebook.

It is 2022. So why are we still talking about the digital transformation of healthcare? Shouldn't we all be well on our way to being digital already and thinking about what is next? The Metaverse? Life and health in space?

Before we get into the reasons, let us deconstruct the word "transformation." According to the Merriam-Webster dictionary, the term means "a complete or major change in someone's or something's appearance, form, etc." It is, in fact, a popular word — one of the top 1% of the words by look-up popularity as reported by Merriam-Webster (n.d.). The data suggest that transformation may well be the need of the day.

We have read about examples of transformation in school — how a caterpillar becomes a butterfly, how plants capture solar energy and convert them into glucose through photosynthesis, and how water becomes vapor. In math, we studied about four types of transformations: translation, reflection, rotation, and dilation.

Transformation is all around us. A blender transforms electrical power into mechanical power. An internal combustion engine in cars transforms fuel into heat energy into mechanical energy that propels the car forward. COVID-19 has transformed itself from alpha to beta to delta to omicron, where each variant challenges the efficacy of vaccines.

The one fact that remains consistent across all these transformations is that the end takes a remarkably different shape from the beginning. It is not a tweak, it is not an adjustment, and it is not a change. It is a "transformation."

By that logic, what should a digital transformation of a business lead to? A new business? New processes? New products? New business models? New customer service models? New supply chains? New payment models? One could argue that all of these are the right answers.

Or are they?

In other words, is digital transformation necessary? If your business has been running successfully for 100 years? If your business model makes you money, and barriers to entry into your business are high? If your product is not for digital consumption?

Even though it is 2022, digital transformation remains a relevant concept. If technology helped businesses do better in the early days, now it has become the driver of business in most industries. The COVID-19 pandemic has only accelerated the change, with healthcare and education being the exceptions.

Healthcare has been one of the slowest entities to embrace digital transformation. The reasons have been discussed *ad nauseam*, so I will not belabor that. The pace of transformation has varied based on the sector within healthcare: hospitals, which are the frontline portal to patients, have embraced digital solutions faster than the sectors that are one step removed from the patients: insurers and manufacturers. This fact supports the hypothesis that customer expectations, rather than revenue or cost, drive the business case for digital transformation in healthcare.

Looking deeper into healthcare occupations reveals a particular trend. Take, for instance, the 2021 compensation data for healthcare occupations as identified by the Bureau of Labor Statistics and the 2020 median base salary of the jobs in healthcare as reported by the US Willis Towers Watson Health Care Compensation Survey. Together, the data show a greater-than-average increase in market demand for radiology, IT development, strategic planning, corporate development, IT administration, data science, and business intelligence. A combination of the two sources as seen in Figure 1 reveals that IT occupations rank in the top 20% of all healthcare jobs from a median salary perspective and, as reported by Willis Tower Watson, are growing at a rate higher than average. A safe

Occupation	**Median Salary ($)**
Physicians and Surgeons	2,08,000
Dentists	1,64,000
Podiatrists	1,34,300
Pharmacists	1,28,710
Optometrists	1,18,050
Nurse Anesthetists, Nurse Midwives, and Nurse Practitioners	1,17,670
Physician Assistants	1,15,390
IT Architecture (Systems Design)	1,14,800
Network Architecture Design	1,12,400
IS and Cybersecurity Development	1,08,700
Data Engineering	1,07,500
Database Administration	1,06,700
Clinical Business Informatics and Project Management	1,02,200
Predictive Analytics/Business Intelligence	1,00,600
Veterinarians	99,250
IS and Cybersecurity	1,08,700
Network Control/Administration	98,600
Physical Therapists	91,010
Radiation Therapists	86,850
Occupational Therapists	86,280
Genetic Counselors	85,700
Audiologists	81,030
Speech Language Pathologists	80,480
Nuclear Medicine Technologists	79,590
Dental Hygienists	77,090
Registered Nurses	75,330
Occupational Health and Safety Specialists and Technicians	72,530

Fig. 1. Median salary, healthcare professions, 2020.

Source: 2020 US Willis Towers Watson Health Care Compensation Survey and Bureau of Labor Statistics: *Occupational Outlook Handbook: Healthcare Occupations.*

Occupation	Median Salary ($)
Chiropractors	70,720
Medical Sonographers and Cardiovascular Technologists and Technicians	70,380
Orthotists and Prosthetists	70,190
Radiologic and MRI Technologists	63,710
Dieticians and Nutritionists	63,090
Respiratory Therapists	62,810
Occupational Therapy Assistants and Aides	60,950
Clinical Laboratory Technologists and Technicians	54,180
Exercise Physiologists	50,280
Physical Therapist Assistants and Aides	49,970
Athletic Trainers	49,860
Surgical Technologists	49,710
Licensed Practical and Licensed Vocational Nurses	48,820
Recreational Therapists	47,710
Medical Records and Health Information Specialists	45,240
Massage Therapists	43,620
Dental Assistants	41,180
Opticians	38,530
EMTs and Paramedics	36,650
Phlebotomists	36,320
Veterinary Technologists and Technicians	36,260
Medical Assistants	35,850
Medical Transcriptionists	35,270
Pharmacy Technicians	35,100
Psychiatric: Technicians and Aides	33,140
Nursing Assistants and Orderlies	30,830
Veterinary Assistants and Laboratory Animal Caretakers	29,930
Home Health and Personal Care Aides	27,080

Fig. 1. (*Continued*)

conclusion that can be drawn from these data is that the engines of digital change in healthcare, especially in hospitals, are accelerating. Whether it is in the form of enabling virtual visits, remote monitoring, or remote work, the wheels are churning. Fait accompli? Feels like it. Is it enough? Maybe not yet!

3. A Recent Healthcare Experience

Day 1: My 75-year-old uncle recently slipped on ice and fell. His home was three hours away from where he slipped, ultimately hurting his arm. Blessed with relatively good health and a strong will, he didn't think much of it and decided to finish the task he was there for. Despite the pain in his arm, he drove three hours and got back home in the evening. His arm was swollen, so his wife called my wife, who is a physician, to get an opinion. My wife suspected a fracture, but given the current COVID-19 load in emergency rooms, suggested a consult at an orthopedic Urgent Care.

A Google Maps search showed only one Urgent Care nearby that could do an X-ray, but it was closed for the day. The next best option was more than 20 miles away. Given the situation, my wife recommended waiting overnight based on her preliminary assessment. There wasn't a way to make an online appointment, so the only option was to wait until the next morning to give the Urgent Care Center a call.

Day 2: The next morning, my uncle was given an appointment for later that afternoon. In the meantime, we called an orthopedist and made the earliest available appointment for the day after. Again, no online scheduling was available.

Lo and behold, the X-ray showed a double fracture below the elbow — both the radius and the ulna were broken. Urgent Care suggested an orthopedic consult. Thankfully, we had an appointment for the next day.

Day 3: The consult with the orthopedic doctor brought troubling news. He recommended surgery and referred the case to a specialized orthopedic group. My cousin got on the phone with the set of doctors to arrange an appointment, but they had none available for the next four weeks. So, it was time to call other orthopedic surgeons to try to get an appointment for the next day. Ultimately, my wife had to play the physician card to get my uncle the care he needed.

Day 4: The orthopedic surgeon evaluated the fracture and scheduled a surgery for the Friday of the following week, eight days away. In the meantime, my uncle needed to get his cardiac clearance and take care of other pre-surgery formalities.

Days 5 to 11: After a few unsuccessful attempts, the family network strikes again and gets involved to find this time a cardiologist to get a stress test done in time for cardiac clearance. A feat accomplished: The stress test is scheduled for the day before the surgery!

In the meantime, my uncle, who is hurting, watches us navigate the complex healthcare system to get him to surgery, almost as a bystander in the situation.

Day 12: The surgery takes place and the healing process begins. Was this situation exacerbated by COVID-19's load on emergency rooms? Certainly. Did it expose how difficult it is to navigate a healthcare system with no other single point of entry other than the ER? Absolutely. Did trying to navigate the system leave a bad taste in everyone's mouth? You bet. Did the healthcare system earn anybody's trust? No. Did this episode highlight the difference in the digital maturity of healthcare versus other businesses from a customer experience perspective? An understatement!

4. The Typical Hospital Board Room

Chief Executive Officer: My biggest concerns are overcoming COVID-19-induced financial challenges, managing workforce shortages, earning the public's trust, and ensuring diversity and inclusion.

Chief Medical Officer: My biggest concerns are managing the caseload and avoiding physician burnout.

Chief Nursing Officer: Same. My nurses are falling like broken trees.

Chief Digital Officer: The world is going digital. We need to move fast. (Sigh.) No one listens to me.

And so the conversation goes.

The voice of the customer demanding digital engagement has still not made it to hospital board rooms, at least not at a disruptive level. The incumbent system works, the near-term challenges overshadow the long-term investments, and so goes life.

Which brings us back to the following original question: Is the digital transformation of healthcare necessary? In that case, what would enable such a transformation other than innovation and advances in healthcare technology?

Having spent more than 20 years as a consultant and an executive in the industry and now as the director of the Business Leadership Center at the Stillman School of Business, I am firmer in my belief that it comes down to people: both the workforce and the leaders.

5. The Workforce

Physicians and nurses form the core of the healthcare workforce. Becoming a physician or a nurse is one of the most challenging and expensive journeys in the US. It typically requires four years of pre-medical education, four years of medical school, three to five years of residency, and two to three years of fellowship. According to Melanie Hanson (2021) at Education Data Initiative, medical school graduates owe a median average of $200,000 to $250,000 in total educational debt, pre-medical debt included (EducationData.org, n.d.). Becoming a nurse is relatively easier; it typically requires a four-year Bachelor of Science in Nursing (BSN) degree. However, the student debt level still gives us pause: "Graduate nursing students expect to finish school with a median debt between $40,000 and $54,999, according to a 2017 report by the American Association of Colleges of Nursing" (Lane, 2021). Once they graduate and enter the workforce, they set the diagnostic and treatment protocols, make all clinical decisions, and provide and oversee care.

However, if we look at the training curriculum for MD or BSN programs, seldom will we find a mention of or emphasis on the development of a digital skill set. Figures 2–4 are snapshots of the curriculum for three of the top medical schools: Johns Hopkins University, Harvard Medical School, and the University of Pittsburgh Medical Center.

In a similar fashion, Figures 5–7, representing the BSN curricula at three of the top nursing schools, University of Pennsylvania, New York University, and Case Western Reserve University, demonstrate little to no engagement with the digitalized world.

While robust in medical science, none of the curricula include more than a cursory mention of anything related to training in digital skill sets fundamental to running a digital healthcare business, such as telemedicine, clinical information systems, data analytics, digital communications, or change management — skills essential for digitizing the business of

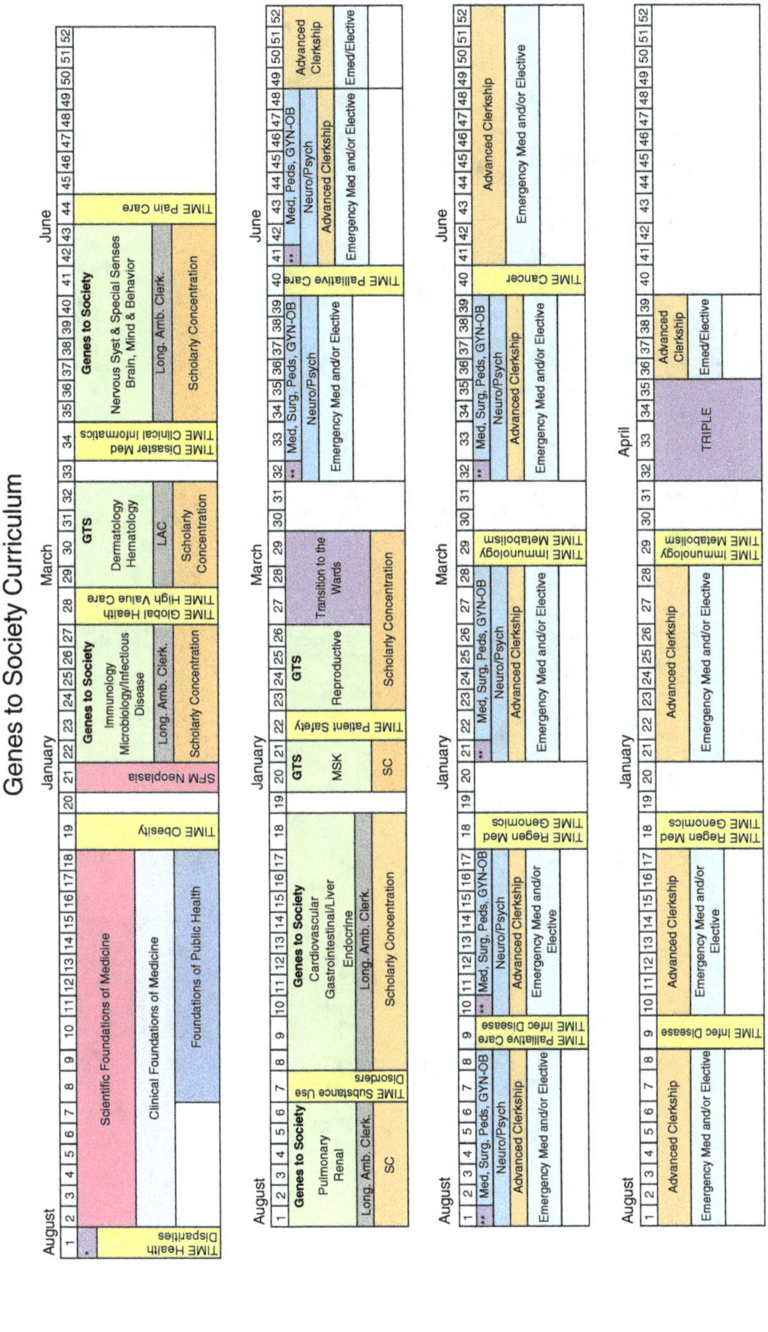

* - Transition to Medical School

** - Preclerkship Education Exercises

TIME - Topics in Interdisciplinary Medicine

TRIPLE - Transition to Residency and Internship and Preparation for Life

Fig. 2. Medical school curriculum, Johns Hopkins School of Medicine (n.d.).

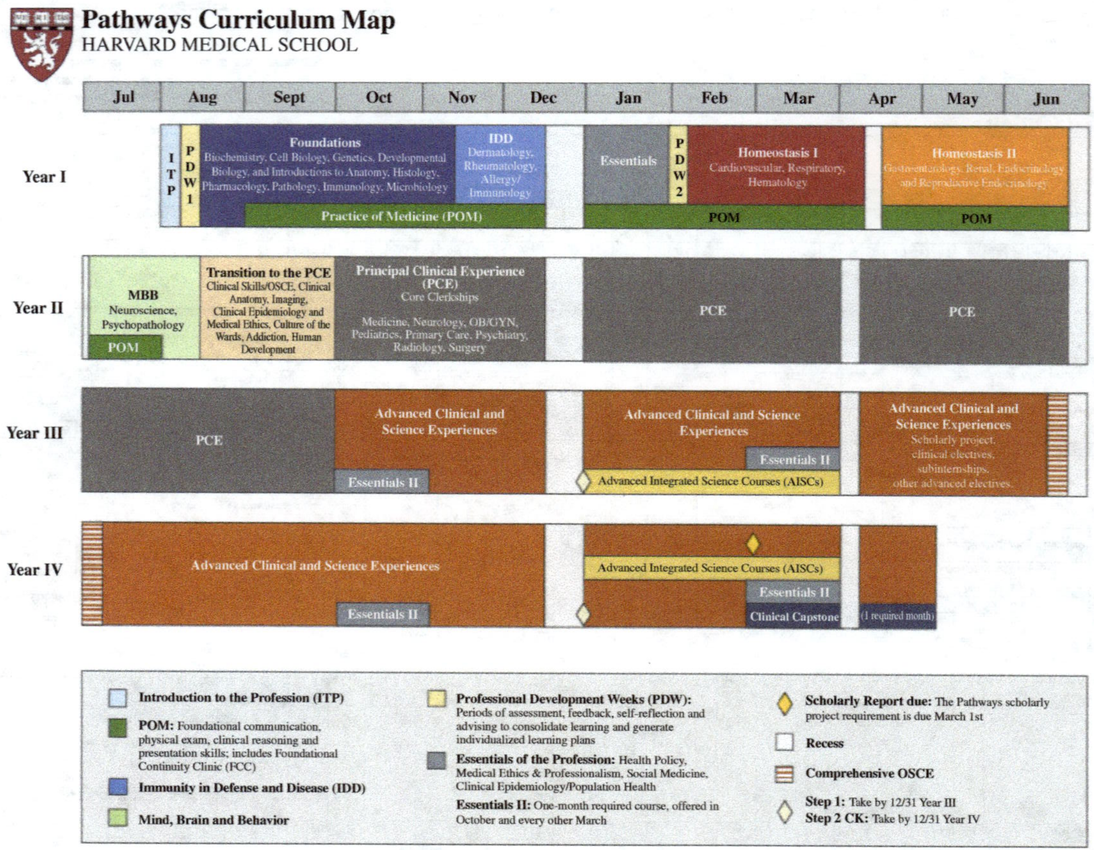

Fig. 3. 2021 Medical school curriculum, Harvard Medical School (2021).

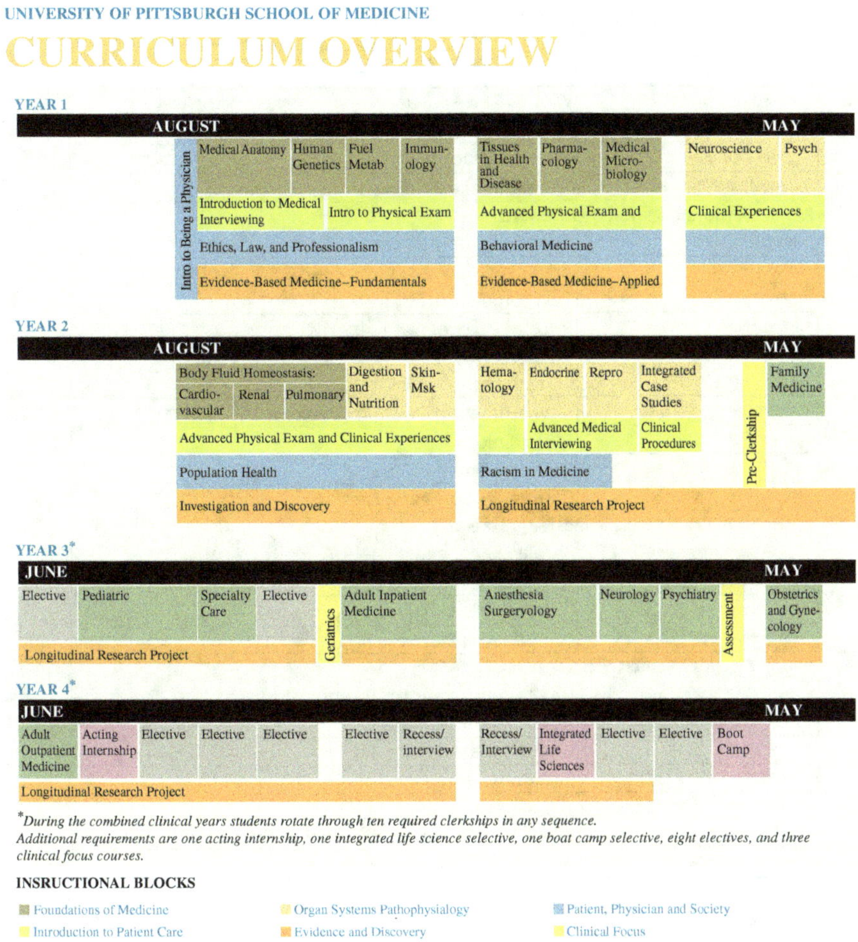

Fig. 4. Medical school curriculum, University of Pittsburgh Medical Center (n.d.).

healthcare. In fact, none of them presents even basic business skills, such as the economics of and money flow in healthcare. Case Western Reserve University's BSN program stands out as an outlier with two courses: Nursing Informatics and Information Technologies in Health.

Once physicians and nurses enter the workforce after years of intensive education, is it fair for us to expect them to be digitally savvy and engage in digital healthcare? In their 30s or later, burdened by debt and a

Course ID	Course Name
First-Year: Fall Semester (17 credits)	
CHEM-UA 120	Introduction to Modern Chemistry
EXPOS-UA 1	Writing The Essay:
SOC-UA 1	Intro to Sociology
NURSE-UN 4	Nursing Cohort Seminar
CAS-Search by Sub.	Social Science Elective
First-Year: Spring Semester (15 credits)	
NURSE-UN 70	Anatomy & Physiology
ACE-UE 110	Advanced College Essay: Educ & The Professions
CORE-UA 4XX	Text & Ideas: Tpcs
PSYCH-UA 1	Intro to Psychology
Sophomore Year: Fall Semester (16 credits)	
NURSE-UN 80	Statistics I
APSY-UE 1271	Developmental Psychology Across the Lifespan
NURSE-UN 75	Microbiology
NUTR-UE 119	Nutrition and Health
CORE-UA 5XX	Cultures & Contexts: Tpcs
Sophomore Year: Spring Semester (16 credits)	
CAS-Search by Lang.	Foreign Language (SPAN-UA, FREN-UA, etc.)*
CAS-Search by Sub.	*Liberal Arts Electives
CAS-Search by Sub.	*Liberal Arts Electives
CAS-Search by Sub.	*Liberal Arts Electives
Junior Year: Fall Semester (16 credits)	
NURSE-UN 239	Health Assessment & Promotion
NURSE-UN 240	Adult & Elder Nursing I
NURSE-UN 1261	Professional Nursing
NURSE-UN 1435	Pathophysiology
Junior Year: Spring Semester (15 credits)	
NURSE-UN 120	Integrating Evidence into Clinical Practice
NURSE-UN 1241	Adult & Elder Nursing II
NURSE-UN 241	Psychiatric Mental Health Nursing
NURSE-UN 1436	Nrsg Pharmacotherapeutic
Senior Year: Fall Semester (15 credits)	
NURSE-UN 1242	Maternity Nursing
NURSE-UN 1243	Adult & Elder Nursing III
NURSE-UN 1255	Pediatric Nursing
NURSE-UN 1248	Contemporary Issues in Health Care
Senior Year: Spring Semester (18 credits)	
NURSE-UN 1244	Community Health Nursing
NURSE-UN 1245	Leadership & Management in Nursing
	UG Nursing Electives
	UG Nursing Electives

Fig. 5. BSN curriculum, NYU Rory Meyers College of Nursing (n.d.).

Year 1:	
NURS061	BIOLOGICALLY-BASED CHEMISTRY
NURS068	INTEGRATED CELL BIOLOGY & MICROBIOLOGY
NURS101	THE NATURE OF NURSING PRACTICE
NURS065	FUNDAMENTALS OF NUTRITION
NURS102	SITUATING THE PRACTICE OF NURSING
NURS163	INTEGRATED ANATOMY, PHYSIOLOGY, AND PHYSICAL ASSESSMENT I
Year 2:	
NURS103	PSYCHOLOGICAL AND SOCIAL DIVERSITY IN HEALTH AND WELLNESS
NURS164	INTEGRATED HUMAN ANATOMY, PHYSIOLOGY & PHYSICAL ASSESSMENT II
NURS165	INTEGRATED PATHOPHYSIOLOGY, PHARMACOLOGY, AND THERAPEUTICS
NURS215	NURSING OF WOMEN AND INFANTS
Year 3:	
NURS230	STATISTICS FOR RESEARCH AND MEASUREMENT
NURS245	NURSING OF YOUNG AND MIDDLE AGED ADULTS
NURS255	NURSING OF OLDER ADULTS
NURS330	THEORETICAL FOUNDATIONS OF HEALTH CARE ETHICS
NURS334	PUBLIC POLICY AND THE NATION'S HEALTH
NURS225	PEDIATRIC NURSING
NURS235	PSYCHIATRIC NURSING
NURS547	SCIENTIFIC INQUIRY FOR EVIDENCE-BASED PRACTICE
NURS330	THEORETICAL FOUNDATIONS OF HEALTH CARE ETHICS
NURS334	PUBLIC POLICY AND THE NATION'S HEALTH
Year 4:	
NURS380	NURSING IN THE COMMUNITY
NURS389	RESEARCH/INQUIRY-BASED SERVICE RESIDENCY
NURS390	LEADERSHIP IN THE COMPLEX HEALTHCARE SYSTEM
Case Study: One of the Following	
NURS354	CASE STUDY: ADDRESSING THE SOCIAL DETERMINANTS OF HEALTH: COMMUNITY ENGAGEMENT IMMERSION
NURS355	CASE STUDY: SELF-CARE OF CHRONIC ILLNESS
NURS356	CASE STUDY: CULTURE OF BIRTH
NURS357	CASE STUDY: INNOVATION IN HEALTH: FOUNDATIONS OF DESIGN THINKING
NURS358	CASE STUDY: NURSES AND THE CHILD WELFARE SYSTEM
NURS359	CASE STUDY: QUALITY CARE CHALLENGES IN AN EVOLVING HEALTH CARE MARKET
NURS360	CASE STUDY: NURSING PRACTICE WITH HIV+ PATIENTS
NURS361	CASE STUDY: BREAST FEEDING & HUMAN LACTATION
NURS364	CASE STUDY: CANCER
NURS365	CASE STUDY: CASE ANALYSIS IN CLINICAL NUTRITION
NURS367	CASE STUDY: PRINCIPLES OF PALLIATIVE CARE
NURS368	CASE STUDY: HOME HEALTH CARE

Fig. 6. BSN curriculum, University of Pennsylvania (University of Pennsylvania, n.d.).

highly demanding, zero-error tolerance profession, how realistic is it for us to expect them to be the innovators, leaders, or enablers of digital practices? Is it fair for us to expect of them what they have not been trained for?

The first change we must make is to introduce digital skill sets in the training curricula for our physicians and nurses. While I understand the complexities involved in updating the curricula, especially when the

Course ID	Course Title	Credits
First Year, 1st Semester		
NURS 115	Fundamentals of Nursing	4
BIOL 114	Principles of Biology	3
BIOL 116	Anatomy and Physiology	3
SAGES	University First Seminar	4
GER	General Education Requirement	3
First Year, 2nd Semester		
NURS 122	Foundations of Practice	3
NURS 201	Nutrition	2
NURS 160	Health Care in the Community	1
BIOL 117	Anatomy and Physiology II	3
CHEM 119	Molecular View of Biology	3
SAGES	University Seminar	3
Second Year, 1st Semester		
NURS 230	Nursing Care of the Adult	5
NURS 211	Introduction to Pharmacology I	1.5
NURS 250	Aging in Health and Illness	2
NURS 210 or NURS 260	Teaching Learning in the Community *OR* Evidenced Based Policy in the Community	1
CHEM 121	Chemical Biology	3
SAGES	University Seminar	3
Second Year, 2nd Semester		
NURS 212	Introduction to Pharmacology II	1.5
NURS 342	Medical Microbiology	4
NURS 317	Psychiatric/Mental Health	3.75
NURS 240	Nursing Care of the Adult II	4.75
NURS 210 or NURS 260	Teaching Learning in the Community *OR* Evidenced Based Policy in the Community	1
SOCI 203	Human Dev: Med & Social	3
Third Year, 1st Semester		
NURS 315	Parents & Neonates in Health and Illness *AND*	4.5
NURS 316	Children & Adolescents in Health and Illness	4.5
	OR	
NURS 338	Care of Complex, Acutely Ill Adult and Older Adult *AND*	4.5
NURS 339	Care of the Perioperative Patient	3.5
STAT 201	Basic Statistics	3
NURS 310 or NURS 360	Leadership in the Community *OR* Process Change in the Community	1
GER	General Education Requirement	3
Third Year, 2nd Semester		
NURS 315	Parents & Neonates in Health and Illness *AND*	4.5
NURS 316	Children & Adolescents in Health and Illness	4.5
	OR	
NURS 338	Care of Complex, Acutely Ill Adult and Older Adult *AND*	4.5
NURS 339	Care of the Perioperative Patient	3.5
NURS 320	Departmental Seminar	3
NURS 310 or NURS 360	Leadership in the Community *OR* Process Change in the Community	1
NURS 345	Nursing Informatics II	2
GER	General Education Requirement	3
Fourth Year, 1st Semester		
NURS 370	Information Technologies in Health	1
NURS 371	Public Health Nursing	3
NURS 372	Health in the Global Community	3
NURS 373	Global Health Practicum (Capstone)	5
Fourth Year, 1st Semester		
NURS 343	Issues and Ethics	2
NURS 341	Nursing Management	3
NURS 380	Senior Preceptorship	8

Fig. 7. BSN curriculum, Frances Payne Bolton School of Nursing, Case Western Reserve University (n.d.).

digital world continues to evolve so rapidly, the mere inclusion of healthcare IT professionals is not enough to enable the transformation of the field. However valuable, they are not trained in the intricacies of healthcare. Digital transformation requires us to train our core healthcare workforce — the physicians and the nurses — so that they become the true enablers of such a transformation. Otherwise, we are asking deep-sea divers to fly an airplane, and then scratching our heads as to why the plane keeps crashing.

We can't, however, wait for the right workforce to be in place for digital transformation of healthcare to happen. While such a transformation is inevitable given the forceful push of our society toward digitalization, its entrance doesn't need to be abrupt. That is where leadership comes into play.

6. The Leadership

Twenty years ago, as a newly minted MBA from NYU Stern School of Business, nothing felt impossible. The world was for us to take, and we were going to change it for the better! We were smart, we had the skills, and the MBA had opened a new set of opportunities.

For the first 10 years, I was a management consultant working on complex consulting projects focused on strategy and transformation in the healthcare industry. The analysis was always rational, the recommendations always clear, and the final client presentations almost always hit the mark. We were so proud. We were providing the right answers that made sense for the organization. But, when we were going back to the same organizations one, two, or even five years later, it was more of the same.

Then, I got a chance to go in-house. As Head of Innovation and then Global Head of Strategy for Digital Services, it was now my chance to implement what I knew was needed. If I could see it, I was sure everyone else did too. Now, it was my turn to hire consultants. Their recommendations were again highly rational, rooted in analysis, supported by facts and investment analysis that made dollar investments a no-brainer. But the money to invest in digital transformation, as I learned, even in some of the highest positions of authority, was not that easy to come by.

Any transformation requires a purse. The purse strings loosen when its holders believe that the investment is necessary. And it is not one person who holds the purse strings and makes investment decisions in an organization — it is a team effort. Rather, it is a match where short-term revenue wins over the long-term possibility. And in healthcare, digital transformation still gets trumped by other, more urgent needs, as we saw with the board room conversation.

However, I have also learned a few key lessons on what could enable leaders' work in driving digital transformation forward:

(1) Start with clarity of the organizational purpose: Irrespective of the level of the organization, clarity of and alignment to the organization's purpose are critical. The absence of alignment leads to individual agendas, politics, and conflict.
(2) If an organization's purpose is to be the best digital health provider, it may be easier to adapt its goals to a digital future than if it is "Exceptional Care, Close to You."
(3) Have a pragmatic vision and measurable milestones: The less pragmatic the vision, the more difficult it will be to gain organizational momentum. Measurable, declared milestones are important because humans are innately trained to go after targets, and nothing succeeds like success.
(4) Stay innovative: Most mature organizations stay focused on driving their core business, leveraging the process machinery they have perfected over time. In the long run, that becomes the reason for obsolescence. As is posited in innovation literature and discussed in our book, *Redefining Innovation: Embracing the 80–80 Rule to Ignite Growth in the Biopharmaceutical Industry*, organizations should methodically allocate to drive their core business (85–90%), build adjacent businesses (7–10%), and innovate for the future (3–5%) (Nagji and Tuff, 2012). Yes, Wall Street and investor expectations will get in the way, but large organizations have the highest ability to operationalize such an investment philosophy.
(5) Be agile, but not rushed: Leading transformation requires agility, but don't confuse that with rushing to adopt every best new idea since sliced bread. That creates confusion, panic, and mistrust.
(6) Be a leader-coach: People will find it difficult to embrace change. You need to operate as a leader-coach to empower people and enable change. Leading with a coaching mindset, a leader-coach operates and enables organizations to operate from the position of creativity, not reaction. A leader-coach frames and reframes perspectives but remains true to the organizational purpose. And a leader-coach can operate from any level in the organization, coaching up and down.

(7) Lead with courage: Change is difficult, and uncertainty will be high. Resistance will come from multiple directions. A lot of times, there will be no playbook to refer to; you will have to create the playbook. This is where the 80–80 rule comes in: "Being 80% confident that you will only be 80% right the first time should feel normal."

(8) Don't miss the forest for the trees: While it is extremely important to execute different initiatives that are part of the transformation program, it is equally important not to lose sight of the big picture. Another way to say it: Don't forget the organizational purpose as you get deep into divisions, functions, and the rest of the organizational labyrinth.

7. Conclusion

Is healthcare a complex system comparable to a food delivery app in terms of user experience and ease of use? Maybe not. Is there an expectation in the market that the healthcare user experience should be simple and easily accessible at the touch of an app? Absolutely. Can we get there? I am an optimist and think so, but a digital transformation will require a multi-pronged approach. The most important area to focus on is developing the people who can lead this transformation.

References

Frances Payne Bolton School of Nursing (n.d.). BSN curriculum. https://case.edu/nursing/bsn/curriculum (Accessed Aug 22, 2022).

Harvard Medical School (2021). Pathways curriculum. https://meded.hms.harvard.edu/files/hms-med-ed/files/pathways_curriculum_map.pdf (Accessed Aug 22, 2022).

Johns Hopkins School of Medicine (n.d.). Genes to society: A curriculum for the Johns Hopkins University School of Medicine. https://www.hopkinsmedicine.org/som/curriculum/genes_to_society/curriculum-overview.html (Accessed Aug 22, 2022).

Lane, R. (2021). Average nursing student debt. https://www.nerdwallet.com/article/loans/student-loans/average-nursing-student-debt (Accessed Aug 22, 2022).

Merriam-Webster (n.d.). Transformation. https://www.merriamwebster.com/dictionary/transformation#learn-more (Accessed Aug 22, 2022).

Nagji, B. and Tuff, G. (2012). Managing your innovation portfolio. Available at: https://hbr.org/2012/05/managing-your-innovation-portfolio (Accessed Aug 22, 2022).

NYU Rory Meyers College of Nursing (n.d.). Traditional 4-year. https://nursing.nyu.edu/academics/baccalaureate/traditional-4-year?tgid=nyunursing-tabs-2406&tid=curriculum (Accessed Aug 22, 2022).

University of Pittsburg Office of Medical Education (n.d.). Curriculum overview. https://www.omed.pitt.edu/curriculum/curriculum-map (Accessed Aug 22, 2022).

https://doi.org/10.1142/9789811271984_bmatter

Index

www.ingramcontent.com/pod-product-compliance
Lightning Source LLC
LaVergne TN
LVHW010331220926
848484LV00004BB/880